Canadian Cases in Human Resource Management

T. F. Cawsey, Wilfrid Laurier University

G. Deszca, Wilfrid Laurier University

A. J. Templer, University of Windsor

Prentice
Hall

Toronto

National Library of Canada Cataloguing in Publication Data

Cawsey, Thomas F. (Thomas Frederick), 1943–
    Canadian cases in human resource management
ISBN 0-13-088455-3

1. Personnel management — Canada — Case studies. I. Deszca, Gene II. Templer, A III. Title

HF5549.2.C38 2002   658.3'00971   C2001-900842-2

0-13-088455-3

Vice President, Editorial Director: Michael Young
Marketing Manager: Michael Campbell
Associate Editor: Susanne Marshall
Production Editor: Gillian Scobie
Copy Editor: Linda Cahill
Production Coordinator: Patricia Ciardullo
Page Layout: Jansom
Art Director: Julia Hall
Cover Design: Amy Harnden
Cover Image: PhotoDisc

 3 4 5   06 05 04

Printed and bound in the USA.

To Heather, Bert and Mary

Contents

Part 3: Developing Your Workforce Effectiveness   151

Part 4: Enhancing Workforce Relationships   251

Part 5: New HRM Horizons   277

Preface

Senior executives often attribute their success to the way they manage their human resources. In this knowledge-economy world, managing human assets is critical and connected with the long-term competitive advantage of organizations. Successful organizations usually demonstrate an up-to-date knowledge of human resources management (HRM) concepts and techniques, a strong commitment to the implementation of modern approaches and procedures in HRM, and a high level of skill resulting from the continuing practice of sound HRM. Knowledge, commitment, implementation, practice, and skill: these factors contribute significantly to the success of HRM and the success of organizations in the modern world.

The authors of this casebook believe that the case method of education provides an opportunity for participants to improve their knowledge and skill in human resources management. The variety and complexity of cases encourage broad thinking about the practical issues faced by the individuals in these cases. At the same time, implementation practice can be developed vicariously as students develop action plans and tactics to handle the case issues. While we cannot explicitly develop commitment through the use of cases, we do believe that participants will develop a commitment to good practices—rigorous analysis, conceptual thinking, systems thinking, and contingency planning—as well as a commitment to a broad humanistic philosophy. The cases enable students to apply the principles of HRM gained through the parallel study of any one of several HRM textbooks to a variety of real-life corporate situations. With practice, participants' skills in HRM increase, developing their professionalism and encouraging them to test and further develop these skills in their future management careers.

In compiling the casebook we have explored some of the problems, issues, and opportunities confronting human resources managers by describing actual situations of modern business life. Our objective has been to produce complex and challenging—though clearly stated—situations involving managers in the Canadian business community. The resulting cases are rich in detail, yet sufficiently brief to be discussed in a standard class period.

We have tried to provide teaching materials that engage students and require them to struggle with the conflicts faced by today's managers. Growth vs. safety, equity vs. productivity, fair play vs. moving ahead—perceptions of these and other apparent "trade-offs" emerge in the cases to follow. We believe that the active involvement of participants in analyzing the situations presented and developing appropriate strategies provides the opportunity for superior skill development.

We have also tried to provide materials that span the conceptual, strategic, and technical areas within HRM. Each case deals with a particular situation that relates to a specific HRM function or skill. However, in nearly all cases, participants are required to relate the activities of the HRM professional to the key success factors and the business strategy of the firm. As well, they must consider the complexity of the entire situation—not just a limited or specific issue.

The text is designed primarily for college and university students who want an appreciation of how the HRM function operates in modern corporations. Other people may also find the cases interesting and useful. Several of the cases have been discussed at academic conferences to broaden our understanding of the issues.

The casebook contains 24 cases, sufficient to support a one-term course in HRM. The cases are written to allow for variation in the depth and coverage of the issues and concepts. For a course at the MBA level the primary focus would, in our view, be on the strategic aspects of the problems presented. At an undergraduate or community college level, more time might be spent on understanding the techniques used and the skills necessary in the human resources field. The cases are sufficiently rich and varied that the casebook could also be used as a supplementary book for an organizational behaviour course which had a functional HR orientation. As well, individual cases could be used in many different ways in different management and organizational behaviour courses.

The cases are arranged in five sections. Four of these cover the major areas of the human resources function but are organized by outcome rather than by function. Managers wish to understand HR from a strategic perspective; they wish to create effective organizations and to develop that effectiveness through HR systems. Finally, they wish to enhance their workforce relationships by ensuring a safe and supportive environment now and in the future.

Underlying the outcomes mentioned above are the traditional functions and roles of the human resources department: planning and staffing an organization; recruitment, selection, and orientation in a firm; training and development; performance management; and employee maintenance. The final section deals with current issues: quality of work life; the introduction of team management; mergers; and the "downsizing" of organizations.

This sequence of cases follows the outline of the major popular texts in HRM, though the headings reflect an outcome orientation, not a functional one. We believe the outline provides a logical overview of the human resources field from an outcomes or objectives perspective. Many instructors may choose to use only some of the cases. Doing so should pose no problem as the cases stand alone and may be used individually.

A teacher's manual accompanies this casebook and provides a comprehensive guide to the use of these cases in particular. Instructors who are familiar with the case method may find this manual a useful supplement to their own class preparation. Instructors who are less familiar with the case method will find the manual invaluable. It provides the instructor with class outlines, assignment questions, outlines of the major issues in each case, action alternatives and their consequences, links to conceptual materials, and, whenever possible, follow-up events to the case.

Acknowledgements

We acknowledge the help that we have received from Canadian business managers, without whose assistance these cases could not have been written and released. We acknowledge the support given by the School of Business and Economics at Wilfrid Laurier University and the Faculty of Business at the University of Windsor in the preparation of this text.

We thank our academic colleagues and fellow case writers: Pauline Brockman; Céleste Brotheridge; Kathleen Cawsey; Bill Cooper; Loren Falkenburg; Joyce Johnston; Natalie Lam; Patrick Larbi; Kenneth Loucks; Elizabeth Lunau; Chad Mance; Rosemary McGowan; Stuart Munro; John Podrebarac; Eileen Polson; Michael Robertson; Francine Schlosser; Bernadette Schell; Tom Stone; Katarina Tegling; Helena Wennberg; and Eric Vanderbrouke.

We acknowledge a particular debt to Mike Ryan, previously with Pearson Education Canada, who saw the need for this casebook and sought our cooperation. Finally, the initiative and professionalism of the staff at Pearson Education Canada, especially Susanne Marshall, were invaluable in bringing this casebook into being. We hope that the efforts of all who have contributed to the book will help to continue raising the level of HRM and organizational effectiveness in Canada.

The cases in this book are meant to provide a basis for analysis and discussion, not examples of correct or incorrect handling of HRM situations. They are copyrighted by the listed authors unless otherwise noted.

About the Contributors

Tupper Cawsey is professor of business at Wilfrid Laurier University. He has been associate dean of business at Wilfrid Laurier University, MBA program director, director of the Laurier Institute and area coordinator of the Management and Organizational Behaviour Area. Dr. Cawsey was recognized in 2001 as one of Canada's top five business professors with the Leaders in Management Education award, sponsored by Bell Nexxia, PricewaterhouseCoopers and the National Post. He is a recipient of the 1994 David Bradford Educator Award and the 1990 Wilfrid Laurier University "Outstanding Teacher Award." Dr. Cawsey is chairperson of the board of directors of Lutherwood CODA, a not for profit organization in Kitchener-Waterloo. His consulting and research interests focus on the management of organizational change and on managerial careers. He has written widely in these areas.

Gene Deszca is professor of business administration and the past director of the MBA program at Wilfrid Laurier University. He has published and/or presented over 100 papers, monographs, and technical papers. Two recent examples are the co-authored pieces: *Managing the New Product Development Process: Best-in-Class Principles and Leading Practices* (with H. Noori and H. Munro); and *The Career Management Guide* (with T. Cawsey). Current research involves organizational change, career processes of knowledge workers, and the development of high performance organizations. He has been instrumental in the development of the Society of Management Accountants of Canada's post-university professional accreditation programs.

Dr. Andrew Templer is professor of management in the faculty of business administration at the University of Windsor in Canada. His research interests are in the evaluation of human resources, reward systems and the social impact of technology—including telework and distance learning. He is the author of over 50 papers, which have been published in such journals as *Personnel Psychology*, *Human Resources Professional*, *International Journal of Management*, and the *Journal of Managerial Psychology*. He is a member of the editorial board of Career Development International and is currently a member of the board of directors of the Human Resources Professionals Association of Ontario.

Pauline Brockman is an MBA graduate from the University of Windsor.

Céleste Brotheridge is currently a Ph.D. candidate at the University of Manitoba and an assistant professor at the University of Regina.

Kathy Cawsey is a Ph.D. student in Medieval English at the University of Toronto.

Bill Cooper is a professor of business at Queen's University. His research interests include career processes, power in organizations, research methods, and the history of management ideas.

Loren Falkenberg is an associate professor at the University of Calgary in the faculty of management. She teaches in the area of human resources and organizational dynamics.

Joyce Johnston is a manager in the public sector and was a business student at the time this case was written.

Natalie Lam is associate professor of business at the University of Ottawa. She teaches and researches in the area of human resources.

Patrick Larbi is a graduate of the University of Ottawa.

Kenneth E. Loucks, Ph.D., is professor of business strategy in the faculty of business, Brock University, St. Catharines, Ontario. Ken specializes in the strategic management of economic development institutions.

Elizabeth Lunau is an MBA graduate from the University of Windsor.

Chad Mance is a graduate of the University of Ottawa.

Rosemary McGowan is an assistant professor of Business at Wilfrid Laurier University and a doctoral student at York University.

Stuart Munro is an MBA graduate from Wilfrid Laurier University and a professor at Sheridan College.

Eileen Polson is an MBA graduate from Wilfrid Laurier University and an independent consultant in Kitchener-Waterloo.

John Prodrebarac is an MBA graduate from Wilfrid Laurier University and a senior manager with an industrial manufacturer.

Michael B. Robertson is currently an investment facilitator/business analyst with the Niagara Enterprise Agency in Niagara-on-the-Lake. He is presently pursuing a master of business administration at the Schulich School of Business at York University.

Dr. Bernadette Schell is director of the school of commerce and administration at Laurentian University and the Management Development Center and the author of three books, including *A Self-Diagnostic Approach to Understanding Organizational and Personal Stressors*.

Francine Schlosser is a Ph.D. candidate in management sciences at University of Waterloo. Currently her research explores the ways in which employees perceive and accept wireless handheld technologies.

Tom Stone is professor of business at Oklahoma State University and the author of several textbooks on human resources.

Katarina Tegling is a graduate of the University of Ottawa.

Eric Vandenbroucke is an MBA graduate from the University of Windsor.

Helena Wennberg is a graduate of the University of Ottawa.

## part one

Human Resource Management as a Strategic Function

Some readers may have come across Peter Townsend's now classic book, *Up the Organization*. The book was arranged in alphabetical subject areas, and his comment under "Personnel Management" was the crisp: "Fire the lot of them." This may have been jaundiced but reflected the author's view at the time that the personnel department contributed nothing to an organization, except in overhead costs. Has anything changed since then? The answer is not straightforward or simple and involves both good and bad news.

The good news is that perspectives of human resources management (HRM) in Canada have changed. Earlier negative conceptions of "personnel administration" are disappearing. There is more recognition of human resources as a legitimate part of management and, increasingly, of top management. Executives now recognize that people provide the competitive edge and that commitment to and full utilization of labour resources are essential.

The bad news is that these changing perspectives have not always resulted in a shift in actual practices—especially in the area of strategic planning. It is probably still true in many organizations that while business planning is taking place upstairs, the HR department may be found downstairs making name tags for the annual company picnic.

Nevertheless, forward-thinking organizations today have a human resource function that plays an integral role in their strategic activities. Strong arguments have been made that organizational performance will depend upon the fit between human resource practices and the strategic components of that organization. Thus, the task of the senior human resource professional is to understand the organization's strategy and to play a senior management role in ensuring that the human resource capabilities are present in the firm.

More recently, arguments have been proposed that the role of strategic HRM is to develop flexibility in the organization. Organizations are faced with uncertain and changing environments, and HR can help best by building the capacity to change and cope with different environments.[1]

Regardless of this argument, evidence continues to mount that workforce empowerment is connected directly to organization performance. And HRM is often central to the creation of an empowered workforce. Those who wish to read more on this connection should look at Pfeffer's classic, *The Human Equation*.[2] In addition, Patterson, Wall, and West's empirical study of manufacturing performance is an interesting examination of the impact of empowered workforce behaviours.[3]

HRM IN A TIME OF CHANGE

In Canada, human resource practices are affected by the turbulence around us. The old adage, "change and decay in all around I see," seems particularly pertinent to the Canada of today. Mega-mergers are creating new financial institutions that, with the growth of electronic banking, no longer even require a physical presence in the landscape. Global partnerships in the auto and other industries are not only eliminating the differences between nationalities and cultures but also making it quite difficult to distinguish between foreign and domestic manufacturers. Downloading of government services, restructuring, and changing political alliances have even blurred the lines between the public and private sectors in Canada. The result is a growing complexity in the world of work in a number of areas:

1. A more competitive business environment—especially in the need for strategic interventions and planning to meet the challenge of change.

2. The growing complexity of socio-political problems that require an improvement in the skill levels of key organizational participants.

3. Major changes in corporate philosophy requiring a more proactive approach to people management. These include:

   • changes in approaches to problem solving and the value of work;

   • shifts in the nature of work;

   • the growth of "just-in-time" and cost-recovery systems; and

   • the increasing use of team and contract working arrangements.

The shift towards strategic HRM is occurring for many reasons. Some of these are described below.

---

[1] Wright, P. M. and S. A. Snell. "Toward a Unifying Framework for Exploring Fit and Flexibility in Strategic Human Resource Management," Academy of Management Review, vol 23, no. 4, 1998, 756-772.

[2] Pfeffer, J. *The Human Equation*. (Boston, Mass.: Harvard Business School Press, 1998).

[3] Patterson, M., M. A. West, R. Lawthom, & S. Nickell. *Impact of People Management Practices on Business Performance.* (London: IPD, 1998).

New Technology

The geometric growth in new technology, particularly information technology, is resulting in a profound change in the nature of work and of HRM. Entire careers, such as the bank teller, telephone operator, or typesetter, have disappeared, to be replaced by automated systems operated by fewer, high-skilled employees. Computer networking and reporting systems allow for cross-national team projects structured without traditional supervisory channels and evaluation programs. HRM is shifting towards teleworking and self-managed review programs that make much more use of external specialists and consultants.

Expectations of Quality and Service

Restructuring and changing demographics in Canada have produced organizational stakeholders with ever-increasing expectations of quality and service. Customers are just as willing to adopt the products of a quality supplier in Tijuana as in Toronto—and the Tijuana supplier may even be contacted first if its Web listing is more accessible to search engines. Customers calling for service from their local Sears in Vancouver may quite likely be making pickup arrangements with an operator in New Brunswick. In this environment, HR functions that are not seen to add value to the organization and offer exemplary service will simply not survive. HR professionals will have little choice but to carry out regular assessments of effectiveness, both of the overall HR function and of the "people practices" throughout the organization.

Globalization

Cross-national mergers and alliances are making it increasingly difficult to determine where Canadian HR practices end and international HR practices begin. Consider the difficulty of coming up with integrated HR systems in the new corporate mergers that characterize the Canadian landscape. HR strategies have to work in Canada and yet be congruent with effectiveness criteria throughout the world. The good news is that Canadian HR professionals who have learned how to make the most of cultural diversity within Canada will have a genuine competitive advantage in the global arena.

THE VALUE OF HR PROFESSIONALS

One of the questions that arises in many of the cases in this book is *why introduce an HR professional?* The key lies in a demonstrated contribution to business competitiveness and the successful management of change. In addition, organizations that set up effective HR functions seem to have two characteristics in common:

First, the senior management includes someone willing to champion the cause of HRM and the need for professionals. This is usually the top manager or owner but may be a senior vice-president or director.

Second, there are sufficient organizational resources to facilitate professional HRM. This is sometimes as basic as having the organizational "slack" to afford the hiring of an HR professional but more usually follows from the willingness of the champion (point 1 above) to set aside such resources.

THE CASES IN PART 1

The cases in this first section capture situations faced by human resource managers as they struggle with their strategic role in helping organizations cope with complex environments and dramatic changes. It may be easy to describe the global shift in the HR function. It is much more difficult to specify what a particular manager should do in his or her firm to improve the firm's performance, the status of the HRM function, or the well-being of the firm's employees.

In the cases provided, participants have the opportunity to plan actions that address the above issues while working to achieve multiple corporate, departmental, and personal objectives. That is, participants can specify what they would do in each situation, keeping their organizational strategy in mind. Traditionally, HRM has been taught as a series of functions, e.g., HR planning, recruiting, selecting, and so on. Unfortunately, by examining these functions one at a time, undue emphasis is placed on individual activities rather than on corporate mission and strategy or on the outcome and results expected by senior management and the board of directors. A better method of dealing with HRM is to think strategically in terms of environmental scanning and organization matching, and to view the HRM function from a variety of perspectives, thereby generating multiple insights into what action should be taken.

The primary task is to understand the overall strategy of the firm, and to view HRM manoeuvres as an integral piece of the whole. The HRM executive must be able to identify the corporate strategy and recognize how it affects the HR function and vice versa. Some organizations may have their strategy clearly spelled out. Many do not. The strategy of the firm is a complex, variable plan that exists mainly in the minds of top managers. HRM executives may be officially unaware of many significant aspects of the plan. They need the skills and wisdom to identify the firm's strategy and relate it to HRM policies and programs. Only then can HRM is play a major role in the company.

The twin and often contradictory objectives of HRM provide another perspective from which to view the subject—how to maintain the organization vs. how to make it more effective. Historically, HR managers have dealt with maintenance systems, such as pay policies, health and safety, and benefits. More recently, however, HRM has become involved with issues relating to organizational effectiveness, such as HR planning, productivity improvement, and organizational redesign.

A further consideration is the method by which the HRM function deals with top management. Too often in the past, "personnel" managers were reactive and passive—a posture reinforced by a traditional maintenance role. Most CEOs today, however, expect their senior HRM people to demonstrate an active stance towards issues and events, in keeping with the current needs of the company.

A final perspective from which to view the role of HRM is its orientation—specialist professional vs. organizational management. Individual areas within HRM have become increasingly specialized, such as software, legislation, or benefits, and require specific technical skills and knowledge. While these skills are necessary, it does not follow that a top HRM executive should be a specialist or have a predominantly professional perspective. A general management perspective may be required to deal with the variety of human resource problems, issues, and opportunities faced by today's corporations.

Thus, numerous perspectives provide a dynamic view of the strategic role of the HRM function. They encourage a broad approach to the analysis of all the cases in this book, particularly the three in this first part. These three cases offer points of view from which to appraise the HRM function and evaluate the role of the HRM leadership in very different settings: large public organizations in Ontario (Hallington and HRDC Niagara) and a small private company in western Canada (Frontier).

Hallington Utilities Services provides the participant with an opportunity to think about the rapidly changing environment facing public service companies in Ontario—privatization, downloading of services, and a dramatic increase in competitive pressures—and how this can affect human resources strategy. A new HR manager has joined Hallington and finds what appears to be a busy and efficient HR function, but one that has not assessed its match with corporate strategy in some time. All action to be taken needs to be placed in the context of the organization and its environment. Questions need to be asked, such as: What sort of an organization is this? What sorts of people are needed, and what value-added contributions can the HR function be expected to make? The case contains a lot of information, and the skill that is required is focusing on just those strategic issues that will make a real difference to Hallington's competitive advantage down the road.

Frontier Printers, Inc., in contrast, is a case dealing with a small company that is in danger of miring in its own success. Once again, however, unless strategic HR decisions are made, Frontier will not be in a position to capitalize on the introduction of new technology and growth opportunities. The company has little choice but to shift from its small, informal operation to a more formalized structure, but it cannot allow such change to lead to a loss of either flexibility or the customized service orientation that has been a major part of its success. Unlike Hallington, with its very busy HR function, Frontier does not as yet have a full-time HR professional, and Frontier's president views the search for such a professional with some trepidation.

The final case in this section returns us to the public sector.

Empowerment and Workforce Adjustment in the Niagara Area Office of HRDC reports on a case of successful staff reductions over a number of years that culminate in too many employees opting for the exit packages that have been made available. Assessment and actions are needed that will address budget issues, stabilize the workforce, and allow it to effectively get on with the delivery of the services it is mandated to provide.

ACHIEVING A STRATEGIC HRM PERSPECTIVE

Strategic human resources management is not just an activity, but rather an overall philosophy and way of managing. Strategy is the glue that holds together everything that the HR function does. As you analyze the cases in this book, look for the following characteristics of a strategic HRM perspective:

- Human resources "costs" are seen as investments, not expenses.
- Human resources management is proactive, not reactive or passive.
- Human resources functions are explicitly linked to other organizational functions.
- Human resources strategy links HR activities together in a dynamic system.
- There is a focus on using strategic planning to further both individual and organizational goals.

Hallington Utilities Services

Eric Vandenbroucke

Andrew Templer

Marion Forbes, the recently appointed senior human resources manager at Hallington Utilities Services (HUS), sat back at his desk and contemplated his newest and greatest challenge to date. In front of him lay a memo from John Swatridge, CEO of HUS, welcoming him to the organization but outlining his concern that the current department of human resources at HUS was not ready for the challenges that lay ahead.

ORGANIZATION BACKGROUND

Hallington Utilities Services is the utility that distributes electrical power to customers in the municipality of Hallington, a medium-sized city in Ontario. HUS was created on January 1, 1979, amalgamating five municipal utilities. As well as serving Hallington, HUS services the surrounding rural areas and has a service territory of approximately 545 sq km. Its peak electrical load was 205.5 MW in July 1999.

Low-cost power available to all across Ontario was the dream of Sir Adam Beck, a businessman and mayor of London, Ontario, in 1903. Three years later, he became the first chairman of the Hydro-Electric Power Commission of Ontario, a precursor of the new Ontario Hydro Services Company.

In the mid-1990s, the Ontario government decided it should move to deregulate the electrical power market because residents and businesses in Ontario were paying the third-highest electricity generation rates in Canada, with no choice of suppliers. Energy costs were an integral part of many businesses and could, in certain instances, account for 5 percent of total spending—an important competitive business issue. The government believed that energy generation technology had evolved to the point where this essential customer service would be better provided through multiple suppliers. An entrepreneurial structure would allow utilities to operate on a more commercial footing. In addition, deregulation and privatization would spur investment, open American markets to Ontario-based power suppliers, and reduce the level of electricity-related debt on the provincial ledgers.

As a precursor to deregulation, HUS was reorganized. It now responded to a Board of Directors, which, in turn, was responsible to its shareholders (HUS was still owned by the area municipalities) and the customers. The Board adopted the vision:

> Excellence in customer service with competitive electricity rates and a knowledge of power that is first class.

COMPETITIVE CHANGES

Under the new *Energy Competition Act*, the Ontario Energy Board (OEB) would oversee the new competitive market, with a mandate to provide customer protection, ensure codes of conduct, and grant licences for generation, transmission, distribution, wholesale marketing, and retailing. The Act carried over existing provisions for reliability and safety from the current system and provided additional safeguards for the new marketplace. Electric utilities in Ontario, including Hallington, would no longer have Ontario Hydro as the sole supplier of electricity. These utilities would be able to procure power from various sources on the open market at prices that would benefit Ontario customers.

Under the new legislation, HUS had to separate its "wires business" from the energy retailing business. The legislation ensured a level playing field for competition while making sure that monopoly activities were not used to subsidize other parts of the business. HUS continued to be responsible for maintaining a reliable distribution network. HUS had a continuing "obligation to connect" customers to its distribution wires. HUS also looked after hydro reliability and public safety through inspecting, repairing, and maintaining the distribution lines.

Ontario Hydro had been the main supplier of electricity in Ontario and currently controlled 85 percent of the province's generation capacity. With the restructuring of the electricity industry, Ontario Power Generation Inc. was formed from the power generation components of Ontario Hydro and was required to decontrol some of the generation it owned. These measures were intended to create a competitive wholesale electricity market by having a number of different generating companies selling into the Ontario market.

In addition, imports from other provinces and American states could supply 20 percent of peak demand requirements, or approximately 4000 MW. Plans were underway to increase this capability by 2000 MW within three years.

In a significant change of business, Hallington had begun offering retail products to the public as well as delivering regular hydro services. It was now supplying electrically powered items, such as electric water heaters and fireplaces, and cordless garden tools, such as hedge clippers and lawn mowers.

CURRENT ISSUES

With the recent move to a more competitive environment, there was concern that HUS would face major restructuring and reorientation challenges. Pressures to reduce costs, increase the level of outsourcing, identify key competitive advantages, and begin privatizing the organization were all issues that Hallington Utilities could no longer afford to ignore. In fact, these issues were so controversial that many Hallington employees were beginning to be concerned about their future within the organization. This concern could have a serious effect on morale.

Presently, HUS was organized into four departments: electrical acquisitions, distribution, retail operations, and administrative services. Human resource management was part of the administrative services department, which also included the areas of information systems, and finance (see Exhibit 1.1). Most of its 275 employees were located in either the distribution or the clerical function. Of the 275 employees, about 160 would be classified as "outside workers," and the other 115 would be clerical, professional, and managerial.

MARION FORBES

Marion Forbes, the recently appointed senior human resource manager at Hallington Utilities Services (HUS) sat back in her desk and contemplated her newest and greatest challenge to date. Marion recalled the discussion with John Swatridge, CEO of HUS, welcoming her to the organization but outlining his concern that the current Department of Human Resources at HUS was not ready for the challenges that lay ahead.

Upon graduation, she took a job as a human resource specialist with a major public utility. After several promotions, she applied for the position of director of administrative services with HUS. She did not get this job but was offered the position of senior HR manager instead. Senior management at HUS decided, for the moment, to neither fill the director of administrative services position nor give Marion the title of director of human resources. They promised, however, that she would be considered for the position of director of administrative services at some point down the road. The promise of eventual appointment into the director position persuaded Marion to join HUS. She was highly motivated to prove herself in HR, since winning the director position would give her considerable status and the responsibility for a variety of areas, including HR. In this position, Marion knew she would learn a great deal and face significant challenges.

The previous head of human resources, Fred Watkins—whose title had been "personnel director"—had been with the utility since its formation. Prior to its incorporation, he had worked as a technician and lead hand for one of the predecessor municipal utilities for 14 years. Fred was ambitious and hard-working and had managed to complete an undergraduate business degree by attending evening courses over a seven-year period. He joined HUS as a supervisor but moved to human resources as the manager of industrial relations following the certification of the outside workers in 1983. He became the director of personnel in 1985. The "personnel department," as it was called under Fred's direction, was quite traditional in its orientation and approach, with Fred maintaining an active role in labour relations. During the 1990s Fred became increasingly nervous about the potential changes at HUS. Following "discussions" with Swatridge in 1999, he decided to take early retirement.

Exhibit 1.1
Organization Chart: HUS

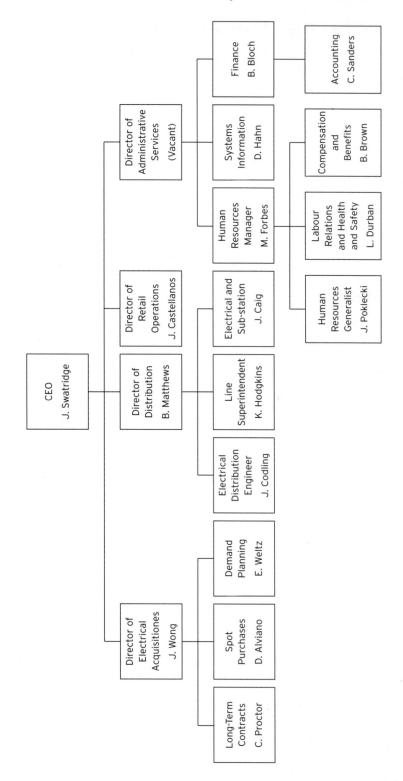

THE MEETING WITH JOHN SWATRIDGE

Marion's most immediate concern in her new position was to carry out an organizational assessment at Hallington, with the purpose of determining what needed to be done in human resources. What should be the HR strategy at HUS? In other words, what human resource processes, procedures, and systems needed to be halted, updated, or created in order to assist HUS to successfully adapt to its new environment? She decided that her obvious first step should be to meet with John Swatridge, the CEO at HUS.

Marion had had numerous conversations with Swatridge on the phone but not much one-on-one contact since her job interview and welcome to the organization. From their conversations, Marion had gained the impression that Swatridge was a no-nonsense, by-the-book type of executive. Little seemed to amuse him, and his only focus in their conversations had been to find solutions to the problems they had been experiencing within the organization.

As the secretary escorted Marion into Swatridge's office and before Marion could consider what to say, a voice rang out, "Welcome Marion, what can I do for you?"

After some initial pleasantries, the conversation quickly turned to the current status of the organization. "I read your memo, John," Marion stated, "and I realize that if I am to do anything in my new position, I need to know how human resources management can help the organization achieve its long-term goals. Now, to do that, the best place to start is probably for me to get a better understanding of what your present concerns are with the organization."

"Not a problem," Swatridge replied, "I've thought about it and, right now, there are three major issues that worry me. The first is the issue of privatization, the second is the possibility of downsizing, and the third is the talk about a unionization drive of the clerical staff."

"Can you talk a bit more about these issues?" Marion asked.

"Certainly," John replied.

Privatization

"While the managers may be worrying most about downsizing and the union drive, I think these are really small potatoes in comparison with the major impact of globalization and privatization," Swatridge began. "As I've become more aware of how the global economy is affecting our business, privatization seems to be growing more and more likely. As the market becomes more competitive, we as a utility organization need to explore every option available to remain competitive. Does that mean privatizing? Maybe, maybe not. At this point, though, if privatizing can lead to increased revenue for the organization and a way to cut costs, then that's most likely what will happen. Certainly, the government has a philosophy that moves us in this direction."

"I would certainly have agreed with you before the *E. coli* outbreak in Walkerton," Marion interjected, "but after that disaster, I'm not so sure. The government seemed well on its way to privatizing water utilities, but now it seems uncertain. How has this affected public perception?"

"Ever since the Walkerton disaster and the subsequent enquiry, residents everywhere, especially in Hallington, have become very concerned about the quality of all utility services that are provided to them," Swatridge continued. "And then, the California debacle has not helped. That publicity has added to the uncertainty. The fact that it wasn't a true privatization doesn't seem to come through—privatization just seems to have come to be associated with power shortages and potential price increases rather than reductions![1]

"One thing that has happened since the Walkerton incident is that the government's quality control measures for all municipalities and utilities have become stricter. Higher and tougher standards are being enforced to ensure that something like that never happens again. Thankfully, we have plenty of systems and procedures in place to ensure that an incident like that will never take place in Hallington. However, these events have certainly clouded the waters. Privatizing utilities will be much more difficult, in my opinion, as a result of public concern about quality control. At the same time, we will face a much more open competitive marketplace with our suppliers!"

Downsizing

Barely pausing, Swatridge went on to discuss the next major issue. "For a year or so, the Board at Hallington Utilities has been considering some possible downsizing within the organization. We clearly aren't being as efficient as we could be, which means changes will eventually have to be made. We have benchmarked our staff to a power-generated ratio, and we are above average. Of course, this is a difficult measure to use because of the area that we service. Bigger utilities are much more concentrated. But our added cost per megawatt of energy seems out of line.

"Obviously, nothing's been decided, but there does seem to be a need to at least reduce our staff somewhat in order to get our costs down. One thing I will say is that I am concerned with how the employees are handling this issue.

"About a month ago, we conducted some focus groups regarding employees' general feelings about the organization. While I was not surprised to find a concern about job security, I was taken aback by the number of employees who expressed concern over the lack of planning for the future in HUS. For the most part, the results were quite consistent, though there were differences because of the varying positions and the years of service of respondents. Younger workers were much more worried about their security than were older workers, who mentioned, as an option, taking an early retirement package if it's offered.

"I found it particularly surprising that professional and skilled employees admitted to thinking about switching jobs. They said they needed to take responsibility for their own careers in the absence of a clear future at HUS."

Unionization

Swatridge cleared his throat before continuing. "Lately, there have been some rumblings about a possible union drive. Now, one of the things I am most proud of is the fact that the clerical and professional employees at Hallington have never wanted or needed a union. Like most utilities, we have unionized outside workers, but we have not had an inside union. The fact that we are not unionized is unusual for an organization of our size and in our industry. I am sure this is partly the result of the strong independent spirit of the folks

---

[1] Walkerton: Refers to an outbreak of *E. coli* bacteria in the small town of Walkerton, Ontario, in 2000 and the inability of the town's water supply control procedures to predict or contain it.

California: Refers to the power brownouts that occurred in California as the result of inadequate funding and pricing problems that some analysts had linked to deregulation.

who originally settled in the Hallington area and partly that our employees get competitive wages and benefits, good vacation and holiday time, and work in an environment that is positive and enjoyable. However, with the concern over privatization and employees' worries about downsizing and job stability, I guess the unionization issue was bound to arise. For the most part, I wouldn't buy into that too much, as I think we can cope better than most. Sure we have problems, but what organization doesn't, right?"

Before Marion could decide whether or not she agreed with her boss's sentiments, Swatridge's secretary interrupted, and it was clear that Marion's time was just about up.

"Is there anything else you think I need to know?" Marion asked.

"There is one thing. About a week ago, I received a memo from the head of the electrical acquisitions department, Jim Wong. He informed me about a department-heads' meeting that had taken place recently. Apparently, the reason for the meeting was concern over the electrical futures purchasing responsibilities that the administrative staff within his department were now required to perform. In the past, all of this commodity buying was performed through Ontario Hydro, but with approaching privatization, this responsibility had fallen upon the electrical purchasing staff. The purchasing staff were used to traditional product purchasing activities and were not trained to handle the trading of electrical power units. A completely new mindset and dramatically different competencies were required.

"Apparently, other department heads also had the sense that similar changes would be required of staff across HUS. HR's response seems to be that all our training budget is committed now, and the department isn't ready to 'just throw together a few new training programs.' Jim's memo made it clear that the department heads were very concerned about their employees' preparation for the changes coming to the utility.

"This is definitely an issue I need to look into," Swatridge concluded. "Unfortunately, I am a little busy right now, and it has been pushed back. Maybe you could investigate this issue for me?"

THE PLANT TOUR

With that, Marion was off on a self-guided tour of the facility. She wanted to obtain the employee perspective. The following is a summary of some of her discussions.

Steve Knott: The Issue of Downsizing

The first employee that Marion ran into was Steve Knott, a 49-year-old father of three and a general labourer with Hallington Utilities. Knott had been with the organization for over 26 years and was considered by many to be a hard-nosed but hard-working employee.

Throughout their discussion, the same issues kept coming up: "If this fricking organization lays me off, you might as well throw me off a bridge," Knott quipped. "I've been here over 25 years, and you think my job is safe—not likely. They'll protect all those young kids who think they know it all and leave us old folk out to dry! All I've been hearing for the past six months is the organization might be downsizing and then they might not be downsizing. For heaven's sake—make up your minds! And I'll tell you this, if they lay me off, I've got no chance. I have no skills, no experience outside of this organization, and no updated education. You think I'll be able to find another job? Forget about it! You might as well sign me up for welfare and throw me in a nursing home, 'cause my life is over!"

Though the drama built up by Knott's speech was a little much, Marion believed that Knott was serious about the issue and wasn't putting on an act. Was Hallington Utilities handling the issue of downsizing properly? What was the company telling its employees, and how was the communication process being handled inside the organization? Clearly, the issue was of great concern to the employees and was most likely affecting morale. Marion noted the issue and moved on.

Colin Moore: The Issue of Motivation

The mailroom seemed like an odd place to visit, but Marion decided that the more diverse the group of employees she interviewed, the better the feel for the organizations she would have. Colin Moore had been employed as a mail sorter with Hallington Utilities for over eight years and, for the most part, was quite positive about his experience. However, there was one issue he was concerned about: "I love it here, but we've got compensation problems," Moore said. "Our system is outdated, it's barbaric, and it does nothing to reward solid performance. Why would I work hard to differentiate myself from the others when there's no opportunity to be compensated for it? I may only be a mail sorter, but I'm no dummy; I've enrolled in a technical supervision program at the local college. As soon as something comes up outside— I'm gone. All those outside guys get big bucks compared with me, and I work hard at what I do. Just because they have a union, they end up with more money!"

"How can you argue with that?" Marion wondered. Marion knew that HUS relied on a Hay system of compensation. She had heard that many of the job descriptions were out of date and that few employees understood the basics of how their pay ranges were set and the factors that went into setting those ranges. Of course, the union scales were another issue!

Norm Zenglein: The Issues of Recruitment and Training

If there was a more enthusiastic and energetic person than Norm Zenglein in the world, Marion had never met him. Norm was a 27-year-old section head within Hallington Utilities and was regarded as an up-and-comer. Though he had only been with the organization for two years, he was already one of its most productive and efficient supervisors. Unlike Steve Knott, in Marion's first conversation, Norm's concerns were with recruitment and training.

"Hey, if you want to be the best, you need the best people working for you," Norm explained. "My dad taught me that. Good man, my father. Anyways, if you want the truth, here it is: Hallington Utilities is one of the worst recruiters and trainers of any organization I have ever worked for. The needs of the organization rarely coincide with the people they are recruiting, and when we do get quality people, we can't train them well enough to do the job. Clearly, whatever system they are using for recruitment and training is out of date. Now, don't get me wrong, I like working here. But if they want to be successful in the future, they are going to have to do a better job of recruiting and training their new employees. Last year, we hired a bright graduate from a community college. We made all sorts of promises about the future and then had her do clerical work for six months. No wonder she left. And then there was George. How did he get hired? We couldn't have done reference checks on him, or we would have discovered his drinking problem!"

Marion was concerned about the "gossip quality" of some of this information and wondered how valid it was. "Nevertheless, another employee, another separate and distinct problem," she thought. From her conversation with Norm, Marion realized that one of the things Hallington Utilities really required was an update—or perhaps even major over-hauling—of most of its current HR systems. It was not surprising that this was mentioned by the focus groups that Swatridge talked about.

Lance Durban: Issues of Contract Administration and Labour Relations

Lance Durban had been the manager in charge of labour relations and health and safety for seven years. Lance told Marion that prior to the departure of the director of personnel, he had spent most of his time dealing with health and safety matters and having Fred second-guess him on labour relations matters. As a result, he had learned to defer any significant decisions or roles to Fred and had acted primarily in a research and support function. Now that Fred had left, Lance was keen to get on with the job. "Fred did a great job keeping the peace, but I continue to be amazed at all of the unwritten arrangements and side deals that Fred made. This informality may have been useful in smoothing things over and keeping the union leadership and certain individuals happy, but it also created perceptions of favouritism and inconsistency. I'm trying to clarify and codify practices as I come across these deals so that the arrangements don't haunt us further. It is not easy, though, because you have to stumble on the arrangements before you even know they are there. People aren't very forthcoming when it comes to letting you know about the sweetheart deals."

Lance also mentioned the challenges related to health and safety. Until last year, HUS had a pretty solid record in this area. But since then, there had been a 14 percent rise in lost time accidents and a 17 percent increase in the number of health and safety related incidents. Lance was unsure what was causing this, and he believed it was an area that needed close scrutiny. "I don't know if it is declining morale, deficient training, health and safety committee problems, or supervisory inattention. Whatever it is, we need to sort it out soon. I keep asking those involved, but all I'm getting is finger-pointing thus far."

Janet Poklecki: Communication and Training Issues

Next, Marion sought out another direct report from Janet Poklecki, a human resource gen-eralist at HUS. Janet had been with Hallington Utilities since 1985, and Marion had heard rumours that Janet wanted Marion's job. After all, she had the seniority at HUS and had done a good job. She was proud of her work as well as the department's. Marion would need to spend considerable time with her to make certain she was OK reporting to her. But for the moment, Marion wanted to continue her initial tour and assessment of HUS.

Marion found Janet with her desk piled high with recruitment folders and time-management training brochures. Marion was surprised that the time Janet spent talking to her would have to be accounted for in detail in Janet's time-management reporting sched-ules. Despite this hassle, Janet was willing to talk to Marion and quickly made clear that her concerns lay mostly in the area of communication.

"We just don't communicate well with each other," Janet complained. "And by "we," I mean management and the employees. Whether it's the issue of downsizing or privati-zation, nobody seems to know what's happening. Sure there are newsletters and memos sent by management, but they never really tell us what's going on. It's frustrating, and most of all, it hurts morale. I find it particularly tough that I am so busy with our recruitment and training activities that I just don't have time to help employees plan ahead. The one time I do hear from employees is during our lunch breaks, and I can see how this poor communication affects morale and, more importantly, productivity. Something has to change, or else.

"I think our new training program will make a huge difference to the organization. It is so exciting, and I am certain that John is going to be thrilled with the results. I plan on meeting with him next week to update him on how it is going. The program will help employees deal better with time management. I have been designing the program for almost a year now, and it has really taken a lot of my effort to develop. The program consists of three different seminars that the employees have the option of taking, as well as a follow-up program to assess its effectiveness. I think it is something that could benefit all of our employees at Hallington, even management. I want to persuade John to authorize management attending. Also, I am just getting started on one of my new initiatives, which is to design another training and development program for the organization relating to teamwork. I think it is an important part of business today and could be a useful program at Hallington. As you can probably tell, there are a lot of good things going on with HR right now!"

"That's great," Marion thought. "At least I know what HR staff have been spending their time on, and I am impressed at the carefully crafted training programs they have developed. But how do these activities help HUS deal with the issues worrying the CEO and department heads, and in addition, how do I explain all this to Janet?"

Bob Brown: Compensation Issues

As a final stop, Marion looked into Bob's office. Bob was a long-service HUS employee who had been transferred into human resources seven years ago to look after compensation and benefits issues. As Marion entered, Bob quickly switched programs on his computer, and Marion wondered what Bob was working on.

"What's up in compensation today?" asked Marion.

"Oh, it is always the usual stuff," replied Bob. "People always complain about what they earn. Just the other day, I had a manager trying to get around the system because she said we were going to lose a good employee. We can't just regrade jobs or give pay raises because someone gets an offer from somewhere else. It's not my job to find money for these people; I am busy enough as it is, making certain that payroll is up to date. When people join on, they never seem to fill out the forms right, and I keep finding errors. People also make lots of errors on forms related to the benefits programs. I end up spending my time on the administration of these programs. I just send the forms back until the information is correct. Frankly, I just can't keep up and have asked for part-time assistance. Can you help me with this? You should be able to pull some strings there, can't you?"

Marion wondered about this request. Just where did that fall into his new role?

Heinrich Voelker: Union Concerns

As Marion headed back to her office, she ran into one of the union vice-presidents, Heinrich Voelker. He challenged Marion to improve things at HUS. "You guys sit up in your offices and pretend you know what is happening. You have no idea what is really happening out there with my guys. This winter has been freezing, and six people have been off with frostbite. No wonder lost time accidents are up. You can't have that and expect people to be committed. We try to make suggestions and are ignored—all you are concerned about is your fancy offices and special parking spots—you just have no idea about the real problems of getting electricity to people! And Swatridge! He is just paranoid about this new Board structure! If he got out into the field more, he wouldn't have to worry so much about the Board. When people phone in because their power is out, you can't be worrying about budgets and efficiencies. You have to get the power back on, and this new overtime policy is crazy. It's your rules not ours, but to think you can restrict overtime is nuts—especially this winter. And the focus is nuts. Last week, one of my guys brought back a truck at 11:30 and his supervisor was all over him. The job was done, and he needed to wash up before lunch. What was he supposed to do—hang around until 12:00 and then come back? It's just an example of how rules oriented our supervisors are. Worried about the minutes and not the job that is done!"

Marion listened to this diatribe for a while and wondered how much was real and how much was positioning. It was clear that some of the status differences grated—too much emphasis on the privileges of management and on the clerical employees and not enough focus on service quality, it seemed.

THE DILEMMA

As she walked back to her office, Marion thought about what she had learned so far. She had heard some very different perspectives from various employees and some major issues raised by the CEO, all, in their own way, trying to cope with the inevitable changes facing HUS. She wasn't at all sure that she was ready to answer the question of how prepared the HR function was to address these issues. On her journey, Marion had found a human resource department that was busy doing all kinds of different things. What exactly should her role be? What should be the role of her department? How could she make a real impact on the organization?

If defining these problems was difficult enough, finding solutions was going to be another story. "The issue I need to focus on," Marion thought, "is whether HUS wants a good HR department, or whether it wants an HR department that helps the organization achieve excellence." Whatever the answer, Marion knew that as the new kid on the block, she would have to tread carefully. As she thought of all that she had seen, she reflected on what she had recently read in an HR book referring to the necessary "discipline of abandonment"—that organizations have to learn the discipline of discarding certain responsibilities so that they can take on new and more strategic ones.[2]

Upon her return to her office, Marion sat down and pulled out a pad of paper from her desk and proceeded to scribble the words: "New HR Visions and Plans for HUS."

Ironically, the only other thing that ended up on that pad of paper on that first day was a big question mark.

---

[2] Weiss, David. *High-Impact HR: Transforming Human Resources for Competitive Advantage.* (Toronto: Wiley, 1999), p. 38.

Frontier Printers, Inc.

Tom Stone

Loren Falkenburg

It is the end of a long day; however, Bonnie Pfizer, president of Frontier Printers Inc., is unable to break out of her thoughts and clear her desk. She is worried that if she doesn't initiate some significant changes in management practices, Frontier Printers will mire in its own success. Frontier is in a position to capitalize on the introduction of new technology and growth opportunities if the company can shift from being a small, informal operation to one with a more formalized structure. However, Bonnie is afraid the introduction of more formal management procedures may lead to a loss of flexibility and a lower customer service orientation.

Bonnie has known for the last year that changes were needed; however, the exit interview she just finished with the lead press operator has brought her to a decision point. The press operator has accepted a job with one of Frontier's competitors because he believes there is no opportunity for growth in Frontier. Extremely frustrated at losing this valued employee, Bonnie is questioning what she could have done to retain him as well as the delivery person who quit because he didn't see any opportunities to learn to operate a press.

As she reflects back on the exit interview, she recognizes the irony of the press operator's reasons for leaving. The company has experienced more than 50 percent growth in the number of employees in the last three years, and revenues are growing at projected rates. Frontier has been introducing new technology that requires the development of technical skills. With the growth and introduction of new technology, there are good career and skill-building opportunities for the employees. The future looks great, if only Frontier can find and retain skilled workers. She knows that changes are needed so that she can better plan for obtaining the skills and knowledge needed for the technological changes, better manage employee performance, and build a more formal training and development program.

Recognizing that she and her partner (her father) do not have the expertise to make the needed changes, she is uncertain how to proceed. The company is not large enough to justify a full-time human resource professional, but Bonnie wonders if she will be able to find someone she could trust with the company information, who understands the issues of small businesses, and who has the skills needed to guide the company through the necessary changes.

COMPANY HISTORY

Frontier Printers, Inc. is a commercial printing company located in a small city in western Canada. The company has been operating in the community for almost 60 years. At the end of the last fiscal year, sales revenues were $1.2 million with 21 employees or $57 000 per employee. Six months later, 23 employees were on the payroll, including two part-time workers. Sales are expected to reach $1.5 million by the end of this fiscal year.

The company currently has two owner/partners, Bonnie Pfizer and her father, Randall Bonev. Frontier Printers had been languishing under the ownership of a large manufacturing corporation when Randall and his wife bought it eight years ago. Four years later, Bonnie joined the company as vice-president of sales and marketing. Mrs. Bonev worked in the business until her death two years after Bonnie joined the company. After her mother's death, Bonnie bought the outstanding shares and became president of the company. Currently, Randall is responsible for all the financial and production activities of the company, and Bonnie looks after planning, sales, marketing, and the management of human resources.

There is only one other management employee, the production manager, Thomas Bridenstine. He has been with the company for almost 25 years, and has worked his way up through the ranks to his current position. He is a loyal and hard-working employee who is well respected by Bonnie and her father, as well as by all the employees. His responsibilities include purchasing of production materials, all aspects of production scheduling, and supervision of production employees.

In addition to the managers, in the front office there are two "outside" sales persons, one for printing and one copying. There is also a billing/personnel administrator and two customer service representatives. One of the customer service representatives works part-time, about 28 hours per week. The production area employs 15 people.

When Bonnie became president, she developed the following mission and vision statements for Frontier Printers, Inc.:

Mission Statement

OUR BUSINESS is to provide printing and related services, which facilitate communications between our customers and their customers.

OUR CUSTOMERS choose us because we provide outstanding quality, excellent service, and comprehensive capabilities. They depend on us to be a resource for information and services that provide them with a consistent image that contributes to their business success.

OUR MARKET is all business in western Canada.

OUR MISSION is to delight our customers by exceeding their expectations for quality and service, including product quality, industry expertise, delivery time, value, friendliness, and helpfulness of employees.

Vision Statement

By 2000, Frontier Printers, Inc. will be an established, vertically integrated company that provides one-stop service for its customers, including printing, copying, small-run colour work, colour separations, design, photography, advertising, and mailing services.

Frontier Printers is considered a medium-sized, commercial sheet-fed printer that produces custom printing jobs. Its typical products include brochures, newsletters, envelopes, letterheads, forms, booklets, annual reports, mailers, postcards, folders, and business cards. A production copier was added last year to provide for the black-copying requirements of Frontier's small and medium-sized customers. The addition of colour-copying and mailing services is planned for the end of this year.

Full-colour, or process-colour, printing is Frontier Printers' speciality. Approximately[1] 80 percent of the company's printing business includes at least one colour other than black. Business forms represent about 20 percent of the business. Multi-part forms are printed in the plant, or outsourced when quantities are greater than 2500. Another 20 percent of the printing business consists of stationery items, such as letterheads, envelopes, and business cards. The remaining 60 percent is made up of marketing or communication materials, such as flyers, mailers, brochures, and financial reports.

Since Bonnie joined Frontier as vice-president, the company has pursued the expansion of its customer base as well as the addition of products and services desired by an increasingly technical marketplace. The addition of equipment, services, and outside sales representatives, as well as an aggressive marketing campaign, increased sales by 25 percent in the first year and by 23 percent in the second year. Last year, a copy shop was added to serve the printing customers requiring high-quality copying. Target sales for this year require another 25 percent increase, which will partly come from the addition of copying revenues. It is anticipated that mailing services will be added by the end of this year, since over 75 percent of the products produced by Frontier are ultimately mailed out by the customer. In addition, equipment will be added that will allow the production of colour separations. This equipment will not only reduce cycle time on colour printing by two to five days, it will also allow Frontier to provide services to artists and printers in their market area. The vertical integration should be completed within two years.

---

[1] Frontier Printers Inc. does not currently have systems in place to accurately measure and record production costs and results. Percentages are estimated. A production tracking/costing system is planned and will be installed when profitability and cash flow permit.

FRONTIER'S MARKET

Printing is a regional business; even simple printing jobs involve many production variables, and a face-to-face interaction between the customer and the printer is often essential. Proofing must be completed by the customer, which requires hands-on activities, such as the review of colour samples and large layout sheets. Records are maintained by the printer, and reprints are substantially less expensive to the customer, so long-term relationships are common. This makes new customers difficult to attract and maintenance of current customers critical.

Frontier Printers has served its market in western Canada for 58 years. It has a reputation for high-quality work and exceptional service. Frontier serves a market that falls between two larger urban areas where there are more printing companies. It has the greatest size and colour capabilities of any printer in its market area. The city in which it is located has a vital and diversified economy with many thriving small- and medium-sized businesses. Many of these companies ship products nationally and internationally. These companies generate a large demand for printing services.

There are two other sheet-fed printers in the same city, as well as an office supply company that takes in printing and outsources it to another location. There are a few small printers in the surrounding communities, but Frontier has the greatest capabilities. Some printers from the larger cities have sales representatives calling on Frontier's local customers and those in the surrounding small towns, creating some competition. Frontier, however, is normally competitive with its pricing and, generally, supported by the local businesses.

WORKFLOW ANALYSIS

The printing process requires several steps, which are outlined in the following section. Exhibit 2.3 provides a diagram of the production process.

Sales (Department 1): 3.5 employees
Skill Requirements: On-the-job training

There are two positions in the sales department: sales representatives (SR) who meet with customers outside the plant and customer service representatives (CSR) who handle customers at the counter and over the telephone. More specifically, the SRs call on major customers, make new contacts, provide quotes, deliver proofs, and coordinate projects with customers. Their customer service orientation is critical to Frontier's reputation for high-quality service. CSRs provide services similar to the SRs; however, their contact is with smaller customers and/or telephone requests. They screen telephone calls for potential sales leads that require an outside sales contact (SR).

Both CSRs and SRs require the development of an order ticket when a sale is closed. An order ticket is the vehicle for communication with all other departments, as it provides the information needed to do the printing work. Once a printing job is completed and the billing is done, CSRs file the order tickets. Reprints are an important part of Frontier's business, so order tickets are kept on file for eight years.

Purchasing (Department 2): 1 employee
Skill Requirements: Extensive on-the-job training

After an order is completed, it is sent to the production manager's desk for review and ordering of any necessary materials. The production manager also reviews incoming supplies and matches orders to materials. Once the materials are ordered, he schedules the production of the order according to the customer's requirements. He is also responsible for ordering and maintaining the supplies kept as inventory.

This step is bypassed for copy shop orders where quick turnaround time requires use of supplies from inventory.

Art and Typesetting (Department 3): 2.5 employees
Skill Requirements: Technical school training,
computer skills, on-the-job training

The work in this department includes typesetting, graphic art, layout, and production of camera-ready copy. From a customer draft or description, typesetters/designers lay out artwork in a manner that is "readable" by the press. Creativity is required of typesetters/ designers as often customers are uncertain as to what the end product should look like. An important part of Frontier Printers' service reputation is the extra effort extended in this department.

Typesetters/designers must maintain customer files in chronological order so that they may be retrieved for reprints or updates. The computer system is backed up weekly to ensure that files are preserved.

When a customer or artist provides camera-ready copy, this step is bypassed and the material is sent to the pre-press department. If an order is for photocopying, it goes directly to Department 8.

Pre-press (Department 4): 3 employees
Skill Requirements: On-the-job training, computer skills

This department produces proofs as well as photographs through camera work and production of film, stripping, and plating. These processes are labour intensive. Pre-press technicians paste camera-ready copy onto large sheets, called flats, and then photograph them with a camera. From the camera, negatives are produced and "burned" onto thin metal plates. These plates are what the press uses to "read" what is to be printed; each type of press requires a different arrangement of copy. Attention to detail is critical as mistakes can lead to a costly waste of time and materials.

Press (Department 5): 5 employees
Skill Requirements: On-the-job training, computer skills

The presses are run by skilled technicians called press operators. The processes in this department include running the plates on the press, die-cutting, and thermography; foil stamping and embossing are outsourced. Each press operator works with a particular press and is responsible for maintaining and repairing that particular press. Colour density and consistency must be constantly monitored to ensure that a quality product is produced. Mistakes in this department are also very costly as the paper is ruined once an impression is made incorrectly.

Bindery (Department 6): 2.5 employees
Skill Requirements: Minimal on-the-job training

Bindery workers complete all aspects of the bindery process, including scoring, cutting, binding, folding, gluing, padding, collating, and inserting. The bindery process requires less skill than in some of the other production departments; however, a mistake in the bindery can completely destroy a product. Quality must be monitored, as problems can arise during folding and cutting.

Shipping (Department 7): 1 employee
Skill Requirements: Minimal on-the-job training

In this department, a shipping clerk ensures that all finished products are given a final quality review and then packages the products for shipment or delivery. Deadlines are often an issue for the shipping clerk. When shipping is completed, the order ticket is sent to the sales department for review (Department 1), and then to billing (Department 9).

Copy Shop (Department 8): 1.5 employees
Skill Requirements: Minimal on-the-job training

The copy shop was opened a year ago to serve the black-copying needs of its business customers. An SR is responsible for managing this department as well as doing outside sales. Two part-time employees, called copier operators, do the actual copying under the supervision of the sales representative.

Billing (Department 9): 1 employee
Skill Requirements: Bookkeeping skills, computer skills

A bookkeeper, the billing administrator, sends a final bill within a few days of the completion of a printing job. Billing is based on the order ticket, via shipping and sales, for each completed job, as well as any invoices from outsourced components, and is done several times a week. After billing is completed, all order tickets are sent back to Department 1 for filing and follow-up. Copy shop (Department 8) billing is done once a month.

The billing administrator produces monthly statements; as well, the system software can provide management reports and a customer history, if requested.

FUTURE ISSUES

Technological Changes

Frontier is competitive with other printers with its current technology. Some of the equipment involves leading-edge technology, while other equipment is almost as old as the company itself. Using the old equipment is the most efficient way to do some printing work. At the same time, the future of printing is in digital technology. Currently, large (or web) printing companies have the technology to go directly from the art and typesetting department to film, which bypasses about 75 percent of what the current pre-press department spends its time on. Frontier Printers has plans to go "direct-to-film" by the end of this year. This would eliminate the need for two of the employees in the pre-press department. This technology would require additional technical skills in the art and typesetting department. The ability to go directly from the art and typesetting department to plates would eliminate the other 25 percent. This technology is currently available, but not widely used due to the expensive equipment required. As prices stabilize and competitive pressures persist, all printing companies will need to invest in these technologies.

A "job-tracking" system is also planned for some time next year. This system will enhance customer service and provide accurate costing information. Orders would be entered on a computer terminal, instead of on a paper "ticket," and be tracked all the way through the production process. This change would require every employee to be trained in the use of the associated computer terminals and software.

The goal is to add mailing services by the end of this year. Mail service equipment is highly computerized, and programming it requires analytical skills specific to software conversion. The addition of this department will require a manager and another employee with specific computer skills, as well as one or two bindery workers.

Changes in Managing Employees

Frontier Printers' reputation and profitability are dependent on providing the best possible service to its customers. The company slogan "…..leading the way in quality and service" means that these two things must be reflected in each employee's actions, every day. Bonnie knows that as the business grows, more formal policies and procedures for hiring, assigning work, training and development, and performance evaluation are needed.

Hiring Process

When an employee is needed, Bonnie and her father discuss the required skills and abilities and then compare these with the skills of current employees. If the needed skills and abilities are not available within the current employees, they review the job applications they have on file. These applications are normally from "walk-in" applicants. If there are applications from qualified candidates, they are contacted for an interview. If there are no applicants with the necessary qualifications, an advertisement is prepared for local newspapers. Two weeks has generally been long enough to obtain applicants with the necessary skills. Some employees have been hired through temporary personnel agencies to ensure that the company had 90 days to review work habits and abilities before placing these employees on the regular payroll.

Responsibility for the final selection decision is determined by the type of employee needed. The idea of testing employees for abilities has been discussed but is not currently done. If the new employee is to work in the production area, Randall and Thomas Bridenstine complete the hiring process. If the employee is for sales, customer service, or multiple areas, Bonnie is involved. Randall interviews all candidates once they are finalists for a position. Thomas has final approval for production employees, while Bonnie has final approval for all other employees. Thomas and Bonnie complete the reference checks.

This simple process has been adequate for the company. This is supported by a turnover rate of less than 5 percent per year. However, as the company grows and the need for technically skilled employees increases, Bonnie thinks that the current process will not lead to Frontier getting the most qualified employees. As Frontier Printer's reputation and profitability are dependent on providing the best possible service to its customers, the company cannot afford to make poor hiring decisions; in the future, each decision must be based on an appropriate match between the candidate's background and the company's needs. Bonnie isn't sure what type of process is needed to ensure that the most qualified candidates are hired.

Work Assignments

Bonnie and Thomas deal each week with employee issues such as responsibility and salary. Often, employees are at odds over who is responsible for a certain task, particularly the less desirable tasks, delaying the completion of projects. Bonnie realizes that as the company grows, employees will need to have a more formal understanding of their specific responsibilities and expected outcomes. As she thinks about issues around work assignments, she remembers the frustration she felt with Sarah Hickman right after she was hired. Initially she was pleased with Sarah's editing skills, but within a few weeks Bonnie realized that Sarah was sometimes less than pleasant with customers, both in person and on the telephone. After a few complaints, Bonnie had to spend several hours with Sarah counselling her on how to handle customers' requests and inquiries.

Bonnie is puzzled as to whether formal job descriptions would help clarify responsibilities or would lead to a loss of needed flexibility. Currently, Frontier operates somewhat like a job shop where some jobs may require non-standard operations. Frontier has a reputation for finding creative approaches to solve customer problems and for its flexibility to adjust to unexpected customer deadlines. She is concerned that formal job descriptions might lead employees to limit their work to only those tasks contained in their job descriptions and, thus, reduce the creativity and flexibility Frontier now has.

Performance Evaluation

Several employees have been terminated due to poor performance. Documentation of these terminations is weak, and Bonnie is concerned that the company could be exposed if these employees or others feel that they were wrongfully fired. Given the informal nature of operations at Frontier, the standards of performance have not been clear and fired employees might be able to argue that they were wrongfully terminated because they did not know their performance was inadequate. She wonders if there might be an effective way to communicate performance standards in order to reduce the frustration that she and others feel when they have to spend time correcting problems arising from poor performance.

Training and Development of Employees

The company has no formal qualifications for any jobs, and the training is done on an informal, *ad hoc* basis. As Bonnie reflects back on the resignations of the press operator and the delivery person, she speculates that a more formal outline of skills and abilities and formal cross-training programs might have motivated these employees to stay with Frontier. For example, the delivery person simply did not show up at work one day. When he failed to show up the following day, Thomas telephoned him at home to learn that he was quitting because he wanted to be a press operator and was not being given the opportunity. Thomas was unaware that this employee was interested in learning to operate a press. This employee would have likely made an excellent press operator, and Bonnie wondered what could prevent this type of situation from occurring again.

Bonnie thinks that cross-training employees in computer skills will become essential as the company requires more specialized computer expertise. Without cross-training in computer skills, the company will lose flexibility in managing its operations and, if employees do leave, valuable time could be lost while finding or training another individual in the needed skills. For example, Randall and Ida Harris are the only employees who know how to use the software for billing, payroll, or financial reports; consequently, if one of them were to become ill, it would be difficult to find a short-term replacement. Another problem area is that only Randall and Thomas know the software package for estimating pricing; however, as the company grows, Thomas will need backup help in pricing.

DECISIONS

Bonnie knows she must start making these changes tomorrow. As she leaves the building, she thinks she has a handle on some of the issues, but isn't really sure where to start, where to get advice, or what policies and/or procedures need to be developed. She wonders what issues should be addressed first and how to ensure Frontier Printers, Inc. is able to manage the anticipated growth.

Exhibit 2.1

The Printing Industry

The printing industry is divided into the three major categories summarized below. Printing companies are defined by the equipment they use because this determines the types of products they are able to produce and the types of customers they are able to serve. A glossary of industry terms is included in Exhibit 2.2.

Copy Shops and Quick Printers

These shops focus on the retail end of the business, with their primary customers being individuals and small businesses or organizations. They handle small printing jobs, usually quantities of less than 1000, with production copiers or small printing presses. They are capable of doing black or colour copying. Black-copying is most efficient for quantities of less than 2000 if quality is not critical, and colour-copying is generally suitable for reproducing colour in quantities of less than 200 when high quality is not necessary. Normally they print on letter or legal-sized sheets of paper, with many shops having small printing presses for small quantities of envelopes or other types of printing. Sometimes franchise or chain shops will take in more complex or higher-quantity printing orders and outsource them to a national printing centre. Therefore, these shops can be potential competitors of larger printers in their market area. Also, some consumers, unfamiliar with the differences, will choose copying when printing would be more economical.

Commercial Sheet-Fed Printers

These printers serve small- to medium-sized customers who require printing quantities of 1000 to 100 000. This category of printers utilizes printing presses that run large sheets of paper, normally 58.4 cm by 91.4 cm. Most of these printers can accommodate any type of printing on paper, including process (full) colour. This gives them a much wider range of products and makes higher-quantity runs more economical. The customers served by sheet-fed printers generally have greater printing knowledge and higher expectations for quality results than those who use copy shops.

Web Printers

These printers serve large customers with very large volume needs (greater than 10 000). Web printing presses utilize large rolls of paper, some weighing as much as 900 kg. The presses feed the paper from the roll through a "web" of turns and processes, giving the most flexibility for a variety of applications. The extensive set-up and labour-intensive nature of this process requires huge quantities to make this efficient. Large national companies and advertising agencies, as well as most national magazines, use web printers to produce their products. These same companies, however, would likely use a sheet-fed print shop to produce their business stationery and internal forms. The quantity of the run is what determines the choice.

Copying utilizes xerographic reproduction technology involving optics and toners, while printing utilizes film and metal plates which assure 100 percent detail and maximum quality. Printers of all sizes differentiate themselves based either on low cost or on quality and service. The printing industry is competitive and the market area in which a company operates determines the price that can be charged for products.

Exhibit 2.2

Glossary of Terms

Black-copying   See 'Copying'.

Camera-ready   Layout of customer draft or description in a manner that can be "read" by the press. This includes separating one colour from another and generating clean text and artwork that can be photographed.

Commercial printing   Printing for business customers.

Copying   Also called xerography. An electrophotographic reproduction process that uses a selenium surface, electrostatic forces, and toner to form an image.

Die-cutting   The process of using sharp steel rules to cut special shapes for labels, boxes, folders, etc. from printed sheets.

Embossing   Impressing an image in relief to achieve a raised surface.

Foil stamping   Application of thin, metal "foil" using a heat process. Used instead of ink, it gives a metallic finish to text or art.

Plating   Thin metal plates are "burned" with the stripped, camera-ready artwork using a chemical process. The mirror image of the artwork is left on the plate. A separate plate is required for each colour of ink.

Printing   Application of ink by press using metal plates, rubber mats (blankets), oil, and water. Also called lithography or offset printing.

Process colour   Printing process that utilizes four colours—cyan, magenta, yellow, and black to create all colours.

Scoring   Impressing or indenting a mark with a rule in the paper to make folding easier.

Sheet-fed printers   Printing companies that utlilize presses that require large sheets, normally 58.4 cm to 91.4 cm wide.

Stripping   The pasting of camera-ready copy onto large sheets, called flats, which will be photographed with a camera.

Thermography   The creation of raised printing by the application of fine wax beads to wet ink. A heat process melts the wax beads to form the raised texture.

Web printers   Printing companies that utilize presses that require large rolls of paper that run through a multi-directional web.

Xerographic reproduction   See 'Copying'.

Exhibit 2.3

Workflow at Frontier Printers, Inc.

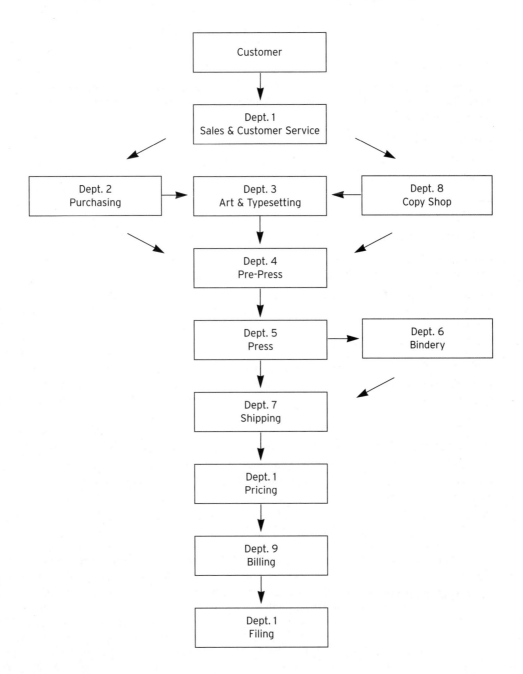

Empowerment and Workforce Adjustment at Human Resources Development Canada

Kenneth E. Loucks

Michael B. Robertson

INTRODUCTION

On a warm Friday afternoon in late June of 1997, Laura Sillinger, the associate deputy director, Ontario Region, for Human Resources Development Canada (HRDC), sat and read for the third time the memo she had just received while contemplating what the next five days would be like. She had been summoned to Ottawa to make a presentation to the deputy minister, HRDC, on the following Wednesday regarding the most recently completed fiscal year. The timing of the meeting was not extraordinary; these reviews were an annual occurrence, but the main topic had never been overtly presented. Specifically, the deputy minister wanted to hear justification for the wildly excessive severance numbers he was being asked to give to his "political overlord." There were allegations of mismanagement implied in the call to this meeting, and Laura knew she would have to be very careful in her accounting for what had been an extremely difficult time of change for the organization.

Laura had recognized that this would be an important issue and had started preparing for just such a presentation 10 weeks earlier. The past year had been one of organizational turmoil across Ontario. The previous federal budget had called for the reduction of 5000 employees from HRDC nationwide, and Ontario's portion was to be 1100. In the end, Ontario severed some 1800 people from the ranks, and this exodus had warped the fabric of the entire network. At the federal level, the costs were extraordinary. The severance of 700 extra employees in a fiscal year would produce a budgetary shock. While there is a recognizable cost benefit to the early severance of employees, it is only realized on a long-term, amortized basis.

The organizational change reached every corner of the system, affected every area, and changed every local office, permanently. She could still feel the fear of an entire organization, as people watched close friends leave, their careers unfinished, and others retire before anyone thought it would be necessary.

In preparation for the Ottawa meeting, one of the first calls she made was to the director of the Niagara area office in St. Catharines, Ontario. Niagara had experienced cuts that exceeded those of other regions of the province, and yet important gains had been made in service quality and efficiency. In fact, over the previous five years Niagara had severed 147 employees of a workforce that originally totalled just over 260. The area had just terminated approximately 60 people due to the latest round of budget cuts, yet showed a significant increase in performance in terms of service delivery.

Impressed, the ADD asked the area director to put together an account of the events of a tumultuous year and an assessment of the present state of the organization in Niagara. She felt that a critical analysis of this document was essential to her presentation, and she knew there were lessons here for the entire organization as it looked towards the next millennium. As she put the memo in her briefcase preparing for a working weekend, she wondered if those lessons could be learned now.

BACKGROUND

Located between the southwestern shore of Lake Ontario and the northeastern shore of Lake Erie, the Niagara region includes a geographic area of approximately 1800 km^2. Historically, Niagara had relied on large international manufacturers to drive its economy for over 45 years following World War II, until the local branch plants began to downsize and close due to the recession or corporate restructuring brought about by the now well-known changes in the global economy. The corresponding economic impact, in particular job displacement, was severely felt in the latter half of the 1980s and the early 1990s. These developments resulted in both an increase in the volume of traditional "employment insurance services" delivered by HRDC and a requirement for new or enhanced employment-creation services. Coping with the emergence of this "Rust Belt" environment put the Niagara office on early alert in recognizing the need for change.

Until the early 1990s, the pace of workforce reduction at HRDC in Niagara resulting from the diminution of financial resources had been manageable through normal annual attrition and the flexibility inherent in the temporary or contracted portion of the workforce. Displacement could take place without affecting people's sense of job security. The management team understood the implications of the impending introduction of the Resource Allocation Model (RAM) for the Ontario region in the fiscal year of 1992–1993. RAM was an expenditure model whose most significant variables were client population and general population. RAM was based on a formula of regional indicators, the most heavily weighted of which was the unemployment rate, and suggested that regardless of the basket of services being offered by each HRDC office, an office in Timmins would not be allocated the same resources as an office in Toronto. RAM's anticipated effects upon the Niagara office strongly suggested the likelihood of workforce reduction.

The new area manager had a clear perception of the need to adapt to trends that appeared to be the tip of the iceberg. His leadership style valued entrepreneurship and employee empowerment through participation and cooperation. A course of action to involve his management team first, and then the front-line staff, was initiated.

"Unfreezing," removing the sense of security that an established culture creates, and sensitizing the organization was started at a three-day management retreat held in Niagara-on-the-Lake. At this retreat, the vision of a new organization operating under a management area perspective was established and reinforced by asking managers to fill different positions at different times. This broke down job ownership, and a cadre of managers was created with a new perspective of broader service demands and keener insight into the needs for a flexible workforce.

During 1992 and 1993, proactive, participative forward planning was undertaken with the formation of an area task force consisting of the managers in Niagara. Subcommittees were formed to address the key issues the Niagara office was likely to face. Simultaneously, productivity improvement was encouraged through the use of microcomputer hardware and the development of software and by increasing the skill level and financial support for what was then a small technology unit resident in HRDC Niagara.

IMPLEMENTATION PROGRESSES

As this process of transformation and planning progressed, externally imposed resource reductions were accelerating and increasing in magnitude. Over time a number of issues and practices, some unconventional in HRDC if not the entire civil service, were discussed, developed, and acted upon. These included:

- restructuring to meet **service and performance** requirements through such devices as centralization, partnerships with community agencies such as the Career Placement Centre, and program design and development;
- increasing **volume of throughput** through changing work methodologies by such devices as client self-service areas and no-counter offices;
- productivity **improvement** through multi-skilling of personnel and the implementation of technology; and
- **lean production** through flatter organizations with greater flexibility and faster response times.

The process contributed to a focus on outputs and a commitment to quality service. The shift from custody and supervision of inputs, inherent in traditional practices, to management of outputs was subtle at first but profound in impact both operationally and culturally. Increasingly, client services and the quality of those services became the focus for all planning and the litmus test of decisions.

Essentially, the organization was turned upside down and viewed from the customer's point of first contact. The culture embraced was not only one of a new "commitment to quality service" as the overriding mission of HRDC Niagara but also one that recognized the centrality of the human resource development approach to achieving that mission through an empowered workforce.

ADJUSTMENT "SHOCK WAVES"

Throughout the period when the area was undergoing transformation, a number of events created "shock waves" that served to feed the forces of resistance. This led the staff to question the wisdom and equity of what was being done. These included: the loss of all temporary positions through the RAM; the loss of "permanent" positions through successive large-salary budget reductions; culture shock due to the Hamilton office amalgamation and then separation from the region and, ultimately, denial and reinstatement of incentive package applications.

While RAM's introduction in 1992 had been anticipated, its magnitude had not. It required a major reduction in personnel that, given the magnitude and logistical constraints, could only be accomplished by removing the majority of the contract staff. Niagara had a large loss of personnel but, due to changes in the service mix, little or no loss of work to do.

The remaining staff of permanent employees, while insulated, was alerted to the beginnings of a **climate of severance**, which would become considerably stronger in the ensuing years. They were seeing friends and family losing jobs with no reduction of work to be done. In fact, there had been a significant *increase* in workload as a result of the downturn in the region's economy. There was still a growing trend in the demand for "insurance" operations, while the need for new skill and effort towards enhanced "employment" services was increasing rapidly.

The RAM-generated budget for 1993 required further staff severance resulting in both the first permanent staff being targeted for severance under the existing "cash-out" provisions of the workforce adjustment legislation of 1991 and non-replacement of persons leaving through normal attrition. This was a major shock in an area that had an employee profile where 60 percent of permanent staff had over 20 years of service. HRDC Niagara historically had a long-term, stable workforce with a sense of loyalty in a geographic region that was remarkable for its continued economic instability.

Should these "cash-out" provisions for reduction not have provided sufficient candidates, an involuntary separation process would have had to be invoked. The alternative available for workforce reduction in the absence of any seniority provisions in the public service was a "reverse-order merit-rating system."[1] This was viewed by all concerned as a divisive, inhumane process requiring up to nine months to complete and serving only to work against any positive elements in the relationship between staff and management. The new style of empowerment was in its early phases and was put to a severe test as the workforce was called on to achieve the staff reduction on a voluntary basis.

Diminishing resources coupled with severe recession-induced workload increases signalled the need for increased productivity to meet performance targets. It was in this environment that management was asking staff to take a positive, proactive, and entrepreneurial approach to preparing for improved services and performance in the face of almost certain further reductions in staffing and financial resources. In effect, they were being asked to adopt and embrace a **culture of development** in a **climate of severance**.

---

[1] The "reverse-order merit-rating system" evaluated and rank-ordered employees based on externally developed performance measures. In this way, it identified those employees with the lowest performance ratings and targeted them for termination.

In recognition of the need to provide staff with support in this new environment, "Power of Transition" workshops were arranged for all staff in the Niagara area. This workshop had been developed at the national level in an effort to provide organizational change exposure to regional and area offices. It was used as a means to acclimatize the staff and further facilitate the establishment of a new corporate direction towards change.

At this time, management relied heavily on the use of staff committees both for input in helping to shape the new direction and as a means of engaging staff and thus eliciting their ownership of the change process. Committees were used extensively to address specific issues regarding different areas of responsibility. Participation was solicited and received from all staffing levels of the operational departments particularly affected.

The area office began to experiment with service delivery options designed around the remaining employee base, and the technology unit was given a much higher priority at this point. The first action was to staff the unit with highly qualified personnel who were at once designers, builders, and managers. This allowed the rapid introduction of microcomputer-based systems as an aid to front-line client service delivery and exemplified a move towards a new vision built upon a self-service philosophy. The result was that, with the assistance of the tuition reimbursement plan offered by the national office, over 90 percent of staff became literate and functional in this critical area.

In the fall of 1993, forecast salary budget cuts of \$359 220 for 1994–1995 required the severing of more permanent staff members. These reductions, requiring a large number of severances under the "cash-out provisions," again were fully subscribed on a voluntary basis. At this time, details of a new "service delivery model," created over the previous nine months, were presented to the regional office. This model showed sweeping organizational change with the implementation of technological innovation, but it permitted maintenance and enhancement of the area mission while absorbing the reductions. The meeting facilitated approvals for the "cash-outs" and tacitly endorsed both the new service delivery model and the transformation of the management organization in Niagara.

In late February 1994, a vision of organizational redesign, sweeping technological innovation, and job reclassification that would require extensive retraining was communicated to staff of the Niagara area. The "Client Service Officer" position was created, which combined the responsibilities of the job classifications Agent 1, E&I Officer, and Client Service Representative. Clients would see one line staff member much of the time, and the service time required for each client would be drastically reduced. Employees would be given multiple skills through training to assist in this initiative. And by January 1995, experimental positions were established to begin the first stage of implementation for this "new-look" staff at the Canada Employment Centres in the area.

During the transformation process, which began in 1992, productivity and performance targets continued to be met and exceeded. Concurrently, a "programs and services review" was performed in the management area, the findings of which were published in April of 1994. This document resulted from the involvement of over 60 employees of HRDC Niagara from all levels of the organization. In 20 consultative meetings, over 220 recommendations regarding the operation of HRDC were made and published in a 127-page document. This study went well beyond the local area in scope to include the regional and national areas of responsibility in an effort to give those parties a grassroots perspective as the organization was heading into the national social policy reform debate led by the then minister for human resource development Lloyd Axworthy.

The budget brought down in 1995 by Finance Minister Paul Martin was a major shock to the working environment in the public service. It demanded the reduction of 45 000 civil servants of which 5000 would come from HRDC nationally. The Niagara region was informed that its salary budget would be reduced by $1 036 250. While a reduction had been anticipated, one of this magnitude would have been impossible to forecast. Some adjustment assistance was afforded by amended workforce adjustment (WFA) legislation that offered early leaving incentives through the creation of the early-departure incentive and early-retirement incentive packages. A key organizational enhancement was formed at the beginning of this year, with the creation of the WFA committee (WFAC). This committee was made up of the area's managers and director and union representation from all HRDCs in Niagara. Its purpose was to jointly identify all human resource impacts in the area resulting from the federal budget and to make decisions on the best approach to solving these problems. The line staff was empowered through their union's participation on this committee to help make important decisions regarding their employment lives.

At this time, the Hamilton and Niagara offices were amalgamated as a result of regional reorganization, with the Niagara management team taking the lead in the newly constituted "area." Organizational change initiatives for Niagara were slowed down or put on hold as the management team concentrated on rationalizing two office infrastructures and aligning two very different organizational cultures. One major hurdle was that the Hamilton office had not previously downsized in any way other than by normal attrition. The Niagara management team, with its radical new vision, was viewed with suspicion and mistrust.

Retraining to create a multi-skilled workforce, however, was continued during this time in spite of resistance from some front-line staff. This initiative was viewed with suspicion in light of the fact that no other management area was attempting organizational change of this magnitude. The job design transformation also posed significant challenges from an administrative perspective. Human resource legislation and policies born of the *Public Service Act* were created in an environment of specific "siloed" jobs. This mechanistic structure could not allow for the easy movement of staff into the multi-skilled and multi-responsible positions that were now required by the Niagara area office. As a result, staff were required to "compete" for jobs in the new structure, which created an atmosphere of tension, suspicion, and fear.

Some staff members viewed this organizational transformation as an affliction and asked why this was "being done to them" in the face of such a major organizational "shake-down." Competing for newly designed positions created to perform the same tasks served to amplify an already uncertain environment regarding job security.

The reductions required in Niagara for the 1995–1996 fiscal year were of such magnitude that they were undersubscribed on a voluntary basis. Management initiated a reverse-order merit-rating process to identify surplus employees in the affected departments of the organization. The process was extremely divisive and was necessarily exacerbated by the "multi-skilling" job competition. It saw employees openly "playing off" against one another on the basis of performance. This also served to create a chasm between staff and management that was widened by the amalgamation of the Hamilton and Niagara management areas. Organizational change initiatives were suspended and management's presence diminished considerably.

The end result was a mood of fear and distrust between the now very separate groups. The merit-rating process would take eight months to complete, adding significantly to what was already a tension-filled climate.

In late 1995, HRDC national headquarters introduced the concept of the human resources investment fund. The Niagara Human Resources Coordinating Committee (HRCC) was asked to be part of a pilot to develop an approach to the formulation of business plans for HRCCs with a changed mission, primarily focused on the provision of enhanced employment services. Key to this was the assumption that all services would be provided in concert with a number of community partners and built upon assets already present in the geographic region. The plan identified the need to introduce technological innovations to the employment side of the operation and more importantly signalled the need for employment staff to follow the same multi-skills training that the insurance staff had received in early 1995.

The employment staff perceived the introduction of multi-skilling as a tremendous threat to their employment environment. They, too, vocally questioned why they were being forced to change so radically when no other HRDC area office was doing so.

For the 1996–1997 fiscal year, the Niagara management area received another salary reduction of $705 780. However, the Hamilton area was reconstituted as a separate management area once again. The only relief for the Niagara area was that the previous year's reverse-order merit-rating process was perceived as so unpleasant by area staff that the salary reductions were fully achieved through voluntary separations. In anticipation of the final year's salary reduction from the 1995 federal budget for Niagara, the management team began planning for the 1997–1998 budget year in May of 1996 with the full participation of the union. A "total disclosure" policy was practised in regard to all budgets allocated to the area, and human resource planning became the responsibility of the entire organization. As part of its strategy, management was prepared to assume a level of risk in managing the budget in the event that sufficient volunteers were not available to leave under the workforce adjustment program. This was to be accomplished by anticipating that a percentage of the budget would be freed up based on traditional, unplanned, unpaid leave of absence situations that occur on an annual basis. By October 1996, sufficient volunteers had not come forward even to the level that the management team was prepared to risk, so "all-staff" meetings were held throughout the area indicating a projected salary shortfall for 1997–1998 of $545 000. Staff were advised that the reverse-order merit-rating process would be necessary, and by the end of that month, 22 applications for the WFA program were in hand.

Even with the 22 applications, the management team had not met their total salary reductions for the coming year. They were, however, prepared to "risk manage" the balance of the reduction through the unpaid leave strategy.

A further complication was also affecting morale among staff members in relation to their job security. As part of the area's service delivery network strategy, some of the smaller human resource centre offices in the area were slated to close, to be replaced by third-party delivery agreements that would provide the continuation of rudimentary HRDC services. While practical in terms of optimizing the area's salary budget, the initiative was seen by many staff and the union as a sellout of their jobs, eventually leading to involuntary separations for many staff. In addition, the move was seen as adding to an already escalating amount of work for the staff that remained in the organization with the perception that management was indifferent to the situation. Morale diminished and a growing mistrust of management became evident in debates regarding further organizational changes in area meetings and in union-management meetings.

On March 5, 1997, the regional office informed all area directors that applications for the WFA program would not be approved due to an oversubscription to the program. All 22 applications from the Niagara area were, therefore, no longer being considered for approval. This decision sent a shock wave throughout Ontario. Outrage spilled into the open, the intranet crackled, and the media circled. People had made life-altering decisions based upon their applications. Some had sold theirhouses in an effort to relocate for future employment. Others had retirement plans prepared based upon the severance package they were to receive. Local and area managers were left to take the full brunt of the staff's ire for a circumstance that was totally incomprehensible, since budget cuts had been responsibly met and no previous applications had ever been denied. The sudden, unexpected refusal was seen as a denial of all that had been done to humanely achieve the organization's mission and financial objectives.

The staff that were unaffected by the decision reacted as well, for when the applications were refused, the budget shortfall still needed to be addressed. There were two alternatives that were assumed; either there was more money available that area management had "squirrelled" away, or no job was safe. Staff feared that area management would make decisions unilaterally regarding the budget deficit and that staff would, again, be the ones to pay the price.

As the "shock wave" was still reverberating two days later, a second communication was received from the regional office reversing the decision. All 22 applications were approved, but a moratorium was placed on all future severance applications.

THE CURRENT SITUATION

The effect of these decisions was still being felt almost three months after they were made. Staff mistrusted not only the decisions that their managers made and the reasons behind them but also their ability to manage in the local environment where decisions made locally could be arbitrarily changed at other levels of the organization. Henceforth, management's credibility in terms of operational change would be severely questioned.

And yet, the success of the Niagara area's initiatives was readily apparent by the beginning of 1997. Performance targets were largely exceeded and a more effective and efficient workforce had been established, assisted in large part by the implementation of advanced technological tools. Measures such as speed of pay were vastly improved; insurance productivity had soared to over 1200 clients per staff member; and the return on investment for investigation and control had exceeded $12 for every dollar spent. All this was achieved with 147 fewer staff members as compared with the 1991 complement.

Laura Sillinger could not escape the feeling that she was facing a "no-win" scenario. On the one hand, she managed an organization that was deeply scarred and extremely suspicious due to the extraordinary nature of the recent restructuring process. On the other, she had an area that was functioning at levels never before experienced in HRDC Ontario. She knew that over the next few days, she would have to carefully rationalize the process that brought about an organization that lived in a climate of fear in the context of its potential to become one that delivered the highest quality of service. Could she do this to the satisfaction of the deputy minister next Wednesday?

## part two

Building a Competitive Workforce

The best companies now know without a doubt where productivity—real and limitless productivity—comes from. It comes from challenged, empowered, excited, rewarded teams of people. It comes from engaging every single mind in the organization, making everyone part of the action, and allowing everyone to have a voice—a role—in the success of the enterprise. Doing so raises productivity not incrementally but by multiples.

—Jack Welch, General Electric

No one ever admits to being a bad human resources planner. Nevertheless, planning is among the topics to which we pay the most lip service. Few organizations admit to ignoring planning for their employee needs. Yet, we have only to think for a moment about the dismal hiring and firing record of many companies to realize that this is a major problem area. Most of us in the Western world tend to be action orientated—we like to do things first and then think about them afterwards. There are pressures in the world of business favouring this tendency—in particular, the short-term nature of financial reporting and the dramatic impact of continuous change on all our best-laid plans. In addition, human resources forecasting is *not an easy process*—a point that is illustrated throughout the cases in this book.

IMPORTANCE OF HR PLANNING

Does the fact that forecasting is difficult mean that we can get away with no planning? Absolutely not! Consider that there are three aspects to effective human resources management: a close link between overall business and human resources strategies, forward planning of human resource needs, and the efficient use of human resources. Peter Drucker once said, "Recruit in haste, repent at leisure." This section of the book deals with the planning for and acquisition of human talent. Manage this well, and your organization benefits immensely. Manage this poorly, and all other good human resource practices are much more difficult because the talent you have is not what you need.

HR activities exist within a business context and are there to support an organization's objectives. These HR activities must be part of an overall planning process. It is not enough to have strategies in place. Implementation is critical. Effective organizations know what the people needs of their various projects and activities will be and prepare a plan to meet these needs. Thus, human resources planning attempts to meet needs at all points in the business planning cycle. Finally, effective HRM recognizes the value of people as part of the corporate assets of an organization, assets worthy of tender, loving care. Individuals need to be challenged with meaningful responsibilities that enable them to contribute as efficiently as possible.

There is little doubt that with the pressures of new technology, labour legislation, government intervention, globalization, and the ever-present demands of change, strategic human resources planning will become *more important*, not less important, in the future. Human resource planning is essential to ensuring that all the various human resource activities are geared effectively to company needs.

STRATEGIC STAFFING

A forward plan for developing a competitive workforce, integrated within organization strategies, is a critical component of ensuring effectiveness. Staffing becomes strategic when plans for staffing needs are developed according to the overall strategic direction of the organization. These plans are implemented through such staffing techniques as recruitment, selection, promotion, transfers, and, if necessary, downsizing. The intent is that every person employed in an organization is there because he or she has something to contribute to the overall organizational objectives.

Strategic staffing is not an option in times of change. As organizations become more flexible, with changes occurring rapidly, managers might be tempted not to plan for staffing at all, but rather to act spontaneously. If there is to be any meaningful alignment of HRM with organizational strategy, this temptation must be resisted. When conditions are changing rapidly, careful analysis and planning of future staffing are all the more important. Of course, such planning needs to be flexible and adaptive.

In contrast to some of the rather fixed and formalized staffing procedures of yesterday, organizations are adopting more informal, "open market" approaches, which allow employees to bid for positions and enable managers to act quickly in filling them. Companies will use the staffing process that best suits their immediate needs, including: succession planning, targeted development, focused internal search, job posting, and informal staffing.

THE JUST-IN-TIME MODEL

In his book, *HR Strategy*, James Walker uses the term "just-in-time talent" to refer to a growing trend in strategic staffing to have the people a manager needs just when they are needed.[1] Companies seek to have the required talent—with just the right skills, knowledge, abilities, and experience—to meet their needs. This involves maintaining just the right inventory of staff and the right flow of talent to meet labour demand. As you can guess, the concept of just-in-time staffing adopts JIT terminology from the manufacturing industry and applies it to the world of HRM.

Just-in-time staffing does raise some difficult ethical considerations. What may be a great concept for manufacturing engineers and accountants may not be quite so much fun for employees. There are legal considerations in Canada limiting the ability of organizations to fully practise just-in-time staffing. Perhaps even more important, however, is the reality that it makes good sense to balance the immediate efficiencies promised by just-in-time staffing against the longer-term effectiveness of employees. Such effectiveness is a function of empowered employees who feel they have a real stake in the organization. Commitment and satisfaction are bound to dimish when employees are treated as simply inputs to the production process.

THE LIMITS OF RATIONAL MODELS

It is rather straightforward to say that the policies of the HRM function must fit the needs of the organization. It is much more difficult to ensure that what actually happens reflects changing corporate strategy. By never losing sight of the firm's key success factors, HRM can contribute to organizational adaptation and effectiveness. Most human resource plans follow a logical, rational model, but this is usually only the beginning of a complex planning process, one that proceeds on the assumption that plans can be specified accurately in advance. It assumes that managers and others will act logically. It also assumes that the very act of planning does not affect the situation dramatically. None of these assumptions is necessarily true. Organizations change constantly, and change will frustrate those who want to specify exact plans. Managers are notorious for responding to their "gut feeling" about a problem; they often reject a logical solution or choice because it "doesn't feel right," or "out of loyalty." Information from the planning process leaks out to employees who then respond in ways that undermine the plan.

As a result, human resource planning is a less exact procedure than one might expect. The person promoted by the superior may not necessarily be the one chosen on the basis of a rational match of skills and job requirements. A predicted shortage of skills in an area may not materialize, or individuals may recognize the shortage and move to correct it before it happens. Both these situations demonstrate that a planning model that recognizes both rational and non-rational components is more appropriate to the area of HRM.

RECRUITMENT

In this age of "lean and mean," many organizations have systematically reduced their number of permanent employees. Instead, they are turning to various alternative forms of contingent employment. These include part-time, contract, teleworking, and virtual Web hir-

---

[1] Walker, J. *HR Strategy.* (New York: McGraw-Hill, 1992).

ing. Such developments have increased the strategic role of HRM in the hiring process, and human resource professionals should examine their recruitment strategy to ensure that it meets the needs of the organization.

There is considerable controversy over the need for "realism" within the recruiting process. If the company is oversold, the candidate becomes disillusioned and unhappy on the job. To prevent this situation, organizations should engage in "realistic job previews." During the recruiting/interviewing process, the job and company should be described as accurately as possible. In turn, job interviewees are usually advised to present an accurate description of themselves—their interests, skills, and objectives—to interviewers. If candidates oversell themselves, the organization will also be disillusioned and unhappy with the reality.

The key to any selection process is the matching of job and individual. Job analysis determines the requirements and characteristics of a position. These need to be matched carefully with the abilities and needs of the individual. This process is simple in concept but difficult in practice, because it is difficult to forecast the demands of a position over a long period or predict the performance of individuals with accuracy. And in today's changing world, job descriptions are often static and become dated as organizational needs change.

Once an individual has joined the firm, a socialization process begins: The individual learns the norms, values, and expectations of the firm. The process may actually begin before the individual officially joins the company. It may commence through a formal orientation procedure or in an unstructured way on the job. However it happens, human resource professionals need to recognize that a "psychological contract" is developed between the individual and the firm. This unwritten contract involves the mutual expectations of both parties. It is thought that an excellent way to orient a newcomer is to develop as explicit an understanding of the psychological contract as possible among the new employee, the employee's supervisor, and the human resource professional. If there are differences in the expectations of these three parties with respect to the employment decision, those differences can be discussed and resolved when the contract is explicit. If the contract is only implicit, however, differences may fester without resolution and create morale, productivity, and turnover problems whose real source may never be known.

It is important to note that the advent of contingent work relationships has had a dramatic impact upon the types of psychological contracts that are established in Canadian organizations today. The expectation of life-long employment has given way to mutual contracts of organizational contribution and skill acquisition predicated upon much shorter time horizons.

THE CASES IN PART 2

The cases that follow provide opportunities for the participants to make decisions on developing competitive workforces through strategic human resources planning, recruiting and selecting job candidates, and orienting newcomers to jobs and careers.

GENTRO Limited deals with human resource planning and development in an entrepreneurial, fast-growing firm. It is not clear that the old processes of developing managers will be appropriate, given the reorganization of the company and the changing technology in the industry. The key questions raised are, what sort of managers will be needed, and where will Gentro find them?

L-D Tool & Die is a small and successful manufacturer of custom moulds with a sizable export business. Dramatic growth has resulted in an acute shortage of skilled workers; the company has been unable to recruit the necessary expertise locally, and new directions in recruitment are clearly desired. With the demographics of the Canadian workforce, skill shortages will be a common occurrence in many organizations today.

Family Medical Group of Companies describes a business in the dynamic and changing health-care environment of Canada today. It must incorporate a new manufacturing division within its traditional distribution business. The new director of HRM is charged with the responsibility of creating an HR plan in a company with no prior experience of strategic planning.

Recruitment Procedures at Olsen Long deals with the annual hiring of graduates for a major chartered accounting firm in Canada. Participants are required to define and characterize the job opening and evaluate the available applicants in relation to the job description.

The Norris Company: "Just a Typical Day" takes participants through a day in the life of a plant manager. Participants are asked to identify the essential tasks of that manager, given the nature of his industry and environment. The question "What is the manager's job?" is not straightforward and must be addressed before a change in plans can be made.

In **Burnaby Glass Decision**, a significant promotion decision has to be made that involves a radical rethinking of the managerial role in the company, as well as an in-depth analysis of the job–person matching process.

Finally, **A Matter of Fit** allows participants to observe the problems that occur when the expectations of a new MBA graduate are out of sync with those of the firm. The task in this case is to understand what went wrong and to improve the orientation and hiring processes for the future.

GENTRO Limited

Gene Deszca

GENTRO's CEO and its Board had come to a difficult realization. GENTRO's continued capacity to grow rapidly was at risk because of its inability to find and develop talented individuals. In the past, GENTRO had relied on acquisitions to grow but the integration of acquired companies was becoming difficult. Management would not walk away from good opportunities, but they knew they needed to do a better job digesting and leveraging the corporate assets they had already acquired. If their current operating units were to grow, people needed to learn how to talk and work with one another. Strategic management and leadership skills were in scarce supply, and presently, managers seemed to have little time for anything other than trying to keep up with their business units.

Although GENTRO was privately owned by a small number of shareholders, its access to capital resources was significant. And over time, it had demonstrated its willingness to make significant capital investments. However, extending this investment mentality to human capital did not come easily to senior management. The CEO had recognized the talent problem and had recruited Kerry Merstone as the director of member development. The CEO and the Board were anticipating receiving Kerry's size-up of the situation and her recommendations for action. While the Board knew there were managerial talent problems, they were far from a consensus concerning what should be done.

KERRY MERSTONE

Kerry had arrived at GENTRO with an undergraduate degree in industrial psychology, a recent MBA, and eight years of experience in management development with two packaged-goods firms. She had worked three years with a consumer-products subsidiary in training needs assessment and supervisory training and then five years with B&A in the design and delivery of management development programs. She resigned from B&A to pursue an MBA because she found that her lack of formal management education restricted her upward mobility. Kerry graduated in the top quartile of her class and joined GENTRO in September 1999, after being actively pursued by GENTRO for several months. GENTRO's interest was stimulated by a study on the company she had completed as part of an MBA elective in marketing research. The professionalism, analytic insight, and interpersonal competence that she had demonstrated had attracted the attention of the CEO and the vice-president of marketing and organizational growth. They became her corporate sponsors.

In Kerry's first month, she had visited half the operating units, interviewing GENTRO managers. In addition, she had reviewed organizational documents, introduced herself to other key players at head office, and attempted to develop a feel for the organizational politics and strategy of the firm. Kerry now faced the challenge of developing an acceptable plan for dealing with the human resource issues that the firm faced.

GENTRO'S EVOLUTION AND CURRENT STRUCTURE

When GENTRO was formed in 1971, it manufactured electrical and mechanical components for the North American auto industry, i.e., Ford, General Motors, and Chrysler. GENTRO now comprises 19 relatively independent operating units, located in North America (six plants in Canada, eight in the United States), Europe (three plants), and Mexico/Brazil (two plants), and its head office was located near Toronto. The operating units were organized into three divisions (automotive—eight plants, aerospace—four plants, and industrial products—seven plants). The organizational structure is outlined in Exhibit 4.1.

Originally there had been 23 operating units, but in 1995, seven of the automotive operating units were merged into three to gain synergies and economies of scale. At that time, four of the original unit managers were let go with generous exit packages. Except for those three merged units, the operating units were based on the original acquisitions. Of the 19 operating units, 12 had unit managers who had owned the unit prior to acquisition, seven unit managers had been promoted into their current roles when three of the original owners retired at the time of purchase, and another four resigned from their units because of health issues. The acquisitions of 10 of the operating units had occurred over the last nine years at a rate of about one per year.

Each operating unit serviced its own, separate set of clients. This focus resulted from GENTRO's organizational ideology (local autonomy, decentralized control, and local accountability) and the process used to drive GENTRO's growth. GENTRO's head office acted as the strategic director, the bank, and the ultimate governance authority, but unit managers (often the original entrepreneurs) were given the autonomy to run their units as they saw fit. Unit managers were then held accountable for the end results and rewarded on their performance. Salaries of unit managers were somewhat less than the industry average, but bonuses (based on the unit's year-end profit performance) typically moved their total compensation into the top quartile. Unit managers pursued profits relentlessly and were quick to compare operations across plants.

Unit managers had complete responsibility for the operations of their unit. As well, they held a substantial proportion of outstanding shares. In fact, the unit managers represented the third-largest group of shareholders with 17 percent of the voting shares of the firm.

The past ten years had been a period of dramatic growth, with sales growing from $18 million to $832 million between 1989 and 2000. During that period, profits increased from $0.3 million to $63 million, and staffing levels had climbed to approximately 6100 employees (only 42 in head office). The 19 operating unit managers reported to the president through one of three divisional vice-presidents. In addition to their divisional responsibilities, each of the divisional vice-presidents was also responsible for an operating unit. That is, they held double responsibilities, divisional vice-president's and operating unit manager's.

There had been efforts to increase the level of planning and information system integration within each of the divisions, and these efforts had met with some success. Within the divisions, the information systems people now talked with one another, and the chief operating officers had held semi-annual planning and strategy conferences for the past three years. Divisional vice-presidents had created industry-level promotional programs and an e-business-to-business task force/design team. However, the vast majority of initiatives continued to be nested within the operating units. Operating units jealously guarded the retention of ultimate responsibility for their own performance and profitability, and they competed aggressively for bragging rights concerning the size of their performance bonuses.

Head office activities were funded by levies from the operating units. Major organization-wide decisions tended to be made (or at least confirmed) either at the annual corporate conference or through one of three standing executive committees (investments and asset management—referred to as the GENTRO Bank, the planning and strategy committee, and the communications/IT committee). Six months previously, human resource concerns were added to the planning and strategy committee's mandate.

The operating unit managers, the president, the CFO, and the other vice-presidents attended an annual corporate conference where major strategic decisions were discussed and made. Discussions at the conference were always lively, with unit operating managers challenging each other to improve performance and comparing the most recent rankings of performance results.

Membership on corporate committees was decided upon at the annual corporate conference. Most operating unit managers had mixed emotions about serving on these committees. The committees did provide opportunities to influence corporate decisions. However, the committee process was foreign to how most of the unit managers operated and took considerable time away from their operating unit. Terms varied from two to three years, and no one (with the exception of the CEO and the CFO) served on the same committee for more than two consecutive terms. A typical committee would consist of three to four operating unit managers and two senior executives. Corporate officers from head office played supportive roles on the three committees.

With the growth projected in the auto industry, the relative weakness of the Canadian dollar, and the continuing impact of NAFTA, GENTRO planned on continued growth, provided the company could learn how to support and manage it. GENTRO had a reputation for excellent client relationships based on its ability to address customer needs in a timely and innovative manner. Because of its reputation for excellence in manufacturing and quality, GENTRO was brought in early on projects and was able to sustain modestly higher margins than its competitors. Sales were expected to exceed $950 million by 2000 and $1.5 billion by 2004.

Human resources remained a primary responsibility of the independent operating units, and there was little in the way of an integrated strategy for addressing and managing human resource concerns. Human resource planning at the operating unit level was *ad hoc*, reflecting the entrepreneurial focus of the unit operating managers and their direct reports. Some of the larger operating units committed time and resources to staff development, but many relied on recruitment, on-the-job training, and performance bonuses to retain key personnel.

Kerry Merstone saw her prime initial tasks as identifying human resource issues and challenges and recommending an integrated approach for dealing with these matters at both the corporate and local levels. As one of only three senior female managers (out of a total of 24), she wondered what reception her recommendations would receive when it came time to issue them.

MANAGEMENT DEVELOPMENT AT GENTRO

Kerry discovered a wide variety of practices during her initial interviews. The number of employees in operating units varied from 250 to 500 employees. Technical development practices varied, depending upon the nature of the equipment and what was being produced in the plant. Management development practices were likewise fairly *ad hoc* and idiosyncratic to the unit and the manager in charge. The primary vehicle for development was on-the-job experience, supported occasionally by educational programs (e.g., workshops, tuition subsidies) and other development aids (e.g., conferences, books and video purchases, payment of professional fees). Approximately 50 percent of individuals in a post-secondary education program were able to access some level of financial support, and 30 percent of accredited professionals (e.g., engineers, accountants) had their dues reimbursed by their unit employers. Support for management development seemed to be higher in the North American units than it was in Europe or South America. The automotive sector had developed a supervisory training program that was shared internally within parts of the division.

Some managers in the automotive sectors mentioned that the supervisory training program had proven to be a useful way to prepare new supervisors for the challenges that they would face. However, their sentiments were not universal. Others complained about the amount of time involved (12 sessions of three hours each), while some participants commented that it would be nice if their managers were sent to the training program first so that they could practise what was being preached.

One unit manager in automotive noted the importance of autonomy and local decision-making power when it came to management development.

> Management development starts with the freedom to hire and develop your own people. You can spend money on development programs until the cows come home, but if you don't get a chance to groom the talent you need, you're behind the eight ball. Once you've selected the people you want, the key is to put them in jobs that mould them in the right ways. Production planning, operations support, shift supervision, sales, and customer service are great places to start in this business because you get to know things from the ground up. Participation in task forces and the management team are also very useful in people development, provided they have the right personality to take advantage of such approaches. Courses and education subsidization are expensive and pretty ineffective—you spend the money to get someone trained, and either the training turns out to be impractical or the individual packs up and leaves.

A manager of one of the industrial product units echoed the above sentiments and reflected on the importance of personal initiative on the part of the employee.

> I select my employees very carefully. Once they are here, though, they often fail to measure up to their potential. Those who've got what it takes know the importance of long hours, volunteering for extra assignments, asking lots of questions, and learning by digging in. Asking questions, volunteering, and working hard gets the hungry ones lots of support. People will take the time to explain things if someone shows they are truly interested and if they know how to ask without ticking people off. I don't mind investing in educational programs for such individuals if it will help both them and us, but I sure can't afford to do it for everyone.

When it came to the use of formal external courses, it was clear that there needed to be a good reason before support was forthcoming. This was particularly true for external management development programs. While there was no budget line that reported educational support in most of the operating units, most believed that funding for external management training programs was carefully rationed. One engineer from an industrial products division unit spoke of the frustration many junior managers felt concerning the lack of support for advanced education. When she mentioned to her boss that she was planning to enroll in a local part-time MBA program, the response was that no financial support was available presently and that it was hoped this program wouldn't get in the way of work or require special privileges. Another engineer (currently enrolled in a part-time MBA program) reported that his supervisor would roll his eyes whenever ideas were offered that sounded like they had come from his program. "This is the real world—let's keep theory in the classroom" was the typical response.

Funding for technical training related to equipment and processes was easier to obtain, as was instruction related to safety, computers, and ISO-related matters (most units had sought out and received ISO or equivalent certification as a response to current or anticipated customer requirements and competitive pressure). If possible, individuals were expected to get permission and pursue the training on their own time. Reimbursement (varying from 50 to 100 percent) was received upon the successful completion of courses. When managers required others to attend specific training, funding was always at the 100 percent level.

In general, individuals had an easier time gaining support for formal, external programs if they either possessed or were pursuing professional accreditation. Next came those working on degrees. As noted earlier, it was the common expectation that coursework (including classroom attendance) would be done on the employee's personal time. Some senior managers resented the expectation of support.

> Why should I be expected to help my most valuable employees go to school, just so they can increase their marketability and leave? Other firms are doing it, so I feel the pressure to go along. … It doesn't seem fair. For three years I paid for an MBA program for my sales manager, only to see the person walk six months later to one of our other divisions. They get the career advancement, and I get stuck with the bill and the cost of finding a replacement. (Chief Operating Officer, Aerospace Unit)

Managers reported that they thought management development worked better when it was put directly to use. One unit manager described how he mentored an individual pursuing the CMA (Certified Management Accountant) program in his operation. Every few weeks he would review the course field projects she was working on and discuss them with her in detail. As a result, a number of internal improvement projects were initiated, the CMA candidate became more committed to the organization, and her skills were enhanced.

While some operating unit managers regularly used formal external courses to develop their staff, they were the exception. Rather than take individuals off the job, senior managers stated that they tried to accomplish similar ends through mentoring, the provision of challenging assignments, and performance management. Sometimes the professional relationships would extend to off-site social activities, such as a barbecue by a backyard pool. Here, initiatives could be talked about in a more relaxed atmosphere. Since not everyone received equal exposure to the senior managers in a unit, some felt ignored and undervalued. All 19 operating unit managers reported the active use of performance management as a development tool. But junior and middle managers experienced a different reality. While some form of goal setting and feedback was practised in most venues, 40 percent of those interviewed reported that formal performance management largely disappeared after the first few years of employment. An aerospace unit, two of the automotive units, and one of the industrial products units were clear exceptions, with performance management used as an integral part of their management processes. These latter operations also linked bonuses and increments to the performance management process in a clear and active fashion.

On-the-job learning and development were viewed positively by most individuals, and many felt performance management had the potential to be an important component in growing the talent the firm needed. However, as a quality manager in the industrial products division noted, most of these activities were directed towards what one did now—not the future challenges one should be getting ready for:

> I'm viewed as an egghead in this organization because I'm always reading or taking courses … I do this to get myself sharp. Many people around here can do their jobs in their sleep, but how is that going to help when they have to wake up? We let people get complacent as long as they do their job well. We don't push people to better themselves, and then we get surprised when they aren't ready to take on something new. We also make it difficult for people to get exposed to new things. The attitude is "why move someone who is doing a good job—that will just disrupt things." For example, I'd love to have more contact with the sales force and our customers so that I could see the challenges they face first hand. However, I'm told that this can't be done just now and that I should focus on my current job. I've been asking for three years.

Effective staff development also required a willingness to delegate. While most unit managers believed they delegated well, a majority of their subordinates reported otherwise. They saw their managers as wanting to do things themselves while complaining about the lack of time and help. When they did attempt to delegate, they were perceived as doing it poorly, assigning activities in a piecemeal fashion, with ineffective direction. They were also reported as likely to second-guess the work of others and were often found redoing work to suit themselves.

For their part, several of the unit managers reported that they only delegated to certain individuals because they were the only ones that could be counted on to exercise initiative and think for themselves.

> What's the point of delegating when you have to hand hold all the time? … It's quicker and less frustrating to simply do it yourself. The other day, I got a call from one of the purchasing clerks, asking if she should place a reorder for tubular steel because we were running low. What did she think we should do—close down production? (Senior Plant Engineer, Automotive Division)

Due to the pace of their work and their drive for success, GENTRO's managers found it difficult to find time for improvement initiatives that could be used to both develop the people and improve the organization. They reported that staffing levels were always very tight, with a focus always on the targets they were striving to meet. One sales manager (Industrial Products) noted that she had wanted to revamp her unit's customer communication program for about three years now but never had found the time or resources to do so.

> Making your numbers is extremely important in this organization. We've always run very lean. When everyone is flat out, it's hard to get around to many of the things you know you should do. We do well, but a lot of the things don't get done because we haven't got anyone to delegate to. A lot of money could be made if we only had the time to do some of these things.

New initiatives also were difficult to launch for the same reasons, and managers found they lacked the time and resources to get out and see what other organizations were doing—even other managers/professionals in their own organization. As a result, many individuals (particularly those responsible for inside functions) reported that they felt out of touch. There had been a few attempts over the years to bring managers/professionals involved in similar functions together, but these efforts had not been sustained.

While many junior and middle-level managers reported experiencing frustration when it came to their development, others spoke more positively about their immediate supervisors. For example, one plant accountant (Aerospace) reported that his manager always found time to expose him to new challenges (e.g., task forces, special projects, vacation coverage), help him shore up weak areas, and give him feedback on how he was doing. He very much appreciated this, but he wondered if there also were formal courses he should be taking to prepare himself for promotion. Managing the overtime would be a challenge, but he felt his manager would support him.

> My manager has mentioned many times that she thinks we run far too thin at GENTRO. Rather than look outside in a panic for help, she can't understand why we don't make it more attractive to hire a few extra people and develop the talent within. There is no shortage of need and we'd be in a lot better shape if we had sufficient staff to develop backups that would allow us to deal with vacations and illnesses. Rather than having all these "temps" running about and our overtime budget groaning, we'd probably save money.

Managers in two of the automotive plants argued that employee development didn't have to cost an arm and a leg. They noted that participants attended the supervisory management program on their own time and that it was taught by local community college instructors at a reasonable rate. Further, they pointed out that they also made use of university co-op placements (to search for talent as well as address special projects) and management development initiatives. The principal management development activity they proudly referred to was one that took approximately two managers each year and systematically rotated them through the functional areas in their two plants over a 15-month period. While there were some incremental costs, individuals on these rotational appointments were given challenging projects above normal job requirements and were expected to add value. There had been seven participants in this program over the past four years and all reported that it had been both exhausting and exceedingly rewarding. Unit operating managers in the two units reported that they were very satisfied with the results. They believed it opened peoples' eyes, contributed to improvements, and resulted in very able managers. However, both were concerned about their ability to continue to challenge and retain these talented individuals.

> Our development initiative puts our dollars where our mouths are. When you develop good people you also risk losing them, but is that such a bad thing? The simple act of developing others

makes your firm and your own people better because it makes them think about what's important and how to do it more effectively. (Chief Operating Officer, Automotive Unit)

It makes you plan more so that you can take advantage of those skills—if we don't do that then we deserve to lose them…. We're too damn parochial in this organization. We hide talented people rather than expose them to other managers, and then we get angry when they get frustrated at being blocked and go to work for a competitor. (Controller, Automotive Unit)

One of the challenges Kerry observed during her field visits was that most middle managers in the operating units were unaware of what the organization as a whole was up to. They didn't know where challenging career opportunities were that might interest them, and they didn't even know what units were actively recruiting. Autonomy and decentralization had lots of merit, but people became alienated when they were the last to hear about opportunities and when they were actively discouraged from applying.

My friend is a very talented design engineer who was employed in one of our industrial products units. An opening came up for the same job in one of our other units that paid $7000 more and he wanted to apply. His boss told him that he wouldn't support his application because they needed him in his current job. They couldn't pay him more, because he was already at the maximum salary rate for his current position. He was advised to be patient. After a year of inaction he left to work with a competitor for $9000 more. When they finally found a replacement for him, the starting salary had to be raised by over $10 000 to attract someone with the right background. (Service Manager, Industrial Products Unit)

Obtaining talented people was only part of the challenge. Utilizing, leveraging, and retaining their capacities was almost as daunting an undertaking. Were GENTRO's managers open-minded to new approaches? Were they frightened of the talent? Were they worried about not being able to keep up and understand? Kerry heard enough in her travels to suggest that these were questions she should give serious attention to. Hiring people who were not a threat seemed to happen all too often. It occurred under the guise of keeping recruitment and salary costs down or hiring people with the right attitude.

One final issue that emerged during her initial round of meetings involved the role of the divisional vice-presidents. All of these individuals had spent their careers growing their personal operating units and had limited experience developing and managing the strategic direction of multiple plants within a more broadly defined industry sector.

The move from managing your own operating unit to trying to run a whole division is huge. It's a different skill set and a lot less fun. First, you have to think much more broadly and strategically, and second, you have to be a master of politics in order to get things implemented. We know how to get things done within our units and local markets but mobilizing other operating unit managers within a division is like herding cats. (Vice-President, Marketing and Organizational Growth)

HEAD OFFICE'S ROLE IN PEOPLE DEVELOPMENT

Kerry found that there was general recognition of the need for head office support for human resource planning and development. However, recognition was a long way from commitment and practice. As one automotive unit manager put it:

It's like we're all entrepreneurs, running our own operations—trying to outdo one another. We sit down at corporate, start to plan, and next thing you know we're committing ourselves to numbers that scare us. Funny thing, though. The only one egging us on is ourselves. We talk about the importance of doing those things that will sustain us, but we're driven by the numbers. We get there by being lean, running flat out, focusing on the bottom line, paying attention to customers and production, being very competitive, and ignoring everything else.

We talk planning, but we love doing. The reward system is clear—making and beating your numbers is what counts. That's where the bonuses and bragging rights come from.... No one gets praised at the annual strategy conference for developing great people, but they certainly do for beating other units and industry benchmarks on growth and profitability measures.

Some managers mentioned the need for corporate to begin charging units that weren't developing their people or were losing them. Others thought that one way to get people to pay attention would be to really reward managers who took the time and effort to develop staff. Still others thought there should be money for training, backup, and co-op positions and that there should be a required commitment of training dollars in each operating unit (say, 1 percent of sales or the cash equivalent of two or three working days for each employee in the unit). Some argued that these funds should become accessible to other operating units if they were not used by the unit supplying the funds.

Some managers who were particularly concerned about the matter talked about the huge commitments top companies like IBM made in human resource planning and people development.

Other firms have corporate VPs responsible for centralized human resource planning systems and senior training programs—we don't even possess a centralized list of the people we employ. It's no wonder good people get fed up and leave. When there's turnover or we run into a "people" crisis, we quickly get concerned about this matter. However, as soon as the Band-Aids are on, we forget and become busy and arrogant again. (Aerospace Unit Manager)

Finally, a group of influential managers believed that the matter should be left to the chief operating officers and head office should stay out of it.

Every time we move away from letting unit managers make the calls and act entrepreneurial, we get into trouble. Why do you think head office can do a better job finding and developing people than we can, and why do you think we'll do a better job if we have a budgetary gun to our head? We've exchanged managers with other units, gotten together to support technical training when it made sense, and talked with our suppliers and others to find the people we've needed. I'd rather have some shortages and occasional pain than a head office that hung around pulling people out of work, running programs, and otherwise getting in the way. (Chief Operating Officer, Industrial Products Unit)

One unit Kerry found that was particularly supportive of head office involvement had developed its own systemic approach to the problem. Managers in this unit began with their own talent inventory. In this, they recorded each employee's educational and professional background, accomplishments, skills and abilities, readiness for new assignments, demographic information (age, gender), salary level, current assignment, and other relevant information (courses taken and so on). Next came the annual performance management update. At this review, past performance against targets was discussed, development activities and initiatives were highlighted, and specific objectives (performance and development) were established for the upcoming year. Output from these reviews were used to update the talent inventory, allocate merit bonuses on individual and team bases, and plan the training and development initiatives (in-house and external programs, developmental assignments, and so on) for the upcoming year.

We are committed to using these reviews to work on the development of winners. We don't see why anyone should be left behind, because if they are, we all lose. It created some turnover and it's been expensive, but it's paying dividends now. Critical functions have backups, people are excited and engaged, and performance is getting ratcheted up. Two years ago, we were losing market share and our margins were shrinking. Now our customer service is the best in the industry, we've regained our market share and then some (23 percent growth last year), and our profit margins are 40 percent above the industry average, even though our prices are at the industry average. If you (Kerry) could leverage what we've been doing and get everyone at GENTRO sharing information, treating development seriously, and using the process to build their businesses, then we'd kill the competition. That's because most of them are worse than we are when it comes to human resource development. (Corporate Controller, Automotive Unit).

Staff shortages, combined with the emphasis on technical as well as managerial knowledge, meant a fair amount of aggressive recruitment from competitors and suppliers. This, in turn, led to recommendations for head office recruitment support from some of the operating units. However, this sentiment was not universal. As one chief operating officer (Automotive) noted, "Buying talent is what you have to do when you've been too lazy to develop your own. Unless something strange has occurred, hiring from outside is a poor substitute for internal development. Corporate shouldn't bail them out for not having done their job."

A very contentious human resource matter revolved around what role head office should play in facilitating the internal transfers of talented individuals between different operating units. Some viewed activities in this area as tantamount to raiding while others thought it was essential for individual development and making future growth possible, particularly in conjunction with the demographic reality of impending retirements and a hot labour market. All agreed that if there was to be greater action in this area it required careful planning and support for the individuals involved and their families. Currently there was no shared human resource database, employees didn't know what opportunities were available outside of their own unit, knowledge of available talent was informal and unstructured, information flow was by word of mouth, and planning and support for transfers was *ad hoc* and largely non-existent. Some degree of centralized, organization-wide human resource information existed only for chief operating officers and senior unit members who were involved with the management of the information and accounting systems. This was because GENTRO had learned (the hard way) of the consequences of having operating units that could not talk to one another.

The only time we transfer someone is when we're in a pickle or when someone has managed to get noticed by one of the anointed. Six months ago, our production manager was transferred into our East Coast aerospace plant to take over for someone who'd died of a heart attack. No one helped him sort out the logistics of his move, there were hassles with emigration concerning his family, there were problems getting his house sold, and the reimbursement for moving expenses was so mishandled that the Canada Customs and Revenue Agency threatened to treat the expenses as employment income and tax him accordingly. It's a wonder his family stayed with him and he didn't have a heart attack. (Customer Solutions Manager, Industrial Products Unit)

RELATED HR CONCERNS

GENTRO's middle and senior-level managers had been asked to focus on management development matters in their meetings with Kerry Merstone. However, when she reflected on these discussions, two related themes also surfaced—(1) structural concerns related to the industry, and (2) the organizational structures and processes that would enhance competitive advantage.

In all three divisions, managers reflected very similar thoughts about what was happening in their respective sectors. Globalization, supply chain management, and customer and competitor rationalization (through mergers, acquisitions, and organizational failures) were producing larger, more powerful customers and competitors. The pressures/demands for price, quality, and service were escalating, and firms which wanted to survive had to do one of three things—get acquired, get big, or become very adept at addressing niche needs. GENTRO's strategy had been to do the third—but on an international basis. They reasoned that if they could supply global players with timely, quality solutions to their niche needs better than anyone else, they would end up winners. Thus far, things seemed to be working, but was it sustainable? The key to GENTRO's success had been to solidify its place in desired customers' hearts and minds by acquiring small entrepreneurial niche players who deepened GENTRO's product mix. How could GENTRO maintain the critical spirit and skill set as aging ran its course, hungry new competitors entered the marketplace from anywhere on the globe, changes occurred in technologies and products, and yesterday's niche solution became today's commodity?

Concerns about industry trends naturally gave rise to the consideration of how best to structure its activities. What structure would best allow GENTRO to sustain and grow itself? Some argued that the current approach was just fine and that one of the realities they had to face was that not all units would or could survive over time. As one unit manager said, "We certainly don't want to create structures and processes that protected weak units." These managers believed that GENTRO would be much better off to err on the side of entrepreneurial and technical zeal, to hive off faltering units that no longer fit, to nurture growth where conditions were right, and to take advantage of the flexibility and adaptability that characterized the current structural approach. In these managers' minds, most structural interventions that attempted to shield units only created larger head offices, inefficiencies, and competitive impairment.

Others believed that head office needed to take on a larger role if the seeds of GENTRO's success were to bear full fruit. They pointed to the need to take advantage of the synergies that were available, to learn from one another's experiences in the marketplace, to grow talent and technological muscle, and to otherwise contribute to each other's capacity to compete effectively. They believed GENTRO's size and complexity needed to be reflected in the centralized services offered by head office and the structure of the organization itself. These individuals reasoned that if the entrepreneurial units were to win over time, they needed access to systems and supports that would improve their competitive staying power. This was not possible if they were simply left to act on their own. While this position was clearly articulated by a number of the chief operating officers, there was no unanimity in this camp concerning what the structure should be, what centralized services should be offered, and whether or not those services should be required or voluntary.

WHAT NEXT?

During her interviews with GENTRO managers, Kerry Merstone had become all too aware of the diversity of human resource opinions and practices that coexisted within the firm. The question was what to do about this diversity and what to recommend to the Board. The ideal solution was proving to be elusive.

Exhibit 4.1
GENTRO Ltd. Partial Organization Chart

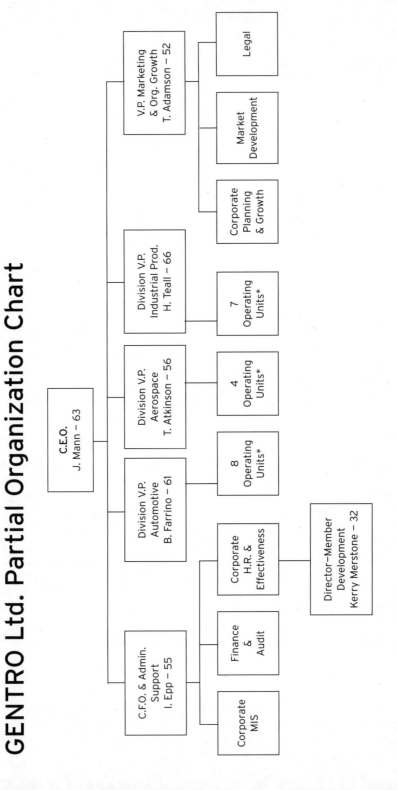

C.E.O.
J. Mann – 63

C.F.O. & Admin. Support
I. Epp – 55

Division V.P. Automotive
B. Farrino – 61

Division V.P. Aerospace
T. Atkinson – 56

Division V.P. Industrial Prod.
H. Teall – 66

V.P. Marketing & Org. Growth
T. Adamson – 52

Corporate MIS

Finance & Audit

Corporate H.R. & Effectiveness

Director–Member Development
Kerry Merstone – 32

8 Operating Units*

4 Operating Units*

7 Operating Units*

Corporate Planning & Growth

Market Development

Legal

*See Exhibit 4.2 for the breakdown of operating units.

Exhibit 4.2

GENTRO Ltd.

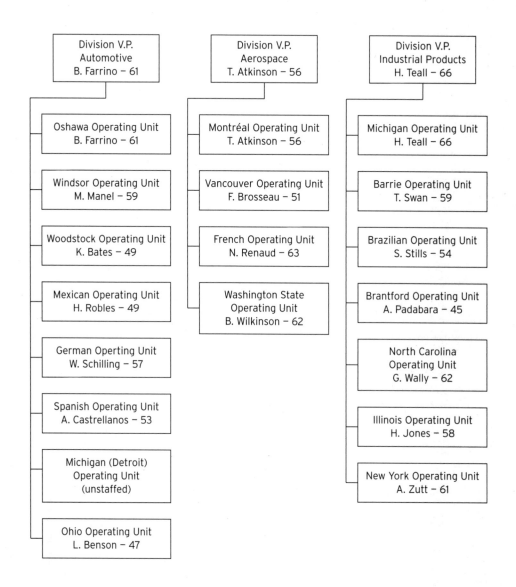

Division V.P. Automotive B. Farrino – 61	Division V.P. Aerospace T. Atkinson – 56	Division V.P. Industrial Products H. Teall – 66
Oshawa Operating Unit B. Farrino – 61	Montréal Operating Unit T. Atkinson – 56	Michigan Operating Unit H. Teall – 66
Windsor Operating Unit M. Manel – 59	Vancouver Operating Unit F. Brosseau – 51	Barrie Operating Unit T. Swan – 59
Woodstock Operating Unit K. Bates – 49	French Operating Unit N. Renaud – 63	Brazilian Operating Unit S. Stills – 54
Mexican Operating Unit H. Robles – 49	Washington State Operating Unit B. Wilkinson – 62	Brantford Operating Unit A. Padabara – 45
German Operting Unit W. Schilling – 57		North Carolina Operating Unit G. Wally – 62
Spanish Operating Unit A. Castrellanos – 53		Illinois Operating Unit H. Jones – 58
Michigan (Detroit) Operating Unit (unstaffed)		New York Operating Unit A. Zutt – 61
Ohio Operating Unit L. Benson – 47		

L-D Tool & Die

Natalie Lam

Patrick Larbi

Chad Mance

Katarina Tegling

Helena Wennberg

L-D Tool & Die (LDTD) is a small and successful manufacturer of custom moulds. The company has a sizable export business to companies in the United States and Europe. This growing business is presently experiencing an acute shortage of skilled workers and has been unable to recruit the necessary expertise from the Ottawa region (capital of Canada). An examination of the industrial sector to which it belongs gives some insight as to some of the reasons.

INDUSTRIAL SECTOR OVERVIEW: TOOL & DIE–PLASTIC INJECTION MOULDING

The tool, die, and mould (TDM) makers are in the business of making and repairing cutting tools, dies, and fixtures that are subsequently used to cut, form, or process materials—usually metal, glass, wood, paper, or plastics.

The plastics products industry, a TDM sector business, is composed of establishments whose main activity is transforming synthetic resins and plastic materials into a wide range of finished products, parts for other manufactured goods, and intermediate products consisting of shapes and forms made by a variety of fabricating methods. While applications for plastics are found in virtually all end-use market segments, the packaging, construction, and automotive markets account for nearly 80 percent of the industry's output. The industry's largest input cost is raw materials—mostly synthetic resins—which represent more than 50% of direct costs. Labour accounts for about 15 percent of input costs (Society of Plastics Industry of Canada, www.cpia.ca).

The plastic injection moulding industry is a subsector of the plastic products industry. The subsector comprises some 345 establishments with a total workforce of approximately 6700. Most of these companies are private, Canadian-owned, owner-managed, and usually made up of small shops employing an average of 20 people each. Eighty percent of the subsector in Canada is located in southern Ontario (mainly Windsor), with other firms located in Québec, British Columbia, and the Prairie provinces. Shipments of moulds and dies, totalling $610 million in 1996, are sent mostly to the United States, primarily for the automotive industry.

A number of external factors continue to apply pressure on the subsector. The most significant challenges facing the industry are (1) a shortage of adequate human resources, and (2) technological change.

Human Resources

Plastic injection mould-making companies have traditionally performed specialized tasks and hence employ people who have several years of experience in the field and are highly skilled in the crafts. Experienced workers are scarce in supply because Canadian apprenticeship training programs have not been producing sufficient numbers of qualified personnel to fill the positions that are either being vacated by retiring personnel or are being created by growth in the industry. More recently, computer applications are finding wider acceptance in tooling companies and are subsequently transforming the skill requirements. However, high product quality, custom designs, quick delivery, and after-sales service remain key attributes in this subsector.

Technological Factors

Technology is becoming an increasingly competitive factor in this subsector along with product quality and performance (see Exhibit 5.1). While the technology continues to be generally available, its implementation, operation, and maintenance require high levels of skill at the shop-floor and management levels. The introduction of high-powered, high-speed computer-aided design and computer-aided manufacturing (CAD/CAM) demands a large capital investment. Some community colleges and university engineering programs produce graduates who are knowledgeable users of these applications and who are quick learners in the TDM industry. However, these graduates lack the required experience that would otherwise enable them to provide immediate TDM business impact.

COMPANY PROFILE

LDTD manufactures and designs customized moulds and plastic parts for the plastic products industry. The company was founded by Laurie Dickson in the late 1980s after a careful market survey in the Ottawa area and in Montréal to assess the market potential for his customized moulds. LDTD has been headquartered in Kanata, Ontario, since its inception. The fast-growing "high-tech" companies in the Ottawa-Carleton region have provided new market opportunities for local tool and die shops. LDTD's tool shop will expand to 1394 m^2 next March.

The company is jointly managed by Laurie Dickson and his partner Dave Tate. The two partners have established strategic objectives for the business:

- Flexible and adaptable to customer needs

- "Solutions-oriented"

- Constantly able to meet present and future challenges

In addition, the long-term corporate goals for the firm include:

- Expanding plant size to 2323 m^2 within three years

- Being a "key player" in the Canadian plastics industry

The labour pool within the company consists of skilled and unskilled workers, as the firm employs 30 unskilled moulding machine operators. The skilled workforce is made up of one mould designer, one computer numerically controlled (CNC) machine programmer, one CNC machine operator, four mould makers, and eight mould-making assistants (see Exhibit 5.2). The company presently has a multicultural workforce that includes workers from Canada, Jamaica, Britain, France, and Israel.

Upper management has cultivated a team-oriented working environment in which a loyal workforce feels a sense of ownership in the company's future. Laurie Dickson has specified organizational objectives related to his employees:

- Preserving the informal but stable working environment, where employees work efficiently under less supervision

- Fostering a learning atmosphere and organizational culture, where employees are able and encouraged to undertake challenging projects that add to self-esteem.

Since beginning its operations, LDTD has acquired a solid reputation for fulfilling customer requirements and delivering high-quality custom designs and moulds. Via word of mouth from satisfied customers and its own aggressive sales approach, the company has developed an impressive customer base—e.g., Canadian Plastics, Black & Decker, Smith & Wesson, Akona, Braun, and Standard Building Components. LDTD is also the largest manufacturer of diving equipment in Canada and produces plastic medical products for export to Sweden, Germany, Australia, and the Netherlands.

There are four similar companies in the Ottawa-Carleton region: Calcutron, Ottawa Mould Craft, Kontech Plastics, and ETM. Calcutron is equipped with moulding machines but employs only one mould maker. Kontech Plastics is involved in plastic injection moulding but does not make its moulds in-house. ETM has two mould makers but only fabricates moulds for internal use to make proprietary products. Ottawa Mould Craft is LDTD's main competitor because this manufacturer offers services and customized solutions equivalent to those provided by LDTD. There is enough business for all the competitors; the real competition is about finding enough skilled workers, rather than competing over customer contracts. The unwritten rule amongst these local competitors is "non-raiding" and "no stealing" of each other's employees. Involvement in raiding practices would only create hostile relations between the companies and lead to expensive employee "buy-back" deals.

Therefore, the key success factor in this growing business sector is dealing with the labour shortage in a proactive manner. LDTD continues to refuse business because the company cannot find sufficient quantities of properly skilled workers capable of producing moulds to customer specifications.

RECRUITMENT OF NEW LABOUR AT L-D TOOL & DIE

The company's rapid growth has created a need to recruit additional skilled and unskilled workers. The firm recently installed four new moulding machines and now plans to hire six unskilled machine operators within the next six weeks. There is a sufficient supply of this type of labour, and the job openings are expected to be filled quickly. However, the recruitment of an additional three or four experienced mould makers is becoming problematic for LDTD. The ideal mould maker should have approximately 10 years of mould-making experience in the plastics industry. These mould makers should be able to work with little or no supervision and develop creative designs to meet customer requirements. Preferably, applicants should be able to program the advanced computerized mould-making machines according to design specifications.

Finding the desired applicants appears to be an almost impossible task. This difficulty has befallen LDTD because of the combination of industry characteristics and internal inefficiency. The whole industry is facing this recruitment problem and the reality is an insufficient supply of experienced workers (see Exhibit 5.3 for Ontario's occupational prospects for tool and die makers). There are also indications that enrollment in trade schools has not risen in accordance with the pace of growth in the industry. Traditional forms of recruitment such as word of mouth no longer suffice; employers such as LDTD are discovering that they will have to find new and innovative channels of recruitment. The trend towards higher skill levels in production jobs will also require employers to place a greater emphasis on continuous education and training of their employees.

LDTD is a small firm that has not been able to devote enough time and money to its recruitment practices. Laurie Dickson has too many areas of responsibility (he is involved in every aspect of the business, especially in securing work contracts) and consequently has little time to involve himself in recruitment and other HR practices. No adequate recruitment planning is currently in place at LDTD, and these issues are handled in an *ad hoc* manner. Presently, there is no specific individual responsible for HR issues, such as recruitment and selection. In general, Laurie Dickson will engage in recruiting activities when the need arises. Dave Tate is too heavily involved in the administrative, financial, and marketing sides of the business to be able to devote any time to HR.

Previous attempts by LDTD to attract new mould makers involved varying recruitment methods but all efforts were unsuccessful despite generous wage offers. Laurie Dickson is prepared to pay $45 000 to $50 000 CDN per year for qualified people. This base salary is above the industry average of $35 980.

The company has posted advertisements in *The Toronto Sun* (see Exhibit 5.4) and has "spread the word" among current employees and via the local industry network that job openings exist for qualified applicants.

Laurie Dickson has established a fruitful relationship with Algonquin Technical College, but he does not believe that recent graduates from a two- or three-year technical college trade program possess the requisite skill set and practical experience to be immediate and effective contributors. Given the urgency of meeting contract delivery dates, LDTD is seeking self-responsible and self-motivated mould makers who will not need extensive on-the-job training.

The recruitment methods that LDTD has utilized thus far are clearly not achieving the desired results.

SELECTION AT L-D TOOL & DIE

Since L-D Tool & Die is a small machine tool shop, it is constrained by both financial and human resources. The company's selection process is, by necessity, short, and most of the selection of new employees is the responsibility of Laurie Dickson. In addition to being the owner and thus having a major stake in finding the right employee, he knows the trade and is also involved in the shop in a supervisory capacity, with hands-on knowledge about the jobs.

In selecting candidates, LDTD does not make use of standardized tests. Generally, Laurie Dickson will ask the candidates to demonstrate their skills on some of the machines. He always holds unstructured interviews with each applicant, with questions about previous experience to assess the candidate's problem-solving skills. Applicants are often asked how they would solve a specific problem for a potential customer. LDTD seeks self-reliant and highly skilled workers. Laurie Dickson feels such indicators can help assess how an applicant will perform on the job.

After the interview, Laurie usually takes the candidate on a tour of the shop and gives him/her a brief overview of the company, its culture, and his philosophy of how the company is run. Most of the time, Laurie would have made a decision on the candidate by the end of the interview, although the candidate would not be informed immediately. When hired, new employees are normally subject to a probationary period.

The *ad hoc* nature of the selection process at L-D Tool & Die has, so far, not had any negative impact on the company's performance. The candidates hired are motivated. Turnover is low. One result of this *ad hoc* process, although unintended, has been the creation of a multicultural workplace.

LDTD FACES A RECRUITMENT CRISIS

Laurie Dickson has just had to turn away two very lucrative work contracts (again!). He could not guarantee to meet the completion deadlines, due to the acute shortage of skilled and experienced mould makers. Traditional recruitment channels, such as word of mouth and newspaper advertisements, do not seem to be enough to fill the job vacancies. It is clear that L-D Tool & Die needs to review its recruitment and selection practices, but Laurie Dickson does not even know where to begin.

Laurie Dickson pulls out a package he recently received from a contact at the University of Ottawa. The professor, at Laurie's request, had sent him information she thought might help him in his recruitment efforts. He has not had the time to open it, much less read the materials! The package contains information packages from CAMM (Canadian Association of Moldmakers, www.camm.ca), CPIA (Canadian Plastics Industry Association, www.cpia.ca), and SPE (The Society of Plastics Engineers, www.4spe.org). (Abstracts from the information packages are found in Exhibit 5.5.)

Besides the package, Laurie also has several invitations to job fairs at technical colleges nationwide on his desk. A current employee has mentioned that it might be a good idea to contact some of the ethnic organizations that operate in the Toronto region. Since LDTD is in acute need of additional mould makers, Laurie Dickson has pulled out the last-entered newspaper advertisement from his files. However, it is not yet decided where the company should advertise. Recently, some of his competitors have begun to use the Internet for marketing their products and services. Competitors in the Toronto and Windsor regions are utilizing headhunting firms to find skilled and experienced labour.

Laurie Dickson looks at the mass of information on his desk and lets out a big sigh. Where can he get three to four experienced mould makers immediately? He cannot afford to turn down any more work contracts. The company is expecting to grow, and the recruitment situation will only get worse.

Exhibit 5.1

Canadian Industry Profile: Machine Shop Industry

From:
http://www.hrdc-drhc.gc.ca/sector/english/industryprofiles/308/busenv.shtml

Machine Shop Industries are primarily engaged in manufacturing machine parts and equipment, other than complete machines, for the trade. This industry includes machine shops providing custom and repair services. Establishments primarily engaged in rebuilding or remanufacturing automotive engines are included here.

Principal activities and products:
- Camshaft regrinding;
- Crankshaft regrinding;
- Engine rebuilding;
- Machine shop;
- Machining, custom work;
- Manual transmission rebuilding;
- Metal boring and drilling, custom;
- Metal grinding, lapping and honing, custom; and
- Metal punching, custom.

Companies in this industry rework metal equipment and products, in some cases for sale to manufacturing customers. Newer forms of technology are spreading rapidly in this industry. New forms of technology and substantial amounts of research and development into new products and new production technology are directly related to customer needs, especially in the auto industry.

This is an industry characterized by a large number of small establishments. Levels of concentration in this industry are low. Total establishments in 1996 were 1,482 compared to 1,668 in 1990. Statistics Canada estimates 41.6 percent of the establishments in the industry were in Ontario, 29.2 percent in Quebec and 11.7 percent in British Columbia.

Companies in this sector do a large amount of custom work, in addition to more standardized parts and equipment production. With the intense competition in this industry and the spread of newer production machinery, success depends on being able to meet increasingly stringent standards for product quality and machining tolerances. Given the cost of new equipment, this trend may favour larger enterprises.

A major factor in the growth of productivity in this sector as well as other metal fabricating sectors, has been the use of computer technology in the production process. Computer-assisted design and manufacturing (*CAD/CAM*) is increasingly being adopted in this industry. Newer microprocessor-based machines are replacing older computer numerical control (*CNC*) tools and machines as closer tolerances and less rework become important factors with customers.

It is likely that the spread of *ISO 9000* certification in all the metal fabrication sectors, as well as the *QS 9000* standard in the case of auto industry customers, will speed up the replacement of manual processes with automated ones. A result is a rise in the minimum levels of literacy and numeracy required in these industries.

Significant amounts of the production of this industry go into the auto industry, and this is forcing smaller machine shops into alliances with larger operations as the auto industry rationalizes its supply system into tiers. Tier 1 and Tier 2 suppliers control quality standards in this industry and impose standards such as *QS 9000* on their own suppliers, which is forcing a round of investment in new machinery and processes.

Reports suggest that shortages of skilled labour will hit this industry hard in coming years. Some Quebec companies have begun to adopt co-operative programs to deal with an anticipated shortage of skilled workers as older workers retire. Similar programs have begun to appear in other parts of the country as well.

Information from *Industry Profiles* from Human Resources Development Canada is reproduced with the permission of the Minister of Public Works and Government Services Canada, 2001.
Web site: *http://jobfutures.ca/jobfutures/noc/7232.html*

Exhibit 5.2
L-D Tool & Die Organization Chart

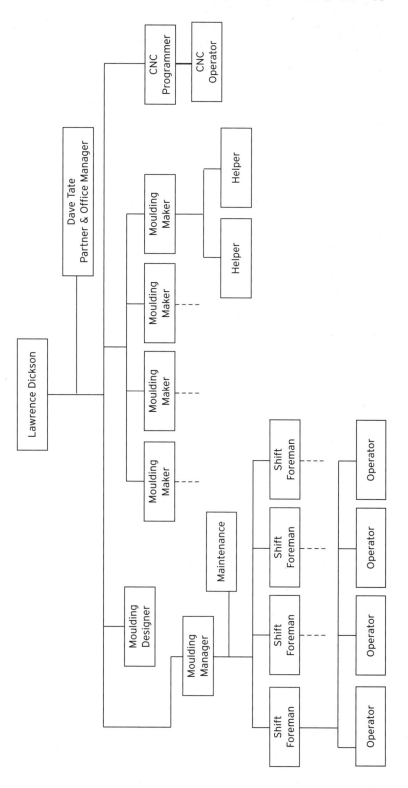

Exhibit 5.3

Ontario's Occupational Prospects

7232 Tool and Die Makers

Persons in these occupations make and repair cutting tools, dies, and fixtures subsequently used to cut, form, or process materials, usually metal. From technical drawings and specifications, they calculate or have the computer calculate required dimensions and tolerances, set up and operate metal-working machinery, machine the tools to close tolerances, apply heat treatments, assemble and test the tool or die, and verify the conformance of the finished product to specifications. In many shops, a tool and die maker may specialize in one or more of the above activities. Changes in technology have increasingly required the operation of computerized numerically controlled or computer programmable machinery.

Labour Market Conditions

The work is indoors and involves some exposure to noise and hazards requiring the use of safety equipment. Physical activities may include lifting and carrying parts of up to 23 kg, and periods of standing and handling material and machinery. Nearly all employment of tool and die makers is in manufacturing, mainly in metal fabricating. These jobs tend to be full-time with little seasonal variation. A five-day work week of 40 hours is normal, and shift work may be required in this occupation.

The experience with shortages earlier in the 1980s, the older age profile of those in the occupation, and the skill level and training duration bode well for future job opportunities. In the near term, to 1997, the recovery in the provincial economy is expected to contribute to job opportunities specifically for Tool and Die Makers with Computerized Numerical Control/ Computer Alternated Manufacturing skills.

Education and Skill Requirements for Employability

A tool and die making apprenticeship program is offered in Ontario. The apprenticeship lasts four years and a Grade 10 education is the minimum program entry requirement, although most employers now insist on Grade 12 or community college education. Traditionally, the tolerances commanded in crafting tools and dies required skills in mathematics and measurement. However, investment in new technology, undertaken by many firms, has seen a growing need for additional skills and knowledge in computer controlled equipment. This has prompted experienced tool and die makers to upgrade their skills in these new technologies.

The ups and downs of the business cycle have an effect on apprenticeship. During times of economic slowdown, employment declines due to layoffs, and cutbacks occur in apprenticeship training. This diminishes the number of new tradesmen entering the occupation and hence the available labour pool when the economy picks up.

Highlights from the 1991 Census Statistical Summary

This occupation is 95% male and is overwhelmingly concentrated in southwestern Ontario's manufacturing sector. Ninety-seven percent of employment was full-time. Employment was well distributed through all the prime age groups.

1991 Census Data (Ontario—Unless Stated Elsewhere)

		Worked in 1990			Average Income		
		Total	Male	Female	Total	Male	Female
Total		13 350	12 695	655	$35 340	$36 100	$20 400
			(95%)	(5%)			
Full-Time	(97%)	13 010	12 385	625	$35 980	$36 720	$20 970
Full-Year	(74%)	9 845	9 455	390	$38 620	$39 270	$22 770

Age Groups	Employed	(%)
Ages: 24 or less	915	(9%)
Ages: 25 to 29	1525	(16%)
Ages: 30 to 34	1555	(16%)
Ages: 35 to 39	1090	(11%)
Ages: 40 to 44	1180	(12%)
Ages: 45 to 49	1155	(12%)
Ages: 50 to 54	920	(10%)
Ages: 55 to 59	720	(8%)
Ages: 60 to 64	425	(4%)
Ages: 65 and up	90	(1%)

Geographic Distribution	Employed	(%)
Northern Ontario	115	(1%)
Eastern Ontario	1805	(14%)
Southern/Western Ontario	7300	(55%)
Metro Toronto Region	4130	(31%)

Main Industries (1 % or Greater)	Employed	(%)
Manufacturing	10 816	(92%)
Trade	572	(5%)

Educational Level (Canada)	Employed	(%)
Trades Certificate	7 590	(47%)
Post Secondary Non-Univ.	2 340	(14%)
University Non-degree	60	(0%)
Bachelors	190	(1%)
University Post-Graduate	60	(0%)
Other	5 995	(37%)

Information from Canada Job Futures from Human Resources Development Canada is reproduced with the permission of the Minister of Public Works and Government Services Canada, 2001.
Web site: http://jobfutures.ca/jobfutures/noc/7232.html

Exhibit 5.4

L-D Tool & Die Advertisement in The Toronto Sun

TOOLING FOR PLASTICS
CNC Operator/Programmer
Mould Maker
Mould Designer
3 positions to fill immediately in
Ottawa at L D Tool & Die. Require
at least 8 years experience in
plastic injection mould making
environment. Call 613-591-1474
or Fax resume to 613-591-8683.

Family Medical Group of Companies

Pauline Brockman

Andrew Templer

It's a bright April morning, and Bill Maron smiles towards the sun shining into his office. "Finally," he thinks to himself, "the missing piece to the puzzle that's going to have us move forward." But before Bill has long to dwell on this moment of satisfaction, the phone rings. It's his secretary Monica. "Nancy Meyers has arrived for your 9 a.m. meeting," Monica chants. After a brief moment, Bill turns his attention back to the issue at hand. "Thanks, Monica. Show her in."

Nancy is Bill's newest employee at the corporate head office of Family Medical. She was hired less than two weeks ago to be the director of human resources. Nancy has several years of human resources experience and particular expertise in human resource planning. Nancy has worked for major companies in the transportation industry throughout Canada and has gained a reputation for her energy and practical attitude. Bill needs Nancy to develop a comprehensive human resource plan for his two divisions (distribution and manufacturing). Continuing problems with morale, turnover, succession planning, and training have kept Bill from concentrating on his next endeavour: a new division that would provide home-nursing services.

Bill has just finished his daydreaming when Monica brings Nancy into the office. "Good morning, Nancy," Bill offers cheerfully with a firm handshake. "Have a seat," he says as he motions to the leather chairs in front of him. "I understand you are just the person to solve our HR problems."

Although Nancy was given selected information about the company and the challenges during her interviews, there is key information that Bill wants to share with her before she plunges into her new responsibilities. Nancy will also need to speak to the vice-presidents of each division. But, nevertheless, the appropriate place to start is at the beginning. Bill begins by giving Nancy a brief history of the company.

FAMILY MEDICAL DISTRIBUTION

The original company, Family Medical Distribution, was created by the grandfather of Bill's wife, Helen. The company began operations in 1924 selling medical supplies, such as syringes and bandages, to local hospitals in the Kingston region. For 45 years, the company maintained its quiet but consistent presence in the local medical community. Over this time, the company built a solid reputation for quality products and reliable service, which the owner credited to his dedicated employees. Probably as a result of the company's small size, employees often felt like family members and stayed with the company until retirement.

Customer service was largely responsible for the company's early direction. The owner's philosophy was to satisfy the needs of the customer—regardless of what it might entail. Bill can't help but smile to himself when he recalls one of his favourite stories. Helen's grandfather, Mr. Halton, spent considerable time and energy to find and import a number of special religious articles from Europe as a favour to the nuns at St. Joseph's Hospital. It was these extraordinary business decisions that convinced Bill that Mr. Halton was as interested in building a socially useful organization as in making a reasonable income—evidenced by the modest bottom line each year on the income statements.

Bill shakes his head now when he thinks back to 1969 and how he came to purchase Family Medical Distribution. At the time, Bill was 30 years old and had a promising career as a Chartered Accountant with Ernst & Young. He worked long hours and enjoyed the challenges and perks of public accounting. Bill thought he'd be an accountant for life. Looking back now though, Bill is thankful for the bullish style of his father-in-law. When Mr. Halton became ill and passed away suddenly in 1968, it had been Helen's father who convinced him to take the risk and purchase the business. Helen's father believed that Bill had the youthful energy and determination to take control of the foundering company.

BILL'S EARLY YEARS

In the first few years, Bill had no choice but to learn about his company by rolling up his sleeves and getting involved. With only eight employees, Bill's role was far from glamorous (see Exhibit 6.1). Bill would often take customer orders, speak to vendors, and hunt for products in the warehouse—all within the same hour. Bill also spent countless hours on the road talking to customers and suppliers.

Bill's new surroundings had also been a bit of a letdown. The plush, modern facilities of Ernst & Young were out of reach for Family Medical. In fact, Family Medical Distribution consisted of a 1672 m^2 warehouse and a single open-concept office for all staff to work in—including Bill. The office space was full of assorted old furniture that needed to be shunted around to allow staff enough room to manoeuvre from the coffee station back to the warehouse.

Despite the humble initial stages of ownership, Bill was driven to make his investment a success. Bill spent countless hours at Family Medical Distribution. He was determined to make the company grow beyond the boundaries of the Kingston region.

Thankfully, the efforts began to pay off. In the 15 years following 1969, Bill began to realize measured success. Family Medical Distribution had grown out of its original facilities when the company expanded into the rest of Ontario (especially Toronto) and later into the rest of the country through strategic acquisitions. By 1984, the company had become a true "national entity" with a distribution network that stretched from coast to coast. Branch offices in Vancouver, Winnipeg, Montréal, Fredericton, and St. John's were now supplying hundreds of Canada's leading hospitals with quality medical products and systems (see Exhibit 6.2). Family Medical Distribution's reputation for service and quality had also grown nationally.

NEED FOR CHANGE

But Bill wasn't satisfied. By 1984, he craved a new entrepreneurial challenge. He had grown passionate about the medical business and the new technologies that were making significant improvements to medical treatments. Among the many changes, surgeries were becoming less invasive and hospital stays shorter. Bill's fervour for new technologies was not a secret. Family Medical Distribution had become a known supporter of leading-edge technology.

A few years earlier, Bill had received a frantic call from the emergency room supervisor at Toronto Hospital. Although it was quite late in the day, Bill, as usual, was in the office. A young accident victim was being transferred to Toronto Hospital and was in desperate need of a special non-invasive ventilator. Although considered new technology, the equipment was the young girl's best chance for a full recovery. Bill immediately ran back to the warehouse to gather the required equipment and accessories and headed to Toronto. Bill recalls the night vividly. It was 7:20 p.m. The sky was black with snow clouds, and Bill was determined to get to Toronto and make a difference.

He did. The girl survived. That special trip to Toronto had a lasting effect on Bill and strengthened his desire to make a difference in the medical community. As a distributor, Family Medical was limited in its ability to significantly advance technology. That trip to Toronto had given Bill the vision and desire to create a new division of Family Medical: a company responsible for developing and manufacturing innovative, new medical products.

ADDITION OF FAMILY MEDICAL MANUFACTURING

Over the years, Bill had been approached by physicians many times to consider partnering in the manufacture and distribution of a particular invention. Bill was always careful to balance his interest and excitement against the potential risks. Such ventures typically require a substantial capital investment and particular expertise that was, at the time, not available in Family Medical Distribution.

Nearly two years after Bill's memorable trip to Toronto, an invention caught his attention—and the timing was right. Family Medical Distribution was operating smoothly and generating a reasonable income. Bill was presented with an idea that would help asthmatic patients, by more effectively delivering their medication through puffers. Like many great inventions, the principle behind the product actually appeared rather simple: a plastic holding chamber attached to the patient's puffer. The chamber would hold the medication until the patient was ready to inhale. Bill immediately funded the additional research necessary to perfect the prototypes and further analyze the market opportunities. After two years of laboratory research, the simple little product had become a complex, but nonetheless successful, innovation. In 1986, the AeroTube was launched and the new business division formalized under the name Family Medical Manufacturing.

NEED FOR HELP

By 1996, Bill was exhausted. The drastic funding cuts to the health-care community by both the federal and provincial governments in the 1990s had been squeezing the profits out of Family Medical Distribution. The company reacted to the industry chaos and drastic sales slump by reorganizing internal operations and refocusing the overall corporate direction. The company needed to make some radical changes in order to reverse the negative sales trends (see Exhibit 6.3).

Meanwhile, Family Medical Manufacturing continued to grow at an almost uncontrollable rate. The sales and marketing departments were aggressively promoting the AeroTube internationally. Within the past six years, the AeroTube had expanded its sales network to over 50 countries. New product-line extensions had been developed, but the resources were not available to begin producing and promoting the products. Although profits were significantly ahead of projections (see Exhibit 6.3), the growing pains within the company were becoming increasingly more obvious.

The demands of both companies were taking their toll on Bill. The pace was relentless, and despite working seven days a week, he could no longer keep up with the responsibilities of each company. After careful consideration, Bill decided he had no choice but to hire a vice-president for each company. Bill needed to relieve himself of many of the day-to-day tasks of each company to allow him time to manage the enterprise's overall direction.

NEW VICE-PRESIDENTS

Early in 1997, Sam Collins was promoted to vice-president of Family Medical Distribution. Sam had joined the company 15 years earlier and had successfully risen through the ranks. Sam was first hired as a sales representative for the province of New Brunswick and was a natural at building rapport with his customers. Sam had an easygoing personality and a sharp wit that customers loved. After eight years in the field, and some coaxing, Sam agreed to join head office in Kingston to become a marketing manager. Although leaving his roots in Maritime Canada was difficult, Sam made a successful transition into his new position. After this initial move, Sam continued to progress through the company, accepting opportunities as senior marketing manager, district sales manager, and director of marketing. Sam has always been considered a trusted and loyal employee. When Bill needed to create the vice-president's role in Family Medical Distribution, Sam was his obvious choice.

A few months later, Bill hired Mark Olsen to become the vice-president of Family Medical Manufacturing. Finding the right person for this position had been a bit more of a challenge. Bill needed to find someone with the experience and vision to continue expanding the markets for the AeroTube product line, yet who also possessed the technical ability to manage both the production and R&D departments. Mark's previous employer had been a related manufacturing company in the Kingston area. Mark had been quite successful as that company's director of the manufacturing and engineering operations. Although Mark is a relatively young vice-president at 45 years of age, his charm and approach to business have earned him respect. Mark studied engineering while at university, which has been helpful in overseeing the activities of the R&D division. Bill has been counting on Mark to grow the AeroTube line and expand the markets for new products.

"This is where I need your help, Nancy," offers Bill. "Family Medical Distribution is starting to make a financial turnaround but really needs some HR help to deal with the change process and the resulting fallout of staff. As well, Family Medical Manufacturing really needs your help to develop an appropriate structure to cope with the growth. Both companies have made some strategic mistakes recently, which have resulted in the loss of some key staff to the competition. The environmental changes and our lack of organization have been very stressful for the staff. I think some staff have simply grown tired of waiting for top management to work out the problems. I really think addressing our human resource issues will help each of the companies gain control. I want to feel confident that both companies are on solid ground before we enter the home-nursing market."

Bill stopped for just a moment before proceeding. "Before I get ahead of myself, I really should give you some background on our human resources department."

NEED FOR HUMAN RESOURCES EXPERTISE

"In addition to hiring Sam and Mark in 1997, I also realized there was a need to formally establish a human resources department. The human resource issues in each of the companies had become increasingly more time-consuming and complex. It had become obvious that the need for human resources management had grown beyond an amateur's role and required a professional."

Bill stopped for a moment, and Nancy could see a cloud come over his eyes. Bill shook his head. "Unfortunately, the HR department has been a bit of a disaster. The HR manager we hired has been on leave for the past 13 months. The human resources associate, Claire Jackson, has done a wonderful job and taken charge of the department, but the issues the department needs to address are just too much for her. In the past year, Claire has been spending almost all her time interviewing for vacant positions and handling the orientation and paperwork of the new employees. At any given time, she has a minimum of ten vacancies that she is working to fill. The growth in the manufacturing division has kept steady pressure on Claire to find quality staff, FAST. Although Claire has a clerk to help with the day-to-day paperwork, she really has not been able to deal with all the issues in the department. The training and development programs have really suffered. As well, we have not done any strategic planning or forecasting for either of the companies."

"You can now understand how delighted I was when you accepted the challenge and joined Family Medical. We certainly need your expertise in developing a human resource plan for the companies. We promoted Claire recently to the manager's position so that she would be ready to help you. I know you will find her a tremendous asset. The bottom line is, Nancy, the department is in desperate need of your leadership, and the company is in desperate need of your expertise. We need a solid human resource plan in order to move forward. I need the current problems addressed before I can create the home-nursing division.

"I'd like to give you a chance to prepare some preliminary information for the human resource plan before we meet again. I also know that you need to meet with Mark and Sam to gather their perspectives on things. Would it be okay to meet in two weeks to discuss the plan?"

NANCY'S INITIAL ACTIONS

Bill had been very clear; he wanted Nancy to develop a human resource plan to encompass both the manufacturing and distribution divisions. Nancy had to get moving—she just did not have the luxury of time to painstakingly review her every option. Bill wanted to meet with her in two weeks. She decided that the obvious place to begin was by finding out what her human resources manager and the two vice-presidents thought. Nancy asked Claire to write a brief memo to her outlining the pertinent issues in the human resources department (see Exhibit 6.4) and kept notes of the extensive interviews she had with Sam and Mark (see Exhibits 6.5 and 6.6).

With less than 10 days to go until her meeting with the president, Nancy closed her office door, turned off her phone, and began work on her strategy for the Family Medical Group of Companies.

Exhibit 6.1

Partial Organization Charts

Family Medical Distribution
December 31, 1967

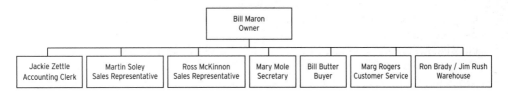

Family Medical Group of Companies
April 30, 1999

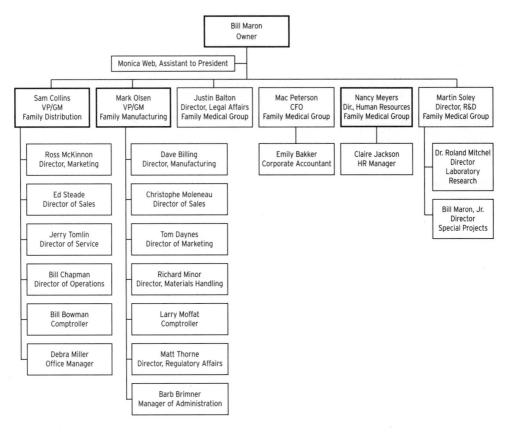

Exhibit 6.2

Timeline—Family Medical Distribution

1924   Family Medical Distribution created by Herbert Halton, a former stock keeper for the Kingston General Hospital.

1968   Herbert Halton dies after a brief illness at the age of 70.

1969   Bill Maron purchases the company with a bank loan and the family house as collateral.

1971   Family Medical successfully expands the Ontario market with key customers in Toronto, Ottawa, London, and Windsor.

1975   Family Medical Distribution purchases a local distribution business in Montréal, Quebec. Under the purchase agreement, the 12 staff members in Montréal become the newest employees of Family Medical.

1977   Kirkland Medical is purchased in Vancouver, British Columbia. The business and staff become the western branch for Family Medical Distribution.

1978   A small operation in Winnipeg, Manitoba, is converted to Family Medical Distribution. Few customers are gained through the acquisition, but Family Medical Distribution is now able to comfortably supply all the western provinces.

1982   McArthur Medical Supplies is purchased. Both branches (Fredericton, New Brunswick, and St. John's, Newfoundland) are converted to Family Medical Distribution.

1986   Family Medical Manufacturing is created. Family Medical Group of Companies name is established to represent the corporate company.

Exhibit 6.3

Family Medical Group of Companies
Profit (in OOOs)

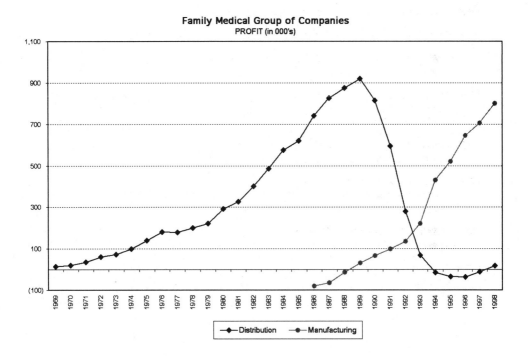

Family Medical Group of Companies
PROFIT (in 000's)

Exhibit 6.4

Notes to File:

Sam Collins Interview

DATE: April 28, 1999

BCC: Bill Maron

RE: <u>Interview with Sam Collins</u> (Family Medical Distribution)

- Company has now grown to about 145 employees with most working in the sales, marketing, and operations departments. Many of the employees hired during Bill's early years continue to enjoy successful careers with the distribution business.

- Family Medical Distribution still has a solid reputation in the medical community but has been faltering in past five years due to government cutbacks in the medical industry. The restructuring has meant that hundreds of hospitals across the country have closed, while others have been forced to significantly reduce their number of beds.

- Sam feels the company has lacked a strategic focus and become "lazy" in the years leading up to the budget cuts.

- Sam is committed to returning Family Distribution to its former profitability. Sam feels personally responsible to deliver the bottom line to Bill.

- Family Medical Distribution has had to reposition itself as a specialty distributor of high-end medical products and systems in order to survive. The goal is to represent only key suppliers in Canada in the key areas of Critical Care, Anaesthesia, Respiratory Care, and Surgery.

- As a result of these industry stresses, there has been a significant change in the company's corporate culture. The new atmosphere is one of cost restraint and continuous change. The company has had to reduce its inventory and improve its processes to remain competitive in the increasingly smaller market.

- Sam has spent considerable effort evaluating the operations, sales, and marketing departments. He feels these areas will be the keys to turning the company around. He thinks the staff needs to work "smarter" and not "harder."

- Until recently, the company had operated for many years with relatively few changes. Many of the employees had a considerable amount of seniority, had risen through the ranks, and had hoped to retire from Family Medical. In the past two years, however, the external forces have created a need for change in the organizational mix and structure of the company. About five or six long-term employees have been terminated. Some of the vacancies have been filled from within the company, but the staff is still generally feeling nervous and uncertain. Sam has been pushing hard to focus the company and turn the company around.

- Sam is a bit hesitant about the role and value of an HR department. His past two years have been very disappointing with problems around hiring methods, confidentiality, knowledge/expertise, and lack of support for the new company Vision.

- Sam is willing to consider an HRP for Family Distribution but is more concerned with making the company profitable again.

Exhibit 6.5

Notes to File:

Mark Olsen Interview

DATE: April 27, 1999

BCC: Bill Maron

RE: Interview with Mark Olsen (Family Medical Manufacturing)

- The pace has been hectic since Mark joined Family Medical Manufacturing two years ago. The company is very successful having continuously exceeded its growth and profit projections each year.

- The AeroTube is currently marketed in over 50 countries and secures about 47 percent of the market for valved holding chambers worldwide. The lab has also completed successful prototypes for two new products to be launched in the next year. One product will allow intubated patients in a hospital to receive their medications orally through puffers. The company is close to receiving approval from Canada's Health Protection Branch. The other product is a much larger version of the AeroTube and will soon be launched to veterinarians for use on animals with breathing problems.

- Bill still remains fairly involved in the day-to-day operations of Family Medical Manufacturing. This is the company that has brought him international recognition. Bill still approves all research projects that take place in our laboratory.

- The company has just moved into its "state-of-the-art" manufacturing facility in the past year. The building has been a showcase for other such companies in the region and boasts all the modern amenities including a programmable pass-card entry system, contemporary cafeteria with home-cooked meals, and a research & development lab worth over $3 million.

- The company now employs approximately 180 people (55 percent on the production line who work one of two shifts per day). The company also employs over 12 engineers and six laboratory technicians.

- Mark believes that staff is generally happy and that the company is positioned for yet another "better-than-expected" year.

Exhibit 6.6

Memo from Claire Jackson

INTEROFFICE MEMO

Date: April 23, 1999

To: Nancy Meyers

From: CLAIRE JACKSON

RE: Human Resource Issues

CONFIDENTIAL

The following list is a summary of the urgent/priority Human Resources issues that I have been working on in the past two months:

Family Medical Group (Corporate)

Our request for a part-time HR Assistant has been declined once again, and the purchase requisition for the HRIS has been put on hold until Mr. Maron gives further authorization.

Family Distribution

The staff at Family Distribution seems to be unsettled. Several staff members have left the company through terminations and voluntary resignations within the past two years. Most recently, Dorothy Haffrey was terminated after 16 years of service. Dorothy has had several formal complaints in her permanent record over the years for inappropriate behaviour and language. Despite several warnings her behaviour has not changed. Three weeks ago she swore at the Director of Marketing in the presence of a supplier. Although the staff does not generally condone Dorothy's behaviour, I believe they are genuinely concerned about their own futures.

The staff at Family Distribution has also been applying aggressively for posted openings at Family Manufacturing.

Family Manufacturing

Four formal complaints have been submitted about the hiring practices at Family Manufacturing. These employees feel that they have been overlooked for key openings despite being able to fulfill the education and skills required for the positions. In all cases, the positions were filled by former employees of King Manufacturing (Mark Olsen's former employer). I completed the entire first round interviews and have reviewed the files carefully. The positions have all been filled with incumbents who can "hit the ground running." Mark felt Family Manufacturing did not have the time or luxury of training an internal employee.

Laura Davies, Senior Administrator, has tendered her resignation effective June 11th after not being successful in her application for the new Office Manager position. She has been a strong contributor to the overall administration of the company and has steadily been accepting increasing responsibility. During an informal meeting Laura shared the source of her unhappiness. Barb Brimner, the new Manager of Administration, inadvertently mentioned that Mark had promised her the position before the opening was posted. Laura has obviously perceived the hiring process to be unjust.

Recruitment Procedures at Olsen Long

Tupper Cawsey

Andrew Templer

Applications for student accounting positions for next year pour into the human resources department at the Toronto office of Olsen Long throughout September and October. David Phillips, director of human resources, and his staff face the important task of pre-screening the applications of candidates for the first-round campus interviews scheduled for mid-October. David has to work quickly. University placement officers require campus recruiters to submit lists of students they wish to interview at least two weeks prior to the scheduled interview date.

COMPANY BACKGROUND

Olsen Long is one of Canada's largest chartered accounting firms with more than 4000 personnel, including 350 partners. The company's services are tailored to meet the needs of all clients, from small independents to large corporations. As the Canadian founding partner of one of the world's largest international accounting firms, Olsen Long offers its CAs a wide variety of job opportunities and its clients a broad range of services on a national and international basis. The firm's decentralized management style allows its 60 offices (see Exhibit 7.1) to exercise a high degree of autonomy at the local level, but to ensure consistency among offices, the firm supports and coordinates its human resources nationally.

INDUSTRY BACKGROUND

Public accounting has undergone many changes in the past few years with the introduction of computers into every facet of business. In addition, there has been increased competition from non-CA firms providing a variety of services such as data processing consulting and computer software applications, as well as service organizations providing systems design, data processing, control software, and information delivery. These changes have forced CA firms to become proficient and innovative in computing solutions in order to improve efficiency in the delivery of service.

Auditing services, once expensive and time-consuming, have become more price-competitive and less of a focus in public accounting firms. Price has become an even more significant factor in clients' buying decisions for all services offered by public accounting firms. Due to the increased number of companies merging, CA firms have been competing aggressively to become the sole auditor of the newly formed, larger companies. To combat intensified competition, some public accounting firms have hired marketing managers to promote their image and services.

INDUSTRY AND COMPANY REQUIREMENTS*

A student has several hurdles to overcome in order to earn the CA designation. In Ontario the first step in the process is for students to register with the Institute of Chartered Accountants of Ontario (ICAO) as a graduate of a recognized Canadian university or a university outside of Canada that has met the Institute's standards. The student is required to have successfully completed a number of specific university credit courses before qualifying as a CA student.

Upon graduation from university, students are required to secure apprenticeship opportunities with CA firms approved by the Institute to earn practical experience. Students will spend the next 30 months (or 2.5 years) developing their skills in all the keys areas of accounting. Students can move through the ranks of Junior Accountant 1, Junior Accountant 2, and Junior Accountant 3 to reflect progression through the 30-month period. During this apprenticeship program, the CA student is required to complete a one-week staff training program in their first 12 months in the designated training office. As well, they must pass exams at the summer school in Toronto, where students are required to pass the School of Accountancy exam. Both exams, one multiple choice and the other case-style, are difficult with only 75 to 80 percent of students passing each step. Failure to pass either exam will require a student to rewrite before earning another spot in summer school and a chance to rewrite the School of Accountancy exam.

The last hurdle for the student is passing the Uniform Final Examination (UFE), which is set nationally and has about a 60 percent pass rate. Upon successful completion of this final exam and the 30 months of experience with a public accounting firm, a student will finally earn his/her CA designation. Upon graduation, a new CA could choose one of many career paths offered at Olsen Long: audit, taxation, receivership and insolvency, computer services, valuations and mergers, business advisory services, management consulting services, computer auditing, research and training, quality control, forensic accounting, and human resources.

---

*The specific steps to becoming a CA vary by province.

To be eligible for promotion in Olsen Long, a student *must* have attained his or her CA designation. Once the designation has been earned, his or her advancement could proceed to the level of supervisor, manager, and eventually partner (normally within about 10 years).

Considerable competition to attract the highest-quality CA students exists among all top public accounting firms in Canada. Economic differences within public accounting firms and industry result in a large number of CAs leaving public accounting upon earning their designation for better earnings elsewhere. Hiring CA students who will remain loyal to Olsen Long is important for attaining long-term company objectives.

THE SELECTION PROCESS

The selection process plays a significant role in attracting high-calibre accounting professionals and is taken very seriously by Olsen Long's human resources department. In late spring each year, David Phillips determines the number of recruits needed for September of the following year with the help of his computerized human resource planning system. The system's time frame encompasses a 12-year period commencing each September; forecasts for three to five years are normally used. The results of the analysis are incorporated into the Toronto office's annual strategic business plan. The number of recruits required for next September is estimated to be 60.

Over the summer, personnel assistant Lilly Heinz arranges the interview dates on campus, lines up interviewers, and has the company literature prepared for the upcoming fall interview session. All Ontario universities but one hold their placement programs in the fall. Students send their applications on standard Canadian Association of Career Educators and Employers (CACEE) forms. David commented that using the same form for all applicants makes pre-screening easier and quicker. A number of staff perform the task of pre-screening applicants from larger universities, cross-checking to ensure accuracy and consistency. Applications from smaller universities are usually pre-screened by the director himself, or by Sandy Payne, the personnel manager. While computer screening of résumés is possible, Olsen Long does not do this.

The human resources staff check for concise, well-written answers on the CACEE forms. They look for applicants with the desire to pursue professional careers as accountants and with some knowledge of the accounting profession and of Olsen Long. The job description for student accountants reads as follows:

> A Student Accountant will initially work as a member of a group responsible for serving a variety of clients. The majority of the work will involve the audit and preparation of financial statements. As the Student Accountant becomes more experienced, he or she will be given increased responsibility on larger and more complex assignments. On-the-job training, along with professional development programs, will assist the Student Accountant in achieving a high level of technical competence and sound judgment.

While previous summer employment experience is important, pre-screeners are aware of the difficulty students face in obtaining jobs. However, they expect applicants to have achieved increased levels of responsibility if they remained with the same employer for more than one year. They view summer employment as an indicator of students' initiative to support themselves during university and to develop new and existing skills. Applicants with a strong academic background are preferred because the CA program is rigorous; however, lower grades could be compensated for by active participation in extracurricular activities. *Olsen Long does not consider it essential for the applicant to have a business degree and welcomes students with other academic backgrounds.*

Not all applications arrive through the university placement offices. Occasionally, first interviews are given to students who make a direct application to Olsen Long. Also, contact through a partner, staff member, former employee, or a client frequently results in an interview. In the past, a few students have called the Olsen Long office after being rejected at the pre-screening stage (see Exhibit 7.2 for a summary of the recruitment process). If the applicant could convince David that his/her application should not have been overlooked, a first interview might be granted.

Each year David conducts two orientation sessions for staff members who volunteer to perform first interviews on university campuses. The first session is a planning meeting to discuss tactics for the entire recruitment program. Next, a day-long interviewing training session is held where prospective interviewers participate in videotaped practice interviews with newly hired student accountants to hone necessary interviewing skills. Concurrently, the interview evaluation form to be used is distributed and explained, so all interviewers are equipped for the upcoming recruitment period (see Exhibit 7.3).

With a total of approximately 1000 CACEE forms expected to reach the Toronto Olsen Long office during the year (the majority in the fall), David wonders if the human resources department's system of pre-screening could be more efficient. He is concerned that promising candidates might be rejected at the pre-screening stage, possibly as a result of reviewing too many applications at once. In September, as he read the first 10 applications from the growing pile on his desk (see Exhibit 7.4 for copies of the student applications), David had wondered which candidates to choose for the first interviews in October.

Exhibit 7.1

Number of Offices in Canada— Breakdown by Province

Province	Number of Offices
British Columbia	10
Alberta	5
Saskatchewan	3
Manitoba	3
Ontario	22
Quebec	6
New Brunswick	4
Nova Scotia	4
Prince Edward Island	1
Newfoundland	2

Exhibit 7.2

Recruitment Process Summary Timetable

Summer	Establish number of students required
Summer	Prepare literature for recruits and universities
September	Conduct meetings with volunteer interviewers
September	Attend career days and receive CACEE forms
September–October	Pre-screen CACEE forms
October	Notify universities of first-interview choices
October–November	Conduct first interviews
November–December	Conduct second interviews
December	Extend job offers or send rejections

Exhibit 7.3

Applicant Evaluation Form

Name _____   Degree _____

University _____

Note: Rating should exclude comparisons with students from other universities.

   Rating Scale   1 = Outstanding

                         2= Very Good

                         3 = Good

                         4 = Conditional

                         5 = Unsatisfactory

Rating

1. **Academic Achievement**   ☐

   Average: 3rd Year _____   Cum. _____

   ICAO Hours: Now _____   Grad. _____   Start Date _____

2. **Leadership**   ☐

   Drive, Assertiveness, Confidence, Energy, Past Positions, Potential

3. **Interpersonal Skills**   ☐

   Self-expression, Tact, Quality of Questions and Responses

4. **Overall Rating**   ☐

Recommend Office Interview   Yes _____   No _____

Office Desired   1st Choice _____   2nd Choice _____

Comments: _____

_____

_____

_____

Interviewer

Name: _____   Date: _____

Office: _____

Exhibit 7.4

Student Applications

change?

Approved by	CACEE Application for Employment	◉ Full-time ○ Summer ○ Co-op ○ Internship ○

Name of Organization
Olsen Long

Position(s) sought
Junior Accountant

Name of Educational Institution
York University

General Information

Surname
Sisley

Given Name(s)
Mark Andrew

Address until 30 Apr 00	No. 416	Street Norwood Avenue		Tel. 416-567-2612
	City Oakville	Prov./State ON	Postal Code M4T 1Z3	E-mail

Permanent Address (If different from above)	No.	Street		Tel.
	City	Prov./State	Postal Code	E-mail

Are you legally eligible to accept employment in Canada?
◉ Yes   ○ No
Documentary evidence may be requested after a job offer is made.

When are you available to start work?

Would you accept employment anywhere in Canada?
○ Yes   ◉ No

Preferred location(s)
1. Oakville
2. Toronto
3.

Education

Post Secondary or other institutions attended. Begin with most recent.	Faculty, Department, Division or School	Discipline or Programme (Major)	Degree/Diploma/ Certificate	Date obtained or expected
York University	Science & Mathematics	Computer Science	B.Sc.	06/00
York University	Admin. Studies	Accounting	BBA	06/99
University of Ottawa	Computer Science	Computer Science	B.Sc.	

G.P.A. for your most recently completed academic year _____ on a scale of _____ (Percentage or letter equivalent _B+_).

G.P.A. for all courses completed to date (cumulative average) _____ on a scale of _____ (Percentage or letter equivalent _B+_).

Highlight skills relevant to the position(s) sought.
Strong computer skills (programming, database management, software programs such as Word, Excel, AccPac, Simply Accounting, Lotus 1-2-3)

Educational Experiences and Accomplishments

Describe your relevant courses, project work, theses, publications, and presentations. Include awards and scholarships.

Dean's Honour List (1996/97)

Extracurricular Activities

Describe your extracurricular activities including class or campus offices held, volunteer experience, memberships in clubs or organizations, leadership roles, sports activities, hobbies, etc. (You are not required to mention the names of organizations that indicate race, ancestry, place of origin, colour, ethnic origin, citizenship, creed, sex, sexual orientation, age, marital status, family status, political beliefs or disabilities).

Participation in sports such as flag football, softball, hockey and bowling.

Hobbies and Special Interests: computers, science fiction books, cooking, camping, computer games

Work Experience

Please describe all work experience (paid and unpaid) starting with most recent.

General Helper   Private Company - Donald Brodeur
        Position   Name of Organization

Oakville   ON   11/95 to 04/99
City   Province/State   Dates

Minor plumbing, repairs, interior painting, scrap removal

☐ Summer
☒ Part -time
   # of hours/week: 10
☐ Co-op
☐ Internship
☐ Volunteer
☐ Full -time
☐ Other: (Specify)

Plumber's Helper   Jerrold Mechanical
        Position   Name of Organization

Oakville   ON   11/95 to 04/97
City   Province/State   Dates

Plumbing repairs, material deliveries, Furnace, oil tank and water tank
removals

☐ Summer
☒ Part -time
   # of hours/week: 15
☐ Co-op
☐ Internship
☐ Volunteer
☐ Full -time
☐ Other: (Specify)

Student Programmer   The Computer Communications Group
        Position   Name of Organization

Oakville   ON   01/94-01/94 & 09/94-12/94
City   Province/State   Dates

Developed application programs, worked on CALRS system
Learned communication skills and how to work with people

☐ Summer
☒ Part -time
   # of hours/week: 10
☐ Co-op
☐ Internship
☐ Volunteer
☐ Full -time
☐ Other: (Specify)

Labourer   Ford Motor Company
        Position   Name of Organization

Oakville   ON   06/93 to 08/94
City   Province/State   Dates

Worked in the Engine Plant on the line
Learned what hard work is!

☐ Summer
☐ Part -time
   # of hours/week:
☐ Co-op
☐ Internship
☐ Volunteer
☒ Full -time
☐ Other: (Specify)

Summary

Demonstrate your suitability for position(s) sought, by outlining your career objectives and elaborating on the factual material already presented. Show how your experience (educational, extracurricular and work) is relevant to the position(s), organization, and/or field of work for which you are applying.

My career goal is to become a Chartered Accountant. I would like to work in the computer auditing function and possibly as a computer systems consultant. The ultimate career accomplishment would be to become a partner.

When I went to the University of Ottawa, I did not have any real career goals in mind. My only reasons for going to university were to please my family and because I had an aptitude for mathematics. I was accepted to a very good programming co-op computer service, but I quickly found out that I did not want to work as a computer programming.

Through a friend, I found a job with Jerrold Mechanical. At the time my goal was to become a plumber. I returned to school and study business when I decided that plumbing was not the career that I wanted to follow. Talking with other students in the business program helped me to learn about the C.A. profession. I found the accounting courses interesting and I became more committed to becoming a C.A. To help achieve this goal, I decided to acquire a strong background in computers.

My greatest asset is my willingness to work hard. I feel that I am capable of becoming a Chartered Accountant who would be an asset to your firm.

_____   _____
              Date   Signature

Approved by		CACEE Application for Employment	○ Full-time ● ○ Summer ○ Co-op ○ Internship ○

Name of Organization
Olsen Long

Position(s) sought
Junior Accountant

Name of Educational Institution
McMaster University

General Information

Surname
Jerrod

Given Name(s)
Eric Robert

Address until	No.	Street			Tel.
30 Apr 00	23	Stroud Avenue			905-529-2461
	City	Prov./State	Postal Code		E-mail
	Hamilton	ON	M3T 2X4		

Permanent Address (If different from above)	No.	Street		Tel.
	City	Prov./State	Postal Code	E-mail ajerrod@hotmail.com

Are you legally eligible to accept employment in Canada?
● Yes   ○ No
Documentary evidence may be requested after a job offer is made.

When are you available to start work?

Would you accept employment anywhere in Canada?
○ Yes   ● No

Preferred location(s)
1. Toronto
2. Winnipeg
3.

Education

Post Secondary or other institutions attended. Begin with most recent.	Faculty, Department, Division or School	Discipline or Programme (Major)	Degree/Diploma/ Certificate	Date obtained or expected
McMaster University	BUsiness	Commerce & Finance	B.Comm.	04/00

G.P.A. for your most recently completed academic year ____ on a scale of ____ (Percentage or letter equivalent __B−__).

G.P.A. for all courses completed to date (cumulative average) ____ on a scale of ____ (Percentage or letter equivalent __B−__).

Highlight skills relevant to the position(s) sought.
-Good computer skills
-Easy to get along with
-Motivated to exceed expectations
-Good communication skills
-Able to meet deadlines

Educational Experiences and Accomplishments

Describe your relevant courses, project work, theses, publications, and presentations. Include awards and scholarships.

Extracurricular Activities

Describe your extracurricular activities including class or campus offices held, volunteer experience, memberships in clubs or organizations, leadership roles, sports activities, hobbies, etc. (You are not required to mention the names of organizations that indicate race, ancestry, place of origin, colour, ethnic origin, citizenship, creed, sex, sexual orientation, age, marital status, family status, political beliefs or disabilities).

When not attending classes, much of my time isspent playing baseball and touch football with friends in my neighbourhood. Living directly adjacent to a baseball field and having already established a position on such local sports teams as shortstop and quarterback, I didn't join any formal McMaster intermural teams. I do however have a membership at the local Golds Gym. Coinciding with these sports, I try to play as much golf as possible on the weekends, usually averaging about 18 holes a week. DUring the fall term, I purchased a membership for tennis instruction and play on the local courts as much as possible.

I spend many of my evenings answering the phone for my father's business. This responsibility of course, has limited my membership in the Commerce Student's Association and other university organizations and teams.

Work Experience

Please describe all work experience (paid and unpaid) starting with most recent.

Circulation Info. Systems Clerk   The Spectator
          Position   **Name of Organization**

Hamilton   ON   06/95 to 10/97
City   **Province/State**   **Dates**

Via the telephone and computer, duties included resolving customer
complaints, updating carrier route information and general public
relations. The diversity of the customer complaints necessitated
effective communication skills and tact to alleviate such greievances.
Indeed, this experience taught me to be more receptive to people's
ideas and wishes which will inevitably be an asset in future
company-client relations.

- ☐ Summer
- ☒ Part-time
   # of hours/week: 20
- ☐ Co-op
- ☐ Internship
- ☐ Volunteer
- ☐ Full-time
- ☐ Other: (Specify)

Circulation Aid   The Spectator
          Position   **Name of Organization**

Hamilton   ON   04/94 to 06/95
City   **Province/State**   **Dates**

The primary purpose of this position was to confirm that new customer
orders had been serviced by carriers. As training focused on effective
public relations, my ability to associate and relate with new people
has improved considerably which should provide helpful in meeting
potential clients. This experience with P.R. will permit me to make
such clients feel more at ease with the company and assure them of the
vast resources at their disposal.

- ☐ Summer
- ☒ Part-time
   # of hours/week: 20
- ☐ Co-op
- ☐ Internship
- ☐ Volunteer
- ☐ Full-time
- ☐ Other: (Specify)

Carrier Leader   The Spectator
          Position   **Name of Organization**

Hamilton   ON   05/93 to 04/94
City   **Province/State**   **Dates**

This job focussed on commisssion sales and also required occasional
service inquiries to be made. A great deal of diligence was required
as often 70 calls would have to be made during a 5 pm - 8 pm shift. By
experiencing actual sales and learning to convince the consumer that a
purchase of the product was in their own best interests, this position
offered an insight into effective selling procedures.

- ☐ Summer
- ☒ Part-time
   # of hours/week: 15
- ☐ Co-op
- ☐ Internship
- ☐ Volunteer
- ☐ Full-time
- ☐ Other: (Specify)

          Position   **Name of Organization**

City   **Province/State**   **Dates**

- ☐ Summer
- ☐ Part-time
   # of hours/week: ___
- ☐ Co-op
- ☐ Internship
- ☐ Volunteer
- ☐ Full-time
- ☐ Other: (Specify)

Summary

Demonstrate your suitability for position(s) sought, by outlining your career objectives and elaborating on the factual material already presented. Show how your experience (educational, extracurricular and work) is relevant to the position(s), organization, and/or field of work for which you are applying.

Although actual involvement in the accounting workplace would serve as the best means for determining which facet of accounting was best suited to my individual skills, the B.Comm program has proven to illustrate the challenging nature of financial reporting and taxation. Financial accounting and auditing invariably pose special demands upon the individual, including heighteneed interpretive and writing skills as well as requiring meticulous research and consultation. As my work experience and education have taught me how to effectively prepare reports and given my interest in problem solving, this had led me to the conclusion that the accounting profession best satisfied my short and long term objectives and coincides with my personal strengths.

Although recognizing the fact that a firm must believe that a new employee can pass the C.A. examination in order to be of value to the firm, my marks are not truly indicative of my academic potential. In particular, my final grade in Introductory Accounting is well below my average upon entering the examination. Prior to the exam, my average was close to 80%, however, I was involved indirectly in an automobile accident which caused me to be 25 minutes late for the exam, which I subsequently wrote under considerable duress. Also, in my third year, I was negatively affected by the fact that I helped with my father's business before school and in the evenings while he recovered from surgery. His period of convalescence was approximately 4 months. I am therefore convinced that my 4th year academic standing will show substantial improvement.

My thorough knowledge of sports and participation in various sporting activities should proved to be an asset in developing rapport with certain clients. Also, my constant progression through the corporate structure of The Spectator reflects a willingness to learn and a desire to accomplish my personal goals. In this respect, I hope to be able to utilize my verbal and writing skills in preparing financial statements and reports.

_____   _____
                Date   Signature

Approved by	CACEE Application for Employment	● Full-time
		○ Summer
		○ Co-op
		○ Internship
		○

Name of Organization
Olsen Long

Position(s) sought
Junior Accountant

Name of Educational Institution
University of Windsor

General Information

Surname
Cassar

Given Name(s)
Michael James

| Address until | No. 78 | Street Emerson Drive | | Tel. 519-824-0896 |
| _____ | City Windsor | Prov./State ON | Postal Code N7X 2J3 | E-mail cassar@uwindsor.ca |

| Permanent Address (If different from above) | No. 46 | Street Fairbanks Avenue | | Tel. 905-728-4516 |
| | City Oshawa | Prov./State ON | Postal Code K8M 2X9 | E-mail |

Are you legally eligible to accept employment in Canada?
● Yes   ○ No
Documentary evidence may be requested after a job offer is made.

When are you available to start work?

Would you accept employment anywhere in Canada?
○ Yes   ● No
Preferred location(s)
1. Toronto
2. London
3.

Education

Post Secondary or other institutions attended. Begin with most recent.	Faculty, Department, Division or School	Discipline or Programme (Major)	Degree/Diploma/ Certificate	Date obtained or expected
University of Windsor	Business	Accounting	B.Comm.	May 2000

G.P.A. for your most recently completed academic year _____ on a scale of _____ (Percentage or letter equivalent 79).

G.P.A. for all courses completed to date (cumulative average) _____ on a scale of _____ (Percentage or letter equivalent 77).

Highlight skills relevant to the position(s) sought.
Organized, dedicated, team-player
Year-end audit experience
Strong computer skills (Microsoft Word, Excel, Lotus 1-2-3_
Involved in extracurricular activities

Educational Experiences and Accomplishments

Describe your relevant courses, project work, theses, publications, and presentations. Include awards and scholarships.

I received the 3rd Year Micheal Dueman Memorial Award sponsored by Deloitte and Touch for involvement in extracurricular actvities and academic achievement.

I was also a Teaching Assistant for Professor Trudell for Third Year Cost Accounting.

Extracurricular Activities

Describe your extracurricular activities including class or campus offices held, volunteer experience, memberships in clubs or organizations, leadership roles, sports activities, hobbies, etc. (You are not required to mention the names of organizations that indicate race, ancestry, place of origin, colour, ethnic origin, citizenship, creed, sex, sexual orientation, age, marital status, family status, political beliefs or disabilities).

Coordinator of Business School Graduation Formal

Class President. Directed many operations of the class including social activities, fund-raising, formal and communications; Chairman of Frosh Week '98, overseeing organization of Business department events; President, Commerce Society

Business Manager for 'The Lance' (school newspaper)

Communicty Youth Choir; Director of Public Relations, Master of Ceremonies

Oshawa Softball Association. Coach of little league (9-11 year olds)

I also enjoy skiing, racquet sports, music, and carpentry

Work Experience

Please describe all work experience (paid and unpaid) starting with most recent.

Student Accountant   Deloitte and Touche
     Position   Name of Organization

Windsor   ON   July 1999 to September 1999
City   Province/State   Dates

- ☒ Summer
- ☐ Part-time
-    # of hours/week: ___
- ☒ Co-op
- ☐ Internship
- ☐ Volunteer
- ☐ Full-time
- ☐ Other: (Specify)

Participated in year-end audit. Concentrated on computer programming. Various task requirements for a partner.

Mechanical Maintenance   Ontario Hydro
     Position   Name of Organization

Oshawa   ON   May-September 1997 & 1998
City   Province/State   Dates

- ☐ Summer
- ☐ Part-time
-    # of hours/week: ___
- ☐ Co-op
- ☐ Internship
- ☐ Volunteer
- ☒ Full-time
- ☐ Other: (Specify)

Provided customer service in the paint and hardware departments

Able to demonstrate product, advise and offer suggestions about the use of home improvement needs

---

          Position   Name of Organization

City   Province/State   Dates

- ☐ Summer
- ☐ Part-time
-    # of hours/week: ___
- ☐ Co-op
- ☐ Internship
- ☐ Volunteer
- ☐ Full-time
- ☐ Other: (Specify)

          Position   Name of Organization

City   Province/State   Dates

- ☐ Summer
- ☐ Part-time
-    # of hours/week: ___
- ☐ Co-op
- ☐ Internship
- ☐ Volunteer
- ☐ Full-time
- ☐ Other: (Specify)

Summary

Demonstrate your suitability for position(s) sought, by outlining your career objectives and elaborating on the factual material already presented. Show how your experience (educational, extracurricular and work) is relevant to the position(s), organization, and/or field of work for which you are applying.

By becoming extremely involved in extra-curricular activities, both at school and in the community, I have further developed both my interpersonal and communication skills. I have also learned a great deal about managing time and activities, reasoning with others, and effectively working with many different personalities.

Being elected as the Class Presdient has been the highlight of my university career and a tremendous opportunity to practice important skills. Through the network of other executive on various committees I have learned about organizing, delegating and dealing with responsibility. Similar to this, I have owned two small businesses which have exposed me to hiring, marketing, dealing with customers, and staff motivation. The organizations were small, but the experience was invaluable.

Most importantly, wining the Micheal Dueman Memorial Award and working for a summer with an accounting firm confirmed to me that I am making a career choice that I will be happy with and dedicated to. I am looking forward to applying my skills and experience to an accounting career with a respectable firm like Olsen Long. I know that a successful career is not something that just happens, it is something you earn.

I understand that any omission or misrepresentation with respect to this information may be cause for denial or immediate termination of employment.

_____   _____
            Date   Signature

Approved by		**CACEE Application for Employment**		● Full-time
				○ Summer
				○ Co-op
				○ Internship
				○

Name of Organization	Position(s) sought
Olsen Long	Junior Accountant

Name of Educational Institution
Carleton University

General Information

Surname	Given Name(s)
Hatt	Jo-Ann

Address until	No.	Street		Tel.
May 2000	212-521	Addington Street		613-235-4067
	City	Prov./State	Postal Code	E-mail
	Ottawa	ON	K2C 3J4	jhatt@sympatico.com

Permanent Address (If different from above)	No.	Street		Tel.
	410	Ambleside Drive		613-549-9788
	City	Prov./State	Postal Code	E-mail
	Kingston	ON	K7J 2F5	

Are you legally eligible to accept employment in Canada?

● Yes   ○ No
Documentary evidence may be requested after a job offer is made.

Would you accept employment anywhere in Canada?

○ Yes   ○ No

Preferred location(s)
1.
2.
3.

When are you available to start work?

June 2000

Education

Post Secondary or other institutions attended. Begin with most recent.	Faculty, Department, Division or School	Discipline or Programme (Major)	Degree/Diploma/ Certificate	Date obtained or expected
Carleton University	School of Business	Business	Bachelor, Business Admin.	June 2000

G.P.A. for your most recently completed academic year _____ on a scale of _____ (Percentage or letter equivalent __78__).

G.P.A. for all courses completed to date (cumulative average) _____ on a scale of _____ (Percentage or letter equivalent __78__).

Highlight skills relevant to the position(s) sought.
Able fo perform Accounts Payable functions
-experienced in balancing payroll and commission reporting
-comfortable in a Customer Service environment
-Responsible for handling of cash
-Good computer skills

Educational Experiences and Accomplishments

Describe your relevant courses, project work, theses, publications, and presentations. Include awards and scholarships.

```
-Took a Professional Business Writing Course through the Toronto School of Business
(Ottawa Campus)
```

Extracurricular Activities

Describe your extracurricular activities including class or campus offices held, volunteer experience, memberships in clubs or organizations, leadership roles, sports activities, hobbies, etc. (You are not required to mention the names of organizations that indicate race, ancestry, place of origin, colour, ethnic origin, citizenship, creed, sex, sexual orientation, age, marital status, family status, political beliefs or disabilities).

```
Commerce Lecture and Speaker Series:  Financial Officer
-managed a budget of $5,000
-organized the fund raising campaign
-participated in committee decision-making

Carleton's Business Conference:  Delegate and Hostess
-attended the conference and participated in seminars and informal topic discussions
-welcomed guest speaks to conference and assisted with their presentations

Commerce Communications
-publicized Commerce events

Carleton's Student Police Organization (1998)
Commerce 'Buddy' System (1996-1997)
High School Liaison Program (1995-1996)
Music, Internet, Outdoor sports
```

Work Experience

Please describe all work experience (paid and unpaid) starting with most recent.

Accounting Clerk   LePage
    Position   Name of Organization

Kingston   ON   Summers 1997, 1998, 1999
City   Province/State   Dates

Responsible for Accounts Payable-received invoices which I dispersed
for proper approval, issued payments and maintained records. Assisted
with commissioned employees payroll by maintaining accounts of
commissions earned, inputing payroll information and balancing payroll
reconciliation.

- ☒ Summer
- ☐ Part -time
-    # of hours/week: ___
- ☐ Co-op
- ☐ Internship
- ☐ Volunteer
- ☐ Full -time
- ☐ Other: (Specify)

Sales Clerk   Shopper's Drug Mart
    Position   Name of Organization

KIngston   ON   June 1995 to Sept. 1996
City   Province/State   Dates

Responsible for cash sales and customer relations. Handled customer
purchases and complaints. Stocked shelves, maintained inventory, gift
wrapped and arranged displays for in-store promotions.

- ☒ Summer
- ☒ Part -time
-    # of hours/week: 15
- ☐ Co-op
- ☐ Internship
- ☐ Volunteer
- ☐ Full -time
- ☐ Other: (Specify)

Student Security   Carleton University
    Position   Name of Organization

Ottawa   ON   Sept. 1998-present
City   Province/State   Dates

I supervised students at campus events for crowd control and
enforcement of the University's Code of Conduct

- ☐ Summer
- ☒ Part -time
-    # of hours/week: 12
- ☐ Co-op
- ☐ Internship
- ☐ Volunteer
- ☐ Full -time
- ☐ Other: (Specify)

Head Cashier   Kingston Speedway
    Position   Name of Organization

Kingston   ON   Sept. 1994-Sept. 1998
City   Province/State   Dates

Responsible for paying cash to winning driver and balancing cash
allocation. Promotion from banker position where responsibilities
include counting and bundling money and balancing to computer totals.

- ☒ Summer
- ☒ Part -time
-    # of hours/week: 16
- ☐ Co-op
- ☐ Internship
- ☐ Volunteer
- ☐ Full -time
- ☐ Other: (Specify)

Summary

Demonstrate your suitability for position(s) sought, by outlining your career objectives and elaborating on the factual material already presented. Show how your experience (educational, extracurricular and work) is relevant to the position(s), organization, and/or field of work for which you are applying.

Attaining the Chartered Accountant designation will necessitate that a successful candidate be able, hard working, committed and associated with a good firm. In terms of ability, my consistently high marks in accounting and successful completion of courses indicate that I have the capabilities to learn, understand and perform in the accounting field. My involvements in extracurricular activities have shown me the importance of time management. I understand what it is to work hard as I have maintained grades, committee positions, part-time employment and a social life. I am also prepared to work hard in the future in order to achieve my goals.

I understand that any omission or misrepresentation with respect to this information may be cause for denial or immediate termination of employment.

_____
Date

_____
Signature

Approved by	**CACEE Application for Employment**	● Full-time
		○ Summer
		○ Co-op
		○ Internship
		○

Name of Organization	Position(s) sought
Olsen Long	Junior Accountant

Name of Educational Institution
University of Toronto

General Information

Surname	Given Name(s)
Hayes	Kristy

Address until	No.	Street		Tel.
April 2000	710-220	Ferndale Avenue		905-770-8147
	City	Prov./State	Postal Code	E-mail
	Mississauga	ON	M3I 2Z1	

Permanent Address (If different from above)	No.	Street		Tel.
	306	Pugsley Avenue		519-786-2143
	City	Prov./State	Postal Code	E-mail
	Kingsville	ON	N0T 3S4	K_Hayes@golden.net

Are you legally eligible to accept employment in Canada?

● Yes   ○ No
Documentary evidence may be requested after a job offer is made.

Would you accept employment anywhere in Canada?

○ Yes   ● No

Preferred location(s)
1. Toronto
2. Calgary
3. Vancouver

When are you available to start work?

September 2000

Education

Post Secondary or other institutions attended. Begin with most recent.	Faculty, Department, Division or School	Discipline or Programme (Major)	Degree/Diploma/ Certificate	Date obtained or expected
University of Toronto	Arts and Science	Commerce & Finance	B.Comm.	Oct. 2000

G.P.A. for your most recently completed academic year ____ on a scale of ____ (Percentage or letter equivalent A-).

G.P.A. for all courses completed to date (cumulative average) ____ on a scale of ____ (Percentage or letter equivalent A-).

Highlight skills relevant to the position(s) sought.

I have worked in an accounting department for the past 6 summers where I have learned a great deal of practical knowledge about Accounts Payables, Petty Cash, posting Journal entries, compiling reports and providing control functions.

I have strong computer skills (Microsoft Word, Excel, and AccPacc) and an excellent work ethic.

Educational Experiences and Accomplishments

Describe your relevant courses, project work, theses, publications, and presentations. Include awards and scholarships.

```
-Received the Mitchell A. Brady Bursary for attaining the highest grades in my third
year accounting courses.
-Received the Senior Accounting Award, Business Proficiency Award and the Math Award at
graduation from Kingsville Distric High School
```

Extracurricular Activities

Describe your extracurricular activities including class or campus offices held, volunteer experience, memberships in clubs or organizations, leadership roles, sports activities, hobbies, etc. (You are not required to mention the names of organizations that indicate race, ancestry, place of origin, colour, ethnic origin, citizenship, creed, sex, sexual orientation, age, marital status, family status, political beliefs or disabilities).

```
-Member of Senate Committee on Scholarships and Student Aid
-Project Manager for Fund-raising Committee- AIESEC
-Marker- 3rd year Operations Research Course
1998/99-Research and Resources Officer- International Finance Club
1998-Marker- 2nd year Statistics Course
    -Commerce '00 Social Committee, Brain Trust Program
1996/97
-U of T's Symphonic Band
-5 years as an Assistant Brownie Leader for the Girl Guide Movement
-Qualified leader through the Girl Guide leadership training program
-Treasurer for the Centennial Secondary School Bands and Student Council

-downhill skiing, sailing, squash, music
```

Work Experience

Please describe all work experience (paid and unpaid) starting with most recent.

Control Assistant   Allied Chemical Canada Ltd.
          Position   Name of Organization

Windsor   ON   May 1999 - September 1999
City   Province/State   Dates

☒ Summer
☐ Part-time
-Productions record control   # of hours/week: ___
-Off-standard material control
-Industrial planning   ☐ Co-op
-Designing, programming and implementing computer software, and   ☐ Internship
training others to use it   ☐ Volunteer
                                                             ☐ Full-time
                                                             ☐ Other: (Specify)

Accounting Clerk   Allied Chemical Canada Ltd.
          Position   Name of Organization

Windsor   ON   June 1998 - September 1998
City   Province/State   Dates

☒ Summer
☐ Part-time
-summer relief for 3 departments   # of hours/week: ___
-involved verifying approving payment of Accounts Payable
-prepared material receipts reports   ☐ Co-op
-controlled petty cash   ☐ Internship
-prepared Journal entries and posted to the fixed Assets Ledger   ☐ Volunteer
-production records control   ☐ Full-time
-keyed accounting data   ☐ Other: (Specify)

Accounting Clerk   Allied Chemical Canada Ltd.
          Position   Name of Organization

Windsor   ON   Summers, 1995, 1996, 1997
City   Province/State   Dates

☒ Summer
☐ Part-time
-verified and approved payment of Accounts Payable   # of hours/week: ___
-prepared material receipt reports
-created a job and prepared a job description and job training   ☐ Co-op
-keyed accounting data   ☐ Internship
-placed purchase orders   ☐ Volunteer
-prepared US content and drawback studies   ☐ Full-time
                                                             ☐ Other: (Specify)

Playground Leader   City of Windsor Department of Recreation
          Position   Name of Organization

Windsor   ON   June 1994 to August 1995
City   Province/State   Dates

☒ Summer
☐ Part-time
-planned and implemented a recreation program for 4-7 year olds   # of hours/week: ___
-involved supervising activities
-provided counselling   ☐ Co-op
                                                             ☐ Internship
                                                             ☐ Volunteer
                                                             ☐ Full-time
                                                             ☐ Other: (Specify)

Summary

Demonstrate your suitability for position(s) sought, by outlining your career objectives and elaborating on the factual material already presented. Show how your experience (educational, extracurricular and work) is relevant to the position(s), organization, and/or field of work for which you are applying.

The last three years at the University of Toronto have been invaluable to me, not only in providing the sound background and analytical skills essential in the Chartered Accountant profession, but also in the development of communication, teamwork and organizational skills. I have particularly enjoyed working on the International Finance Club as it has broadened my understanding of international business, as well as affording me the opportunity to interact more closely with leading individuals in the business community. Fulfilling my responsibilities on the committees I have been involved in, as well as marking a course, tutoring and maintaining high academic standards, has required a great deal of commitment, self-discipline and enthusiasm.

The various summer jobs I have held at Allied Chemical have given me the opportunity to build on these skills, as well as to develop a strong working knowledge of all aspects of an accounting system in a manufacturing environment.

I feel that this experience will prove to be an excellent preparation for this profession and I am looking forward to learning more about the opportunities available in your firm.

I understand that any omission or misrepresentation with respect to this information may be cause for denial or immediate termination of employment.

_____   _____
              Date   Signature

Approved by		○ Full-time

CACEE Application for Employment

- ◉ Full-time
- ○ Summer
- ○ Co-op
- ○ Internship
- ○

CACEE

Name of Organization	Position(s) sought
Olsen Long	Junior Accountant

Name of Educational Institution
Wilfred Laurier University

General Information

Surname	Given Name(s)
Martinelli	Anthony

Address until	No.	Street		Tel.
April 30, 2000	34	Sunningdale Drive		519-746-0462
	City	Prov./State	Postal Code	E-mail
	Kitchener	ON	N2L 3K2	martinel@hotmail.com

Permanent Address (If different from above)	No.	Street		Tel.
	City	Prov./State	Postal Code	E-mail

Are you legally eligible to accept employment in Canada?
◉ Yes   ○ No
Documentary evidence may be requested after a job offer is made.

Would you accept employment anywhere in Canada?
○ Yes   ◉ No
Preferred location(s)
1. Toronto
2. Mississauga
3.

When are you available to start work?
May 2000

Education

Post Secondary or other institutions attended. Begin with most recent.	Faculty, Department, Division or School	Discipline or Programme (Major)	Degree/Diploma/ Certificate	Date obtained or expected
Wilfred Laurier University	School of Business	Commerce & Finance	BBA Co-op	Oct 2000

G.P.A. for your most recently completed academic year _____ on a scale of _____ (Percentage or letter equivalent 75).

G.P.A. for all courses completed to date (cumulative average) _____ on a scale of _____ (Percentage or letter equivalent 76).

Highlight skills relevant to the position(s) sought.
- 4 years of related accounting experience (posting entries, preparing reports and statements, verifying claims)
- Strong academic skills (Dean's List in 1997-GMAT score of 620)
- Demonstrated leadership skills through volunteer and extracurricular activities (Team captain on Laurier's Varsity Soccer team in 1996 and current Vice President of the Student Investment Club)

Educational Experiences and Accomplishments

Describe your relevant courses, project work, theses, publications, and presentations. Include awards and scholarships.

The Dr. Norton Melson Prize
Dean's Honour List
The Watkins Scholarship-HIgh school graduation scholarship for the highest grade average (92%)
The Professor John Matheson Scholarship for excellence in mathematics (93%)

Extracurricular Activities

Describe your extracurricular activities including class or campus offices held, volunteer experience, memberships in clubs or organizations, leadership roles, sports activities, hobbies, etc. (You are not required to mention the names of organizations that indicate race, ancestry, place of origin, colour, ethnic origin, citizenship, creed, sex, sexual orientation, age, marital status, family status, political beliefs or disabilities).

I enjoy all sports but have a significant interest in soccer. My abilities as a leader and organizer was acknowledged in 1996 when I was appointed team captain of the Laurier Varsity Soccer team. I also play soccer on organized teams for residence and the School of Business and Economics.

I am co-founder and currently Vice President of the Student Investment Club. The club was formed in 1996 to acquire knowledge of stock market transactions. I was involved throughout the initial planning and organizational stages. I strengthened many skills through this experience, such as competent leadership, objective decision-making and the ability to recruit new members.

I also collect sports cards and enjoy reading biographies and books on sports.

As a co-op student, these activities were difficult to incorporate in the school year.

Work Experience

Please describe all work experience (paid and unpaid) starting with most recent.

Accounting Clerk		D.W. Ingram Real Estate & Insurance Ltd.
Position		Name of Organization
Kitchener	ON	98 to present
City	Province/State	Dates

I am responsible for the administration of all accounting ledgers and the issuance of all cheques through our office. I prepare bank reconciliations monthly, unaudited cash flow statements, and most statements required by insurance regulatory bodies. These tasks require accounting skills, an ability to work independently and a certain degree of competence. Also, I am in constant contact with clients. This has helped me develop effective interpersonal communication skills and confidence with people.

☐ Summer
☒ Part-time
  # of hours/week: ___
☒ Co-op
☐ Internship
☐ Volunteer
☐ Full-time
☐ Other: (Specify)
___

Expenditures Clerk		Ontario Ministry of Revenue
Position		Name of Organization
Kitchener	ON	5/98 to 8/98
City	Province/State	Dates

I was responsible for verifying ministry officials' travel claims and preparing manual and computer cheques. I worked under the Chief of Finance on special assignments such as balancing budgetary ledgers and calculating expenses of ministry officials. This position required administrative skills such as working independently with minimum supervision, assuming responsibilities and cooperating with co-workers.

☐ Part-time
  # of hours/week: ___
☒ Co-op
☐ Internship
☐ Volunteer
☐ Full-time
☐ Other: (Specify)
___

Expenditure Clerk		Ontario Ministry of Revenue
Position		Name of Organization
Kitchener	ON	5/97 to 8/97
City	Province/State	Dates

I was assigned accounting duties such as preparing computer input, checking math of expenditures and preparing manual and computer requisitions for payment. I also was a liaison between ministry personnel and outside firms. This position required communication skills, cooperation with both office staff and outside firms, and the ability to work independently on assignments.

☐ Part-time
  # of hours/week: ___
☒ Co-op
☐ Internship
☐ Volunteer
☐ Full-time
☐ Other: (Specify)
___

Salesperson & Bookkeeper		Rudy's Tailor Shop
Position		Name of Organization
Kitchener	ON	5/95 to 6/97
City	Province/State	Dates

The company is an owner-operated retail clothing store specializing in made-to-measure suits and catering to a small but elite group of clients. My responsibilities included the preparation of display shelves as well as insuring the timely completion of customer orders. I was also responsible for the accounts payable and accounts receivable. The position required some account knowledge and interpersonal communication skills.

☐ Summer
☒ Part-time
  # of hours/week: ___
☐ Co-op
☐ Internship
☐ Volunteer
☐ Full-time
☐ Other: (Specify)
___

Summary

Demonstrate your suitability for position(s) sought, by outlining your career objectives and elaborating on the factual material already presented. Show how your experience (educational, extracurricular and work) is relevant to the position(s), organization, and/or field of work for which you are applying.

My goal is to acquire the practical experience necessary in obtaining the designation of Chartered Accountant. My education, supplemented by my work experience and extra curricular activities, has provided me with the knowledge and abilities which are essential for success in the required position. I feel that membership in a reputable organization such as Olsen Long would help me in the pursuit and attainment of my career goals. Once I have obtained my Chartered Accountant designation, I would like to join on of the specialty areas offered by your firm.

My most practical experience has been with D.W. Ingram Real Estate and Insurance Ltd. I was hired to improve the firm's cash procedures. I independently reviewed existing accounting methods and determined that a more appropriate system of record-keeping was needed. This required an ability to identify problems and implement solutions using good judgement and creativity.

Although Chartered Accountants are experts in many specialized areas (i.e. tax, auditing, consulting) it is important for one to have an understanding of the basics of accounting. The diversity of the two offices I have worked for has given me the opportunity to appreciate this fact since I observed the operation of two completely different systems using the same basic rules.

As an active member of the Students Investment Club, I have developed an entrepreneurial spirit which is essential in the business world. One should be able to find opportunities and use these to his/her advantage. As the appointed chairman of meeting and liaison between club members and the investment broker, I have had to display qualities such as leadership and good judgement.

I will graduate from **Laurier** and will have obtained all the required courses. The fact that I have maintained a B/B+ average and have scored a 620 on the GMAT proves that I have the required academic background for this field. I appreciate your consideration of this application and look forward to meeting with you soon.

_____   _____
            Date   Signature

Approved by

CACEE

CACEE Application for Employment

- ◉ Full-time
- ○ Summer
- ○ Co-op
- ○ Internship
- ○

Name of Organization	Position(s) sought
Olsen Long	Junior Accountant

Name of Educational Institution	
McMaster University	

General Information

Surname	Given Name(s)
Masse	Gregory Richard

Address until _____	No. 78	Street Maple Drive		Tel. 416-628-4163
	City Dundas	Prov./State ON	Postal Code M4S 7T1	E-mail

Permanent Address (If different from above)	No. 275	Street Princess Anne Street		Tel.
	City London	Prov./State ON	Postal Code N5Z 3M5	E-mail GMASS@yahoo.com

Are you legally eligible to accept employment in Canada?

◉ Yes   ○ No

Documentary evidence may be requested after a job offer is made.

When are you available to start work?

January 2000

Would you accept employment anywhere in Canada?

○ Yes   ◉ No

Preferred location(s)
1. London
2. Toronto
3.

Education

Post Secondary or other institutions attended. Begin with most recent.	Faculty, Department, Division or School	Discipline or Programme (Major)	Degree/Diploma/ Certificate	Date obtained or expected
McMaster University	Business & Science	Science & Commerce	B.Sc.	Jan.00

G.P.A. for your most recently completed academic year ____ on a scale of ____ (Percentage or letter equivalent B-).

G.P.A. for all courses completed to date (cumulative average) ____ on a scale of ____ (Percentage or letter equivalent B+).

Highlight skills relevant to the position(s) sought.
- Experience in an Accounting Department
- Enjoy problem solving and providing customer service
- Good computer skills (Lotus 1-2-3, Simply Accounting, WordPerfect_
- Good communication skills

Educational Experiences and Accomplishments

Describe your relevant courses, project work, theses, publications, and presentations. Include awards and scholarships.

I received a Junior Achiever's Award from the London Chamber of Commerce in September 1999 in recognition of successfully organizing and fulfilling my own business enterprise. Each year the Chamber solicits nominations for businesses that were started by students aged 15 to 24 years. Award recipients are invited to the Chamber's annual awards banquet in September.

Extracurricular Activities

Describe your extracurricular activities including class or campus offices held, volunteer experience, memberships in clubs or organizations, leadership roles, sports activities, hobbies, etc. (You are not required to mention the names of organizations that indicate race, ancestry, place of origin, colour, ethnic origin, citizenship, creed, sex, sexual orientation, age, marital status, family status, political beliefs or disabilities).

Although I am apresently enrolled in the commerce department, I have continued to maintain my interests in the sciences. I have retained the position of Treasurer for the Science Council for the past three years. Part of my duties entailed the preparation of a budget, presentation of financial information, as well as the authorization of all cash transactions. I was also in charge of selecting and purchasing faculty sportswear.

Outside of my studies at McMaster University, my extracurricular activities include spending time purchasing, restoring and enjoying my antique vending machine collections.

I have also played organized hockey for the past three years on a weekly basis and am an avid rollerblader and downhill skier.

Work Experience

Please describe all work experience (paid and unpaid) starting with most recent.

President   GRM Iron and Steel

Position   **Name of Organization**

London   ON   May ' 99 - September '99

City   **Province/State**   **Dates**

I created, organized and implemented my own business. Accomplishments:
-formulated the idea of iron and steel grill work on easy access windows
-applied for and secured a loan with the Student Venture Capital Loan program
-registered the company with the Ontario government
-Arranged and purchased an insurance policy
-Created advertisements and flyers. Delivered flyers door-to-door
-Provided strict personal handling of all clientele
-installed bars and ensured customer's satisfaction with follow-up visits
-paying back the loan within the time allotment

☐ Summer
☐ Part -time
# of hours/week: ___
☐ Co-op
☐ Internship
☐ Volunteer
☐ Full -time
☒ Other: (Specify)
   own company

Position   **Name of Organization**

City   **Province/State**   **Dates**

In general, this experience has allowed me the chance to further my business skills from the other side of the accounting desk, as well as increasing my knowledge in the various aspects of owning and operating a business.

☐ Summer
☐ Part -time
# of hours/week: ___
☐ Co-op
☐ Internship
☐ Volunteer
☐ Full -time
☐ Other: (Specify)

Accounting Clerk   Lambton Homes

Position   **Name of Organization**

London   ON   May 1996 - September 1997

City   **Province/State**   **Dates**

As an Accounting Clerk I was in charge of the Accounts Payable functions. I was able to apply my academic knowledge to the processing of invoices, preparation and posting of journal entries and the verification of the monthly statements from thirty to forty of the sub-contracted trades. If discrepancies arose with one of the trades, dealing with the public proved to be an important attribue that was mastered well.

☐ Summer
☐ Part -time
# of hours/week: ___
☐ Co-op
☐ Internship
☐ Volunteer
☒ Full -time
☐ Other: (Specify)

Position   **Name of Organization**

City   **Province/State**   **Dates**

☐ Summer
☐ Part -time
# of hours/week: ___
☐ Co-op
☐ Internship
☐ Volunteer
☐ Full -time
☐ Other: (Specify)

Summary

Demonstrate your suitability for position(s) sought, by outlining your career objectives and elaborating on the factual material already presented. Show how your experience (educational, extracurricular and work) is relevant to the position(s), organization, and/or field of work for which you are applying.

Although I had originally been enrolled in the sciences, I have decided that I definitely want to work towards becoming a Chartered Accountant.

The process which led me from Science to Commerce was initiated not only by a newly found appreciation for the concepts of accounting, but was also affected by the inspiration received from one of my professors.

Having a father who has been a successful Chartered Accountant for twenty-five years has instilled upon me most beneficial assistance in pursuing my endeavors of becoming a Chartered Accountant. Always having access to such business-related material as "The Financial Post", "The Financial Times", "C.A." and "Fortune" has given me the opportunity to keep well-informed with theh day-to-day happenings in the world of business, as well as being a constant source of significant information which has helped to increase my interests and knowledge.

Subsequently, this personal attribute will prove extremely advantageous to both myself, as an accountancy student and employee, and to Olsen Long as an employer. The main advantage will be in the extracurricular experience I will be able to put to use both academically and practically. Learning will never cease to take place outside of my "9-5" office position, but wil rather be an important aspect of my day-to-day life.

I am confident that this added experience outside of commerce will aid in making me an excellent candidate for Olsen Long since I am now sure of the type of career I am striving for -- that of becoming a dedicated Chartered Accountant.

_____   _____
              Date   Signature

Approved by	CACEE Application for Employment	● Full-time
		○ Summer
		○ Co-op
CACEE		○ Internship
		○

Name of Organization	Position(s) sought
Olsen Long	Staff Assistant

Name of Educational Institution
Brock University

General Information

Surname	Given Name(s)
Plant	Dayna Lynn

Address until	No.	Street	Tel.
30/04/00	171	Riverside Avenue	905-682-3341
	City	Prov./State Postal Code	E-mail
	St. Catherines	ON M6A 3S5	

Permanent Address (If different from above)	No.	Street	Tel.
	21	Meadowlane Cr.	905-876-2199
	City	Prov./State Postal Code	E-mail
	Milton	ON M1X 8P3	DPLANT@hotmail.com

Are you legally eligible to accept employment in Canada?
● Yes   ○ No
Documentary evidence may be requested after a job offer is made.

Would you accept employment anywhere in Canada?
● Yes   ○ No
Preferred location(s)
1. North York
2. Mississauga
3. Hamilton

When are you available to start work?
May 1, 2000

Education

Post Secondary or other institutions attended. Begin with most recent.	Faculty, Department, Division or School	Discipline or Programme (Major)	Degree/Diploma/ Certificate	Date obtained or expected
Brock University	Administrative Studies	Accounting	BBA	04/00
Brock University	Physical Education and Recreation	Recreation & Leisure Study	BRLS	12/98

G.P.A. for your most recently completed academic year _____ on a scale of _____ (Percentage or letter equivalent _72_).

G.P.A. for all courses completed to date (cumulative average) _____ on a scale of _____ (Percentage or letter equivalent _74_).

Highlight skills relevant to the position(s) sought.
-Entrepreneurial skills through the creation and implementation of own business
-Strong interpersonal and communication skills
-work well independently or with teams
-actively involved in athletic teams (volleyball, soccer, basketball) and personal competition (diving)

Educational Experiences and Accomplishments

Describe your relevant courses, project work, theses, publications, and presentations. Include awards and scholarships.

```
Campus Recreation Outstanding Volunteer Athlete Award (1997, 1998, 1999)
Barbara Shiley Female Athlete of the Year Award upon graduation from high school
```

Extracurricular Activities

Describe your extracurricular activities including class or campus offices held, volunteer experience, memberships in clubs or organizations, leadership roles, sports activities, hobbies, etc. (You are not required to mention the names of organizations that indicate race, ancestry, place of origin, colour, ethnic origin, citizenship, creed, sex, sexual orientation, age, marital status, family status, political beliefs or disabilities).

```
Volunteer for the Southwestern Ontario Regional Sports Council
Researched potential for volunteer sports administrator training program.

Convenor of Kernahan Park Secondary School Girl's Gymnastic Competition
Organized the one-day meet for 120 competitors, developed a new scoring system and was
responsible for 20 scorers on the day of the meet.

NCCP technical and practical qualifications.  Coached (volunteer) for the Brock Diving
Club and the Oakville Diving Club.

Member diver of the Oakville Diving Club for 4 years.  Competed in diving meets across
Ontario.

Hold the current Bronze Medallion for the Interuniversity Athletic Competition.

Hobbies and interests include swimming, boating, camping, skiing, reading, cooking, and
intramural sports such as baseball, hockey, basketball, curling and volleyball.
```

Work Experience

Please describe all work experience (paid and unpaid) starting with most recent.

Customer Service   Laurier Drug Mart
       Position   Name of Organization
Milton   ON   06/99 - 08/99
City   Province/State   Dates

☒ Summer
☐ Part-time
   # of hours/week: ___
Operated cash register
answered customer telephone requests   ☐ Co-op
placed orders to suppliers   ☐ Internship
stocked shelves with orders received   ☐ Volunteer
maintained customer charge account   ☐ Full-time
                                            ☐ Other: (Specify)
                                            _____

Administrative Assistant   Oakville Aquatic Club
       Position   Name of Organization
Oakville   ON   06/98 to 08/98
City   Province/State   Dates

☒ Summer
☐ Part-time
   # of hours/week: ___
-Analyzed present system of recording coaches on computer. Made
changes and documented procedures for user transcribed tapes   ☐ Co-op
-Performed clerical and office duties   ☐ Internship
                                            ☐ Volunteer
                                            ☐ Full-time
                                            ☐ Other: (Specify)
                                            _____

Administrative Assistant   Canadian Amateur Diving Association
       Position   Name of Organization
Toronto   ON   06/97 to 08/97
City   Province/State   Dates

☒ Summer
☐ Part-time
   # of hours/week: ___
Wrote and had printed a manual titled "How to Start a Diving Club"
-Compiled 2 policy manuals for use by: ☐ Co-op
1. CADA volunteers and   ☐ Internship
2. CADA field workers   ☐ Volunteer
                                            ☐ Full-time
                                            ☐ Other: (Specify)
                                            _____

Springboard Diving Instructor   Brock University
       Position   Name of Organization
St. Catherines   ON   1995 to 1997
City   Province/State   Dates

☐ Summer
☒ Part-time
   # of hours/week: ___
Instructed people aged 4 to adult in the skills of springboard divins
-Class size varied from 4 to 18 students   ☐ Co-op
                                            ☐ Internship
                                            ☐ Volunteer
                                            ☐ Full-time
                                            ☐ Other: (Specify)
                                            _____

Summary

Demonstrate your suitability for position(s) sought, by outlining your career objectives and elaborating on the factual material already presented. Show how your experience (educational, extracurricular and work) is relevant to the position(s), organization, and/or field of work for which you are applying.

It is my desire to become a Chartered Accountant because I am an avid learner and would like a career that would offer both challenge and responsibility.

Throughout five years of high school, I maintained myself on the honour roll. As a unniversity graduate from the Sports and Leisure Studies program at Brock University, I held a steady grade average in the mid-seventies in each of my four years. I therefore, have shown a consistent performance which is a result of self-discipline, motivation and hard work. After careful career considerations, I have chosen to become a Chartered Accountant.

Although I have demonstrated a heavy sports interest, I find my commerce courses intriguing. For this reason, I have also chosen to continue my studies in this area.

Through my sports involvement, I have acquired teaching skills through coaching and have been in many positions where I was required to deal with the public, particularly students' parents. I learned tact and acquired the ability to act as a liaison between the diving organization and the parents.

Due to the heavy work and class schedules over the past few years, I have demonstrated the ability to work well under pressure when required. When not under pressure, I look for new projects to tackle. I am self-motivated and enjoy challenge.

Thank you for your consideration of my application. I welcome the opportunity to attend an interview with your firm to discuss career prospects.

I understand that any omission or misrepresentation with respect to this information may be cause for denial or immediate termination of employment.

_____   _____
            Date   Signature

Approved by		● Full-time

CACEE Application for Employment

○ Full-time ●
○ Summer
○ Co-op
○ Internship
○

Name of Organization	Position(s) sought
Olsen Long	Junior Accountant

Name of Educational Institution
University of Western Ontario

General Information

Surname	Given Name(s)
Sexton	Bart Robin

Address until	No.	Street		Tel.
June 2000	728	Montgomery Drive		519-985-0898
	City	Prov./State	Postal Code	E-mail
	London	ON	N5X 2W3	sexton@sympatico.ca

Permanent Address (If different from above)	No.	Street		Tel.
	City	Prov./State	Postal Code	E-mail

Are you legally eligible to accept employment in Canada?	Would you accept employment anywhere in Canada?
● Yes ○ No	○ Yes ● No
Documentary evidence may be requested after a job offer is made.	Preferred location(s)
	1. London
When are you available to start work?	2.
May 2000	3.

Education

Post Secondary or other institutions attended. Begin with most recent.	Faculty, Department, Division or School	Discipline or Programme (Major)	Degree/Diploma/ Certificate	Date obtained or expected
Wilfrid Laurier University	Continuing Education	Accounting	N/A	May 2000
University of Western Ontario	Business	General Management	HBA	May 1999

G.P.A. for your most recently completed academic year _____ on a scale of _____ (Percentage or letter equivalent   73).

G.P.A. for all courses completed to date (cumulative average) _____ on a scale of _____ (Percentage or letter equivalent   75).

Highlight skills relevant to the position(s) sought.
3 Years of Summer Experience at a Chartered Bank with increasing levels of responsibility
-solid oral and written communication skills
-good understanding about field of Chartered Accountancy
-strong computer skills (AccPac, Microsoft Word, Excel)

Educational Experiences and Accomplishments

Describe your relevant courses, project work, theses, publications, and presentations. Include awards and scholarships.

Extracurricular Activities

Describe your extracurricular activities including class or campus offices held, volunteer experience, memberships in clubs or organizations, leadership roles, sports activities, hobbies, etc. (You are not required to mention the names of organizations that indicate race, ancestry, place of origin, colour, ethnic origin, citizenship, creed, sex, sexual orientation, age, marital status, family status, political beliefs or disabilities).

While at Western University, I maintained a keen interest in, and active support of the various educational, social and charitable activities of the Commerce Society. I was also very involved in residence affairs, and intramural sports.

```
(1998-99)  Senior Class Representative (Student/Faculty Committee)
           Researcher (Student Tenants Association)
(1997-98)  Delegate-Business Conference
           Community Services Committee Member
           Heart and Stroke Fund Canvasser
(1996-97)  Chairman-Men's Residence Policy Committee
           Business Orientation Leader
```

I enjoy outdoor activities such as downhill skiing, camping and canoeing. I remain active as a program evaluator for the Ontario Camping Association and have had a lifelong involvement in Boy Scouts.

Work Experience

Please describe all work experience (paid and unpaid) starting with most recent.

Bank Teller
Position

Bank of Montreal, Wharncliffe Rd. Branch
Name of Organization

London
City

ON
Province/State

May 1999 to August 1999
Dates

☒ Summer
☐ Part-time
  # of hours/week: ____
☐ Co-op
☐ Internship
☐ Volunteer
☐ Full-time
☐ Other: (Specify)

Normal cash-handling duties at London's second main Bank of Montreal branch. In addition, was responsible for some auditing work and posting corrections arising out of the normal operations of various departments.

Customer Service Clerk
Position

Bank of Montreal, Sherwood Forest Mall
Name of Organization

London
City

ON
Province/State

May 1998 to August 1998
Dates

☒ Summer
☐ Part-time
  # of hours/week: ____
☐ Co-op
☐ Internship
☐ Volunteer
☐ Full-time
☐ Other: (Specify)

Efficient and courteous processing of all customer transactions, as well as the marketing of bank services and benefits to customers whenever possible. Relief pool activity involved work at branches throughout the City of London.

Bank Teller
Position

Bank of Montreal, Wharncliffe Road Branch
Name of Organization

London
City

ON
Province/State

May 1997 to August 1997
Dates

☒ Summer
☐ Part-time
  # of hours/week: ____
☐ Co-op
☐ Internship
☐ Volunteer
☐ Full-time
☐ Other: (Specify)

As above. Sundry duties were dispatching of U bills and clearing. Miscellaneous duties included filing of cheques, signature cards and DDA particulars.

Camp Counsellor/Bushcraft Director
Position

Camp Tawingo
Name of Organization

Huntsville
City

ON
Province/State

May 1996 to August 1996
Dates

☒ Summer
☐ Part-time
  # of hours/week: ____
☐ Co-op
☐ Internship
☐ Volunteer
☐ Full-time
☐ Other: (Specify)

Responsibility for activity programming covering one camp section (approx. 50 campers)
Responsibility for planning, staffing and directing the camp's four-man woodsmanship and canoe-tripping programs. In addition, normal counsellor duties for an assigned cabin group.

Summary

Demonstrate your suitability for position(s) sought, by outlining your career objectives and elaborating on the factual material already presented. Show how your experience (educational, extracurricular and work) is relevant to the position(s), organization, and/or field of work for which you are applying.

My long range career ambitions lie in the area of management consulting, and I have particular interests in organizational change and design which I would like to pursue in the future. I view the C.A. experience in general as a vital and comprehensive way towards achieving those goals.

I would now like to address any fears which you might have that I am out to "grab a quick C.A." It is my sincere hope that I might eventually join the consulting arm of the firm with which I received my original C.A. training because it is at this level that I feel I could best repay my debt.

In the meantime, I am ready to commit myself to learning as much as possible and sharing what I have to offer with others, while on the general practice staff. I think I can best sum up my capabilities in the following way - I am NOT a detail man, but I DO pay attention to detail. Whether it has been organizing on the job or in various extracurricular functions, I have found that sticking by this rather simple principle can often mean the difference between success and failure.

I look forward to discussing what I hope is a mutual interest in my application.

_____   _____
Date   Signature

Approved by		○ Full-time

CACEE Application for Employment

- ● Full-time
- ○ Summer
- ○ Co-op
- ○ Internship
- ○

CACEE

Name of Organization
Olsen Long

Position(s) sought
Junior Accountant

Name of Educational Institution
York University

General Information

Surname
Washbrook

Given Name(s)
Carrie Ann

Address until	No.	Street			Tel.
April 30 2000	38	Carling Crescent			416-226-0526
	City	Prov./State	Postal Code	E-mail	
	Willowdale	ON	M3L 2J4		

Permanent Address (If different from above)	No.	Street			Tel.
	City	Prov./State	Postal Code	E-mail	

Are you legally eligible to accept employment in Canada?
● Yes   ○ No
Documentary evidence may be requested after a job offer is made.

When are you available to start work?

Would you accept employment anywhere in Canada?
○ Yes   ● No
Preferred location(s)
1. Toronto
2. Toronto Area
3. Hamilton or Oshawa

Education

Post Secondary or other institutions attended. Begin with most recent.	Faculty, Department, Division or School	Discipline or Programme (Major)	Degree/Diploma/ Certificate	Date obtained or expected
York University	Administrative Studies	MBA (Accounting)	M.B.A.	
University of Western Ontario	School of Graduate Studies	M.A. (History)	M.A.	08/94
University of British Columbia	Faculty of Arts	Honours History	B.A.	1990

G.P.A. for your most recently completed academic year ____ on a scale of ____ (Percentage or letter equivalent   A).

G.P.A. for all courses completed to date (cumulative average) ____ on a scale of ____ (Percentage or letter equivalent   A).

Highlight skills relevant to the position(s) sought.
-Excellent research and analytical skills
-Strong computer skills (Microsoft Word, Excel, Lotus 1-2-3)
-Effective oral and written communication skills
-Solid academic achievement

Educational Experiences and Accomplishments

Describe your relevant courses, project work, theses, publications, and presentations. Include awards and scholarships.

Shueller Award for highest marks in accounting courses, York University, 1999

Extracurricular Activities

Describe your extracurricular activities including class or campus offices held, volunteer experience, memberships in clubs or organizations, leadership roles, sports activities, hobbies, etc. (You are not required to mention the names of organizations that indicate race, ancestry, place of origin, colour, ethnic origin, citizenship, creed, sex, sexual orientation, age, marital status, family status, political beliefs or disabilities).

Child Abuse unit for Studies, Education & Services (Chicago)
-Member of Board of Directors; Treasurer of Association; member of Financial Management
Committee
Business Student's Association, University of Chicago
-Member; responsible for convening social events
Society of Graduate Students, University of Western Ontario
-Member; responsible for chairing meetings according to parliamentary procedure
History Society, University of British Columbia
-President; responsible for arranging lecture series and social events
St. Anselm's Anglican Church, Vancouver
-Member of Vesty (board of directors of parish) responsible for financial planning and
control and establishing policy and direction on social issues
Rockefeller Chapel Choir, University of Chicago
-Spent one evening each week rehearsing with choir while an MBA student
Thames Valley Trail Association
-hiking member

Work Experience

Please describe all work experience (paid and unpaid) starting with most recent.

Teaching Assistant-Computer Sci.   University of Chicago
      Position   Name of Organization

Chicago   Illinois   01/99 to 05/99
City   Province/State   Dates

- ☐ Summer
- ☒ Part -time   # of hours/week: 6

Provided individual teaching in computer programming and research packages for business students. Graded programming exams, and supervised assignments on university computer. Lectured occasionally.

- ☐ Co-op
- ☐ Internship
- ☐ Volunteer
- ☐ Full -time
- ☐ Other: (Specify)

Consultant-Historical Research   Parks Canada, Western Regional Office
      Position   Name of Organization

Calgary   Alberta   10/91 to 08/97
City   Province/State   Dates

- ☐ Summer
- ☒ Part -time   # of hours/week: 10

Researched human history of Mt. Revelstoke National Park
Advised Parks Canada on historic site development in Mt. Revelstoke
Produced manuscript report on Mt. Revelstoke's history (300 pages)
Established photo and video collection on history

- ☐ Co-op
- ☐ Internship
- ☐ Volunteer
- ☐ Full -time
- ☐ Other: (Specify)

Researcher-Historical/Legal   Native Brotherhood of British Columbia
      Position   Name of Organization

Vancouver   BC   09/92 to 09/94
City   Province/State   Dates

- ☐ Summer
- ☒ Part -time   # of hours/week: 15

Researched archival and government records for use in land claim negotiations. Prepared written reports (100 pages) individually and in groups. Developed strategy and policies for negotiations with government. Supervised research assistant and secretary.

- ☐ Co-op
- ☐ Internship
- ☐ Volunteer
- ☐ Full -time
- ☐ Other: (Specify)

Teaching Assistant-Communications   Control Data Institute
      Position   Name of Organization

Willowdale   ON   09/92 to 12/92
City   Province/State   Dates

- ☐ Summer
- ☒ Part -time   # of hours/week: 10

Assisted in teaching written and oral business and technical communication skills to post-secondary students. Skills included professional report writing and oral presentations.

- ☐ Co-op
- ☐ Internship
- ☐ Volunteer
- ☐ Full -time
- ☐ Other: (Specify)

Summary

Demonstrate your suitability for position(s) sought, by outlining your career objectives and elaborating on the factual material already presented. Show how your experience (educational, extracurricular and work) is relevant to the position(s), organization, and/or field of work for which you are applying.

I look forward to establishing a career in Chartered Accountancy and would like to continue practicing in a C.A. firm after receiving my designation. Therefore, I am presently looking for a junior accounting position which will provide me with a wide range of the practical skills needed to be a successful accountant. I would also like a broad exposure to many areas of specialization within the accounting profession, to help me make an effective choice about the direction of my future career.

The combination of my education background, work experience and volunteer activities have provided me with useful experience and skills in several areas important to success in business.

My work as an independent researcher for Parks Canada and the Native Brotherhood required the ability to analyze masses of data and organize it into clear, concise written reports. In both of these positions, I was given the minimum of supervision and therefore, in addition to analytical skills, self discipline and the ability to work independently where required. My master's thesis in history also provided invaluable experience in this regard. My background in the social sciences and as a technical communications instructor provided me with the skills in verbal and written communications for which I was often complemented in the MBA programs. Most recently, I feel that my teaching position in computer sciences not only sharpened my computer skills tremendously, but also gave me valuable experience presenting technical material to large roups as well as individuals.

In addition to the analytical and communications skills outlined above, my work on the board of directors of Child Abuse for Sutdies, Education & Services provided skills in the areas of leadership and interpersonal relations. As chair of the Financial Management Committee of the agency, I was constantly looked to for leadership and managerial decision-making by both the staff and the board members. At the same time as seeking leaderhip, however, the organization followed a consensus decision-making model, and it was always necessary to balance the interests of the board, the staff and the volunteers. This work provided invaluable experience in working with groups, which was particularly useful in the group work required in the MBA program.

My work at Child Abuse for Studies, Education & Services also provided useful experience directly relevant to my future career as an accountant, since I was responsible for drawing up the budge with the Executive Director and preparing the agency's books for the annual audit by the State of Illinois.

I believe that I have a demonstrated record of scholastic, work and extracurricular achievement. I look forward to meeting your company's representative in an interview.

I understand that any omission or misrepresentation with respect to this information may be cause for denial or immediate termination of employment.

Date	Signature

The Norris Company: "Just a Typical Day"

It was exactly 7:30 a.m. when Chet Craig, manager of the Norris Company's central plant, swung his car out of the driveway of his suburban home and headed towards the plant located some 24 km away, just inside the Midvale limits. It was a beautiful day. The sun was shining brightly and a cool, fresh breeze was blowing. The trip to the plant took about 20 minutes and sometimes gave Chet an opportunity to think about plant problems without interruption.

Norris owned and operated three quality printing plants and enjoyed a nationwide commercial business, specializing in quality colour work. It was a closely held company with some 350 employees, nearly half of whom were employed at the central plant, the largest of the three Norris production operations. The company's main offices were also located in the central plant building.

Chet had started with the Norris Company as an expediter in its eastern plant just after he graduated from Ohio State. After three years, Chet was promoted to production supervisor and, two years later, was made assistant to the manager of the eastern plant.

This case is a modified version of "The Case of the Missing Time," which was written under the direction of Tom McNichols of Northwestern University. It is reproduced with the permission of Northwestern University, Evanston, Illinois.

After almost five years in the latter position, Chet was transferred to the central plant as assistant to the plant manager and, one month later, was promoted to plant manager when the former manager retired.

CHET CRAIG'S DAY

Chet was in fine spirits as he relaxed behind the wheel. As his car picked up speed, the hum of the tires on the newly paved highway faded into the background. Various thoughts occurred to him, and he said to himself, "This is going to be the day to really get things done."

Mentally, he began to run through the day's work, first one project, then another, trying to establish priorities. After a few minutes, he decided that the open-end unit scheduling was probably the most important project, certainly the most urgent. He frowned for a moment as he recalled that on Friday, the vice-president and general manager had casually asked him if he had given the project any further thought. Chet realized that he had not been giving it much attention lately. He had been meaning to get to work on this idea for over three months, but something else always seemed to crop up.

"I haven't had much time to sit down and really work it out," he said to himself. "I'd better get going and hit this one today for sure." With new resolve, he began to break down the objectives, procedures, and installation steps of the project. He grinned as he reviewed the principles involved and calculated roughly the anticipated savings. "It's about time," he told himself. "This idea should have been followed up long ago." Chet remembered that he had first conceived of the open-end unit scheduling idea nearly a year and a half ago, just before leaving Norris's eastern plant. He had spoken to his boss, Jim Quince, manager of the eastern plant, about it then and both agreed that it was worth looking into. The idea was temporarily shelved when he was transferred to the central plant a month later.

A blast from a passing horn startled him, but his thoughts quickly returned to other plant projects he was determined to get underway. He started to think through a procedure for simpler transport of dies to and from the eastern plant. Visualizing the notes on his desk, he thought about the inventory analysis needed to identify and eliminate some of the slow-moving stock items, the packing controls that required revision, and the need for a new special-order form. He also decided that this was the day to settle on a printing company to handle the production of office forms. As well, he knew that the new Web-based electronic ordering system needed considerable work. There were a few other projects he couldn't recall offhand but he could tend to them after lunch if not before. "Yes sir," he said to himself, "this is the day to really get rolling."

ARRIVAL AT WORK

Chet's thoughts were interrupted as he pulled into the company parking lot. When he entered the plant, Chet knew something was wrong as he met Al Noren, the stockroom supervisor, who appeared troubled. "A great morning, Al," Chet greeted him cheerfully.

"Not so good, Chet—my new man isn't in this morning," Noren growled.

"Have you heard from him?" asked Chet.

"No, I haven't," replied Al.

Chet frowned as he commented, "These stock handlers assume you take it for granted that if they're not here, they're not here, and they don't have to call in and verify it. Better ask human resources to call him."

Al hesitated for a moment before replying, "Okay, Chet, but can you find me some-one? I have two cars to unload today."

As Chet turned to leave, he said, "I'll call you in half an hour, Al, and let you know."

Making a mental note of the situation, Chet headed for his office. He greeted the group of workers huddled around Marilyn, the office manager, who was discussing the day's work schedule with them. As the meeting broke up, Marilyn picked up a few samples from the clasper, showed them to Chet, and asked if they should be shipped that way or if it would be necessary to inspect them. Before he could answer, Marilyn went on to ask if he could suggest another clerical operator for the sealing machine to replace the regular oper-ator who was home ill. She also told him that Gene, the industrial engineer, had called and was waiting to hear from Chet.

After telling Marilyn to go ahead and ship the samples, he made a note of the need for a sealer operator for the office, and then called Gene. He agreed to stop by Gene's office before lunch and started on his routine morning tour of the plant. He asked each supervisor the types and volumes of orders they were running, the number of people present, how the schedules were coming along, and the orders to be run next; he helped the folding-room supervisor find temporary storage space for consolidating a carload shipment, discussed quality control with a press operator who had been running poor work, arranged to transfer four people temporarily to different departments, including two for Al in the stockroom, and talked to the shipping supervisor about pickups and special orders to be delivered that day. As he continued through the plant, he saw to it that reserve stock was moved out of the for-ward stock area, talked to another press operator about his requested change of vacation schedule, had a "heart-to-heart" talk with a press helper who seemed to need frequent reas-surance, and approved two type and one colour order for different press operators.

Returning to his office, Chet reviewed the production reports on the larger orders against his initial projections and found that the plant was running behind schedule. He called in the folding-room supervisor, and together they went over the lineup of machines and made several necessary changes.

During this discussion, the composing-room supervisor stopped in to cover several type changes, and the routing supervisor telephoned for approval of a revised printing schedule. The stockroom supervisor called twice, first to inform him that two standard, fast-moving stock items were dangerously low, later to advise him that the paper stock for the urgent Dillion job had finally arrived. Chet made the necessary subsequent calls to inform those concerned.

He then began to put delivery dates on important and difficult inquiries received from customers and salespeople. (The routine inquiries were handled by Marilyn.) While he was doing this, he was interrupted twice, once by a sales correspondent calling from the West Coast to ask for a better delivery date than originally scheduled, and once by Jane Court, the human resources vice-president, asking him to set a time when he could hold an initial training and induction interview with a new employee.

After dating the customer and sales inquiries, Chet headed for his morning conference in the executive offices. At this meeting he answered the sales vice-president's questions in connection with "hot" orders, complaints, the status of large-volume orders, and poten-tial new orders. He then met with the general manager to discuss a few ticklish policy mat-ters and to answer questions on several specific production and personnel problems. Before leaving the executive offices, he stopped at the office of the secretary-treasurer to inquire about delivery of cartons, paper, and boxes, and to place a new order for paper.

On the way back to his own office, Chet conferred with Gene regarding the two current engineering projects he had called about earlier. When he reached his desk, he leaned back and looked at his watch. It was 10 minutes before lunch, just time enough to make a few notes of the details he needed to check in order to answer knotty questions raised in the sales meeting that morning.

After lunch Chet started again. He began by checking the previous day's production reports, did some rescheduling to get out urgent orders, placed appropriate delivery dates on new orders and inquiries received that morning, and consulted with a supervisor on a personal problem. He spent 20 minutes on e-mail going over mutual problems with the eastern plant.

By mid-afternoon, Chet had made another tour of the plant, after which he met with the human resources director to review a touchy personal problem raised by one of the clerical employees. Together they also reviewed the vacation schedules submitted by Chet's supervisors, and the pending job-evaluation program. Following this conference, Chet hurried back to his office to complete the special statistical report for Universal Waxing Corporation, one of Norris' best customers. As he finished the report, he discovered that it was 10 minutes after six and he was the only one left in the office. Chet was tired. He put on his coat and headed through the plant towards the parking lot. On the way he was stopped by both the night supervisor and the night layout supervisor for approval of type and layout changes.

THE DAY IN REVIEW

With both eyes on the traffic, Chet reviewed the day he had just completed. "Busy?" he asked himself. "Too much so—but did I accomplish anything?" His mind raced over the day's activities. "Yes and no" seemed to be the answer. "There was the usual routine, the same as any other day. The plant kept going and I think it must have been a good production day. Any creative or special project work done?" Chet grimaced as he reluctantly answered, "No. Today was a typical day, like most other days, and I did little, if any, creative work."

With a feeling of guilt, he probed further. "Am I an executive? I'm paid like one, respected like one, and have a responsible assignment with necessary authority to carry it out. Yet one of the greatest benefits a company derives from an executive is creative thinking and activity. What have I done about it? An executive needs some time for thinking. The projects I so enthusiastically planned to work on this morning are at exactly the same stage as they were yesterday. What's more, I have no guarantee that tomorrow night or the next night will bring me any closer to their completion. This is a real problem, and there must be an answer."

Chet continued, "Night work? Yes, occasionally. This is understood. But I've been doing too much of this lately. I owe my wife and family some of my time. When you come down to it, they are the people for whom I'm really working. If I am forced to spend much more time away from them, I'm not meeting my own personal objectives. What about community and church work? Should I eliminate that? I spend a lot of time on this, but I feel I owe society and God some time too. Besides, I believe I'm making a worthwhile contribution in this work. Perhaps I can squeeze a little time. But where does recreation fit in?"

Chet groped for the solution. "Maybe I'm just rationalizing because I schedule my own work poorly. But I don't think so. I've studied my work habits carefully and I think I plan intelligently and delegate authority. Do I need an assistant? Possibly, but that's a long-term project and I don't believe I could justify the additional overhead expenditure. Anyways, I doubt whether it would solve the problem."

By this time Chet had turned off the highway onto the side street leading to his home—the problem still uppermost in his mind. "I guess I really don't know the answer," he told himself as he pulled into his driveway. "This morning everything seemed so simple, but now…"

His thoughts were interrupted as he saw his son running towards the car calling out, "Mommy, Daddy's home."

Exhibit 8.1

Staff Organization of The Norris Company

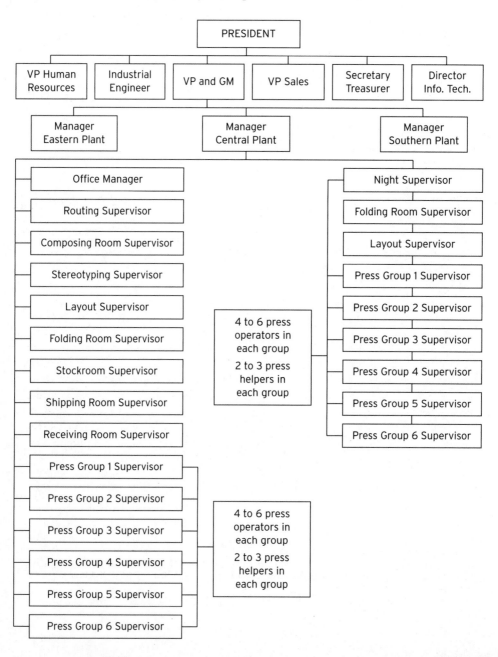

Burnaby Glass Decision

Rosemary McGowan

Tupper Cawsey

It was late Friday afternoon when Peter Williamson, vice-president of Burnaby Glass and Mirror Limited, left the shop room floor. Instead of the usual talk of summer weekend plans, the employees wanted to know when a shop room coordinator was going to be appointed. Williamson's many meetings with the firm's president Jack Hunter and consultant Bill Montgomery had fuelled rumours that a decision was close at hand.

Back in his office, Williamson thought about the hiring decision the company faced. On the one hand, the decision needed careful consideration, but on the other, it had to be made quickly. The firm urgently needed someone to manage a growing and unprecedented backlog of orders that was causing employee friction, jeopardizing future contracts, and creating a staggering workload for Hunter and Williamson.

BURNABY GLASS AND MIRROR LIMITED

Burnaby Glass and Mirror Limited, a custom manufacturer of commercial and residential windows, mirrors, patio doors, and tub enclosures, is located in a light-industrial area in Burnaby, a city of approximately 150 000 that is considered part of Greater Vancouver. Approximately 14 years old, the firm was purchased by Jack Hunter in 1983 with Peter Williamson joining as vice-president one year later. Burnaby Glass' facilities include a "front office" with adjoining retail shop, manufacturing, and storage facilities.

Sales

Sales, generated through service work, contract work, and cash sales, recently reached $6.5 million per year. Contract work accounts for approximately 75 percent of sales and is awarded by commercial customers through a process of tenders. Williamson and Hunter procure and develop all bids. Price, reputation, location, and an "if they like you" factor are key to obtaining contracts. Spring is the "slow" season for contract work because most construction projects start in the spring and glass windows and doors are among the last structural features added to those projects.

Service work involves the repair and installation of windows and doors for residential and commercial customers. Typically, when customers phone the company for a quote, they want to know "how soon the job can be done." Delivery time, therefore, rather than price often determines which company gets the job. Jobs range from $50 to many thousands of dollars, and quotes are on a "take it or leave it" basis. Although orders for service work only represent 15 percent of sales, demand is year-round and growing.

Cash sales of mirrors and framed prints from the retail display area and from windows or doors brought in for repair account for approximately 10 percent of sales. In recent years, however, cash sales have declined as customers have moved to department and specialty stores for mirrors and prints.

Growth

Under Williamson and Hunters' management the firm experienced strong growth. In five years, sales increased from $860 000 to approximately $6.5 million, payroll increased from 12 to 38 employees (see Exhibit 9.1 for current organizational chart), and the facilities are six times their original 223 m^2. Expansion has resulted in additions to the original facilities as well as acquisition of manufacturing and storage warehouses across the street.

Although much of the firm's growth is attributable to long hours and aggressive pursuit of contracts by Hunter and Williamson, explosive growth in commercial and residential construction in the Burnaby and surrounding areas has contributed significantly. Burnaby's proximity to Vancouver and its own natural beauty prompted many people to move their businesses there or take up residence in Burnaby and commute to Vancouver for work. Growth in demand for custom glass products has also spawned a number of local competitors but, according to Williamson, "there is work for everyone." The firm's sales volume placed them within the top five firms in the area. Among the half dozen local companies "everyone knows everyone else" usually as a result of having worked together at some point.

Employees

Of the firm's 38 employees, eight people, including Hunter, Williamson, a CGA, a service work coordinator, and four clerical staff, occupy the front offices. Hunter and Williamson each have many years of experience in the glass industry. Williamson, now in his 50s, had spent many summers employed in his father's custom glass firm.

The 30 shop room employees are all members of the Painters and Allied Trades Union. Of these employees, eight work in the shop during the day cutting and manufacturing products. The remaining employees work in teams, usually of two, at various job sites. Employees of the front office and the shop know each other on a first-name basis, and several of the firm's employees are related (Exhibit 9.2 shows the relatives of those applying for the new position). In past years, the company had a Christmas party and a summer barbecue, but recently they have been too busy to formally organize any social activities. Occasionally, some of the shop room employees get together after work for a beer at the "The Burner," a local pub.

The company's reputation as a fair and equitable employer is supported by its history of low employee turnover. In addition, the Painters and Allied Trades Union has not had a strike in almost five years.

The shop room employees play a key role in determining the firm's reputation for product quality, timely delivery, and profitability. Glass cutting and edging, as well as the fabrication and installation of metal frames, requires precise attention to detail, experience, and skill to minimize breakage, meet customer specifications, and reduce the risk of personal injury. Safety is a key concern for workers in this industry. Breakage is not a big problem for Burnaby Glass. In one large contract, only about 10 glass plates of 600 to 700 that were installed were broken. Although there's no bonus for minimizing breakage, Williamson indicated that "if you don't break it, you don't get in shit."

Scheduling and Workflow

Contract Work

Contract work begins when Hunter or Williamson discover a lead either through their network of contractors or by the request for a quote sent to them. A bid is developed and submitted. At this point, it could take from two days to eight months before the contract is awarded. Williamson estimates that Burnaby Glass wins one out of every seven bids.

Once a contract is won, detailed plans and drawings are prepared by the draftsmen, and materials are ordered. The plans are translated into a manufacturing schedule depending upon delivery dates of materials and due dates for construction.

The sequential series of activities that marks building construction offers Hunter and Williamson a fairly lengthy and predictable lead time for scheduling trucks and assigning staff to the teams who install the work. Once a job has started, teams remain with that project until installation of all units is complete; projects can run from days to weeks. Factors such as construction strikes, weather, and absenteeism can have an impact on scheduling.

As start dates approach, Williamson and Hunter prepare and prioritize written work orders so that cutting and fabrication are done well in advance of the start of a job. This system allows a time "buffer" so that if an emergency arises on an existing job, it can be scheduled in without seriously affecting the start dates of future jobs.

Although each truck is equipped with tools and a ladder, glass panes and fabricated metal products are loaded daily, usually in the morning. Because return trips for loading represent an unprofitable source of downtime for the firm, scheduling of cutting and fabrication are key to operating efficiency. Employees generally load their own glass orders because "each guy knows how he wants it packed." The assignment, care, and cleanup of trucks is a continuing source of conflict. When necessary, two trucks go to one job site to deliver the materials for that day.

Service Work

Service work is generally called in on an emergency basis, as the result, for instance, of a vandal throwing a rock through a store window or a homeowner breaking a storm window. Typically, following the call, the service coordinator goes to the customer's home or business to determine the type and size of glass needed. A call is then put in to Hunter or Williamson for a quote. Hunter or Williamson would then call down to the cutting room floor, to see if the required glass was on hand. If the glass was available and the customer agreed to the quote and delivery time, the job would be given priority on the cutting room floor and it would be cut and prepared for delivery. Usually, cutting can be done in a matter of minutes. In the case of large jobs, such as a showroom window, employees may be recalled temporarily from contract job sites to install the service order.

For out-of-town service or contract orders, an extra panel or two of cut glass is sent to avoid time lost due to broken panels because, as Williamson said, "If a piece is going to break, it's usually for a job that's 100 km away. So, now we just send an extra panel or two, and if they aren't needed, they come back to the shop to stay in storage until they are needed."

Hiring Practices

For many years, the procedure for hiring consisted of contacting the union to see if anyone was available. Recently, however, given the tight employment market, staffing, like most of the firm's operations, was less formal. Individuals would hear through the "grapevine" that the firm was hiring and would phone Williamson. Williamson would decide to hire or not on the basis of a brief interview, a phone call to the individual's previous employer, his "gut feel," and a check with current employees to, as Williamson indicated, "see who knows him and what he's like." Although this approach was driven by Williamson's desire to make decisions quickly, it usually worked because, as Williamson said, "everyone knew everyone in the business." Williamson involved other employees in the hiring decision because they "had to work with the guy," and he felt their input would decrease the risk of costly shop floor resignations if an incompatible person was hired. New employees were on a 60-day probationary period, after which, if they worked out, they were automatically considered to be part of the union. Shop room personnel records were minimal, often listing only the employees' name, birthdate, and previous employer.

Because of the firm's growth, hiring decisions were made quickly, often when "the firm needed a warm body" to drive a truck and work a job. Although he had been "lucky," Williamson admitted that his "gut feel" had led to a couple of poor hiring decisions.

Locally, there was a limited number of individuals with the specialized skills needed by firms like Burnaby Glass. As a result, recruiting among the firms was fairly competitive. It was commonplace for other owners to contact competitors' employees directly with a job offer. Williamson, however, had a personal policy of not recruiting employees from his competitors, indicating that "you quickly develop a reputation as a 'pirate' that would come back to haunt you."

DECISION TO HIRE A COORDINATOR

The decision to hire a coordinator was driven by a number of factors. Williamson and Hunter realized that despite substantial growth, they still shouldered much of the responsibility for the day-to-day operations including hiring employees, scheduling jobs, contacting suppliers, assigning teams, mediating employee conflicts, and developing and tendering bids. As a result, 60-hour workweeks turned into 70- and 80-hour workweeks for Williamson and Hunter, and despite their efforts, jobs were running two to three weeks behind. In an industry where contracts are awarded on the basis of reputation, order backlogs were posing a serious threat to future contracts.

As well, haphazard truck allocation, job scheduling, and job assignment were leading to increased interpersonal conflicts and frustrations. Williamson believed that these problems were also causing decreased productivity and increased absenteeism among the shop floor employees. Finally, Williamson wanted to focus his efforts on contract development and negotiation rather than the firm's day-to-day operations.

Two years earlier, the efficiency of the service work operations had improved after a service work coordinator was hired. Although Williamson and Hunter realized for over a year that they would have to hire a shop room coordinator, they never found the time to do it. Given the value of contract work to the firm, the position of coordinator would be a major position within the firm. They had to hire someone whose authority would be both accepted and respected by the shop room staff and someone who could communicate effectively with both the shop employees and the front office staff. Feeling that they lacked the skill, experience, and time necessary, Hunter and Williamson brought in Bill Montgomery, a consultant specializing in human resources management, to help.

Montgomery sat down with Hunter and Williamson to determine the responsibilities of the coordinator. Their discussions led to a job description that was eventually posted in the shop room (see Exhibit 9.3). It was agreed that the search should initially be internal but could be extended outside the company if no suitable internal candidates were found. In order to make sure that they were interviewing "interested" candidates, they asked all candidates to submit, in writing, their reasons for wanting the job.

Among the perks for potential internal candidates were an estimated 15 to 20 percent salary increase, a company car, and the benefits of working primarily inside rather than outside at job sites.

Applicants

Six of the firm's current shop room employees applied for the position (see Exhibit 9.4). Most applicant letters were brief, handwritten notes stating their desire to arrange an interview for the position.

Interviewing

Although Montgomery conducted the interviewing, Hunter and Williamson attended all interviews. The decision on the final candidate had to be by unanimous agreement of Hunter, Williamson, and Montgomery.

The interviews targeted five basic areas: background information on the candidates, their understanding of the job, their skill and ability to do the job, their interpersonal skills, and their motivations. Excerpts from each candidate's interview are included in Exhibit 9.5.

Now faced with this decision, Williamson felt overwhelmed by the quantity of information on the candidates. He knew that Hunter and Montgomery had made their preliminary decisions and were waiting on his input. Although tempted to go with his "gut feel," he knew that he should use the information obtained in the interviews to arrive at a decision—but how?

Exhibit 9.1

Organizational Chart: Burnaby Glass and Mirror Limited

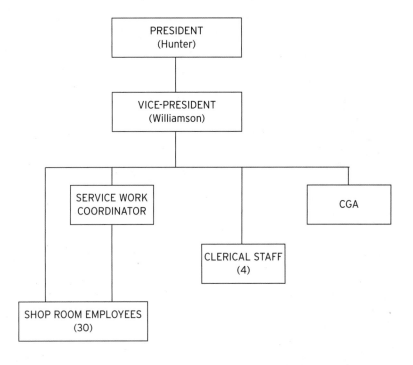

Exhibit 9.2

Employee Relatives within the Firm

Front Office	Shop	Relationship
Charlotte Murray	**Tom Murray**	Aunt–Nephew
	Darryl Wagner, Jeff Wagner	Stepfather–Stepson
	Steve Porter, Frank Turner	Brothers-in-law
		Father-in-law also in shop
	George Ogilvy	No relatives
	Cam Jackson	No relatives

*Bold type indicates applicants for position of shop room coordinator.

Exhibit 9.3

Position Description for Shop Room Coordinator, Burnaby Glass and Mirror Limited

Position Title: Coordinator

Reporting to: P. Williamson

Position Summary: The person in this position will provide an important coordinating role between the office and those measuring, fabricating, and installing the work. He will be required to work closely with Jack Hunter, Peter Williamson, the office manager, the sales staff, and each of the employees fabricating and installing for Burnaby Glass.

Position Duties

Service Work: The coordinator is responsible for ensuring the scheduling and coordination of work in this area. Measurement of work, installation, delivery, pickup of materials, and planning material availability are responsibilities of the coordinator.

Contract Work: Duties in this area are similar to those for service work with the addition of the scheduling and coordination of fabrication of materials.

The coordinator is responsible for the scheduling of orders for cash, service, and contract sales.

The coordinator is responsible for tool control.

The coordinator is responsible for maintaining the stock on hand of caulking, tapes, vinyl, screws/plugs, drill bits, etc.

The coordinator will have significant input on hiring or job reassignment decisions.

Salary and Benefits: Negotiable.

Exhibit 9.4

Applicant Information

Name and Age	JACKSON (40)
Years with the Company	3
Industry Experience	18
Reason for Application	Wanted a change in responsibilities
Major Strengths	Skilled, very experienced; Quality work, that rarely needed a revisit for repairs
Major Weaknesses	No bearing of authority

Name and Age	MURRAY (35)
Years with the Company	1- 1/4
Industry Experience	3
Reason for Application	Felt at a standstill; Wanted to move on in company
Major Strengths	Good interpersonal skills
Major Weaknesses	Technically limited; Not fully accepted by others

Name and Age	OGILVY (47)
Years with the Company	4
Industry Experience	22
Reason for Application	Desire for a less physically demanding job because of previous work-related injury
Major Strengths	Strong organizational skills
Major Weaknesses	Tendency to order people to do things; Not well linked to the other employees.

Exhibit 9.4 (continued)

Name and Age	PORTER (37)
Years with the Company	3- 1/2
Industry Experience	12
Reason for Application	More money; Less physical work
Major Strengths	Astute; Knows job and industry well
Major Weaknesses	At times comes across very strongly; Sometimes doesn't listen

Name and Age	TURNER (33)
Years with the Company	2
Industry Experience	10
Reason for Application	Desire to advance within company
Major Strengths	Good working relationship with others; Technical perfectionist
Major Weaknesses	Viewed as having little authority; Unseasoned

Name and Age	WAGNER (38)
Years with the Company	4
Industry Experience	15
Reason for Application	Wants to move inside after 15 years; "Fool not to try"
Major Strengths	Knows work, knows what needs to be done and can do it; Gets along with most of the other employees; Perfectionist
Major Weaknesses	Perfectionist; Has to be the best and communicates that to everyone.

Exhibit 9.5

Summary of Interviews

Cam Jackson

"I want this job as something different, try it out and see how it works."

"We have to get a system for ordering and keep control of things. When I start, I would meet with Peter and Jack, find out how things are going, get the groups together. For those who don't get along, take them aside on a one-on-one basis. If we still can't resolve the problems, then we'll meet with Peter and Jack. If an employee was constantly late, I'd probably talk the problem over with Peter and Jack. Talking to the men is the hardest part, it could be a real problem handling it."

"The trucks are messy now. We should probably bring them back 15 minutes early to get them cleaned up. People should be told what to do; I don't like people just standing around. If they're not sure how to do something, I'd just show them how to do it. To get around the contradictory orders, we should develop a weekly plan and work on it. Our worst problem right now is a lack of policy."

Tom Murray

"I've been here for 15 months and before that I worked for the competition. Prior to that I worked for 8 years as a lead hand at a construction firm. When I was there I was the union steward and did public relations management, arbitration, and negotiation, and I was involved in personnel issues."

"In my job I learned to operate under pressure, developed my communications skills, and have found that a lot of people have opinions etched in stone and you have to have different perspectives."

"I have some of the job skills but not all of them—I'm not a saviour. But as coordinator, I'd be there to help and develop discussions if there's a problem. From my experience, I know that you just can't walk away from a problem. I'd probably want to put people together to learn and solve the learning needs by matching people. We should develop teams and team leaders on some of the jobs. People learn best through the help of others on the team. We also have to deal with rumours on a one-on-one basis."

"I'm not going to be a puppet. I won't put up with contradictory orders."

"I can't really figure out why I'm here. I guess I'd like to switch to the coordinator position because I feel that I'm at a standstill, want to get contractors to do things, and my experience with the union stuff makes me want to do more than I am now."

George Ogilvy

"As coordinator, I'd need authority to be able to make decisions, some which are worth thousands of dollars. I'd have to be available for answers. I like to make decisions and expect people to follow my say. In Port Coquitlam, I liked being boss of the job because

Exhibit 9.5 (continued)

of the autonomy, ability to make decisions. I take pride in my work and like to see a job from start to finish. I called the shots and if something went wrong, I only had myself to blame. I've never had a problem getting along with anybody."

"I have the ability to straighten out problems, organize, and measure well. I have no reservations about my ability to do the job."

"You have to give employees freedom, have to open eyes as to how you went wrong."

"Usually, I want the people I work with to do it my way; there's no second chance on safety. I'll just tell someone the way it is. We need company meetings. We have to make the trucks the same colour, and colour code the tool boxes, and get the trucks out in the morning."

Steve Porter

"I want this job because it's more money and I don't have to work physically. I want something different. I just bought a speed boat and need the money for it and want time for winter vacations. It doesn't matter to me who gets the job; I can get along with anyone who gets the job; I could get over it if I didn't get it. But don't get me wrong, I want the job, I think that I'm suited for this job; I don't know everything but it can be taught."

"We should know what to send and when so that we could arrange the materials, assign men to jobs. Once a week we should sit down and arrange schedules. The coordinator shouldn't have to fire but should have significant input in hiring decisions. I've hired 'quite a bit' because I know a lot of people."

"Whenever you've got people working with one another, you've always got problems. You should try not to switch the guys in the middle of a project. If they start a job, they should finish it. If a guy is late or absent, you just can't fire him; I guess you can talk to him. If they don't show up, they don't show up. We don't have any company policies on paper for discipline."

"There's many ways to do a job. If they're doing it wrong, then you've got to tell the people; otherwise let it go, the coordinator's not God."

"The coordinator must be someone who knows the business and has an idea of how long it takes. We have to meet at least once a week so the coordinator knows what business is coming and put the stuff on paper, like requisitions."

"Jack and Peter have to back out of the job and leave it to the coordinator. Stop this contradictory stuff."

"Apprentices should stay with one man. Now, there's too much switching and the guys told too many different ways how to do things."

Frank Turner

"We need some general meetings to air things out. We need meetings to develop policies, to let individuals know where they stand. Right now there's a lot of disorganization. We also have to sit down and get rid of the rumours. We have to do planning so that we can anticipate possible future problems."

Exhibit 9.5 (continued)

"I get along with people; I don't have any arguments with anyone; I'm not a one-on-one fighter. If I'm in a dispute, I'll think it over and later enforce it. If the guys are telling me what they need, I have to trust their opinions."

"We have to build teams and harmony, give and take B.S., and keep an even keel around here. Getting along and having fun. I'd turn over the work crews, everyone has to do time with the guy that's hard to get along with."

"We had more enjoyment earlier; now with the changes we're keeping so busy we don't have time for the barbecues and Christmas parties. Periodically, we have to have social events."

Darryl Wagner

"I've worked 15 years 'outside' and was looking to get an inside job. I'd be a fool not to try and get the job. If I don't get this job and 'xxx' does, I probably won't have a job at Burnaby Glass."

"I know what has to be done. There's a need for better scheduling and sequencing and making sure that the materials are available. The materials and equipment are a cause of chaos. People are changing trucks all the time, you've got to assign people to trucks. There's not enough equipment."

"Peter and Jack don't have time to sort out the problems. You need to start with written rules and regulations that you can stand by."

"We often get contradictory orders (from Jack and Peter); we have to start pulling together and sort out our priorities. I'm worried that if I assign people and Jack Hunter disagrees, will he overrule my decision?"

"My way might not be the best so I'll let someone do their job and not force my way on them. You can't push people around. You have to understand the people that are paid to work for you. As coordinator your job is to get the people to get along, try to understand each perspective."

"When I've had a tough interpersonal situation with one person in an uproar, I've found it's best to wait, let things calm down, and then work it out."

A Matter of Fit

AMBA/Andrew Templer

Lydia Verona pressed the elevator button to take her up to the offices of International Career Opportunities Ltd. (ICO) for an appointment with Jake Fusion, their senior out-placement consultant. After graduating cum-laude she was invited to join Eastern Industrial Design as a management trainee. What she had expected to be a promising career with Eastern ended with her firing after just six months on the job.

Lydia was not sure where her interview session with ICO would lead, but she hoped that sharing all that had happened at Eastern would help her make some sense of what had gone wrong and help her prepare for her next step in her career.

JAKE: What kind of job did you look for when you were finishing your M.B.A.?

LYDIA: I had always had an interest in computers and selling and I took every course I could in Internet marketing. I was particularly interested in getting into Web-based promotions because it incorporated all aspects from e-commerce to advertising to selling. I was looking for an established company with a clear career path. It was while waiting for a ski lift that I met the VP of Marketing Design at Eastern. He mentioned that Eastern had recently got into Web marketing and had an opening in their management trainee program.

Adapted from *MBA Executive*, January, 1976, with permission of the Association of MBA Executives.

JAKE: Who actually hired you?

LYDIA: I spoke to the divisional president in the initial interviews and then with human resources. My main contact, however, was the marketing design vice president—he was "responsible" for me.

JAKE: Let's go back to when you started work.

LYDIA: As I mentioned, I was initially hired as a management trainee with a view to an eventual appointment in Web marketing. In the management trainee program, trainees spend four to six weeks in different departments before moving on to Web software development. My assignments were to take me through cost-accounting, Web design and advertising and promotions. I was very enthusiastic about the program and ready to learn everything about Web based marketing. Things began well in my first appointment in the cost accounting department.

JAKE: So tell me about this first assignment.

LYDIA: My time with cost accounting was really largely uneventful. This was a long established area using standardized guidelines for determining the overall costs of doing business. I worked on a project for them costing computer upgrades that received very favourable comment. I was able to apply a number of new skills that I had learned in my M.B.A., but was a little taken aback at the rigidity in some of the rules that the department applied. Once my project was completed I was given a pleasant send-off to my next position with Web design.

JAKE: Can you describe the department?

LYDIA: There were about 30 people, all of whom had university degrees, but few M.B.A.'s, if any. The department head, a woman who had been with the company for 25 years, certainly didn't have an M.B.A. The rest were clerical employees in their 40s. There were many more women in that department than the others, with no particular skills in Web design. As far as I could tell, it was sort of an Internet information support service for the marketing department that had shifted from traditional marketing development into Web design media.

I did realize that there could have been cause for resentment because I was a woman coming in at a higher salary than most of them. I was going to be there only a short time and would be promoted faster. Inevitably some might end up working for me.

But that doesn't explain the atmosphere there. The other women were very uptight and quiet. Some of them also seemed rather paranoid—always worried that people were watching them to see if they were working. They did have a point there. The appearance of working was very important. Even if there wasn't much to do, everyone would flutter around looking very harried and trying to seem busy. The content didn't matter as much.

On the other hand, I'm not exactly loud, but I was more visible than they were. I like people. I work best under pressure when there's a lot to do. There was a definite contrast between those women and me.

JAKE: When did things come to a head?

LYDIA: On my third day of work they accused me of entertaining men in my office. This was based on one after-lunch visit from a friend who came up to see my new office, stayed for two minutes, and left. On the following day, a trainee from the international division came down and talked to me a while. My visitors also looked briefly at a particular product Web design. On the strength of these two visits and the design (which concerned a product discontinued over three years ago), someone complained to human resources. No one in the department said a word to me.

I was called to the human resource department where this guy said, "Well, you've been entertaining all these men in your office and we've got these complaints." My first reaction was to laugh—it was so preposterous. But then I realized he was serious.

JAKE: You probably should have laughed. It would have cleared the air.

LYDIA: I think I did laugh and then waited for him to. He didn't have any sense of humour, though. He then asked, "How could you get an unauthorized person into the building? The security guards can tell if you don't have the proper badge." I told him that we just went up the elevator, and no one had stopped us or checked anything. He continued, "But they can hear what you say in the halls."

I said, "What do you mean they can hear us?" And then he told me that the halls are monitored for security.

I really didn't believe I was hearing all this. I thought someone had put something in my coffee!

I explained that I was responsible for the first man being there for a total of two minutes. The second man was their own employee. And I asked him to tell me who was complaining and I would straighten it out.

He was very reluctant to tell me; he didn't want to promote bad relations between human resources and the Web design department. But I finally got the name from him. It was the lady in charge of the department.

JAKE: Trying to look at the situation from the other side, it sounds as though the human resources manager was uncomfortable with the complaint and didn't really know how to handle it. He wasn't sure what was going on and needed you to resolve the problem.

LYDIA: But he wasn't really interested in what was happening in my office. He was fascinated by telling me the various aspects of the security system, and wondering how anyone could get through. He really went off on a tangent.

JAKE: What did you do then?

LYDIA: I went to the woman who had complained to human resources and tried to talk to her. She said that the studies were classified information, which is as it should be, of course, but I pointed out that this particular one concerned a product discontinued three years ago. She just exploded.

I asked why no one in the department had explained the rules about visitors to me or even asked me who the visitors were. After only three days .I obviously didn't know the procedures.

She said, "We don't deal with you except through human resources, you're just a trainee. We don't even sign your cheques. We just discuss you with human resources and that's it."

At that point I thought maybe I'd made a real mistake in choosing this company.

She later gave a horrible review of my probationary training period there, even though I'd designed a solid Web page based on their data about a particular product. From then on, I had a difficult time in the department. Interestingly enough, my actual work was never criticized—just my "attitude."

I was automatically under suspicion, and the next department I went to was warned to watch me closely. I found this out at my subsequent assignment in the training program. People were almost afraid to say anything good because they would be disagreeing with the consensus, if you see what I mean.

JAKE: There are ways to ask questions that make you an ally and ways that challenge a person's authority. I wonder how the department head interpreted you coming to her to ask about the accusation. The human resources manager's reluctance to give you the name indicates that direct confrontation was not the way the company handled such situations. She may have taken your question, "Why didn't anyone tell me the rules?" as a challenge. Her subsequent reaction certainly suggests that she felt threatened.

LYDIA: But I'd only been there three days. I got there on time, didn't leave early, or take even the full hour for lunch. I did my work and even bugged people to give me things to do.

JAKE: Was there anything else?

LYDIA: There were a couple of outside problems—a paper to finish for school, an illness in the family, and a volunteer project I was managing—which would not normally be the case for most new employees. I may not have looked too happy at my desk, but it didn't affect my work. I don't see what I could have done in so short a time to elicit such a strong reaction.

JAKE: She mentioned a vital point—"We don't even authorize payment for you." It's always a good idea to know whose budget you're part of, who is really responsible for you.

LYDIA: I was in the divisional budget, not Web design's. But I don't think you can expect the people in your product division to know all the ground rules in the other departments. I see your point, but in this case, I don't think it would have made much difference.

JAKE: Was she actually in charge of your training in her department or was there a training program coordinator?

LYDIA: That was a problem. There wasn't really any direction. Although we were supposed to learn certain things about the company and its functions, nobody ever had time to show us anything. They were reluctant to give us projects because no one knew how long we'd be in a given department, so we sat there twiddling our thumbs, and tried to find work.

My vice president had said to ask other people under his jurisdiction for things to work on. So I did, often. And occasionally one of the design engineers would spend some time and give me a decent project. Those were interesting and enjoyable.

The company was not using what the M.B.A. was supposed to bring to the job, whether specific skills or a frame of reference or whatever. The main purpose of the training program seemed to be almost military—to make us conform to the company mould. They were very cautious about the trainees and watched us a lot.

The content of the program was minimal We collated endless statistics and cross-checked URL's, which a high school graduate could have done.

JAKE: What kind of reinforcement did you get from your marketing vice president?

LYDIA: I talked to him many times. The bad review from the head of Web design made his boss (the divisional president) nervous, though I told him some of the odd incidents, which he also thought were peculiar.

JAKE: Such as?

LYDIA: During the second phase of my training, I broke my foot at a party and missed two days of work. The divisional president heard about it and was very upset because I hadn't broken it in an auto accident. He was specific about that—you have to have accidents at the right time and place. This seemed a strange response to me, but I didn't know him well enough to know whether he was partially joking or not.

JAKE: How was your last placement?

LYDIA: I went next to advertising and promotions . The ad people were totally flexible; it was like day and night. One of the ad guys called me in and said, "We heard that something happened back at the ranch; this guy has been calling me up and telling me to watch you. I think it's terrible. What's going on?" I told him my version of what had happened and learned a lot about the company's way of doing things from him.

I got a good evaluation from this department—"She did the work, no problem." But there was the broken foot. I assume this must have been interpreted as a negative by the people back at the corporate offices.

JAKE: Did the personality tensions ease up at all?

LYDIA: They became more positive and I was certainly willing to keep trying. I had invested a certain amount of time and was still very interested in Web software development. I thought that maybe the training period was the worst part and once through it, everything would be fine.

At one of my talks with the marketing vice president, he said, "You know, things are really working out now. I'm getting all these good reports about your work and a letter from Cost Accounting commending a project you did." I was so relieved to hear this. Then ten days later the divisional president fired me because he saw me using the company e-mail system for personal use several times and because I had allegedly fallen asleep in a meeting, which was not true.

JAKE: You've described a lot of surface events, your reaction, and your perception of reactions of people at Eastern. But there are things companies fire for and things they don't fire for. It's a very extreme step. The person who fires you must document why, particularly given the pressures on the company for more women in management. As long as you do acceptable work, most large companies will not fire you.

LYDIA: I specifically asked the divisional president that in the final interview. "Are you sure it isn't my work?" He said, "No, they all say that you are very bright and your work is actually quite good. It's just your attitude." He said that a number of times.

I did use the e-mail system for personal messages, many of which were related to the illness in my family and the volunteer project. Maybe it was the e-mailing that indicated I had a life outside the company.

The other reasons he mentioned, falling asleep in a meeting, were not valid. This particular meeting began at 8:30 a.m. and continued till after 6:00 p.m. The air conditioning was turned off at 5, and we were all getting tired and drowsy, but I did not fall asleep.

JAKE: How did it end?

LYDIA: He said I wasn't serious enough.

JAKE: That's usually code for "You don't consider important what we consider important." Your perception of what was trivial and your accompanying attitude may be why you were fired—what you treated lightly was of major importance to them.

LYDIA: Well, I guess I didn't consider it important to sit in my cubicle and pretend to be busy when I had nothing to do. I expected to be evaluated on my performance. But how can you be evaluated on your performance if you aren't given anything substantial to work on? The great bulk of what we were assigned in Web Design was sheer make-work.

JAKE: What you're talking about is a very common feeling among M.B.A.'s when they finish their degree. They want some meaningful work. But for a long time in many companies you're expected to learn how they do things, to get accustomed to their procedures. They don't want to hear from you about being productive until they feel you're ready for responsibility.

LYDIA: You can put up with those preliminaries and suffer through a "training program" provided the people you're dealing with seem reasonable. But some of those I was working with were irrational. If they won't explain the ground rules to you and don't tell you when you're breaking them but go instead to complain to human resources—I just thought it was very peculiar.

JAKE: Can you see your experience happening to a man?

LYDIA: The e-mails would probably be less of a problem, but I can see a male having the same attitude problems very easily. A male acting the way I did—going to people and asking for work—would not have created hostility. They may have expected their men to be more aggressive than their women. If I spoke up at meetings, I was told I was too assertive; if I didn't say anything, I was told that I wasn't being aggressive enough. That sort of harassment wouldn't happen to a man.

Rather than gender, I think the problem is one of adjusting to the company's regimentation.

JAKE: Lydia, in the final part of our conversation I want us to turn to what you learned from your experiences and where to go from here. During your sojourn at Eastern you must have gathered some pretty useful insights into the company and into yourself?

LYDIA: To give Eastern credit—and I may not have stressed that they are very good at what they do—I learned quite a bit about Web design, about e-commerce, how one company manages growth opportunities with cost-accounting. I also learned that I need a more flexible professional atmosphere in a more aggressive company than that one. I realized that I am more results-oriented than image conscious—more interested in what people produce than what they look like and how they act.

JAKE: How will you look differently for your next job?

LYDIA: I'll ask different questions. As an entry-level job seeker, I was very much in awe of everyone doing the things I thought I wanted to do. I kept asking them about their work but neglected to ask about the frustrations, how long they'd been with the company, what previous work experience they'd had, how flexible the company was. A certain line of questions was left out.

Another thing I didn't do before that I'm doing now is conducting exploratory interviews. I've called friends, contacts, other business school alumni and talked to them informally about their companies. I want to find out the strengths and weaknesses of the companies from someone who knows. People are much more open about their work when it's not a "job" interview.

I'm a little more uptight now and more careful. I want to be sure I'd be happy in a place—almost before I talk to them. The atmosphere is almost as important to me as the job content. After one bad judgement, you want to make sure the next job is the right one.

JAKE: When you say you're going to be much more careful, that seems to be the wrong lesson.

LYDIA: Why?

JAKE: If you get too careful, you won't listen to your own feelings as much. You are trying to get the right thing; you don't want this experience to happen again. But you've got to relax about it. It's dangerous to become too rigid because you'll close off the emotional feedback about a potential new job. That works against you in making a decision.

LYDIA: I'm probably more defensive than I should be—I catch myself sometimes and have to remember that it's not that big a deal.

JAKE: How are you explaining your departure to interviewers?

LYDIA: I say as little as possible and keep away from any negative comments about the company because it sounds like sour grapes. I've told you much more than I'd ever tell a job interviewer. I checked on my recommendation from the company. They are saying that it was a fit problem, which is fair. Now that I have left I have been picking up some comments mentioning Eastern as having a reputation of being uptight.

JAKE: I don't think you want to go into Eastern's reputation: that really isn't relevant. You were part of their management trainee program, but it became apparent that it wasn't the right place for you and you weren't the person for them. That's all you have to say.

Lydia left Jake Fusion's comfortable offices at ICO feeling better for having talked about her time at Eastern. Her next appointment with Jake was scheduled for the following day but she had a lot to think about before they met again. As they parted he had asked her to review their conversation together and come prepared to map out a career strategy together.

## part three

Developing Your Workforce Effectiveness

"The organizations that will truly excel in the future will be the organizations that discover how to tap people's commitment and capacity to learn at all levels in an organization."

—**Peter Senge:** *The Fifth Discipline.*[1]

The cases in Part 1 set the scene for strategic human resources policies, and those in Part 2 examined ways of securing the best possible workforce. The cases in this part of the book examine the role of management in ensuring workforce effectiveness through the use of such human resource interventions as employee development, appraisal, and reward systems.

MANAGERIAL LEADERSHIP FOR PRODUCTIVITY

Productivity remains the watchword in the new millennium. It can be improved through technological innovation, organizational rationalization and redesign, or better management of people and their performance. Global pressures have meant that companies can no longer afford even slightly below-average employee performance, hence the continuing emphasis on the need for better job descriptions, better integration of goal setting and budgeting, and better appraisals of employee performance. As

---

[1] Senge, Peter. *The Fifth Discipline*. New York: Currency Doubleday, 1990, p. 4.

a result of his focus, more attention is being paid to the idea of pay-for-performance and performance management systems, which assist in the management of both high- and low-performing employees.

Management plays a key leadership role in ensuring that all employees participate in achieving effectiveness. This involves building trust and openness, providing a vision and communicating it throughout the organization, and moving decisions to the level of those who must live with the result.

EMPLOYEE TRAINING AND DEVELOPMENT

Today, organizations must plan training activities that develop the capabilities of organizational members. Through the enhancement of staff skills, the organization can accomplish its strategy and develop the flexibility needed to adapt to its environment. As well, human resource planning will help the organization to anticipate skills shortages created by demographic shifts and employee turnover. This, in turn, leads to training and development activities. Finally, the new "contract" with employees doesn't "guarantee a job" but it does "guarantee employability"—and diagnosis of these needs will assist the HR manager in developing training programs.

Employee development is a critical responsibility of management, but too often the HRM function is left alone to consider the latest development "fad" in some forgotten training room. HR's excitement over new training ideas may lead to inappropriate training programs. To gain acceptance of programs, human resource staff may oversell the training and promise more than can be delivered. HR managers must resist these natural impulses and adopt a strong managerial perspective on training and development: Will this training add value to the organization? Will the long-term capabilities of the organization be enhanced? Does the training meet our employees' needs for growth?

In the past, the philosophy that guided the development, conduct, and evaluation of many company training programs suggested that it was solely the company's responsibility to develop employees. Today, a contrasting perspective exists, namely, that it is the individual who should be responsible for his or her own development. But the reality is that the responsibility rests with both parties. The company will develop an individual in order to pursue the company's interests; on the other hand, an individual who lets the organization assume all responsibility risks losing control over his or her career.

In addition, it is important to consider development at both the individual and the macro levels. At an individual level, training emphasizes the skills needed in a particular job—whether it provides new instruction or updates skills of individuals or groups. Understood in this "micro" sense, training proceeds on the basis of the needs and plans of employees. A "macro" view of training, on the other hand, takes into account the organization's objectives and how they may be accomplished. For example, if a bank were to switch its focus from retail to commercial, a major training program would be needed to effect such a strategic shift.

EMPLOYEE EVALUATION

Inherent in the perspective of employee ownership of performance management is effective evaluation. This does not happen by accident. There has to be a supportive setting for evaluation—and, once again, management takes a strategic leadership role. A supportive setting is one in which evaluation is a planned and integral part of every job, managers at all levels and in all functional areas demonstrate their belief in the evaluation process, honesty in evaluation is encouraged, and learning through evaluation is supported. And human resource managers assist in this performance management process.

It's easy to list these points but extremely difficult to achieve them in practice. Most of us don't like to be appraised and feel uncomfortable appraising others. While performance evaluation is used in virtually every Canadian organization, it is fraught with problems, and research shows that companies are rarely satisfied with their appraisal systems. Often, these problems are inherent in appraisal systems.

A major difficulty of appraisal is that the pressure it puts on managers and subordinates actually worsens relationships between them. Not only do managers report that performance appraisal takes time—or, as they are likely to put it, "wastes considerable time"—but employees also report low levels of satisfaction with their appraisals.

Why is appraisal so difficult? Here are some reasons:

- Appraisals are done by two "ordinary humans"—typically, neither is an expert in giving and receiving feedback.

- Performance appraisal often ends up as a test of power between managers and subordinates.

- Frequently, both parties want to avoid actual appraisal. The manager feels uncomfortable "playing God," while the subordinate feels threatened.

- There are often two very different agendas for the appraisal meeting (the manager's and the employee's) and two conflicting purposes of appraisal (development and compensation). These conflicting purposes of appraisal are the biggest problem in practice. It is not easy for a manager to be both counsellor (developing the employee) and judge (rewarding success).

- The appraisal system is doomed because it lacks the supportive climate for evaluation mentioned above, i.e., top management does not really believe in it.

Most performance management systems are based on individual-level feedback and development. However, increasingly work is done in teams and task forces—interdependent groups where an individual focus is inappropriate. In the organizations of today, there is no single performance evaluation approach that fits all situations. Managers need to design evaluation processes to fit specific, often changing, business circumstances. Recently, 360-degree feedback systems have become more common—"the latest answer" in performance management. While these systems provide rich feedback to individuals, the amount of time and energy needed to run such systems is significant. In fast-moving environments, such systems may be inappropriate.

Nevertheless, performance evaluation processes seem to have four common elements:

1. All employees are involved in shaping performance plans and in reviewing accomplishments.

2. The system chosen matches the situation, is logical, and is applied consistently.

3. Employees and managers understand the purposes and processes of evaluation.

4. Managers have a sense of responsibility for evaluating performance.

Performance evaluation gives managers a way to focus employee attention and energies on performance improvement. Through the process, employees identify areas needing improvement, generate improvement ideas, formalize and implement plans, and review progress.

Performance evaluation is not a science. Neither is it intended primarily as a legal defence for decisions adversely affecting employees. While there certainly are legal requirements, as well as the need for a degree of company-wide consistency and discipline, managers should use performance evaluation as their proactive tool. From this perspective, performance appraisal is a vital component of the process of managing human resources to fulfill the organization's strategic objectives.

REWARD SYSTEMS

The old psychological Law of Effect states that people tend to do what gets rewarded. This suggests that reward systems are critical in achieving workforce effectiveness. Amazingly, many managers completely overlook the strategic development of their reward policies. Lawler (Strategic Pay) puts it this way:

> Many organizations are more concerned with doing the wrong things right than with searching for the right pay practices. Pay systems are driven more by history and by what other organizations do than by a strategic analysis of their (organization) needs. What is needed is a set of fundamentally different approaches to conceptualizing and structuring pay systems.[2]

That is, many organizations spend ages trying to get something technically perfect that really does not contribute anything to the organization. For example, they might spend a lot of time perfecting job descriptions or precise work standards, when these are increasingly irrelevant in a time of turbulent change. Perhaps they should, instead, develop a reward system that encourages flexibility and cross-skill training and not worry too much about static job descriptions.

Strategic reward management is probably the most direct way for an organization to communicate its attitude to its employees. The problem is that HRM professionals are faced with conflicting objectives with regard to pay. They wish to pay fairly and equitably for work performed. They wish to provide raises that will satisfy employees and motivate them to improve and develop. And they have a responsibility to respect market conditions, not overprice jobs, and maintain organizational profitability (that is, keep costs down). These three objectives often contradict each other.

A compensation system based on equity will take into account the relative contribution of employees to the organization. Most systems have a job evaluation component that allows for a comparison of different jobs according to contribution. Job evaluation can proceed in a number of ways—by ranking jobs, assigning job levels, or comparing and rating job factors. Whatever the system, the result should be a classification of jobs relative to contribution and market conditions, which can be used to fix pay levels.

A pay system may also emphasize the impact of the market on wage levels. Under this system, a job's value to an organization is determined by the prevailing rate of pay for the job in the market. Unfortunately, market rates can place certain groups of employees at a disadvantage—the basic issue in the "equal pay for work of equal value" debate.

The difficulty in achieving fair pay also extends beyond salary to the area of benefits. Today, benefits can account for 35 percent or more of payroll costs. Employees expect benefit packages that contain not only holidays and medical insurance, but also dental plans, various forms of insurance coverage, and a range of status-linked "perks."

---

[2] Note: For a later version of the same viewpoint, see: Lawler, E.E. *Reward Excellence: Pay Strategies for the New Economy.* (San Francisco: Jossey-Bass, 2000).

In North America, many organizations believe that pay should be based on performance. These companies try to develop systems that tie compensation directly to the output of employees—commission plans, incentive schemes, or bonus arrangements. The rationale for these plans seems straightforward: if you reward individuals for their performance, organizational performance will increase. It comes as a surprise to many managers that the negative effects of such plans may outweigh their benefits. For instance, plans may emphasize aspects of performance that are not easily measured, leading to cheating or unhealthy competition. Or performance may rely on group achievement not individual accomplishment.

Productivity schemes can focus on group or organization-wide efforts. For these schemes to be effective, participating employees must feel that they have some impact on productivity and believe that this impact will be reflected in dollars. The measurement system chosen must reflect real changes in performance, yet be simple enough for most people to grasp. Moreover, the amount of money generated by the plan must make a noticeable difference to an individual's pay. Alas, such plans tend to be more successful when business conditions are good and profits growing, than when business is bad and losses are the order of the day.

Regardless of the problems with relating pay and performance, companies have continued to look for ways to make their payroll costs more flexible and tied to overall corporate performance.

THE CASES IN PART 3

The cases in this section of the text require participants to examine how employee development, appraisal, and performance management systems and, in particular, organization reward initiatives can assist in the achievement of individual and corporate goals and objectives.

Canadian Products Limited (A & B) describes a training program which, despite professional credibility and execution, failed to stir the company. What went wrong, and why? How could the failure have been avoided, and what are the implications for HRM strategy?

AMAX Automotive is concerned with a performance review system that incorporates some of the broadest 360-degree thinking but is extremely time-consuming. Participants have to balance the pros and cons of issues of quality, time, costs, and implementation of appraisal systems.

Stability Bank deals with career development issues facing the HR manager in taking care of three employees in the bank after its recent acquisition of a trust company. Existing HR policies require placement of all trust employees within the bank prior to developing the careers of any existing Stability employees. This policy is causing some difficulties at the Serenity branch.

The next two cases, **Who Will Benefit? The Merging of Benefit Plans at Lutherwood CODA** and **After the Merger—Lutherwood CODA's New Compensation Policy: Making Dollars and Sense**, deal with major compensation strategy issues arising after the merger of two human service agencies, Lutherwood and CODA. Job classes have to merge and a new congruent pay and benefit systems have to be developed from the quite different systems that were formerly in place. Participants have the opportunity both to experience the detail of compensation system design and to find ways to achieve synergy with organizational strategies and objectives.

Martin-Straight Compressors (A & B) presents a difficult company situation in which participants must analyze and evaluate the performance management and merit systems in place. Several alternative options and iterations of these systems have to be examined as part of this analysis.

The final case in this section, **Evergreen Technologies Ltd. (ETL)**, describes a high-tech company that has just won a major new government contract (the Ontario Government "Drive Clean" program) and must set up an effective work group to implement this contract at a time of dwindling human resources and a floundering work-from-home program. The case offers participants the opportunity to apply a wide range of HR strategies in the planning, recruiting, and performance management areas in a setting of high change but also considerable flexibility.

Canadian Products Limited (A)

Tupper Cawsey

Andrew Templer

Sharon Cliff, manager of human resource planning and development for Canadian Products Ltd., wondered what she should do in training and development for next year. Her training program for the previous two years at Canadian Products had been reasonably successful, but this year, she hoped to widen the training to all levels of management.

COMPANY BACKGROUND

Canadian Products is a multi-divisional corporation based in Montréal. Its five divisions design and manufacture a broad line of consumer and industrial products from electronics and home furnishings to industrial equipment (see Exhibit 11.1 for a partial organizational chart). In addition to the five divisions, Canadian Products has several wholly owned subsidiaries that provide it with raw materials and component parts.

Over the past 10 years Canadian Products had an annual compound growth of 8.6 percent. Last year, sales increased 12 percent to $520 million, and net income decreased 16 percent to $4.3 million. The decline in net income was attributed to increased global competition, increased raw material and supply costs, and unexpected startup costs of a new plant in Montréal. While sales of all product lines had increased, the president was aware that the market for their major product line was maturing and sales were projected to flatten in the coming years.

Top management continued to voice their concern for employees within the organization. Canadian Products had grown from only a few employees in 1930 to 1800 in 1963 and now over 3800. One year ago, the company had experienced the first strike in its history. Although a long and painful experience, the strike had resulted in improved employee–employer relations. As part of the improved relations, the president announced in the Annual Report that "the human resources division was broadly introducing training programs for all levels of management. Canadian Products recognizes the divisional needs created by rapid expansion, together with organizational changes made necessary to cope with such growth. Improved communications have resulted at all organizational levels. There has been a conscientious effort to renew one-to-one relationships with all employees. As a result, an improved rapport is evolving with salaried and hourly paid members and also with various union stewards representing employees at our various plant operations."

Concern for employees extended to managerial ranks as well. The company has had a long tradition of promoting from within. As a result, few managers of departmental level or higher ever left the company. Until recently, college degrees were not a prerequisite for success. While the company president had an MBA, many of the divisional general managers had risen from blue-collar ranks.

SHARON CLIFF'S BACKGROUND

Sharon Cliff was born in Arvida, Québec, of anglophone parents. She was fluently bilingual and comfortable in both the French and English cultures as well. Before coming to Canadian Products three years ago, Sharon had worked for the federal government in training and development and had taught several years of high school. She decided to leave the civil service because "I needed a change. I had to do something more than was offered there."

Because of her lack of background in manufacturing, Sharon spent the first two months of her new job asking the various managers what they felt their training needs were. From this initial feedback, Sharon decided that her first training program at Canadian Products would involve the department managers in six days of workshops on a variety of topics. At the workshop, the first two days were spent on management concepts, while subsequent days dealt with such topics as interviewing and supervisor relations. Sharon felt that the program was successful but that it demonstrated the need for training below the department manager and manager levels. "If department managers needed as much training as they did, just imagine how much training the supervisors must need," she mused (see Exhibit 11.2 for a typical divisional organization). Because of this finding, last year's program revolved around supervisor training.

In addition to management training, Sharon ran several job instruction programs for sales personnel, secretarial staff, and the manufacturing operators. Sharon was also responsible for a five-member human resource planning training session.

THE TRAINING AND DEVELOPMENT PLANNING PROCESS

Sharon had found her initial visits with managers very useful as they helped form the basis for her training and development plan. She felt it was important that she determine not only the needs for training and development but also people's attitudes towards the plan. To do this she visited every division and department manager one-on-one and met with groups of department managers and managers. The six weeks of discussions were followed by an incubation period, during which the collected data were interpreted and a plan formulated. A rough draft of the program was then drawn up with an attempt to ensure "meaningful end results." Sharon stressed the need to assess and reassess training programs in order to obtain valid and valuable training. The rough draft of the program was then circulated to the managers and finally sent to top management for approval.

The final decision on the training plan was made by the Operations and Environment Committee of Canadian Products. Sharon felt that the presentation made to top management was only a formality. She didn't think she needed to sell it again at this late stage because they'd had so many chances to see and approve of the program.

A Typical Meeting on the Training and Development Plan

In order to provide an understanding of how training plans are developed, Sharon described a meeting with a divisional manager and his department manager: "A meeting with the general manager would precede the meeting with the whole group by about half an hour. I would sit down with the general manager and discuss my intentions and purposes. I hoped to satisfy the GM's need to initiate training-by-objectives rather than training-for-the-sake-of-training. My idea is to prepare the GM, analyze his thinking, and make him realize the impact he would have on the decision making of his subordinate group and himself. I hoped to make him feel energized enough to ask questions at the group meeting—questions that would show he'd done some thinking. I wasn't trying to control the GM's thinking. I just discussed what the agenda would be—my objectives for holding that bigger meeting.

"I didn't want to put the general manager of Canadian Products in the position of controlling or dominating the group, because I saw him as my prime resource. There were so many training needs that I could see—I didn't wish to take the chair or assume the chief resource person's role. In particular, I didn't want to start telling Harry what Harry needed and Alice what Alice needed right in front of Joe who happened to be general manager.

"That was how the meeting was set up originally. Then I got into the larger meeting with the general manager and the group and introduced what was expected. I began with asking the general manager, 'Since you are the senior person in the organization—what do you need for yourself?' Asking the general manager seemed to get the ball rolling—if the boss were going to open up and speak, they all would. I did this because many people feel inhibited when taken out of their comfort zone and you put a fair amount of pressure on them. It's difficult to answer 'What do you need?' in front of the boss. Many would otherwise have a tough time saying 'I really don't know how to manage' or 'I really don't know how to do a performance review.'

"Frequently, managers can say what other people need, but can't describe what *they* need. I would then sit back and try to listen to the managers as they talked."

Training and Development Needs

The training and development plans for Canadian Products fell into several categories. The first category related to job or skills training. This type of training was carried on within departments and sections of the organization and was handled primarily by line personnel, except for specific skills courses. These were under Sharon Cliff's department.

In addition, the top management was instituting a CQI* system that required further development. Last year, the formal programs concentrated on giving executives CQI concepts, while this year's training was to be concerned with implementation. Sharon still needed to decide the best manner of carrying out these plans.

Many managers also had needs specifically related to their functional areas, since many were new to their jobs. The company's growth meant that managers of major departments frequently had little experience and didn't know each other well. The organization, as a whole needed to develop a feeling of unity and cooperation.

In speaking about the general training needs of the organization, Sharon Cliff found that "managers with even 10, 15, or 20 years also needed help. When I talked to senior managers on a one-to-one basis, they said they needed to communicate more effectively with the president and the Executive Committee. They needed to have better committee meetings that were chaired with more skill. Interestingly enough, every level of management identified the same needs for their bosses. Senior managers said, 'I've been here for 25 years and never had a formal performance review. Why is it critical to do one for my subordinates if my own boss doesn't feel it's important?'

"Only the newest managers had some kind of formal management training. Most managers had attended seminars or workshops over the years but had virtually nothing on management. Generally the first question I asked was, 'Which one of your job functions is responsible for most of your salary?' After a few twisted looks on their faces, their response was invariably 'management.' I asked them how many spent any time learning about management—whether by practice, learning in the classroom, or reading. I found that if a good article happened to come along about managing production supervisors they might read it but nothing more.

"In my meetings with managers, they mentioned a great number of concerns. Some of the managers talked of broader concepts, philosophies, and theories of management while others talked about practical issues in management such as interviewing techniques, appraisals, and performance reviews. They wanted to revise the whole review system and know how to put it into effective practice. In short, the managers needed more help in communication, interpersonal relationships, group decision making and on how to run more effective committees. There was so much to do in management development at every single level that you could almost set up a whole company to do nothing else.

"Canadian Products had a handful of beautiful managers who were being utilized as internal resources. Of those, eight were brand new, and two had been with the company almost since its formation."

SHARON CLIFF'S PERCEPTIONS

Sharon described herself as being looked on as the expert in the organization: "This had some advantages, in that I had credibility," she commented. "But it also had some disadvantages in that everyone saw me as being 'different.' It became difficult to anticipate what people wanted and needed because they expected me to tell them. Of course, that was impossible. Consequently, I had to remain flexible with the program. Frequently the managers' objectives and mine were different and had to be reconciled.

"One thing I feel is extremely important in our work is the need for follow-up and feedback on the job. There's no sense in launching a program unless it is accepted and carried

*CQI: Continuous Quality Improvement

out in a work environment. I insisted on carrying things through to the finish and, therefore, sometimes got into trouble. The trainers before me were very different. One was wholly practical and the other was totally conceptual. I think I'm a conceptualizer, but I like putting concepts into practice. I insist on a commitment by management to follow through.

"I think that I've been fairly successful with this approach so far. People are beginning to trust me within the organization. The other day I was asked to visit one of the subsidiaries, which had not previously invited anyone from the human resources division. This was the first opportunity that our division had to demonstrate our work!

"Sometimes I worry about the opinions the line managers have about me. Some of them doubt my usefulness and are reluctant to send managers on courses. However, the procedures I used in setting up the training and development plan seem to have helped. The paternalistic attitude of many senior managers is perhaps finally disappearing. Until recently, people who were promoted could never lose their job. I know of instances where serious errors have been made in promotions and nothing has been done.

"A couple of things that attracted me to Canadian Products were its philosophy that the employees are its most important asset and the company's concern with social responsibility. After a strike two years ago, a major initiative was undertaken to improve communications within the organization and to solve some of the problems that had been created by rapid growth.

"Personally, I don't know how long I will stay with Canadian Products. I see myself as action-oriented, and I like getting things done. If things don't happen around here, I doubt that I'll stay. My goal is to be vice-president of human resources in some organization before I'm 40 [Sharon Cliff is now 35]. When I left government, I decided that one day I might regret leaving—but I have to try it. I still believe this."

RESOURCES AVAILABLE FOR THE TRAINING AND DEVELOPMENT PROGRAM

The primary resources required for the training and development program were the trainers, which could be drawn from a variety of sources. Internally, two people were available—Sharon Cliff and Bill Silver.

Sharon Cliff, as head of the human resource planning and development department, had five human resource planners and one human resource developer (Bill Silver) reporting directly to her. While some of Sharon's time could be used in training and development work, she had to devote considerable time to planning future programs and supervising the human resource planning section. Sharon felt that, at the very most, one-third of her time could be spent on actual training and development seminars.

Because the human resource planners were used for forecasting, career planning, and recruiting, only Bill Silver was available for training work. Bill had worked in education and administration before coming to Canadian Products. He had a BA in education with eight years of teaching and two years of administrative experience in a school. During that time, Bill had considerable exposure as the football coach. Sharon Cliff was aware of Bill's perceptual and human relations abilities. She remarked that Bill was able to develop a trusting relationship with others very quickly.

In addition to the internal staff, Sharon considered bringing in outside consultants at varying costs. The company had already committed to several days of CQI training with George Odihorne but was also considering Doug Bearett. His field of expertise was time management and his price was close to Odihorne's. Sharon was also considering a local university professor from the business school. He didn't have the industry reputation, but was considerably less expensive. His educational background was certainly sufficient, but Sharon wondered if he would be as credible to Canadian Products managers as the other consultants. Another possibility was a group called Performance Management Inc. from Chicago. Sharon had recently received their folder in the mail, knew they were interested in team building, and thought they might be worth investigating.

If she wished, Sharon knew she could avoid the use of outside consultants entirely by relying on a series of films. Several good series on management concepts could be purchased for approximately $3500 to $10 500 per series. These films would cover most modern management topics, but she wondered how quickly they would become dated.

Sharon Cliff considered all the available resources. Although her department operated on a set budget, departments would be charged for whatever services they used—$90 per person per day for workshops run by staff and varying rates for seminars run by external consultants. There was a definite need for demonstrating the value of training to the company, she reflected.

Exhibit 11.1

Canadian Products Ltd., Divisional Organization (Partial Organization Chart)

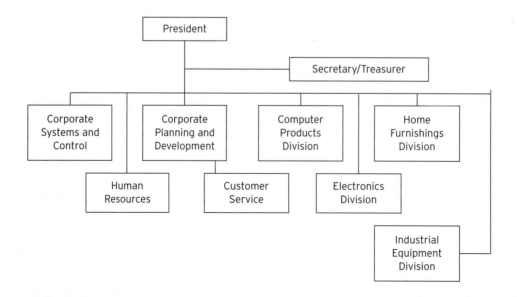

Exhibit 11.2

Canadian Products
Divisional Staff Organization
(Partial Organization Chart)

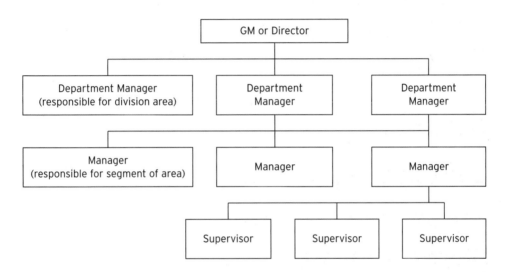

Canadian Products Limited (B)

Tupper Cawsey

Andrew Templer

Sharon Cliff, manager of human resource planning and development for Canadian Products Ltd., was concerned about the progress of her training and development plan for the current year. During the previous two years, she had felt confident that her program had been well accepted and had produced significant results. This year, however, she was both dismayed and exasperated over the responses she was getting to her program. Since it was May, she knew she would have to act quickly if she were to make changes to the training plan.

COMPANY BACKGROUND

Canadian Products is a large multidivisional corporation with over 350 supervisors and managers. In recent years, the company had embarked on an extensive training and development program for several reasons. First, the company had undergone rapid growth during the previous 10 years, and the number of people employed had more than doubled.

Second, the company environment seemed to be changing at a rapid pace. The major product that had fuelled the recent growth of the company was maturing and could not be expected to provide continued sales increases. At the same time, competition from foreign sources was increasing and creating much more competitive market conditions. Top management hoped that the training and development programs would lead to innovation and the initiative to develop new products. An indication of the changes facing the company was given by the previous year's results, released in February. Net profit before taxes was down 16 percent even though sales had increased 12 percent. The profit-sharing bonuses for managers followed a parallel decline.

THE TRAINING AND DEVELOPMENT PROGRAM

Sharon Cliff and her subordinate, Bill Silver, had spent the months of November and December working on the training and development program for Canadian Products. The training and development needs were determined by going to company managers and questioning them about the anticipated events of the coming year.

This process was reasonably complex because of the commitments requested by Sharon Cliff: "I went to each of the bosses or supervisors and told them that if we were to run the training and development program, they must be prepared to follow up on the training. Their subordinates were going to be very frustrated on the course. They were going to want to share with their bosses what they were doing and how they were getting along. After all, their bosses were their major resource. They were the people who did the performance review, merit review, and the whole bit. Supervisors would have to keep track of when their people were going on a workshop and follow up on it casually to find out how they were getting along. They are going to be frustrated at first. CQI* training will be a new process for them and a lot of pressure will be on them to learn it. They know they will be criticized as managers and supervisors if they can't learn and apply the new materials.

"Bill Silver did most of the legwork in visiting the managers because I was focusing on the executive CQI program. When he returned and told me that he had agreement, I said, 'Agreement to what? I need you to summarize every meeting that you had and then follow up in writing. I want you to remind the managers now what you discussed in your meetings just to make sure that we don't have any communication breakdowns.'"

Bill did exactly as Sharon had asked and the phone began to ring off the hook. Manager after manager said, "I don't remember talking about this." Sharon asked Bill where the misunderstanding was, and he was utterly amazed. Sharon said, "Don't be. If a manager has 25 supervisors, can you imagine how much time he has to commit to the CQI process? At least one hour per supervisor. He's just realized what he's got himself into. Obviously he doesn't understand, doesn't have the time, or doesn't want to change how he manages." Sharon sent Bill back for changes.

Bill went back to make modifications in some areas, but some managers still had a hard time with the concept of the training period. One manager realized that he had agreed to have all his supervisors away for the whole day. Thus Bill and Sharon received good feedback and were able to make some good modifications. Two weeks later Bill came back and said he felt that everything had been hammered out. Again, Sharon told him, "Confirm everything again in a speedy memo with a copy to the department managers, general manager, and myself. I think that in six months' time, the sign-offs will be worth their weight in gold—even though I hope not." Once the program was put into practice, Sharon felt she was going to need those backup memos. With a twinge of suspicion, Bill and Sharon launched their program.

---

*CQI: Continuous Quality Improvement

"During this initial period, we made several changes to the program," Sharon offered. "Initially, the training was going to be done with horizontal slices through the organization—only managers at the same level would participate in any one seminar. The bosses would say things such as 'I really don't feel it would be appropriate to have subordinates' or 'I wouldn't feel free to express myself on what I wanted and needed.' Consequently, we originally had the program approved using horizontal slices, but I went to senior management and demonstrated the cost savings that were possible by going with vertical slices in the organization—having three levels of management in the same workshop—as well as horizontal slices. On a horizontal basis, we would need 12 two-day workshops on CQI for senior managers at approximately $4000 per day. On a vertical basis, we could get away with three or perhaps four two-day workshops, which meant a saving of several thousands of dollars. Because of these savings, they changed their minds and agreed to go with the vertical as well as the horizontal slices."

Exhibit 11.3 provides a summary of the training and development program developed by Sharon Cliff. The program includes the use of considerable outside resources. The training and development group was run as a profit centre, where people were charged $90 per person per day for workshop attendance. The plan included six workshop days for approximately 350 managers. When the outside courses were budgeted and the audio-visual materials were ordered, the total budget was around $500 000.

"The philosophy behind the program was a very applied one," stated Sharon. She wished to deal with real-life problems using the CQI approach during the sessions, stating that "it was better to get the people involved in solving their own problems. If you had a production problem, better to get the production people working on that, rather than something else. We would bring in Mr. Manufacturing Manager with his five production supervisors, have them work on their problems, and implement or apply CQI to the problem area. By the end of the year, each of the five should have solved one major problem. They should have learned that using a systematic, analytical approach to problem resolution works very well. If it didn't work at all, they should understand why. At least they should have learned when to use CQI and when not to use it. I didn't want to give the impression that CQI was the panacea for all ills."

Feedback on the Training and Development Program

Sharon Cliff felt that the training and development program was very successful in January and February, especially the first two workshop sessions. The feedback was positive. There was a lot of enthusiasm generated during the workshop sessions, and Sharon was pleased with the way the program was going.

In her opinion, having managers from different levels in the same seminar worked beautifully. People opened up for the first time. No one was amazed that the bosses didn't know all things, and bosses learned a lot that they hadn't heard before.

Sharon commented that the people in one division in particular, customer service, seemed to be having much success. They demonstrated more commitment than other divisions, primarily because of the division manager. They read books, had meetings, spent money bringing in consultants, and developed a keen interest in their program. Sharon said that when you walked into the division, you could feel the difference. It was obvious that good things were happening. Sharon reported that in one case, a person previously considered as non-promotable was developed and promoted to assistant general manager of the division. In other cases, three supervisors went to their superiors and suggested that they were not capable of handling their assignments. It was mutually agreed that certain subordinates were more capable than they were and should replace them. Sharon felt this to be a remarkable indication of the attitudes and climate of that division.

However, not all of the divisions saw the program in the same light. People became disgruntled and would comment, "Why do I need to learn this program? When I return to my department, I don't see my boss doing them and he is going through the same program."

Upon some investigation, Sharon found that in many cases department managers refused to talk with their subordinates about the seminar topics. The managers gave a variety of reasons, ranging from "I don't have enough time" to "It isn't particularly useful" or "It's HR's job." Sharon believed that department managers felt inadequate discussing these subjects except on an informal basis and that their lack of formal knowledge of the management concepts left them hesitant about discussing them with their subordinates.

Amid such training problems, attendance began dropping off. Only seven or eight out of 20, rather than 17 or 18, would attend. Managers would assure Sharon that they would come, right up to the day prior to the sessions, and then not show up. Supervisors were holding meetings and not letting people come. When questioned about the commitment they were showing, they replied that "this was an exception." However, Sharon heard about such "exceptions" all the time. Participation during seminars had fallen off as well. People seemed reluctant to open up, and negative attitudes were apparent. Many managers adopted the attitude that "it was nice to have a day off."

Training and Development Situations

Sharon Cliff reported a typical problem case: "A group of five production supervisors from woodworking sat down and wrote out what they considered to be their major difficulties. They then discussed the problems and decided which one they were going to work on. The problem involved storage of inventory in one supervisor's area. He was running out of space to place items after they came off the finish line. It was a nice problem because of its complexities. A conveyor belt was involved as well as a forklift and boxes. They had a target; they knew their position, the present conditions, and the future condition they wanted. They developed a beautiful solution. I was delighted when this group came out with this plan, as they were a hard bunch to work with. I thought I finally had my breakthrough with them.

"They were so pleased with their discussions they decided they would include their boss. He got excited and said he wanted it done within 10 days. The group was obviously upset and tried to explain that they couldn't do it that quickly. They felt that he had just taken their project away. The group actually preferred to present him with a recommendation and go at their own pace.

"When they came back to the next seminar they didn't want to bring future problems to the boss. One supervisor remarked, 'We discussed other problems with the boss and now we have five extra things to do in addition to our normal work.' These people work hard—most of them put in lots of overtime but they were being turned off. Instead of being excited about identifying and solving problems, they were upset. The boss had reduced the schedule of their action plan from three or four months (a reasonable amount of time) to 10 days. The problem had been there for 15 years and another three months wasn't going to kill anybody. The group would have enjoyed making the changes but the boss destroyed their enthusiasm.

"Another type of problem arose with a group of salaried and office workers. Five supervisors from five different, but functionally related, work areas were together in a seminar. They claimed they had nothing in common. I had them talk about it. Privately they admitted they had a communication problem but they wouldn't open up in the group. However, they were willing to meet on a regular basis to learn about CQI as a concept. I thought to myself, 'That's great. They would have to get together and interact. In this way their communication would gradually improve.' What I forgot was that they couldn't communicate. They wouldn't be able to agree on how to organize themselves. That was precisely what happened. They couldn't decide when they should get together, how they should get together, who should be there, and who shouldn't. Thus they couldn't get past their first problem. It was a disaster.

"One person who had been a supervisor for one month said, 'I've been doing this job for eight years and I don't need a supervisory development program.' I told her that she should discuss it with her boss. She said, 'He doesn't want to hear from me. He never talks to me.' I had had enough of 'He doesn't talk to me,' 'He never has time,' or 'I never see my boss.' After the first two months I had felt very positive—I thought the bosses were doing a good job. Innocently, I believed that they were working with their subordinates. When I started to ask questions, I opened a can of worms. It became very obvious that, in fact, the bosses were not talking to their people."

Sources of Problems

Sharon Cliff felt that there might be several explanations for such problems occurring in the training and development program. First, the department managers were not doing their jobs. They had failed completely in honouring their commitment to follow up the training with on-the-job support and development. In fact, when some subordinates had tried to implement CQI they were told by their bosses to stop: "We don't have time for that stuff in this department." Sharon knew that the environmental problems were leading to organizational pressures for rapid action to increase profits. The change in markets and the decreased profit had created significant emphasis on short-term production.

Besides these problems, Sharon was concerned about the impact of the training group. She knew that in some circles its members were looked upon as preachers rather than as part of management. She knew that her own position as a department manager created some anxiety among the seminar groups. For example, once when she approached a group and asked them how they were doing, she was told (in so many words) to get lost. The group was very concerned that she was checking up on their progress. In fact, she had intended this gesture to be nothing more than a progress review of the CQI plan they were implementing. Instead, it was perceived as a threatening, interfering manoeuvre. Sharon had tried to correct this impression by asking Silver to go around to the groups, but she wasn't certain that the problem had been overcome.

Early in the year, Bill Silver left Canadian Products and was replaced by Tom Erwick. Tom's style was very different from Bill's. He created trust easily, but was much quieter and lacked Bill's 'pizzazz.' Sharon didn't know what effect this change had or would continue to have on the program.

Sharon was very unhappy with the present state of affairs and wanted to do something. At this stage, she wasn't certain what her boss's response would be to program changes. She knew that she would have to make a decision of some sort. She wished all divisions were cooperating as well as customer service. She also wondered what effect this difficult situation would have on her career at Canadian Products.

Exhibit 11.3

Canadian Products Ltd. Summary Training and Development Program

Managerial Level	Type of Training	Trainer	# days	Estimated Cost	Session Numbers	Vertical or Horizontal Slice	Purpose
Executive	CQI	D. Barrett	2	$3000/day plus expenses	1-3	V	To develop an understanding of CQI concepts
Executive	CQI	F. Lafferty	2	$3000/day plus expenses	4-6	V	To begin implementation of CQI
General Manager	CQI	D. Barrett	2	$3000/day plus expenses	1-3	V	To begin implementation of CQI
Department Manager	CQI	F. Lafferty	2	$3000/day plus expenses	4-6	V	To begin implementation of CQI
Department Manager	CQI	D. Barrett	2	$3000/day plus expenses	1-3	V	To begin implementation of CQI
Department Manager	CQI	F. Lafferty	2	$3000/day plus expenses	4-6	V	To begin implementation of CQI
Department Manager	Managerial Styles	S. Cliff	2	Internal	7-12	H	To develop an understanding of their managerial styles
Department Manager	Managerial Styles	P. Baylis	1	$1500/day plus expenses	13-14	H	To increase awareness of managerial styles and their consequences
Managers	CQI	S. Cliff	2	Internal	15-24	H	To introduce the concept of CQI
Managers	CQI	B. Silver	2	Internal	25-34	H	To begin implementing CQI
Supervisors	CQI	B. Silver	2	Internal	35-45	H	To introduce the concept of CQI
Supervisors	CQI	Audio-visual	1	Film purchase $6000	N/A	N/A	To develop an understanding of management

AMAX Automotive

Gene Deszca

Three years after arriving at AMAX Automotive, Andrew Smaltz found himself preparing for his performance review. As the assistant director of human resources, Andrew's portfolio of responsibilities extended across the range of departmental responsibilities, excluding pension and benefits, payroll, and security. Steady and satisfying progress had been made in many of the areas over the past year, but concerns with respect to the performance management system continued to haunt him. He knew it would be a major topic of discussion at his review tomorrow, and he wanted to be prepared with an analysis and action plan that would demonstrate he was committed to addressing the problem.

Andrew, 33 years old and a self-taught mechanic, had spent his working life in the automotive parts business. He had graduated from a community college with a 3-year diploma in business management. Prior to joining AMAX, Andrew had spent eight years with a smaller competitor. He started on the front counter and worked his way up to manager of customer service (two years) and then to assistant human resources manager (three years). This latter promotion suited him because it enabled him to couple his love of the automotive parts business with a more senior management role. Prior to taking this assignment, Andrew had begun working on human resources management courses at the community college in order to get a certificate in human resource management. After two years of evening courses, he had graduated at the top of his class and obtained his certificate.

When AMAX purchased his former employer, Andrew played a key role during the due diligence phase and was helpful in facilitating the subsequent successful integration of the two firms. During this period, he demonstrated patience, insight, and leadership skills. He developed a strong relationship with the director of human resources during this period and was rewarded by being named the assistant director of human resources approximately six months after the acquisition.

AMAX

AMAX, a wholesaler, distributed auto parts to garages throughout Ontario and western Canada. A limited number of the customers were hobbyists, but the vast majority were mechanics. The number of different parts handled by AMAX ran to the thousands and covered all major domestic and foreign cars and trucks. The margins were thin in this competitive, mature industry. AMAX focused on service, price, delivery, and inventory management and attempted to develop and maintain excellent relationships with garage operators and mechanics. Some of the larger garage operators tendered their auto parts business, but that was not the norm in the sector they serviced. AMAX maintained two warehouses (one in Ontario and one in western Canada) and operated 26 distribution and service depots. In addition, it acted as a major supplier to independent auto parts supply firms established in smaller communities. AMAX located its depots within a half-hour driving distance of municipalities that had populations in excess of 300 000. There were 650 people employed by AMAX on a full-time basis.

Robert Wickham, a garage operator/mechanic, founded AMAX in Hamilton in 1953. Over the years it prospered and grew, but majority ownership stayed in the family, and it retained clear signs of its small business roots. It actively and successfully resisted all attempts to unionize its staff by offering benefit and compensation packages similar to those in unionized shops. As was often the case with small organizations, Wickham kept all major decision making to himself, and employees viewed the firm as paternalistic and traditional in its approach to management

When Robert died a year before the acquisition, Henry Fiorino was made president and CEO. Henry was a 43-year-old electrical engineer who had spent the majority of his working life in the firm, largely in supplier management and warehousing. Robert's daughter, Sally, had graduated with a degree in business, joined the firm, and was now VP of sales and marketing. Henry and Sally had been responsible for the acquisition and for championing several initiatives aimed at improving efficiency and effectiveness. These included organizational restructuring around a customer-focused business model, the revamping of the information and technology support operation, the launch of Web-based service and support applications, the improved use of data to enhance marketing and sales initiatives, and the use of telemarketing to service and build small accounts. AMAX was becoming known as an industry leader in using information technology, other forms of technology, and supply chain management principles to better manage inventory.

Henry and Sally believed that the paternalistic practices that characterized their organization and bothered them as employees had to change. They promoted Ed Smith to director of human resources shortly after the death of their father and the early retirement of the former director. Ed was a business school graduate who had been recruited by Sally five years earlier to clean up the operation of the western distribution centre. He was a tough, talented individual who believed in building performance through teams of talented, committed, and empowered employees. He had done a superb job in turning around the distribution centre through the use of teams and empowerment principles. In the distribution centre, he asked several warehouse employees to leave, formed teams, redesigned many of the jobs to improve accountability and authority, and reduced the number of supervisors. He also instituted an active performance management system that included goal setting by individuals and teams and the public posting of performance results. Finally, he used temporary SWAT squads to target improvement initiatives. By the time he left to become the director of human resources, Ed had made the warehouse a very cost-effective and service-oriented operation.

When Andrew first arrived, all senior managers, including Ed, were focused on ensuring that the integration of their first acquisition went as smoothly as possible. The first year was a chaotic one, but within 12 months everyone agreed that the integration had been a success. There were still issues, but key systems and processes had been integrated, operations had been merged, where appropriate, and decisions concerning the future of employees had been made and acted upon (including the release of approximately 100 individuals).

With the acquisition a success, Henry, Sally, and Ed turned their attention to improving the rest of the organization. They aimed at serving their customers more efficiently and effectively than anyone else in the auto parts industry. Ed, Sally, and Henry believed that modern empowerment principles had to be followed to engage the employees and obtain their commitment to this vision. Given Ed's earlier success, they believed the key to this was in the human resource practices of the firm.

Managers were asked to recast their operations in team-based terms and to hold the teams and themselves accountable for performance; business development; customer retention and satisfaction; and employee retention, satisfaction, and skills development. Those who serviced other parts of the firm were asked to think of those parts as their clients. In addition, cross-functional managerial teams were formed around: supplier development, logistics, and inventory management; customer relations and market development; competitive analysis and opportunity assessment; and employee development and organizational effectiveness.

By the time Andrew was promoted, there was a cohesive top-management team that worked well together. Information flowed freely among Ed, Henry, Sally, and Werner Karr (CFO and VP of management information systems). Andrew was on the periphery of this group and had a particularly strong relationship with Ed. Exhibit 12.1 contains a partial organization chart for AMAX Automotive.

HUMAN RESOURCES MANAGEMENT AT AMAX AND ANDREW SMALTZ

The human resources function at AMAX was responsible for wages and benefits administration, health and safety, security, and all the traditional human resource functions (assisting line managers in recruitment and selection, job design, human resources planning, training and development, and so on). Fifteen people reported directly to the director of human resources. Andrew was primarily responsible for organizational effectiveness. This involved organization and employee development and other initiatives designed to promote performance at the individual, team, and unit levels. He was also responsible for facilitating career development initiatives and for handling employee displacement, relocation, and outplacement when these actions were required (a partial job description is contained in Exhibit 12.2). Four people, including a human resources planner and three human resource training and development specialists, reported to Andrew.

The director of human resources described Andrew as straightforward, hard-working, insightful, personable, innovative, and helpful. Further, he could be counted on to maintain confidences. However, many long-time managers and employees saw Andrew as well meaning but still green and perhaps a bit too ambitious and too willing to fall in line with the wishes of Henry and Sally. They also reported that some of Andrew's systems and services created a fair bit of work but not a lot of benefit.

From the time that Andrew joined AMAX, he operated fairly autonomously. Ed Smith was the strategist and visionary in the department. He was ready and willing to listen and advise staff members, but he knew when to back off and let employees run with an initiative. The only thing Ed required was that he be kept informed concerning progress and not be "surprised." Ed had high standards and expectations, but he was not unreasonable. He held himself to these same standards and could be counted upon to listen, support, and develop both his staff and himself.

At the beginning, Andrew played an important role in the organizational integration of structures, systems, and processes and handled the difficulties that resulted from displacement and relocation issues. Subsequently, he helped Ed promote the development of a more team-based structure and facilitated team building in the new senior cross-functional teams. Further, he established a management development program for first-level and middle managers at AMAX that was well received.

Andrew also was responsible for establishing and managing the performance management program. Getting it off the ground was proving to be much more than he bargained for. A year and a quarter after its launch, it was limping along, at best, and ignored totally, at worst. Further, for the first time since his arrival at AMAX, Andrew worried about his reputation. He knew that Ed, Sally, and Henry were committed to making performance management a part of the managerial culture and that they were expecting to see progress in this area.

THE PERFORMANCE MANAGEMENT SYSTEM

Andrew had designed the current performance management system approximately 18 months ago and had begun implementing it 16 months ago. The program itself was purchased from an external supplier and adapted through the assistance of a consultant and a small, *ad hoc* task force on performance management. Prior to this initiative, performance management had been an activity largely left to the discretion of individual managers. Standardized annual performance reviews were required in principle, but they tended to be ignored unless an employee was new or was getting into trouble.

The new program, including the performance appraisal component, was designed to help managers improve the performance of subordinates. The performance management system had a supporting employee information system that could track skills and abilities, developmental activities, career progress, performance, compensation and benefits, and career/development plans and goals. At the beginning of each year, all managers were to sit down with employees individually and in teams. They were to review job descriptions, assess and document the strengths and weaknesses of the team (based upon peer and customer assessment), develop challenging work objectives for the team and themselves, and create meaningful professional development objectives. Managers were expected to meet with employees and teams once a quarter to specifically review progress, make adjustments, and update documentation on progress towards accomplishing the goals.

At the end of the year, managers were expected to take an hour with each employee to review progress, evaluate performance, and assign individual performance bonuses (approximately 0.5 percent of payroll was allocated to this). Both managers and employees signed off on these reviews, and they were filed electronically, with the automatic updating of employee files. Any across-the-board salary adjustments were also to be made at this time. Managers were expected to pursue this same process with the teams that reported to them, with approximately 1 percent of payroll allocated to team-based bonuses. An outline of the overall performance management process is set out in Exhibit 12.3.

To make the reviews more relevant, managers were expected to use some form of 360° feedback for both themselves and their subordinates. It was recommended that all employees solicit written feedback from at least four to seven individuals, including two co-workers, three subordinates (if relevant), and two customers or recipients of their services. The 360° feedback was also to be used for team evaluations. Within one month of completing the annual reviews, managers were expected to recommence the cycle with planning and goal-setting meetings.

Andrew knew that most of the senior managers wanted to improve performance. Ed saw the performance management system as a key route. It was Ed and Henry who had insisted that the review process include 360° feedback and be linked to bonuses. They believed it would help them identify and address problems and areas of weakness, promote the development of individuals and teams, focus attention and effort on performance, and help build a culture committed to customer service and performance excellence.

When the program was launched, consultants were retained to conduct a two-day workshop for all managers who would implement the system. Case discussions and simulation role-plays were used during these sessions. Andrew worked hard during this period to ensure that necessary forms, training materials, and other forms of written documentation were appropriately adapted to AMAX and that documentation protocols were in place. In addition, Andrew held two-hour information sessions with all employees to explain both the philosophy and character of the new performance management system, including what was expected from them, their managers, and the system itself. Finally, newsletter stories promoted and reinforced the introduction of the system. Andrew offered to meet with interested managers and teams to further facilitate the effective use of the new system. Approximately 30 percent of the managers and teams had taken him up on his offer over the past 12 months, but Andrew was concerned about the amount of the groaning and complaining at these sessions.

At the first anniversary of the launch of the performance management system, Andrew became increasingly depressed over the progress achieved. Updates to employee files were not being done in a timely or thorough manner. Only 35 percent of employees had filed any form of employee update within a month of when the reviews should have been completed. Often, bonuses were being assigned in an across-the-board manner, performance review meetings were not being held for the majority of employees in a timely fashion, and when they were held, the discussions seldom lasted more than 15 minutes. The use of 360° feedback was being implemented by no more than 20 percent of the managers. Even senior management expressed difficulty in finding the time to follow the agreed-to process. However, they excused their actions by stating that they engaged in feedback and review on a daily basis with one another and provided one another with regular, informal 360° feedback.

Andrew decided it would be wise to get feedback from others in the organization on why this performance management initiative seemed to be stuck in its tracks. The following were characteristic of the comments he received.

- This review process is far too complex and time-consuming. I seem to have to enter information more than one time and I doubt that anyone will ever put the majority of this information to use, anyway. I wouldn't know what to do with it, even if I really knew how to put it to use.

- Don't get me wrong. I believe it is important to manage performance, but this system is way too complex. I have 34 people who report directly to me. If I was to do what you're asking me to do, how would I ever get any of my other work done? Even this system's record-keeping requirements are 10 times those required by the old system, and I can't see that the benefits are anywhere near worth the cost.

- I like what this new system is trying to accomplish. It works great with new employees or individuals in new assignments, but it doesn't make sense for those who have been with us for years and know how to do a good job.

- This program makes no sense being applied to warehouse employees and those in clerical roles. They don't initiate—they respond to requests and orders and have very little discretion over what they do. I don't think we should be using the same system and forms for everyone.

- I've found the program very helpful. All 11 employees in our depot have participated, and it has helped us to really improve our level of customer service. We now have a formal process in place that lets us know what our customers think, and we've acted on it. For four years we had flat sales; suddenly sales have grown by more than 8 percent. I attribute it to performance management.

- The first time I brought up the subject, everybody ran for cover. However, that was then. By the time we got to the third quarterly review, people had started to embrace the system. They say we should have been doing this a long time ago. I don't know whether we need to keep updating it so frequently or in such detail, but it seems to be working. Even the 360° feedback is making sense, now that we've focused it at the team level on an annual basis. The individual 360° feedback isn't working, but I don't think it's needed as long as we've got it at the team level. The frankness of the discussion there gets down to individual performance very quickly.

- I explained 360° feedback to the employees in my depot and they asked me if I was nuts. The depot was working well and customers seemed satisfied. As far as they can see, this looks like a make-work project from human resources and not something that will help them do a better job.

- It's really interesting to hear what people have to say and watch them learn and improve. It's early and it's awfully complex, but I think there's something here that's worth the effort.

- I don't really understand what I am supposed to be doing with all these forms and review meetings. Rather than spending hours at the call centre navel-gazing and talking about performance, our time is better spent responding to clients and getting the work done.

Andrew pushed his chair back and stared at the comment sheet. What to do ... what to do? He knew he would need to have it sorted out in his own mind by next week when he was scheduled to meet with Ed for his own performance review.

Exhibit 12.1

AMAX Organization Chart (Partial)

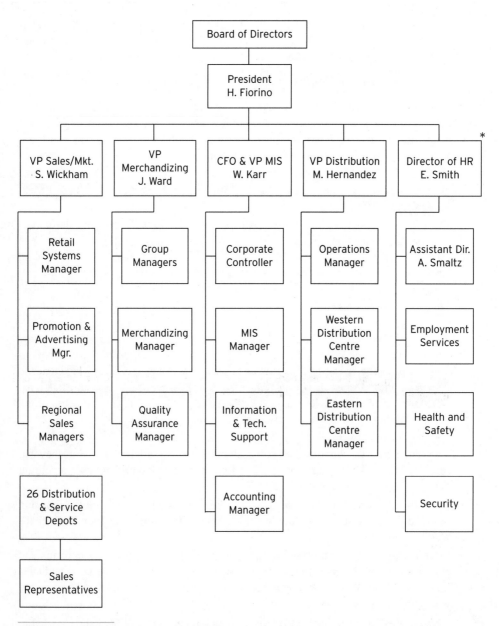

*Both cross-functional and functional teams are imbedded in the structure at appropriate points, for example, the senior management team (president and VP's, CFO's and director of HR).

Exhibit 12.2

Partial Job Description of Andrew Smaltz

Job Description: Assistant Director of Human Resources, AMAX Automotive

Accountable to: Director of Human Resources

Job Incumbent: Andrew Smaltz

Summary of Responsibilities

1. The development and administration of the performance management process and procedures, such that organizational effectiveness is enhanced through improved employee performance.

2. The development and administration of employee/management development programs that enhance current performance capacity, identify opportunities for professional change and development, and help individuals prepare for future challenges and opportunities.

3. Plan and facilitate organizational development initiatives.

4. Manage the human resource planning function and facilitate career development initiatives, including those related to displacement, relocation, and outplacement.

5. Act for the director of human resources, as required.

Exhibit 12.3

Performance Appraisal Process

1. Begin the cycle by reviewing the job description and the challenges that are most pressing at both the individual and the work-team levels.

2. Identify and recommend changes to the job description, if appropriate (i.e., involve more than 20 percent of the job content).

3. Document strengths and weaknesses present at both the individual and the work-team levels. Use team and customer contacts to develop a 360° view of the strengths and weaknesses and the challenges/opportunities.

4. Develop 3 to 5 challenging work objectives with each individual and with each work team.

5. Develop 2 to 3 challenging career/professional development objectives with each individual and for the work team.

6. Meet once per quarter to formally review progress at the individual and the work-team levels.

7. Review performance in depth at the individual and the work-team levels at the end of each 12-month period, or in conjunction with major events, if more appropriate. These reviews should also avail themselves of the benefits derived from the insights provided by 360° feedback.

8. Employees and their managers should sign off on the performance reviews.

9. Bonuses will be assigned based upon performance, and employee files (i.e., the employee information system) will be updated.

10. Managers will launch a new cycle of the performance management process within 30 days of the completion of the annual review.

Stability Bank

Elizabeth Lunau

Andrew Templer

Linda Jones, a human resources manager at Stability Bank, was having a difficult time adapting to her new position. She had only been hired six months ago, but her expectations of a fantastic job in banking were evaporating. Looking out the window of her office in downtown Toronto, she noticed it was raining. "Great," she thought, "even the weather is depressing."

This morning she had had another difference of opinion with her boss, Fred Baines, VP of human resources. All week, she had been looking forward to providing career counselling to three employees. After this morning's meeting, however, she was dreading it. Fred had outlined her responsibilities with respect to counselling the employees. "Right now people are interested in keeping their jobs. Find somewhere to put them, and we can consider long-term career aspirations later," Fred had instructed.

Linda placed her elbows on the desk and hung her head in her hands. "I don't know how I'm going to do this," she thought. "How can I just place people wherever there is an opening? I don't understand. Why can't Fred see that people aren't chess pieces? You have to give them opportunities. Why put them in a position, and then look at counselling them later? If he just used common sense, he'd see that he's doing things backwards!" Linda got up from her desk and walked to the window. Looking down on Bay Street, she watched the throngs of umbrellas moving below. Sighing, she wondered why she had ever accepted this position.

LINDA JONES: HUMAN RESOURCES MANAGER

Linda Jones graduated from business school with an MBA three years ago. She immediately accepted a position with one of her co-op placement employers, VisionTech Software. VisionTech was located in Victoria, British Columbia, close to her family—one of her primary reasons for accepting that employment offer.

VisionTech is a large technology firm specializing in computer software and applications. Linda worked in the human resources department where she concentrated on employee development. She enjoyed her position as she was afforded the opportunity to apply the concepts she had learned in school. The company was forward-thinking and always looking for new ways to do things. Linda felt it was a great opportunity. She had the freedom (and was encouraged) to try new ways of doing things. For her, it was the perfect place to try out different career planning concepts.

Linda had thrived in this environment. Her supervisor had commented in her last performance appraisal that she was innovative in her job, found new ways to help VisionTech employees understand their skills, and was a valuable resource to all employees looking to match their skills and aspirations to future opportunities. While Linda loved her job, six months ago, a headhunting firm had offered her an opportunity she couldn't refuse. A major Canadian financial institution needed someone to head up a large division in the HR department. The position's main responsibility was to help employees cope with problems created by the recent acquisition of a trust company. Most of these problems centred around job redundancy and duplication—there were more employees than positions in some departments, and many positions no longer existed. Linda felt the job would be a challenge. She had dreamed about being able to help employees during times of change. At VisionTech, it was easy to counsel employees. The company was growing rapidly, and every department was looking for new staff; if an employee expressed an interest in a new position, he or she was simply transferred there.

The bank, however, would be different. Now she would face a real challenge. The idea of counselling employees, while constrained by the number of available positions, excited her. She would be able to apply all her knowledge. Linda looked forward to having a more in-depth relationship with employees. At the bank, she knew she would have to really understand the employees in order to place them appropriately. The lack of open positions made putting the right employee in the right job very important.

Linda had accepted the job almost immediately. Even though she was sad to move away from her family, she felt this new position was a way to prove herself. Linda couldn't wait to apply everything she had learned in university. Finally, she would be able to experience HR in an environment of change—just like she had discussed in so many of her MBA classes. While she had no previous experience in the financial sector, she was confident Stability Bank would benefit from her ideas.

FRED BAINES: VICE-PRESIDENT, HUMAN RESOURCES MANAGEMENT

Fred Baines started with Stability Bank as a loan officer in his mid-20s. Over the past 30 years, he had worked his way up through various positions to his current post as VP of human resources. Prior to working for Stability Bank, he had been employed at another financial institution, where he had worked his way up from teller to the loans department.

Fred started working the day after he graduated from high school. He moved to Stability Bank in the 1960s, when a neighbour mentioned the bank was looking for people (and paying a higher salary than he was earning at the time). Fred moved up the ranks through the years, receiving a promotion every three years or so. He had been VP for two years and was quite content in his current position. He knew that, in his field, he was at the top. Someone from the finance or operations area might move up to Chief Operating Officer, but not from human resources. Having achieved his career goal, he planned on waiting out his days until retirement. Based on his years of service, he would be able to retire with a full pension in three years, when he turned 59.

THE EMPLOYEE PLACEMENT PROBLEM

Recently, Fred found his job highly stressful. Stability Bank had purchased Fidelity Trust only a few months ago. The merger resulted in major human resources issues. The CEO had made a commitment to all Fidelity employees that they would not lose their jobs. It was now Fred's job to find placements for all of them. Under normal time pressures, Fred would not find this task stressful—it was easy to find an opening somewhere and look for a person working in a similar area. The problem he faced was that he couldn't place these people quickly enough for the CEO John Smith. John wanted these people working in a job that wasn't an overrun or redundancy[1] the day after the merger was completed. Fred realized that was a bit of an exaggeration, but John was pressuring him to move people as quickly as possible so Stability Bank could focus its attention on other issues.

Finding an open position and matching an employee to it was fairly easy. He was frustrated, however, because no one wanted to move from their city, let alone existing branch. He had always taken the opportunity to move within the bank. He said to himself, "These employees don't realize just how lucky they are. If the bank offers you a position elsewhere, you should grab it. Obviously, Stability employees are not committed to their employer."

FRED REFLECTS ON HIS CAREER

As Fred sat in his office, he wondered what he was missing. "Maybe it's all of these women in the bank," he thought, "none of them want to move their family to another city." Things sure had changed since he was raising a family. His family had moved from city to city as he received promotions... no questions asked. Fred figured that these employees didn't want to progress within the company—otherwise, they would have jumped at the opportunity to be working in a different job.

Fred Baines looked at the picture of his wife and children on the desk. His two children were both married now. His daughter was trying to start a family, while his son already had a baby. He worried about how his future grandchildren would be raised. His daughter-in-law was a lawyer (like his son) here in Toronto, and she had given no indication that she was willing to leave her job to raise her children. He remembered how busy he was when he started his own family. If his wife had been working, no one would have raised the children. He knew he hadn't had the time to devote to it. He regretted not being able to spend the time he wanted with his children. Fred sighed, "Someone had to bring

---

[1] An overrun is a position that is in excess of operational requirements. A redundancy is a position that no longer exists.

home a paycheque to support them. If I hadn't worked so hard, they wouldn't have their current lifestyle. I might not have been there physically, but I have done a pretty good job providing for them."

Shuffling some papers on his desk, he turned his attention back to his job. His most recent difficulties involved the bank's newest HR manager Linda Jones. She was always trying to establish a career plan for these employees. Just because she had an MBA didn't mean she knew everything. It was clear to Fred that she was missing the completely obvious fact that these employees did not need career counselling, they needed a job. He didn't understand why Stability had hired her. Some consulting group had recommended that the bank hire someone to help with employee issues during the merger. He disagreed with hiring someone from outside the financial sector, as the group had suggested. How can someone who hasn't worked in a bank know about banking careers? Fred believed that came from working your way up—just as he had.

Linda reminded Fred of his daughter. Full of energy and ideas. Both of them wanted to change the world. Neither of them seemed able to do things a little bit at a time. Fred was pleased with Linda's work so far, they just seemed to have this recurring difference of opinion. He knew her skills would be valuable at a later date. She would be able to find dedicated Stability employees and promote them. Linda just didn't know how banks worked yet. Maybe at her old company, people could move wherever they wanted. Banks were different, though. An employee put in his or her time and then was rewarded with a promotion. She shouldn't be wasting her time on employees who didn't care about moving up the corporate ranks.

THE MORNING MEETING

Shaking his head, Fred wondered if he had been too harsh on Linda this morning. He had arranged the meeting to discuss her responsibilities in placing three employees from Stability Serenity branch. When Linda started talking about their potential for other areas and what training programs each needed, he had responded sharply, "Right now people are interested in keeping their jobs. Find somewhere to put them, and we can consider longer-term career aspirations later." Fred realized now that this may have been a bit harsh, probably due to all the pressure he was under. Maybe Linda didn't realize these employees weren't promotion material.

Fred looked at his watch. He was late for an appointment with one of the regional VPs. He got up from his desk, grabbed the file and rushed to the elevator. "I'll go and speak to Linda later," he noted, "and we can talk about which employees are looking for promotions. And at the same time we can look at who deserves one."

STABILITY BANK AND FIDELITY TRUST

Stability Bank has been operating in Canada for more than 100 years and is one of the five largest Canadian banks. Recently, Stability purchased Fidelity Trust to expand its business line in the trust services area. Fidelity readily accepted Stability's offer. Fidelity executives knew that Stability had a culture similar to its own. Stability's reputation for commitment to employees was also a key factor. Fidelity knew it would have to merge with another financial institution. It was not large enough to compete in the future and didn't have the capital necessary for the system upgrades required to compete in the current environment.

Fidelity was pleased with Stability's offer—the two companies would complement each other well, and Stability was one of the best possible companies with which to merge.

Stability Bank was committed to its employees. The bank was proud of its record—no one had ever been laid off. While Stability had gone through the same restructuring as other financial institutions, CEO John Smith prided on his company finding alternative positions for redundant employees. John strongly believed that if Stability showed commitment to its employees, the employees would show commitment to Stability.

NEW HUMAN RESOURCES MANAGEMENT POLICIES

John Smith was appointed CEO three years ago. One of his first initiatives in his new post was to reorganize the company's human resources function. In keeping with his beliefs regarding commitment to employees, he redesigned what was then called personnel department. Previously, personnel was more of a placement agency than the division that looked after employee welfare. John renamed the division "human resources" and expanded its duties beyond salary administration and recruiting.

The new human resources division became more and more important during John's first year as CEO. Training programs were implemented for several levels of employees in order to maintain competitiveness in a changing market. New employee incentives were added such as share ownership and profit sharing. A year after renaming the department, John appointed Fred Baines to the newly created position of VP human resources.

John Smith believed the newly created human resources area was a key factor in helping the company adjust to rapid changes in the financial industry. More and more positions were becoming redundant as Stability outsourced and centralized many activities, while also coping with technological change. In order to maintain employee loyalty, John committed the bank to a no-layoff policy. He believed loyalty was key to providing excellent customer service to bank customers. Employees could not provide excellent service if they were worried about their jobs.

John's no-layoff policy immediately caused strain in the human resources department when Stability purchased Fidelity Trust—particularly since former HR policies were maintained. In the past, Stability Bank had ensured redundant employees were placed in new positions at the same responsibility and salary levels. If no positions were available, the employee worked in a different area until a position became open. While the temporary placement may have been at a lower job level, the employee's salary was administered at previous levels. When a position became available, those employees temporarily placed in lower-level jobs had first priority. Other internal or external candidates were only considered when there were no redundant employees for that area. The other side of this policy required redundant employees to accept an open position within their geographic area. Otherwise they could keep their temporary post on a permanent basis and would be administered in the lower salary range.

Even before purchasing Fidelity, this policy had caused some problems. Qualified candidates often could not apply for another position. While the policy did much to ease the concerns of redundant employees, many other employees were becoming frustrated. This problem was exacerbated when Fidelity staff merged with Stability. The bank now had several thousand employees without a job. In the short term, Stability had placed Fidelity employees within the Stability branch network. While this meant that most branches were grossly overstaffed, the move resulted in few other problems. Former Fidelity staff did not appear to be overly stressed.

CANADIAN CONSULTING GROUP

John had realized during negotiations with Fidelity that placing these employees would be difficult. As soon as the merger was finalized, John immediately hired a consulting group to look at the problems associated with the merger. Canadian Consulting Group (CCG) was hired to review any potential merger problems and recommend solutions for Stability. The consultants had made several recommendations, the most important being to hire outside the financial community. The consultants stressed this was especially important in the HR area.

John directed CCG to headhunt some key people from other industries. The consultants located five new employees for Stability. Three of these were employees for the offices of human resources VP (Linda Jones and two others).

John agreed with the consultants that the bank needed some new blood. However, he still needed to solve his immediate problem—where to place all of the Fidelity employees. While he hired the five new employees, he did not want them suggesting changes to current policy until after the Fidelity issue was resolved. First things first, he believed.

John knew the three new HR employees would help Stability have first-rate employee programs. If Fred Baines would only place these employees faster, John could give the division its new mandate: Help employees find careers within the bank. He anticipated HR would be finished moving employees within the next two months, but was pushing Baines to finish sooner. The sooner everyone had a non-redundant job, the faster Stability could implement its career program.

STABILITY BANK IN SERENITY

Linda sat in her car trying to manoeuvre through traffic on the 401. The construction made traffic slow. Luckily, she had planned some extra time for her drive to Serenity in case of any traffic delays. She was looking forward to her drive to Serenity, about two hours north of Toronto. She was heading into cottage country and knew that looking at the fall leaves would help her relax a bit. As she made her way off the 401 to a connecting highway, she began to review what she knew about the Serenity branch.

Serenity was a small community with a resident population of approximately 2000. In the summer, Torontonians and people from other large cities flocked to the area to enjoy a vacation at the cottage. Serenity's location close to Toronto made it an ideal weekend getaway. The local community mainly consisted of retired couples. The area was quite peaceful and located far enough south to be close to major cities and avoid the really severe winter weather.

Only recently, the town had had three financial institutions. One of these was a Serenity Bank branch and another a Fidelity Trust branch. Two months ago, Fidelity's lease had expired, and the staff were relocated to the Stability branch. The branch was experiencing problems with the sudden influx of staff. Normally branches were thrilled to receive extra employees; however, Serenity did not have enough space for everyone. Stability had no plans to renovate or enlarge the branch, as it believed most of the excess employees would be relocated.

THE CALL FROM JANET RICHARDS

Three weeks ago, Linda had received a call from Janet Richards. Janet was an assistant manager at the Serenity branch and responsible for all staffing decisions. Janet was obviously frustrated. She had bypassed proper communication channels and contacted Linda directly (Janet should have contacted her regional VP, who would in turn contact human resources). Linda spoke with Janet for almost an hour. "I don't understand what the bank is doing. I have all these people, and no one has any work! Everyone is becoming lazy! I'm paying people to come in and twiddle their thumbs. When are you going to come and do something about our staffing situation?" Janet asked.

Janet was having logistic problems at her branch. An example of her difficulties was the fact that she only had three teller wickets. Prior to Fidelity staff joining the branch, she had had two full-time tellers. The third wicket was used for part-time staff. Fidelity also had two full-time tellers... bringing the total number of full-time tellers to four. "Fidelity employees are taking the jobs of my part-time employees!" Janet commented. She was faced with having to cut some of her part-time employees' hours. However, according to bank policy, she was not allowed to do that. In addition to guaranteeing jobs to displaced employees, Stability had also made a commitment not to cut part-time staff's hours.

Janet explained that she had used the additional bodies to do extra filing, intermingle the two branches' client records, and other odd jobs. However, now there were no other jobs to do. "My staff are becoming lazy. Rather than taking any task that comes up, they are sitting back waiting for someone else to do it," said Janet.

A SOLUTION FOR JANET'S PROBLEM

After a lengthy discussion, Janet and Linda had come up with two ideas that would give people useful tasks. They had agreed that allowing tellers to job-shadow more senior employees would be a means of keeping everyone busy, while helping people learn other jobs at the same time. This would be useful in the future, especially during the summer when people were on vacation. Their second idea was to get excess staff members to make solicitation calls to existing customers to see if the bank could provide them with any other services.

Linda was proud of how she had handled the situation. It looked like everyone would win in this situation. Those employees involved in job-shadowing would learn new skills, which would make more positions open to them. This would make her job of placing them in other areas much easier. Janet's problem was solved because she now had a pool of people to help out during summer vacations, and her staff were all being productive.

Four days ago, Janet had phoned again, "You know, Linda, I know that you were trying to be helpful when you made your suggestions about job-sharing and solicitation calls, but you have only created more problems for me. Some of the Fidelity staff think I am giving Stability employees training for a promotion. Since they still don't have their own jobs settled, a lot of them are getting upset. Why don't you people send someone down here to fix this situation? It isn't my responsibility."

LINDA TAKES ACTION

After the phone call, Linda immediately discussed the situation (and Janet's problems) with Fred Baines. Fred didn't reprimand her for her suggestions. However, he did indicate that these were the type of problems her training initiatives caused. If she had just got them in somewhere as she was supposed to, she wouldn't be in her current position. Linda and Fred agreed that someone needed to go to Serenity and counsel the employees. Linda had volunteered to go, since it was her suggestions that were being implemented at Serenity.

After calling Janet back to arrange a time, Linda phoned Serenity's branch manager, Preston Dunn. She spoke with Preston for several minutes about the problems the branch was facing. Preston commented that "Janet is highly stressed and tends to make mountains out of molehills." He did request that she still visit the branch, as he had two employees that Janet could not help. Their needs were beyond Janet's authority.

Marjorie Williams was a part-time teller who wanted full-time hours, and Edward Cheng was a loans officer looking for a promotion. Preston stated, "We don't want to lose Edward. He's an excellent employee. But, I think he is getting very frustrated and looking at other banks. Every time a position opens that he is interested in, all of our overruns have priority. He never has a chance. I have spoken with him many times, as has Janet, but I think he believes we are just making excuses not to promote him. Maybe if he heard the reasons from someone higher up, he would understand and stick it out for a bit." "Well," thought Linda, "I certainly have my work cut out for me."

After speaking with Preston, she made a courtesy call to the regional VP's office to make them aware of her visit. While she was talking to the general manager, another employee situation was mentioned. Apparently George Price, the former manager at Fidelity Trust, had been placed in the Stability branch as an assistant manager. He had been quite vocal about his discontent and was demanding an immediate placement as a manager in another city, or at least as assistant manager at a large branch in a major city. Linda had agreed to speak with George regarding his prospects and what type of position he desired.

Linda pulled off the highway into a small town to grab some lunch. She snatched her files off the front seat so she could review them while she ate. She wanted to familiarize herself again with the three employees. She had made excellent time so far and had about half an hour to review her materials.

George Price

After ordering a burger, she sat down in a corner of the restaurant. She ate quickly and opened George Price's file. George was in his late 50s and had moved up the ranks at Fidelity Trust. Most of the Fidelity Trust managers were being relocated to urban centres as commercial officers. However, George did not have any commercial experience. The Serenity community did not have a large business sector. Most of the businesses were family-run, and those requiring financing had gone to the two local banks.

Fidelity Trust's clients had been mainly retirees. They had significant savings, and branch operations had centred around investments. George's main function as manager had been to keep his customers happy. He had not been involved in the actual investment planning side, but rather maintaining customer relationships. As such, he had no education in the investment area. In fact, George's only education was a high school diploma. Fidelity Trust management had encouraged George to take courses, but George wasn't interested in going back to school. Linda found this odd. Apparently George had been having great difficulty lately talking with his customers. Even though he did not do hands-on investment advice, clients still asked him his opinion. He did not understand the new investment vehicles, such as mutual funds. He had commented to Stability management that his job was becoming more difficult because he knew less than his customers.

Linda couldn't understand why George wouldn't take courses in order to service his customers better. She shook her head as she skimmed over the file. "I don't know what to do about him," she thought. "He has no applicable skills and isn't willing to learn any." So far, Linda's only idea was to bring up the topic of early retirement. She knew she had to be careful, though. George was very well networked within the bank. She could not come across as pushing him into that decision, as it would be interpreted as a forced layoff. Linda closed the file, and hoped she would have better luck with Marjorie Williams.

Marjorie Williams

Marjorie was a part-time teller at the Stability branch. She had been working for Stability for more than 20 years and was consistently rated an above-average performer. This year, her youngest child had left home. In the past, she had worked part-time in order to fulfill her family commitments. Now that the kids were gone, she wanted to work full-time. Comments in Marjorie's past performance appraisals (PAs) stated that she was enthusiastic about her job and an excellent team player. Linda looked over the section in Marjorie's PA where she indicated her future career preferences. Linda sighed, "I can't do anything for her either. She doesn't want to do anything but be a teller and will not take a position in another city. Besides, I can't move her anyway until I place all of Fidelity's employees." Linda recalled from her last conversation with Janet that Marjorie was one of the employees doing job-shadowing. She hoped that Marjorie had developed an interest in an area other than teller. Linda thought she might be able to do something if Marjorie were interested in investments. That was an area where the Serenity branch might be able to use another full-time employee.

Edward Cheng

"Well," Linda said to herself, "here's hoping Edward is a bit easier." Edward grew up in Serenity, but had moved to Kitchener to go to Wilfrid Laurier University. While doing his business degree, he had had a co-op placement with Stability in customer service. Upon graduating, he had moved back to Serenity and got a job as a loans officer at the local Stability branch. His first six months with the branch were on a contract basis. Edward proved to be an excellent employee, however, and was offered a full-time position when his contract expired.

Linda reviewed Edward's file and noted that the regional VP's office had singled him out as having excellent future potential. In other words, they wanted to keep him with the bank. Linda wondered about the possibility of making an exception in Edward's case. Maybe something could be arranged with the regional VP that would allow him to be considered along with the redundant employees for upcoming positions.

LINDA'S DILEMMA

Linda got up from her table, put her coat on, and went out to her car. Back on the road, she thought about what she could do for these three employees. "I bet Marjorie would do well on our investment training program... and Edward would excel in the commercial training program. He would get a promotion and some excellent experience," she thought. Linda shook her head. "No use thinking about that," she muttered aloud. Fred had made it perfectly clear this morning that she was to find them a position and worry about the training later.

She decided not to worry about the three employees until after she had spoken with each. She would be in Serenity in another half hour, and she wanted to appear professional rather than frustrated. As she made the turnoff to the town, Linda wondered what she was doing in this job. "Why did they hire me? Anyone can shuffle people around." As she drove into Serenity, she noticed a small computer store on the corner. "Humph," she muttered, "maybe I should just phone VisionTech and see if I can get my old job back."

Exhibit 13.1

Partial Organizational Chart, Stability Bank

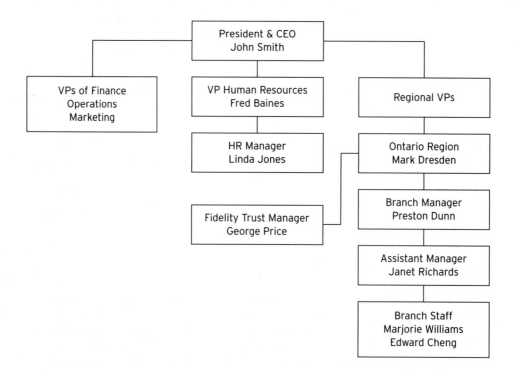

Who Will Benefit?
The Merging of Benefit Plans
at Lutherwood CODA

Tupper Cawsey

Eileen Polson

Eileen Polson paced the floor as she struggled with the dilemma of merging the benefit plans of the newly formed Lutherwood Community Opportunities Development Association (CODA). The merger was well underway; the new organization structure had been announced and the managers appointed. The next crucial step was to merge the human resources systems and, in particular, the benefits plans of the two organizations. Eileen knew that she had a complex task: She had to satisfy the employees of both organizations while developing plans that were fair and acceptable to the Boards of Directors of Lutherwood and CODA.[1] With the financial constraints faced by all social service agencies, she knew that any increase in costs would be difficult to sell to the newly merged Board.

---

[1] While the merger was well underway, the legalities of merger under Ontario law meant that the two Boards of Directors continued to operate separately. Joint meetings were held to ratify merger decisions.

BACKGROUND TO THE MERGER OF LUTHERWOOD AND CODA

Lutherwood and the Community Opportunities Development Agency (CODA) were social service agencies in the Kitchener-Waterloo-Cambridge area. In November 1996, the Boards of Lutherwood and CODA agreed to form a joint task force to determine the feasibility of merging the two organizations.

As a result of the discussions of the joint task force, a set of principles that would guide the merger were developed. The items relevant to HR are the following.

1. We commit to a merger in which planning and implementation will be marked by open communication, acting with integrity, and community participation.

2. We commit to a merger that will ensure the staff are provided with clear information and are treated with respect, sensitivity, and fairness ensuring that the current entitlements are not eroded.

3. We commit to a merger that will be seen as an opportunity to enhance staff opportunities and choices, to make jobs more manageable, and to better align responsibility with resources.

4. We commit to providing supports and fair compensation packages should there be staff adversely affected by the merger.

5. We commit to providing a compensation package that is within the top 25 percent of what our competitors are offering.[2]

The joint task force recommended that the merger proceed, and on June 25, 1997, the Boards of Directors voted to amalgamate. Rev. Dr. Dieter Kays, the CEO of Lutherwood, would become the CEO of the merged organization. Paul Born, founder and CEO of CODA, would remain with CODA until December 31, 1997. During that time, he would act as consultant to the merged organization, serve as leader for the new Project 2000 initiative,[3] but would otherwise withdraw from active participation in the activities of Lutherwood CODA.

During the fall of 1997, Dieter Kays designed an organizational structure for the merged organization and staffed the management positions. A senior management team of five plus the CEO was created by December 1997. (See Exhibit 14.1 for the new structure and the backgrounds of the senior management team.) Although this reorganization meant that senior positions were shuffled and that some senior managers were not included in the senior management team, the new team and structure appeared to be accepted by most in the organization. The merger was expected to become official in April 1998 under a new organizational name, Lutherwood Community Opportunities Development Association.

An employee survey of attitudes to the merger done in early 1998 showed that 24 percent of employees were concerned about losing the core values of each organization, and 23 percent were concerned about job losses. Some 39 percent stated that the greatest hope for the new organization was an improved organization, and 20 percent looked for job opportunities and the chance to develop new skills. The staff reported that they wanted more communication and that they were concerned about the realignment of programs and services

---

[2] Minutes of the Joint Task Force, January 1997.

[3] Project 2000 was an initiative to eliminate poverty in the Kitchener-Waterloo-Cambridge area by the year 2000. The slogan was "2000 families moved above the poverty line by the year 2000."

and the physical relocation of departments and people. They also wanted input into the organizational restructuring and into the development of HR policies and practices.

BACKGROUND TO THE LUTHERWOOD ORGANIZATION

Lutherwood was a non-profit service organization that provided a range of services to children and youth within the Waterloo, Wellington, and Grey-Bruce regions of Ontario. With six primary locations, the agency served over 3000 individuals annually through the residential and day treatment programs, assessment and counselling services, a youth employment and housing centre, and a number of other community-based prevention programs. It operated on an annualized budget of $4 million in 1995–1996 and had a staff complement of 80. The agency received funding from the Ontario Ministry of Community and Social Services, the Attorney General, the Ontario Training and Adjustment Board, the Lutherwood Child and Family Foundation, and a variety of other funders.

Lutherwood was founded in 1970 as a centennial project of the Lutheran Church, Canada. It had developed a reputation for its management systems, its innovative and entrepreneurial approaches, and its caring and professional services.

Lutherwood has been involved in the development of a retirement community called Luther Village on the Park in uptown Waterloo. The development, located on 5.7 ha (14 acres) of land, will eventually house over 700 residents and has a construction value of over $70 million. The site was purchased for $1.4 million. This meant that, at the time of the merger, the organization was heavily leveraged.

The net worth of Lutherwood and Lutherwood Child and Family Foundation is approximately $3.8 million. Over the last number of years, Lutherwood had made a strategic decision to diversify its funding and service mandates, making it less vulnerable to government funding cutbacks and increasing its ability to serve a wider range of clients.

Lutherwood's structure consisted of a Board of Governors who were ratified by the Lutheran Church-Canada East District Board of Directors. A four-member senior management group, headed by a chief executive officer, led the day-to-day operations. Various advisory boards and a parents' committee provided input into programming and policy directions. Lutherwood stated its purpose as "helping people reach their full potential" and expressed its core values as "individual worth, people development, collective responsibility, ability to shape the future, the power of faith, and acting with integrity and mutual respect."[4]

BACKGROUND TO THE CODA ORGANIZATION

CODA was a charitable organization that provided services in employment, self-employment, community development, and community enterprise to over 6000 people annually in the Waterloo, Perth, and Wellington regions of Ontario. CODA had offices in Cambridge and Kitchener and had satellite locations in over 20 neighbourhoods, schools, and townships.

CODA was founded in 1984 by the local labour council and various city, church, and community organizations to deal with the many workers unemployed during the recession of the early 1980s. The organization grew into a multi-regional community economic

---

[4] Lutherwood Strategic Plan, 1995.

development agency with 40 staff, 250 volunteers, and more than 300 donors annually. In recent years CODA had helped nearly 5000 people find jobs, 2000 people upgrade skills, and 1000 people start new businesses.

CODA's budget for fiscal 1996 was just over $3 million. CODA received no core funding but instead relied on contracts, many of which were multi-year. CODA was very skilled at sourcing and bidding on public and private contracts consistent with its mission. CODA owned or managed $800 000 in loan funds and $500 000 in designated reserves. The organization was debt-free.

CODA's vision was "people creating opportunities." Its core values were stated as "access to opportunity, innovation and entrepreneurship, community-based/participant-centred, economic self-reliance, value of partnership, and value of life experience." CODA was managed by a Board of Directors, numerous technical advisory boards, and a three-member management team.

HUMAN RESOURCES AT LUTHERWOOD AND CODA

On March 18, 1997, the joint task force of the two Boards of Directors approved the hiring of a human resources manager for the two organizations. As well, the Boards approved a decision to begin aligning the human resource policies of the two organizations.

Eileen Polson joined Lutherwood on April 1, 1997. Prior to her hiring, human resources had been handled by a part-time HR practitioner, although many of the routine responsibilities had fallen to line managers. This part-time practitioner had come to be seen by management as an advocate for staff.

CODA did not employ any human resource professionals. In fact, part of the reason for the merger was CODA's need to develop management systems and Lutherwood's ability to provide such systems. CODA did have a human resource committee made up of management and elected staff representatives. This committee saw itself as providing advice and commentary on human resource policies at CODA. The committee believed that CODA's management, and Paul Born in particular, had accepted its advice.

During the fall of 1997, Eileen met with staff groups to explain and discuss her HR work plan for the next year. She also wanted to meet as many people as possible to understand the HR issues and approach in each organization. She learned, for example, that at Lutherwood salaries were viewed as private information. When jobs were posted, the job grade was known but not the salary range. At CODA, the salary grid was public.[5]

Eileen also wanted to ensure staff input into her work plan. Without a full-time HR person at Lutherwood, revisions to many human resource management systems had been deferred. So in addition to the integration of benefit, salary, and pension plans as a result of the merger, Eileen's work plan included planning for a performance management system, the implementation of a new salary grid/compensation scheme, and changes to the health-and-safety programs.

Eileen's day-to-day activities took considerable time. Managers of both organizations were delighted to have a resource person to contact for expert advice. Eileen found herself responding to questions regarding recruiting procedures, performance issues, and, in one particularly difficult situation, allegations of misconduct against a manager. As well dur-

---

[5] Source: Company documents.

ing this period, one senior manager was terminated, and the terms of this dismissal had to be negotiated, working with lawyers and senior management.

BENEFITS AT LUTHERWOOD AND AT CODA

Both Lutherwood and CODA had extensive benefits plans. Vacations, paid time off, pensions, insurance benefits, sick leave, group life insurance, accidental death and dismemberment (AD&D) benefits, disability benefits, extended health benefits, and dental benefits were some of the benefits provided.

Vacation Policies and Options

Vacation benefits differed considerably for the employees of the two organizations. As well, CODA supervisors could accumulate overtime up to a maximum of 15 hours carried forward to the next month, while Lutherwood supervisors received one week of vacation in lieu of paid overtime, or "comp time," as it was known.

The current policy for Lutherwood for employees was as follows:

Years of Service	Employees	Supervisors and Designated Positions
1-2	2 weeks/10 days	4 weeks/20 days
3-10	3 weeks/15 days	4 weeks/20 days
11-22	4 weeks/20 days	5 weeks/25 days
23+	5 weeks/25 days	6 weeks/30 days

Lutherwood employees received an extra week of vacation on the 10th, 15th, and 20th anniversary of service.

The current vacation policy for CODA was as follows:

Years of Service	All Employees
1-5 years	15 days
6-10 years	20 days
11+ years	20 days plus 1 day for each year of service to a maximum of 30 days

The cost of the current Lutherwood vacation plan was $168 599, and the current CODA plan cost $90 815 for a combined cost of $259 414.

Eileen was concerned about the differences between the vacation policies of the two organizations. CODA's vacation policy was more generous than Lutherwood's. To understand the impact of changing the policies, Eileen had asked finance to cost out several alternatives. These are shown as Exhibit 14.2.

Eileen wasn't certain which of the options would be preferable. She felt staff should receive enough time to rejuvenate themselves each year as many of the jobs were very stressful. As well, she was concerned about the costs for the children's mental health services area as these staff had to be replaced when they were on vacation. Thus, any increase in vacation entitlement was very expensive for this department.

Additional Paid Time Off

Both organizations provided for a "floater" holiday—Lutherwood's plan allowed the day to be taken at any time; CODA set the day during the Christmas period. Lutherwood also provided two days per annum for family illness (no carry-over), while CODA provided three days for serious household or domestic emergencies. Both organizations provided three days' bereavement leave for immediate family, and Lutherwood added a day if out-of-province travel was necessary. Lutherwood also gave one day's bereavement leave for grandparents, grandchildren, and in-laws.

Lutherwood provided three days for the birth or adoption of a child while CODA provided five days. CODA also provided two days for one's own marriage; one day for the marriage of a child, sibling, or parent; and one day per move (two days per year maximum).

Pension Policies and Options

CODA provided 5 percent of the salary to employees after completion of the first year of employment to be used for RRSP investments. No documentation was required, and as a result, the 5 percent became taxable.[6] Lutherwood's pension plan provided an employer contribution of 5 to 9 percent of salary (based on years of service) plus a 3 percent employee contribution to a defined contribution plan.[7] Of course, the costs of these plans would increase with any increases to salaries. Because of legal limitations, Eileen was restricted in exactly what she could change in the pension plans. Several options are outlined in Exhibit 14.3.

CODA's current pension costs were $62 238, and Lutherwood's were $127 543.

Employee Benefits Survey at Lutherwood and CODA

With the help of Susan Healey of Wright Mogg and Associates (a benefits consultant organization), Eileen had conducted a survey of employees of both organizations to better understand the benefits needs of employees. Exhibits 14.4 and 14.5 provide the responses to the questionnaire.

CODA employees included several written comments on the inadequacy of the vision-care plan, the lack of an employee assistance plan (EAP), and a desire to see improvements to the dental plan. One person wished an increase in pay in lieu of benefits. Several Lutherwood employees wished to have better dental coverage for such things as crowns and bridges. As well, two individuals mentioned the need for cohabiting couples or same-sex couples to be covered. Vision care was considered inadequate by four Lutherwood staff.

Insurance Benefits and Sick Leave

Eileen surveyed other children's mental health facilities and local hospitals to compare Lutherwood's insurance benefit plans. She noted that Lutherwood's was as good as or bet-

---

[6] Eileen had anecdotal evidence that not everyone invested the money. While some CODA staff were diligent about investing the money, others were spending it. In effect, the 5 percent became a salary bonus.

[7] While there are many types of pension plans, two common ones are defined: contribution and defined benefit plans. Defined contribution plans specify the amount that would be put into the plan yearly. The benefit would be determined at retirement. Defined benefit plans, on the other hand, specify the amount of the benefit on retirement.

ter than others. A notable exception was a pension plan that Lutherwood did not pay for but that was often co-paid or employer-paid in other organizations. (Exhibit 14.6 shows the benefits survey results.)

Eileen organized her review of Lutherwood and CODA's insurance benefit plans by creating a comparison table (see Exhibit 14.7). Lutherwood's plan was employer-paid. Its permanent employees were eligible for benefits if they worked 22.5 hours per week or more. CODA employees had to be full-time and permanent to participate in its plan. CODA paid all premiums except for long-term disability (LTD) which was employee-paid. Both organizations required a waiting period of three months for membership. The LTD plans for each organization were very different.

Eileen considered several options before deciding on what to recommend to the Board regarding the pension plans. One option was to choose the best from both plans and provide that benefit to employees. A second option was to choose the lowest-cost option, attractive because of the organization's financial pressures. Eileen chose a middle path, one that she believed to be fair to all employees but that would not create major financial hardship for the organization. Her proposed options are shown in Exhibit 14.7.

As she paced the floor, she worried about her LTD suggestion. Her instinct had been to ask Lutherwood employees to pick up the costs of this program. This was the trend in benefits in most organizations today. LTD costs were projected to rise significantly over the next few years. At the same time, she was concerned that this proposal would not be acceptable to Lutherwood staff as it would be a noticeable monthly deduction from their paycheques.

The costs of the current plans and recommended plan are shown as Exhibit 14.8.

EILEEN'S DILEMMA

Eileen's immediate concern was the senior manager's meeting next week. She had to present recommendations on the new benefit plans to the CEO and her fellow senior managers. While she had tentatively decided on a proposed benefits package, she had to decide how to handle LTD policies. Costs were going to be a major concern, both to senior management and to the new Board, when it was appointed.

Approval by the senior management group was only the first stage. The plans had to be acceptable to employees, and Eileen wondered how to ensure that. Should she take them to the Board before she discussed them with employees? This risked having the plans in place and then having to go back to the Board for changes. However, releasing the details to employees prior to Board approval could alienate the Board and be seen as trivializing its role. This was a particular concern, as Eileen was new and did not know the Board well.

Eileen knew that the new Board would examine her proposals closely. One member was CEO of a local insurance company, and he would have in-depth knowledge of options and costs. Another had been an accountant. Others had social work backgrounds and were familiar with the nature of children's aid societies and the pressures employees faced while working in them.

As one senior manager remarked, "If you get this wrong, we could screw up the whole organization!" While Eileen was confident that the process used was a good one, she was uncertain how employees would react when they saw her proposals.

Finally, she forced herself to sit down and sort out the options. What exactly should she take to senior management? How should she present it?

Exhibit 14.1

Partial Organizational Structure, Lutherwood CODA November 1997

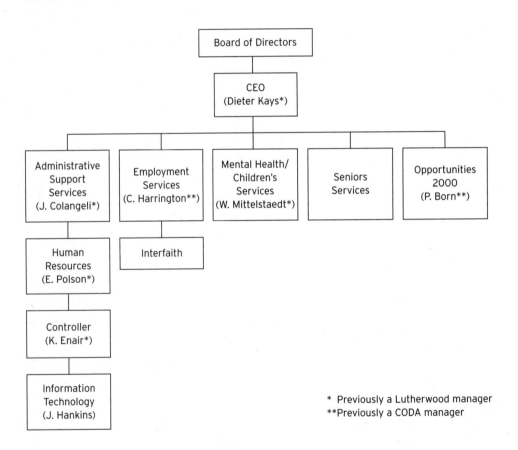

* Previously a Lutherwood manager
**Previously a CODA manager

Exhibit 14.2
Options for Modifying Vacation Entitlements and the Costs of Each

Options	Regular Staff		Supervisory Staff and Designated Positions		Costs
1. Move all Lutherwood staff to CODA vacation policy and keep supervisory differential	1-5 years 6-10 years 11+ years	15 days 20 days Add 1 day per year to a max of 30	1-5 years 6-10 years 11+ years	20 days 25 days Add 1 day per year to a max of 35	$290 336
2. Move all CODA staff to Lutherwood vacation policy, red circle those disadvantaged	1-2 years 3-10 years 11-22 years 23+ years	10 days 15 days 20 days 30 days	1-10 years 11-22 years 23 + years	20 days 25 days 25 days	$264 326
3. Create a new vacation policy while red circling those disadvantaged	1-2 years 3-5 years 6-15 years 16-29 years 30+ years	10 days 15 days 20 days 25 days 30 days	1-5 years 6-15 years 16-29 years 30+ years	20 days 25 days 30 days 35 days	$286 591
4. Create a new vacation policy while red circling those disadvantaged	1-2 years 3-10 years 11-20 years 20+ years	10 days 15 days 20 days 25 days	1-5 years 6-15 years 16+ years	20 days 25 days 30 days	$274 712
5. Create a new vacation policy while red circling those disadvantaged	0-8 years 8-15 years 16+ years	15 days 20 days 25 days	0-5 years 6-15 years 16+ years	20 days 25 days 30 days	$286 499
6. Create a new vacation policy while red circling those disadvantaged	0-10 years 11-15 years 16+ years	15 days 20 days 25 days	0-5 years 6-15 years 16+ years	20 days 25 days 30 days	$280 772

Exhibit 14.3

Pension Plan Options and Their Costs

Options	Details of Plan	Costs
Option 1	Organization contributes 5% of salary. Employee contributes 3% of salary. Staff currently receiving greater than 5% would be reduced to 5%. Enrolment is mandatory. Enrolment is after 6 months of service and includes part-time staff working more than 22.5 hours per week.	$185 820
Option 2	Organization contributes 5% (6 months service to 5 years), 6% (5-10 years service), 7% (10-15 years service), 8% (15-20 years service), 9% (20 + years service). Employee contributes 3%. Grandfather current employees and use Lutherwood's current plan for CODA and employees.	$214 892 at March 31. 1998 $220 477 at March 31, 1999 (changes due to increased years of service)
Option 3	Continue Lutherwood plan. CODA staff have the option of continuing with their current plan (5% RRSP contributions) or joining the Lutherwood plan (and carry forward years of service). If CODA staff waive the Lutherwood plan, costs would be slightly less. New employees would be capped at	$214 892 at March 31, 1998 $220 477 at March 31, 1999 (changes due to increased years of service only)

Exhibit 14.4

CODA Employee Responses to the Survey on Benefits

Question Asked	Yes	No	Survey Responses (28 of 38 surveys returned)				
			Very Important	Important	Not So Important	Not Important
1. How important to you is the group life insurance benefit?	–	–	13	9	4	2
2. How important to you is the AD&D benefit?	–	–	12	10	4	2
3. How important is it that AD&D benefit be obtained on a voluntary basis?	–	–	3	12	3	8
4. Do you belong to the optional life insurance plan?	5	22	–	–	–	–
4a. How important is the optional life insurance plan?	–	–	6	7	6	7
5. How important is the dependent life insurance benefit?	–	–	11	7	5	5
6. Is the level of coverage sufficient under the short-term disability plan?	10	15	–	–	–	–
6a. How important is the short-term disability plan?	–	–	21	6	1	–
7. Is the level of coverage sufficient under the long-term disability plan?	10	18	–	–	–	–
7a. How important is the long-term disability plan?	–	–	24	4	–	–
8. How important is the deductive for extended health care?	–	–	11	10	3	–
9. How important is the 100% reimbursement for extended health care?	–	–	19	6	1	–
10. How important to you is the prescription drug benefit?	–	–	22	4	1	–
11. How important to you is the paramedical services benefit?	–	–	15	8	4	–
12. How important to you is the vision care benefit?	–	–	16	8	1	1

Exhibit 14.4 (continued)

Question Asked	Yes	No	Very Important	Important	Not So Important	Not Important
13. How important to you is the travel assistance benefit?	–	–	10	11	4	2
14. How important to you is the semi-private hospital benefit?	–	–	11	8	5	3
15. How important to you is the 9-month recall examination?	–	–	9	10	2	1
16. How important to you is the RRSP plan?	–	–	27	1	–	–
17. Have you invested 5% into the RRSP plan?	21	3	–	–	–	–
18. Would you be interested in joining a pension plan with a 3% mandatory contribution from you and the organization?	12	10	–	–	–	–
19. How satisfied are you with your current benefits plan?	–	–	9	16	2	1
20. Would an EAP program be helpful to employees?	21	3	–	–	–	–

How important are the benefits? 1 = most important; 6 = least important

Benefit	1	2	3	4	5	6
Extended Health Care	11	4	3	2	1	–
Group RRSP	3	1	1	4	5	7
Dental	1	7	4	4	3	2
Long-Term Disability	4	6	3	5	1	2
Short-Term Disability	2	2	6	5	4	2
Life Insurance	–	1	4	3	6	7

Exhibit 14.5

Lutherwood Employee Responses to the Survey on Benefits

Question Asked	Survey Responses (41 of 61 surveys returned)					
	Yes	No	Very Important	Important	Not So Important	Not Important
1. How important to you is the group life insurance benefit?	–	–	27	12	1	1
2. How important to you is the AD&D benefit?	–	–	26	11	3	–
3. How important is it that AD&D benefit be obtained on a voluntary basis?	–	–	10	13	12	5
4. Do you belong to the optional life insurance plan?	4	31	–	–	–	–
4a. How important is the optional life insurance plan?	–	–	8	13	15	2
5. Is the level of coverage sufficient under the short-term disability plan?	25	12	–	–	–	–
5a. How important is the short-term disability plan?	–	–	33	7	–	–
6. Is the level of coverage sufficient under the long-term disability plan?	22	15	–	–	–	–
6a. How important is the long-term disability plan?	–	–	32	6	1	–
7. How important is the deductible for extended health care?	–	–	30	6	4	1
8. How important is the semi-private hospital benefit?	–	–	19	14	5	3
9. How important to you is the prescription drug benefit?	–	–	37	2	1	–
10. How important to you is the paramedical services benefit?	–	–	24	15	2	–

Exhibit 14.5 (continued)

Question Asked	Yes	No	Very Important	Important	Not So Important	Not Important
Survey Responses (41 of 61 surveys returned)						
11. How important to you is the vision care benefit?	–	–	30	10	–	–
12. How important to you is the travel assistance benefit?	–	–	20	11	7	2
13. How important to you is the no deductible for dental care?	–	–	30	6	2	1
14. How important to you is the 6-month recall examination?	–	–	25	7	5	2
15. How important to you is the orthodontics services benefit?	–	–	21	6	8	3
16. How important to you is the current pension plan?	–	–	37	1	1	–
17. Are you satisfied with the current EAP program?	–	–	21	7	–	1
18. How satisfied are you with your current benefits plan?	–	–	28	10	1	–

How important are the benefits? 1 = most important; 6 = least important

Benefit	1	2	3	4	5	6
Extended Health Care	15	11	4	4	2	–
Pension	15	6	9	3	1	2
Dental	4	11	10	3	7	1
Long-Term Disability	1	4	4	10	10	7
Short-Term Disability	1	2	4	8	13	8
Life Insurance	–	2	5	8	3	18

Exhibit 14.6

A Comparison of Benefits: Lutherwood vs. Other Organizations

Organization	Group Life	AD&D	ST Disability	LT Disability	Ext. Health	Dental	Pension	Other
Luther	Yes 0 EE 100 ER	Yes 0 EE 100 ER	Yes 0 EE 100 ER	Yes 0 EE 100 ER	Yes 0 EE 100 ER	Yes 0 EE 100 ER	Yes 3–8% EE 0% ER	EAP 50 EE 50 ER
Org. 1	Yes 0 EE 100 ER	Yes 0 EE 100 ER	Sick Days 0 EE 100 ER	Mgmt only 0 EE 100 ER	Yes 20 EE 80 ER	Yes 20 EE 80 ER	RRSP 3% EE 3% ER	–
Org. 2	Yes 0 EE 100 ER	No	Yes 0 EE 100 ER	Yes 100 EE 0 ER	Yes 20 EE 80 ER	Yes 20 EE 80 ER	Yes 3–5% EE 3–9% ER	–
Org. 3	Yes 0 EE 100 ER	Yes 100 EE 0 ER	Sick Days	Yes 100 EE 0 ER	Yes 0 EE 100 ER	Yes 10 EE 90 ER	Yes 50 EE 50 ER	–
Org. 4	Yes 0 EE 100 ER	No	Yes 0 EE 100 ER	Yes 100 EE 0 ER	Yes 0 EE 100 ER	Yes 0 EE 100 ER	Yes 6–7% EE 6–7% ER	EAP 100 EE
Org. 5	Yes 0 EE 100 ER	Yes 0 EE 100 ER	No	Yes 0 EE 100 ER	Yes 0 EE 100 ER	Yes 0 EE 100 ER	Yes 0 EE 100 ER	–
Hosp. 1	Yes 0 EE 100 ER	Yes 0 EE 100 ER	Yes 0 EE 100 ER	Yes 25 EE 75 ER	Yes 25 EE 75 ER	Yes 25 EE 75 ER	Yes 4–6% EE match ER	–
Hosp. 2	Yes 0 EE 100 ER	Yes 0 EE 100 ER	Yes 0 EE 100 ER	Yes 0 EE 100 ER	Yes 0 EE 100 ER	Yes 0 EE 100 ER	Yes 5–8% EE	–

Luther = Lutherwood; Org. = Children's Aid Organizations; Hosp. = Hospitals; EE = employee contribution; ER = employer contribution

Exhibit 14.7

A Comparison of Lutherwood and CODA Benefit Plans

Benefit Item	Pre-merger Lutherwood	Pre-merger CODA	Proposed Merged Organization
Life	1 x annual earnings to $250 000	Flat $25 000	1 x annual earnings to $250 000
AD&D	1 x annual earnings to $250 000	Flat $25 000	1 x annual earnings to $250 000
Dependant Life	N/A	$10 000 spouse, $5000 for each child	$10 000 spouse, $5000 for each child
Optional Life	Units of $10 000 to max $250 000 paid by employee, coverage terminates at age 65	Units of $25 000 to max $200 000 paid by employee, coverage terminates at age 70	Units of $10 000 to max $250 000 paid by employee, coverage terminates at age 65
Sick Leave	1.5 days/month to 120-day maximum	1 day/month to 24-day maximum	1.5 days/month to 40-day maximum
Self-Insured Weekly Indemnity	$66^{2/3}$% of earnings to $500/week	Unemployment Insurance Commission	$66^{2/3}$% of earnings to $500/week
LTD	$66^{2/3}$% of earnings to $8000/month (non-evidence max $7500); $66^{2/3}$% of earnings to $500/week, 31-week qualifying period; payment to age 65; 2-year own occupation definition of disability; primary offsets–100% employer paid; 3% COLA	$66^{2/3}$% of earnings to $4800/month (non-evidence max $2500); 17-week qualifying period; payment to age 65; 2-year own occupation definition of disability; primary offsets–100% employee paid, no COLA	60% of earnings to $8000/month (evidence is not required); 31-week qualifying period; payment to age 65; 2-year own occupation definition of disability; primary offsets–100% employee paid; no COLA

Health	Drugs/Supplementary Health Care: no deductible; 80% of 1st $5000 of expenses, 100% thereafter; Vision (max $125 every 2 years); Semi-private hospital; out-of-country—nil deductible, 100% reimbursement Drug definition includes over-the-counter	Drugs/Supplementary Health Care: deductible—$25 single and $50 family per year; Vision (max $100 every 2 years); out-of-country; 100% reimbursement Drug definition excludes over-the-counter	Pay direct drugs card/Supplementary Health Care: 80% of 1st $5000 of expenses, 100% thereafter; Vision (max $150 every 2 years); Semi-private hospital; out-of-country—nil deductible, 100% reimbursement Drug definition excludes over-the-counter
Dental	Basic: nil deductible, 100% reimbursement, unlimited maximum Orthodontic (children only): nil deductible, 50% reimbursement, $1500 lifetime maximum Current fee guide 6-month recall package	Basic: $25 single, $50 family deductible, 80% reimbursement, annual maximum of $1500 per person Current fee guide 9-month recall package	Basic: nil deductible, 80% reimbursement, unlimited maximum Orthodontic (children only): nil deductible, 50% reimbursement, $1500 lifetime maximum Current fee guide 6-month recall package

Note:

Monthly cost of LTD benefit per employee earning:

	CODA	Lutherwood
$30 000	$25.50	$34.35
$40 000	$34.00	$45.80
$50 000	$42.50	$57.25

Exhibit 14.8

A Comparison of the Costs of Lutherwood and CODA Benefit Plans

Benefit	Current Cost		Proposed Cost	
	Lutherwood Annual	CODA Annual	Lutherwood Annual	CODA Annual
Life	$ 5 220	$ 2 208	$ 5 112	$ 3 576
AD&D	792	480	792	480
Dependant Life	nil	1 128	1 704	1,200
LTD*	41 016	11 388	32 724	13 980
Health	45 720	34 080	42 900	29 844
Dental	29 532	15 396	29 244	18 084
Total	$122 280	$64 680	$112 476	$67 164
Lutherwood + CODA costs		$186 960		$179 640

* Note that LTD costs for CODA are paid for by the employees.

After the Merger–Lutherwood CODA's New Compensation Policy

Tupper Cawsey

Francine Schlosser

Eileen Polson knew when she arrived at Lutherwood that her job would be exciting and challenging, and it certainly had been. First there was the start-up phase—getting into and knowing the organization and the players. Then there was the merger between Lutherwood and the Community Development Opportunities Association (CODA) and the role for human resources in helping that merger. Now, as a result of the merger, the compensation systems of the two organizations needed to be unified. While some jobs were unique to either Lutherwood or CODA, other positions were very similar—but paid differently. And she knew that both Dieter Kays, the CEO of Lutherwood CODA, and the Board wanted to move to an incentive or pay-for-performance model of compensation. It was not clear to her what her priorities should be and how she should balance the need for equity within the organization, the demands the organization was facing to match market salaries, and the desire to introduce performance incentives.

Eileen had just received the consultant's proposal for the new Lutherwood CODA compensation package. Should she accept it as is or would she have to change parts or all of it?

LUTHERWOOD CODA

Lutherwood Community Opportunities Development Association was one of the largest non-governmental human service agencies in Waterloo Region, Ontario. It served over 10 000 individuals and families each year through 20 programs in mental health treatment, employment and self-employment training and support, supported housing, and services for youth, family, seniors, and new Canadians. With over 130 staff, a budget of $8 million annually (see Exhibit 15.1 for income statements), and seven offices in Guelph, Cambridge, Kitchener, and Waterloo, Lutherwood CODA was committed to "help someone else build a new life and a better future."[1]

BACKGROUND TO THE MERGER OF LUTHERWOOD AND CODA

In November 1996, the Boards of Lutherwood and CODA formed a joint task force to determine the feasibility of merging their organizations. The rationale for the merger was twofold: Lutherwood would provide administrative systems support (which CODA did not have), and there would be synergies in the employment services area.

As a result of the discussions of the joint task force, a set of principles that would guide the merger were developed. The items relevant to HR were:

1. We commit to a merger in which planning and implementation will be marked by open communication, acting with integrity, and community participation.

2. We commit to a merger that will ensure staff are provided with clear information and are treated with respect, sensitivity, and fairness, ensuring that the current entitlements are not eroded.

3. We commit to a merger that will be seen as an opportunity to enhance staff opportunities and choices, to make jobs more manageable, and to better align responsibility with resources.

4. We commit to providing supports and fair compensation packages should there be staff adversely affected by the merger.

5. We commit to providing a compensation package that is within the top 25 percent of what our competitors are offering.[2]

The joint task force recommended that the merger proceed and on June 25, 1997, the Boards of Directors voted to amalgamate. Rev. Dr. Dieter Kays, the CEO of Lutherwood, would become the CEO of the merged organization. Paul Born, founder and CEO of CODA, would remain with CODA until December 31, 1997. During that time, he would act as consultant to the merged organization and serve as leader for the new Project 2000 initiative[3] but would otherwise withdraw from active participation in the activities of Lutherwood CODA.

---

[1] Extracted from 1998/99 organizational document : Lutherwood Child and Family Foundation, "Building Better Futures."

[2] Minutes of the Joint Task Force, January 1997.

[3] Project 2000 was an initiative to eliminate poverty in the Kitchener-Waterloo-Cambridge area by the year 2000. The slogan was "2000 families moved above the poverty line by the year 2000."

During the fall of 1997, Dieter Kays designed an organizational structure for the merged organization and staffed the management positions. A senior management team of five plus the CEO was created by December 1997. (See Exhibit 15.2 for the new structure.) Although this reorganization meant that senior positions were shuffled and that some senior managers were not included in the senior management team, the new team and structure appeared to be accepted by most in the organization.

On April 1, 1998, the merger was finalized under a new organizational name, Lutherwood Community Opportunities Development Association (Lutherwood CODA).

An employee survey of attitudes to the merger done in early 1998 showed that 24% of employees were concerned about losing the core values of each organization, and 23% were concerned about job losses. Some 39% stated that the greatest hope for the new organization was an improved organization, and 20% looked for job opportunities and the chance to develop new skills. Staff reported that they wanted more communication and that they were concerned about the realignment of programs and services and the physical relocation of departments and people. They also wanted input into the organizational restructuring and into the development of HR policies and practices. Naturally, there was concern over the consequences of the merger—would there be winners and losers as a result?

HUMAN RESOURCES AT LUTHERWOOD AND CODA

On March 18, 1997, the joint task force of the two Boards of Directors approved the hiring of a human resources manager for the two organizations. As well, they approved a decision to begin aligning the human resource policies of the two organizations.

Eileen Polson joined Lutherwood on April 1, 1997. Prior to her hiring, human resources had been handled by a part-time HR practitioner, although many of the routine responsibilities fell to line managers. This part-time practitioner had come to be seen by management as an advocate for staff.

CODA did not employ any human resources professionals. In fact, part of the reason for the merger was CODA's need to develop management systems and Lutherwood's ability to provide such systems. CODA did have a human resources committee made up of management and elected staff representatives. This committee saw itself as providing advice and commentary on human resources policies at CODA. The committee believed that CODA's management, and Paul Born in particular, had accepted its advice.

During the fall of 1997, Eileen met with staff groups to explain and discuss her HR work plan for the next year. She also wanted to meet as many people as possible to understand the HR issues and approach in each organization. She learned, for example, that at Lutherwood, salaries were viewed as private information. When jobs were posted, the job grade was known but not the salary range. At CODA the salary grid was public.[4]

During 1998, Eileen had devoted much of her energy to merging the benefits packages of the two organizations. Eileen had been successful, she believed, in developing a strong benefits package for the new organization and in following the principles articulated by the joint task force. She and the management team had held many meetings with groups of employees, first to gather input on what was critical in the benefits packages, and then to gain

---

[4] Source: Company documents.

acceptance of the proposals. The issue was a complex one since the new plan had all employees pay for their own long-term disability benefits. This was expensive for employees from the Lutherwood side of the organization, as it led to an increase in benefits costs to them of $30 to $60 per month (depending on their salary). Nevertheless, Eileen believed that these changes were accepted by the employees because she was able to provide positive comparisons with other community service organizations. These comparisons showed that it was standard for individuals to pay for long-term disability. The other significant change in the benefits package was the provision of a pension plan for the CODA employees. Previously, CODA employees had received a "bonus" of 5 percent to be used for RRSP contributions.

For 1999, Eileen's objective was to combine the two compensation systems.

COMPENSATION POLICIES AT LUTHERWOOD AND CODA

Both Lutherwood and CODA had relied on a point factor system to establish salary ranges. (See Exhibit 15.3 for a description of a point factor system.)

Lutherwood relied on the "Job Chart System" developed by Justin White at Pannell Kerr Forster Consulting Inc. It considered four factors in a job: skill, effort, working conditions, and responsibility. For the first three, each job was rated on the mental and physical requirements. For responsibility, jobs were rated on the impact of the job and the type of supervision or management involved. Each job was rated by assigning points to each factor and summing the points for the job. The possible job scores ranged from 159 to 4140. These points were then subdivided into 12 grades. For example, job grade 1 included all jobs with 225 to 323 points; job grade 2 included jobs with points from 324 to 388, and so on.

At Lutherwood, there would be four, five, or six steps within each grade. Thus, a person joining Lutherwood might begin in job grade 5 (the classification for that job), step 1. Each year, that person would progress to the next step until he or she reached the highest step in the grid. (See Exhibit 15.4 for the pre-merger salary grid and Exhibit 15.5 for Lutherwood grades and salaries prior to the merger.[5])

CODA had 11 job grades (see Exhibit 15.6 for CODA's pre-merger salary grid and Exhibit 15.7 for CODA grades and salaries prior to the merger). Within each job grade, CODA had 13 steps. Within the job grade, you were assigned a step level based on: the direct experience you had with the job, your education or indirect experience with the job, meritorious performance in the job, and market conditions which called for higher salaries. In practice, steps 10 to 13 were seldom if ever used.

In many ways, the jobs at CODA were unusual. For a social service organization, CODA operated much like a for-profit organization. Many of the employment services contracts resulted in surplus funds that could be retained in the organization, unlike most of Lutherwood's. Many of the positions were very close to the job market, and this led to a heightened awareness of market forces by CODA employees.

When Eileen examined the types of activities of the two organizations, she noted that in both organizations the employment counsellor's role had people doing similar work. In Lutherwood, people in those jobs were classified in grade 4 and earned between $29 000 and $33 000. In CODA, those jobs had four separate grade classifications and could earn between $24 500 and $44 000. Similarly, rates of pay for administrative assistants in

---

CODA ($18 300 to $31 000) appeared different from Lutherwood's grades 1 to 3 positions ($24 300 to $30 700).

Eileen asked Stratford International Management Consulting and Advisory Services to compare the two job evaluation systems. Each system was reviewed for comprehensiveness and compared with other point factors. The consultants recommended that Lutherwood CODA adopt the "Job Chart System." In doing this they recognized that the CODA staff might need to be convinced that the Job Chart System was fair and valid. As well, the Stratford group pointed out that the Job Chart System was heavily weighted towards the mental aspects of work and that there was no consideration for education or experience.

As a result of this comparison, Eileen convinced the management committee to implement the Job Chart System for all jobs in the newly merged organization. The Lutherwood system was chosen because of its ability to classify any type of position. This was important for the organization because it was continually adding new services and divisions, such as Luther Village, a part of seniors services. As well, Eileen hired job chart consultants to help implement the new system. Jobs that overlapped within the two systems and jobs that had not been evaluated under the Job Chart System were targeted for evaluation. This included all positions within employment development services (EDS), Opportunities 2000, and Interfaith.

In July 1998, Eileen notified all staff that the jobs mentioned above would be graded to determine their relative worth. She asked staff to complete a detailed questionnaire outlining the tasks involved in the job and the skill, effort, responsibility, and working conditions of the job. During that July and August, Eileen, Dieter Kays, and the evaluation consultant met with groups of employees, handed out the questionnaire, and answered employees' questions. The questionnaires were to be filled out and returned to human resources, which forwarded them to the consultant. The task lists were sent back and forth between the consultant, human resources, the managers, and the employees to ensure the jobs were described accurately before final review and then signed off by everyone involved.

In August, Eileen appointed a job-grading committee consisting of the chief administrative officer of LCODA, a program coordinator from CODA, a nurse from children's services, an employment counsellor from Lutherwood, a supervisor from day treatment/children's services, and Eileen. The committee was chaired by Eileen. Her intent was to ensure that the committee would be perceived as fair and unbiased.

During the late fall of 1998, Eileen held four focus groups (representing LCODA's staff) to gain feedback on compensation issues and the job evaluation process. Eileen ensured that the focus groups were balanced for job type, length of service, gender, and job level. As well, she ensured that representatives from the old CODA human resource committee were represented.

The feedback from these groups suggested that employees were concerned about the competitiveness of salaries between Lutherwood CODA and other organizations. Groups were split as to whether the organization should pay for seniority or performance, but there seemed to be general acceptance of a system that valued both. Previously, Lutherwood had had a bonus system that was seen as being too subjective. In general, the feedback suggested that performance evaluation should be tied to the job description, but employees were concerned about including work that is difficult to quantify or that supervisors did not observe.

In November 1998, Eileen also identified competitors providing similar services within the region and, with the help of the consultants, did a salary survey for key jobs at Lutherwood CODA. Exhibit 15.8 shows the results of this survey.

THE NEW COMPENSATION PLAN

Throughout the winter, Eileen and the consultants worked to develop the new salary grid. As she worked, Eileen hoped that the grid would adequately address the conflicts between employment counsellors and administrative assistants, in particular.

Eileen considered a variety of options for developing pay ranges. A straightforward approach would be to just pay for performance. Each person would receive one of three pay levels based on acceptable performance, good performance, or exceptional performance. Each level would differ by $5000 to $8000.

A second approach would be to have steps for each job classification. Individuals would progress a step each year until the top step was reached. A modification of this would be to have a step progression to the job rate (often the mid-point of the pay range) and then either an annual bonus based on performance or a performance step with a significant pay increase attached.

A third approach would be to have step progressions to the job rate with the possibility of increases beyond the job rate based on seniority or performance.

The consultants developed a proposed compensation system based on a step model, allowing the employee to move to the top of the range depending on experience and satisfactory performance. Each grade would have four, five, six, or seven steps. At the top of the range, they could receive a bonus based on measurable, value-added activities for the year. (See Exhibit 15.9 for the proposed scheme.) The consultants suggested that the bonuses for front-line staff could be up to 3.5 percent, for management up to 5 percent, and for senior management up to 7 percent.

Eileen was concerned because the proposals meant that about 25 people were now being paid more than the maximum job rate. Several of these individuals were paid thousands more than permitted under the new proposal. When Eileen added all the amounts over the suggested maximum job rates, they totalled over $90 000. How should these salaries be handled? Or was the overall salary structure too low? As well, how should the organization handle people who are at the top step? What would motivate them?

Eileen thought of her earlier concerns about jobs common to "old Lutherwood" and "old CODA" and noted that, under the proposals, administrative assistants were either grade 3 or 4 and counsellor/trainers were grades 7, 8, or 9. She wondered if these classifications resolved the conflicts between those positions.

Salaries and benefits at Lutherwood CODA were around $5 million in March 1999. The implementation of the new model would increase salaries by over $105 000 or by approximately 2.6 percent. (Exhibit 15.10 outlines the costs of the proposed plan.)

As she examined the data, Eileen wondered if the proposal met her objectives. Did it uphold the merger principles? Was it fair to people? Could the organization afford the proposal, and could she sell it to senior management and the Board? Would it attract, retain, and motivate people? Did it reward performance and goal attainment? Did it have enough of a pay-for-performance element, given Dieter Kays' desire to move in that direction?

If the proposal did meet these objectives, Eileen was still faced with the task of selling it to senior management, the Board, and the employees. She wondered what issues she might face there and how she could best anticipate and handle those issues.

Exhibit 15.1

Statement of Revenue & Expenses, Lutherwood CODA
Year Ending March 31, 1999

Revenues	
Ministry of Community & Social Services	$2 753 687
Ministry of Education & Training	1 345 748
Human Resources Development Canada	1 478 223
Regional Municipality of Waterloo	584 417
Health Canada	356 547
Ministry of the Attorney General	90 290
International Fund for Ireland	309 824
Donations	625 505
Fee for service	544 347
Miscellaneous	218 784
Total	$8 307 372
Expenses	
Salaries and benefits	$5 256 513
Cost of goods/services	73 206
Participant costs	866 358
Travel	99 509
Staff development	56 327
Building occupancy	474 121
Purchased services	389 430
Program expenses	114 768
Grants issues	216 294
Professional services	84 129
Advertising and promotion	245 890
Office expenses	336 762
Allocated administrative expenses	27 887
Total	$8 241 194
Excess of revenues over expenses	$67 128

Sources of Funding (percentage)		Spending by Program (percentage)	
Federal Government	22	Employment Services	44
Provincial Government	50	MCSS Core Programs	35
Region of Waterloo	7	Community Programs	10
Charitable Donations	7	Opportunities 2000	4
Other	14	Self-employment Programs	3
		Other	4

Exhibit 15.2

Partial Organizational Structure–
Lutherwood CODA
November 1997

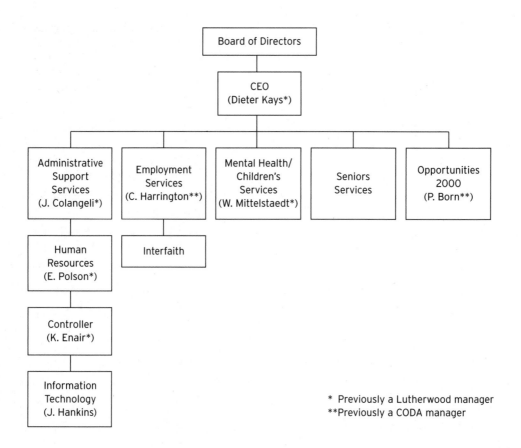

* Previously a Lutherwood manager
**Previously a CODA manager

Exhibit 15.3

Description of a Point Factor System

Point factor means that a number of compensable factors. such as mental skills, physical effort, and education or experience are considered for each job class. A range of point values is assigned to each factor. Point values are then related to salary levels for the jobs. Thus, the job evaluation is a systematic method of establishing the relative worth of jobs in an organization. Point factor systems are popular, as they focus on job requirements, not incumbant qualifications or abilities.

The steps in determining salaries under a point factor system are as follows:

1. Conduct a job analysis that summarizes the relevant work content.

2. Choose compensable factors—items that the organization values and will pay. These factors must be work-related and acceptable to management and employees.

3. Establish factor scales. This step identifies levels for each factor. For example, the Job Chart System has three or four levels of achievement for each factor.

4. Derive factor weights to be used to reflect the differences in importance attached to each factor by the organization.

5. Develop a job evaluation manual, which becomes the benchmark against which jobs are evaluated.

Exhibit 15.4

Lutherwood Pre-merger Salary Ranges (effective March 21, 1996)

Steps	1	2	3	4	5	6	Positions
Grade I	25 000	-	-	27 500	N/A	N/A	Entry-Level Positions
Grade II	26 000	-	-	29 000	N/A	N/A	Secretary I, Clerk
Grade III	27 500	-	-	-	31 000	N/A	Secretary II, Night Shift/Weekend Worker
Grade IV	29 000	-	-	-	33 000	N/A	Counsellor I, Coordinator I,
Grade V	32 500	-	-	-	35 000	N/A	Coordinator II, Analyst I
Mkt Inc. 11.5%	35 000	-	-	-	40 000	N/A	
Grade VI	35 000	-	-	-	40 000	N/A	IS Professional, Coordinator III, Supervisor I
Grade VII	37 500	-	-	-	-	42 500	None
Mkt Inc.	38 500	-	-	-	-	45 000	Specialist I
Grade VIII	42 500	-	-	-	-	50 000	Program Managers
Mkt Inc. 15.3%	47 500	-	-	-	-	57 500	Coordinator III
Mkt Inc. 21.9%	52 500	-	-	-	-	60 000	Specialist II
Grade IX through XII	47 500	-	-	-	-	77 500	Senior Management Positions
Mkt Inc. 26.5%	60 000	-	-	-	-	77 500	

Exhibit 15.5

Lutherwood Grades and Salaries Prior to Merger (as adjusted for confidentiality reasons)

Current Grade	Annual Salary	Current Step	FTE	Hours per PP
I	25 000	2	1	75
	27 500	3	1	75
	12 500	1	0.5	37.5
	12 500	3	0.5	37.5
	27 500	5	1	75
II	27 500	4	1	75
	27 500	4	1	75
	10 000	1	0.4	30
III	27 500	3	1	75
	30 000	5	1	75
	25 000	5	0.8	60
IV	27 500	5	0.83	75
	27 500	1	1	75
	27 500	1	1	75
	32 500	4	1	75
	32 500	5	1	75
	32 500	4	1	75
	30 000	2	1	75
	30 000	2	1	75
	32 500	4	1	75
	32 500	5	1	75
	20 000	2	0.67	50
	31 000	3	1	75
	32 500	5	1	75
	32 500	4	1	75
	20 000	3	0.6	45
	30 000	3	1	
	32 500	4		
	32 500	4	1	75
	30 000	2	1	75
	27 500	1	1	75
	35 000	5	1	75
	32 500	5	1	
	27 500	1	0.9	67.5
	30 000	3	1	75
	32 500	5	1	75
	32 500	5	1	75
	32 500	4	1	75

Exhibit 15.5 (continued)

V	35 000	5	0.867	65
	7 500	1	0.2	15
	35 000	5	1	75
	22 500	3	0.67	50
	35 000	5	1	75
	15 000	5	0.4	30
	32 500	2	1	75
	37 500	5	1	75
VI	32 500	5	0.8	60
	37 500	3	1	75
	35 000	2	1	
	35 000	2	1	75
	37 500	3	1	75
	37 500	3	1	75
	37 500	2	1	75
VII	27 500	5	0.6	45
	20 000	2	0.5	37.5
	35 000	4	0.8	60
	47 500	5	1	75
	52 500	6	1	75
	20 000	2	0.5	37.5
	22 500	5	0.5	37.5
	40 000	2	1	75
	42 500	3	1	75
VIII	45 000	4	1	75
	57 500	4	1	75
	45 000	5	0.8	60
	25 000	1	0.5	37.5
	47 500	4	1	75
	45 000	3	1	75
	47 500	5	1	75
	50 000		1	75
IX	62 500	6	0.8	60
	60 000		1	75
X	57 500	3	1	75
XI	67 500	4	1	75
	70 000		1	75
	70 000		1	75
	20 000		0.5	37.5
	27 500		1	75

FTE = full-time equivalent
PP = per pay
Note: Not all individuals are included in this chart.

Exhibit 15.6

CODA Salary Ranges, effective April 1, 1997

Steps (range from 1 to 13)	1 (minimum)	13 (maximum)
Admin. Assistant 1	18 000	24 000
Admin. Assistant 2	21 000	28 000
Admin. Assistant 3	23 000	31 000
Counsellor/Trainer 1	25 000	33 000
Counsellor/Trainer 2	27 000	36 000
Counsellor/Trainer 3	30 000	40 000
Counsellor/Trainer 4	33 000	44 000
Team Leader 1	36 000	48 000
Team Leader 2	39 000	52 000
Director 1	44 000	58 000
Director 2	50 000	67 000

Exhibit 15.7

CODA Grades and Salaries Prior to Merger (as adjusted for confidentiality)

Start Date	Current Grade	Current Step	Vac. Days	Annual Salary	FTE	Hours per PP
1-Dec-91	AA2	8	20	$25 000	1	75
23-Sep-96		6	15	$22 500	1	75
3-Jun-91	AA3	11	20	$30 000	1	75
1-Oct-96		6	15	$27 500	1	75
16-May-94		6	15	$27 500	1	75
9-Jul-97	CT1	4	15	$25 000	1	75
21-Apr-97		7	15	$27 500	1	75
8-Mar-91	CT2	11	18	$27 500	0.8	60
2-Oct-95		7	15	$32 500	1	75
1-Apr-97		6	4	$30 000	1	75
25-Nov-93		7	15	$32 500	1	75
6-Dec-93		6	15	$30 000	1	75
11-Sep-95		7	15	$32 500	1	75
14-Apr-97	CT3	7	15	$35 000	1	75
17-Feb-92		8	20	$35 000	1	75
1-Oct-96		7	15	$35 000	1	75
13-Sep-93		6	9	$22 500	0.6	45
7-Jan-91		9	20	$37 500	1	75
17-May-93		7	15	$35 000	1	75
17-Feb-97		9	15	$37 500	1	75
26-May-97		6	15	$35 000	1	75
25-Oct-93		6	15	$35 000	1	75
25-Jun-92		6	12	$20 000	0.6	45
22-Feb-93		9	15	$37 500	1	75
1-Sep-94		7	13.5	$30 000	0.9	67.5
22-Feb-93		7	15	$35 000	1	75

Exhibit 15.7 (continued)

6-Feb-95	CT4	5	15	$37 500	1	75
8-Jan-96		6	15	$37 500	1	75
2-Nov-92		8	20	$40 000	1	75
12-Jul-93		7	15	$37 500	1	75
3-Sep-96		7	15	$37 500	1	75
22-Jan-90		9	20	$40 000	1	75
3-Sep-96		6	15	$37 500	1	75
23-Nov-92		10	20	$42 500	1	75
18-Jun-85		9	22	$40 000	1	75
19-Apr-89		9	12	$22 500	0.6	45
20-Mar-95		8	15	$40 000	1	75
13-Sep-86	D2	21	$65 000	1	75	
4-Jan-94	TL2	8	15	$47 500	1	75
1-Apr-88		11	20	$50 000	1	75
6-Oct-97		4	$0			
28-Sep-94		6	$5 000	0.38	28.5	
1-Feb-93		6	$3 200	0.24	18	
30-Sep-97		4	$7 800	0.4	30	
20-Oct-97		4	$25 000	1	75	
8-Oct-97		4	$0			

FTE = full time equivalent
PP = per pay
Note: not all individuals are included in this chart.

Exhibit 15.8
Market Salary Survey, November 1998

(information adjusted for confidentiality purposes)

Comparator Group One: Children's Mental Health Services

Job	Lutherwood		Local Residential Organization 1		Nearby city Organization 2		Large City Organization 3		Local Area Organization 4		Local Area Organization 5		Local Area Organization 6		Local Area Organization 7	
	Min	Max	Min	Max	Min	Max	Min	Max	Min	Max	Min	Max	Min	Max	Min	Max
Psychologist PhD	52 500	60 000	52 500	57 500	50 000	57 500	35 000	42 500	40 000	50 000	47 500	57 500	42 500	55 000	37 500	52 500
Social Worker, MSW	37 500	45 000	40 000	45 000	35 000	42 500					40 000	50 000	37 500	47 500	35 000	47 500
Social Worker, BSW			N/A	N/A											N/A	N/A
Psycometrist, MA	37 500	45 000	N/A	45 000	35 000	45 000			47 500	62 500	42 500	52 500			N/A	N/A
Program Manager	42 500	47 500	42 500	45 000			30 000	37 500	35 000	42 500	35 000	45 000				
Child Youth Worker, Cert/BA	27 500	32 500	27 500	30 000	32 500	35 000			30 000	37 500	35 000	45 000				
Community based CYW, Cert/BA																
Secretary/Admin Assistant	27 500	32 500	32 500	35v000	32 500	35 000	32v500	40,000	27 500	35 000	25 000	30 000				
Supervisor CYW Residential					22 500	25 000	25 000	27 500	40 000	52 500	45 000	30 000				
Full-time employees	80		62		80						160		392			
Union/Non-union	non		both		union		non				union (social work)		both (non for these)		both	
# hrs/week	37.5		40		35		40/35		40		34				37.5	

Comparator Group Two: Self-Employment Programs

Job	CODA		Local Organization 8		Local Organization 9		Local Organization 10	
	Min	Max	Min	Max	Min	Max	Min	Max
Administrative Assistant	21 000	31 000	25 000	35 000	27 500	30 000	17 500	25 000
Business Counsellor/Trainer	30 000	40 000	50 000	57 500	40 000	47 500	35 000	45 000
Program Administrator	32 500	45 000	55 000	60 000	45 000	47 500	45 000	57 500
Full-time Employees	15		24		13		9	
Union/Non-union	non		union		non		non	
# hrs/week	37.5		35		38		40	

Notes to Market Salary Surveys:

1. Lutherwood CODA has a high proportion of staff employed in the positions benchmarked above. Although they are not currently experiencing high turnover in these positions, it is imperative that the organization compensates competitively.
2. The market salary surveys performed on two other key groups of Employment Services and Supervised Access Centres indicated that the Lutherwood CODA compensation was in line with the market. These surveys were completed but have not been included in the case.

Exhibit 15.9

Proposed Compensation Plan for Lutherwood CODA

Lutherwood CODA Salary Ranges

Job Grade	Steps in Each Job Grade							
	I	II	III	IV	V	VI	VII	Mid-points
14	51 000	53 000	55 000	56 000	58 000	60 000		55 500
13	46 000	48 000	50 000	51 000	53 000	55 000		50 500
12	41 500	43 000	45 000	46 000	48 000	50 000		45 500
11	37 000	38 000	40 000	41 000	43 000	44 000		40 500
10	35 000	36 000	37 500	39 000	40 000	–		37 500
9	33 000	34 000	35 500	36 500	38 000	–		35 500
8	31 000	32 000	33 500	34 500	35 500	–		33 500
7	29 000	30 000	31 500	32 500	33 500	–		31 500
6	28 000	29 000	30 000	31 000	–	–		29 500
5	27 000	28 000	29 000	30 000	–	–		28 500
4	26 000	27 000	28 000	29 000	–	–		27 500
3	25 000	26 000	27 000	28 000	–	–		26 500
2	24 500	25 000	26 000	27 000	–	–		26 000
1	19 500	24 000			–	–		

Exhibit 15.10

Costs of the Proposed Compensation Plan for Lutherwood CODA

Lutherwood CODA Summary of Salary Grid Adjustments – Annualized Impact			
Program	Projected Salary "Old Grid" (full year merit) (000's)	Projected Salary "New Grid" (full year merit) (000's)	Total Impact (000's)
Administrative Support Services	605	611	6
Mental Health/Children's Services	2531	2576	45
Employment Services	1690	1728	38
Seniors' Services	204	213	9
Opportunities 2000	202	209	7
Totals	5232	5337	105

Martin-Straight Compressors (A)

Gene Deszca

John Podrebarac

Stuart Munro

INTRODUCTION

After three months with Martin-Straight Compressors (MSC), the new HR manager, Bill Smith, was questioning whether the current corporate compensation program would lead the Chatham business unit to success. He was particularly concerned about the year 2000 compensation budget. He was also worried about several positions that had been left unfilled for several months.

As part of the compensation program, Smith had to allocate a head-office mandated maximum budget increase of 3 percent to a team of approximately 63 salaried employees who had just gone through a major organizational restructuring. A downsizing of employees had resulted in several employees taking on additional responsibilities without additional compensation. Staff workloads had been further increased by voluntary turnover of over 20 percent last year in the managerial/professional (i.e., engineering) ranks. There were currently seven authorized but unfilled middle-level salary positions. The market for engineers was extremely competitive and expected to remain so for the foreseeable future.

The pending sale of MSC made staffing open positions more difficult. Smith believed that to attract and secure new staff, he would have to make creative compensation offers not normally in line with corporate guidelines. He struggled in making these decisions, weighing years of service, current earnings, education, and the future potential of the applicants.

The corporate compensation program linked performance and merit increases. The company's performance management process (PM) had been introduced last year. In this process, the supervisor and the employee created challenging "objectives" set through a dual communication process. Smith was distraught when he discovered that very few employees had considered or formalized their objectives. "How am I going to administer pay increases when objectives have not been set?" he wondered.

Smith was concerned that this year's compensation budget allocation would result in lower morale, decreased satisfaction, and dampened motivation. A quick glance at management's initial merit recommendations showed they would be well in excess of the budgeted guidelines and difficult to defend on any objective basis. He felt that a review of the compensation system was necessary in order to promote achievement of MSC's goals, fit with and support its strategy, and allow it to hire qualified individuals. As well, the company had to link performance with compensation.

BACKGROUND

The Industry

The compressor industry consists of a wide variety of competitors, from independent custom shops to large global compressor companies. Approximately 10 major companies (including MSC) are global competitors. There is significant overcapacity in the industry. The market for industrial compressors can be grouped into four main categories: air-conditioning units for buildings, refrigeration and freezer units, oil-free compressors for those needing gas streams free of contaminants, and portable and stationary industrial compressors for use in such things as service stations and construction products.

Firms in the industrial compressor business compete on the basis of design, manufacturing, service, and price. The margins on standardized compressors have decreased considerably due to the competition. Specialty and custom-designed industrial compressors continue to retain adequate, though thinning margins. MSC excelled here, but its reputation took a beating last year, due to production problems that impaired its ability to deliver on time.

Rationalization in this industry has led to increased competition. Companies have attempted to compete by building long-term relationships with customers. Major compressor manufacturers (including MSC) have extended their services to include acting as service depots and providing maintenance assistance to customers, even on equipment purchased from competitors. However, small independent repair shops have continued to be important in the repair/servicing area, due to their flexibility and ability to quickly respond to customer problems.

The Company

MSC is headquartered in Toledo, Ohio, with 4600 people employed in manufacturing facilities worldwide. With 1999 revenues of approximately US$750 million (US$33.2 million profit), MSC manufactures compressors used in industrial, commercial, and municipal applications.

MSC was formed in 1990 as a joint venture between Martin-Minelli and Straight Compressors. The joint venture resulted in a series of mergers and acquisitions, producing one of the larger compressor companies in the world. On December 30, 1999, Martin-Minelli acquired Straight's 49 percent interest in the joint venture, for a net purchase price of US$620 million.

MSC was subsequently purchased by an American competitor, CompressorRight. This acquisition was announced in February 2000 with a planned closing date in September 2000.

The Chatham, Ontario Location

MSC's Chatham location was a small Canadian facility with approximately 70 salaried and 50 hourly workers. It focused on the manufacture of centrifugal, rotary, and position displacement stationary compressors for heavy industries. Established in 1955, the Chatham plant's history included several mergers and acquisitions. It had always managed to survive, but line employees had become increasingly cynical over the years. For them, both senior managers and owners were temporary residents who looked after themselves. Management also had a reputation for failing to follow through on things it had promised and for backing down in the face of union pressure. (See Exhibit 16.1 for a partial organization chart.)

RECENT DEVELOPMENTS AT MSC CHATHAM

July 1999

A loss of approximately US$2.5 million in 1997–1998 led to several changes in the senior leadership at the Chatham facility. The plant manager, the controller of finance, the manufacturing manager, the human resources manager, and the purchasing manager were replaced. This, coupled with the corporate restructuring, led to the termination of several other salaried employees, including sales and marketing professionals and engineers.

The jobs of the managers who were replaced were expanded, and most of the remaining managerial employees were asked to assume additional roles and responsibilities without corresponding pay increases. The voluntary exit of valuable employees accelerated in the wake of the downsizing. The net effect was a significant increase in the level of organizational stress and workload.

October/November 1999

An acting plant manager moved in from the American parent in the winter of 1999. Between September and November, with the assistance of a national consulting firm, he dismissed the senior managers mentioned above and hired a new plant manager, a manufacturing manager, a controller of finance, a purchasing manager, and a human resources manager. This new leadership team faced many challenges including:

1. A union resistant to change

2. A real loss in experience/knowledge at MSC

3. Seven unstaffed managerial/professional positions—including engineering/design (4), plant supervision (1), and technical support (2)

4. Continuing large financial losses in 1998–1999 (US$1.2 million)
5. Pressures from MSC corporate head office to turn the situation around
6. 22 percent on-time performance
7. Highest warranty costs of all business units within MSC

The management team knew that antiquated approaches to the manufacturing process had to be changed to ones that were much more cost-, quality-, and time-effective.

January 2000

In January 2000, several positions remained unstaffed. As well, the completion of the sale of MSC begun in the fall of 2000 appeared likely. As HR manager, part of Bill's mandate was to move the PM process away from being one of entitlement. In the past, the merit process had been loosely followed, and the most eligible candidates had received greater-than-average merit. Smith recognized that the merit bonus restrictions imposed by head office likely would add to the dissatisfaction and frustration experienced by most managers.

Bill was expected to ensure that only those who truly performed at high levels received higher than average merit, and he had attempted to communicate that change to the managers. However, it would appear that this message had not been heard. Exhibit 16.2 contains the recommended merit increases that Bill had received thus far from the managers of 33 of the eligible recipients. These proposed increases were running in excess of 4.7 percent. Bill knew that none of the merit recommendations would be approved by head office if Chatham's total merit increases exceeded the corporate guideline of 3 percent of the salary budget allocated to the eligible recipients. He was not looking forward to asking the managers to redo their merit proposals in order to bring them into line with the merit budget.

Records (i.e., sign-off sheets) indicated that the 1999 PMs had been reviewed with employees. When Bill investigated further, he observed that very few employees had identified key objectives that were concretely stated. The lack of meaningful, specific objectives made it very difficult to compare and contrast the contributions made by different employees in a fair and objective manner.

Year 2000 objectives currently were being set. At the urging of the new plant manager, managers in all departments were attempting to work more closely together to ensure alignment. Each area aimed at improving quality and on-time performance. For example:

Sales & Marketing

- Accurate forecasting and customer proposals/quotes
- Correct order of materials
- Focus on accuracy of drawings and design specifications
- Realistic and competitive lead times in sync with manufacturing

Purchasing & Materials Management

- Strategic sourcing with key suppliers

- Ensuring delivery times and lead times
- Inventory management
- Subcontracting relationships

Finance

- Accurate forecasting
- Cross-functional relationship with the Front-End Team, the marketing and engineering design team responsible for developing accurate and effective proposals
- Driving to meet forecasted margins
- Accurate data to other departments

Manufacturing

- Implementation of modern manufacturing processes
- Improvement of logistics and shop flow
- Focus on change management with hourly employees and union officials
- Standardization of drawings
- Reduction of scrap and lead times
- Quality workshops, leading to improved quality

Human Resources

- Support all areas in training, staffing, and performance management
- Manage labour relations
- Focus on performance management and leadership development

The name of the acquiring firm was announced in January 2000, with the closing date for the sale set for September. CompressorRight was approximately the same size as MSC. Its CEO publicly stated that there would be several plant closures. Pressure on the Chatham facility therefore was heightened by the sale. However, discussions with the senior managers in the plant convinced Bill that his colleagues really believed that Chatham had a fighting chance for long-term success, if it could only get its act together.

March 2000

In March, MSC's head office renewed its request for the submission of all merit recommendations. It reiterated the requirement that the merit budget be adhered to. Until final approval was received, managers would not be given the go-ahead to communicate the increases to their respective employees.

As noted earlier, the Chatham facility had been faced with several challenges in the past year. The new plant manager was under intense pressure to make Chatham a viable and profitable operation. The Canadian dollar and the plant's location gave it the potential to be an attractive site from which to operate, but not unless it was able to turn itself around and prove it could be a productive, reliable, and profitable operation.

LABOUR RELATIONS

Previous management had avoided conflict with the bargaining unit when it came to negotiations and day-to-day affairs. The new plant manager and his direct reports believed the production culture was one of entitlement and we–they relations. As the plant manager stated, "Too often, the union finds the 'weakest managerial link' in order to achieve its victories."

During the 1990s, management had been zealous in seeking labour peace with its unionized production employees. Seniority and layoff provisions were among the most restrictive in the industry. In 1997 it negotiated a gain-sharing plan that would bankrupt the company within four years if fully implemented. The company bought its way out of this agreement in 1999, at considerable cost and embarrassment. Elected representatives of the unionized production workers appeared to believe that management had little ability and willingness to act to change the productivity situation at the plant.

The flawed gain-sharing plan mentioned above had been designed to motivate hourly employees. The base year was 1997, and the gain-sharing calculations were based on shipments. This plan did not consider waste, rework, product quality, on-time delivery, or shipment profitability. It also did not contain any clauses that protected the business when in a loss situation. Therefore, despite large financial losses in 1998 and 1999, the company found itself having to pay hefty gain-sharing bonuses based upon product shipments.

Despite the current labour climate, senior management continued in its attempt to work with the union membership through meetings, brainstorming sessions, task teams, and open communication. These meetings proved to be particularly frustrating, and it appeared that little progress was being made in changing the views of the local union leadership towards the new organizational realities. Due to the union's resistance to participation in pay-at-risk programs, senior management decided to apply the merit system to only salaried, non-union employees. They reasoned that if they could demonstrate the benefits of the PM process with this group, then maybe, they would have more success with unionized personnel.

THE COMPENSATION SYSTEM

The components of the compensation program for salaried employees included the following:

1. Performance Management Program
2. Job Evaluation—Hay Point System
3. The Corporate Matrix
4. The Corporate Budget
5. Merit Date Transition
6. Management Incentive Plans
7. Merit Communication
8. Union Wages
9. Performance & Compensation System Summary

These are described below.

Performance Management Program (PM)

The PM process for salaried employees was introduced by the acting plant manager in 1999. It focused on the development of SMART (Specific, Measurable, Agreed-upon, Realistic, and Timed) "objectives." Objectives were to be used to align business/department goals with the individual's job responsibilities and activities.

Each employee, in discussion with his or her supervisor, was to identify five to eight job objectives aligned with the company's goals and strategic direction.

The objectives would comprise approximately 70 percent of the employee's job, and each objective would be prioritized and weighted as to its relative importance. The employee could amend or add to the objectives through an informal process, or a formal process called the mid-year review. This was done to ensure that the employees perceived the process as fair and equitable. The other 30 percent of the employee's job was embedded in routine tasks and activities that he or she was responsible for.

The objectives would be rated on a scale from 1 to 5. Ratings were 1 = Unacceptable; 2 = Needs Improvement; 3 = At Standard; 4 = Above Standard; 5 = Commendable. The "At Standard" rating of 3 was considered to be a solid rating, indicating the completion of the objective consistent with MSC's values. The PM process required an overall performance rating for each employee. This was calculated by weighting each objective and multiplying it by the performance rating of each objective.

If completed properly, each employee would have SMART objectives linked to plant and corporate goals. If *all* employees achieved their objectives, the plant would be achieving its goals and ultimately succeeding.

The introduction of this corporate program was an attempt to link performance with compensation. The PM process was intended to reward those employees who performed well.

Job Evaluation—Hay Point System

With the exception of newly created positions, each job at the Chatham location had a position description and an accompanying Hay Point rating. The Hay Point evaluation system rated each job on a variety of factors, allocated points for each factor, and allowed a comparison across jobs based on the allocated points. Bill Smith had inherited these job descriptions and ratings.

The Hay Point evaluation process determined the pay range for each position. More importantly, the employees' position in the pay range had a direct impact on their merit increment potential. The reason for this is explained in the sections that follow.

The Corporate Matrix

The corporate matrix was a guide for supervisors and managers in allocating the budgetary increase, based on the employee's performance ratings. (See the matrix sheet, "Salary Increase Guide," in Exhibit 16.3.)

Two variables played a role in determining each individual's percent merit increase. The increase was based on the employee's current position in the pay range as well as his or her performance rating. The matrix assumed a normal distribution in performance ratings.

For example, (referring to the matrix in Exhibit 16.3), an employee with an "Above Standard (4)" performance rating would receive a merit increase of 6–8%, if he or she was at the low end of the pay range (80 to 88 percent range). Another employee with an "Above Standard (4)" rating, who was at the top of his or her range, would receive an increase of 2 to 4 percent. When managers evaluated their employees, the matrix in Exhibit 16.3 stated that no more than 20 percent of the employees were expected to be performing at an above standard or commendable level. Employees below standard would receive a 0 percent merit increase in most cases.

The Corporate Budget

Each year, head office determined the percent increase for the merit budget, as a percentage of the plant's current salaried payroll. The merit budget for 1999–2000 was 3 percent. The managers were to allocate this among the staff.

The following chart illustrates how the process worked for three fictional employees (at similar points in their salary ranges). If Bill Munro were the top performer and deserved a substantial increase, he could be given more than the budgeted percentage amount, but only at the expense of other employees. If Stuart Jones were the lowest performer, he would receive a proportionately smaller increase. The total dollar value of the increases could not exceed $6750.

Employee	Salary	Budget	Increase	New Salary	% Increase
Bill Munro	$100 000	$3 000	$5 000	$105 000	5%
Stuart Jones	$50 000	$1 500	$ 500	$50 500	1%
Anne Marks	$75 000	$2 250	$1,250	$76 700	1.7%
TOTAL	$225 000	$6 750	$6 750	$231 750	3%

Merit Date Transition

Prior to 1999, merit increases at MSC were administered on the employee's anniversary date. To streamline the process, head office had changed the policy so that all merit increases would occur on April 1 of each year.

Since this was a transition year, employees would receive a portion of their merit increase based on a pro-rated formula.

For example, a person who would normally have received a merit increase on January 1, 2000, would receive 15/12 of the increase on April 1, 2000—the date for the new reviews. Similarly, a person who would normally receive the increase on May 1, 2000 would receive 11/12 of the increase on April 1, 2000. This was put in place to ensure that all employees were treated fairly.

Executive Incentive Plan

Currently, only senior managers participated in MSC's executive incentive pay plan. This plan provided managers with the opportunity to earn up to an additional 50 percent of their base salary. The structure of the incentive was based and weighted on several factors, including their personal PM rating, company and plant profitability, and sales. The makeup of the formula differed from senior manager to senior manager, depending upon what they were responsible for. For example, the director of marketing and sales could receive a bonus of up to 50 percent of his salary, based upon sales (30 percent), his personal PM (30 percent), company profitability (20 percent), and plant profitability (20 percent. The human resources manager also could receive a bonus of up to 50 percent, but the formula for him was different. His bonus was contingent upon his PM rating (40 percent), company profitability (30 percent), and plant profitability (30 percent).

The sales and marketing professionals at the Chatham facility typically had not received bonuses in the past over and above the merit provisions. Recently, however, the company had provided a discretionary bonus for exceptional achievement.

Merit Communication

The human resources manager at Chatham provided a training session to the department managers on how to properly communicate the merit increases to their respective employees. The following lists summarize the "Dos and Don'ts" for communicating merit increases.

Dos	**Don'ts**
• Avoid surprises	• See your paycheque for a surprise
• Be prepared	• Use voice mail/e-mail to communicate
• Reinforce good performance	the merit increase
• Discuss areas to improve	• Make excuses
• Be frank	• Blame it on the budget/HR
• Move on	• Apologize

Despite the training session, Bill Smith was certain that several managers would blame a low merit increase on corporate guidelines, rather than their own performance.

Union Wages

The local bargaining unit had a wage schedule that had been negotiated through the bargaining process. The wage schedule was set to the end of June 2003. There was no performance evaluation or any type of pay-for-performance plan attached to this schedule. As stated previously, the company had "bought" its way out of the negotiated gain-sharing plan. Pay levels in the plant were above average when compared with similar jobs in other unionized settings in Ontario. When compared with others on the basis of plant productivity, wages were exceptionally high.

Performance and Compensation System Summary

MSC's compensation system now linked performance with the merit increase for salaried employees. Prior to 1999, the performance appraisal had been a one-way communication vehicle, and it had not been based on specific performance indicators. The recent changes in the performance management system had created many employee concerns that were primarily linked to the historically high ratings most employees had received. Head office had announced in 1999 that managers were to "raise the bar," rating employees who reach and sometimes exceed their objectives as "At Standard (3)" rather than "Above Standard (4)." (See Exhibit 16.3.)

The compensation system was currently in a transition phase with alignment in merit dates. In addition to the merit budget, discretionary bonuses and management incentive plans were also being used to motivate performance. Managers had received training in how to effectively communicate with their staff to help reinforce performance and minimize negative feelings. This was buttressed by voluntary training and coaching sessions led by Smith in the fall of 1999.

BILL SMITH

Bill Smith was concerned about the potential outcome in communicating the merit increases for the 1999–2000 period. With Chatham's restructuring, several managers had expressed a desire to challenge their Hay Point ratings. Bill knew that the merit announcements, if not very skilfully handled, had the capacity to increase pressure here. Bill also faced the dilemma that very few employees had "objectives" identified in a manner that allowed for a proper evaluation to take place. An added complication was that some managers were questioning the escalating salary offers that were being made to new hires in the managerial and professional areas.

Bill Smith was also concerned about the uncertainty related to the intentions of CompressorRight. The pressure for improved financial performance and uncertainty concerning the future of the plant had caused senior management to place an even greater emphasis on performance.

Finally, Bill felt that, no matter what the compensation program was, the union committee, along with a few employees, seemed to be passively resisting shop floor changes. Something needed to be done to minimize the negative impact they were having. If production could not get its act together, nothing else would matter.

Bill felt responsible for the effective administration and success of the compensation program at MSC. He believed his relationship with the plant manager and most other senior managers was quite positive, but Bill knew the merit issue would be controversial. The plant manager expected to see a merit plan incorporated into the performance management process that differentiated between performance levels and recognized excellent performance. Bill wondered what improvements or changes were necessary to help the Chatham facility become a viable business unit and fulfill its strategic goals and vision. He also wondered what he needed to do to keep people on side and not have the merit process become an alienating experience.

MSC'S VISION

Meet our customer expectations by providing compressors and parts with *zero defects on time*.

Exhibit 16.1
MSC Organization Chart (Partial)

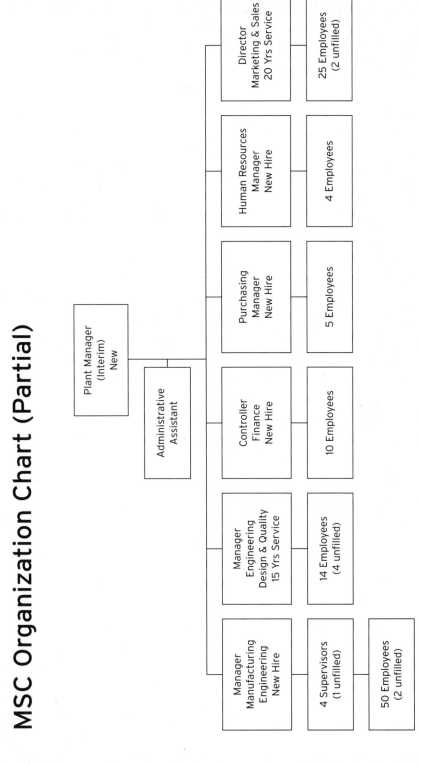

Exhibit 16.2

Recommended Merit Increases

Expected distribution of employee merit increases (n = 33 at time report was generated)	
Percentage Increase	Number of Employees
< 2.5%	1
2.5%–3.25%	11
3.25%–4.0%	11
4.0%–6.5%	8
> 6.5%	1

Expected average = 3%

Merit increases recommended by supervisors (n = 33 at time the report was generated)	
Percentage Increase	Number of Employees
0–1%	2
1–2%	0
2–3%	3
3–4%	19
4–5%	6
5–6%	5
6–7%	3
> 7%	1

Average increase recommended by supervisors > 4.73%

Exhibit 16.3

Salary Increase Guide

PERFORMANCE LEVEL (as measured against job performance)		POSITION IN SALARY RANGE (as a % of mid-point)						
(1)		80%	88%	96%	**100%**	104%	112%	120%
Expected Population **5%**	COMMENDABLE ("5") Exceeds the standards most of the time							
Average Increase Limit **8%**		8–10%	7–9%	6–8%		5–7%	4–6%	
Expected Population **15%**	ABOVE STANDARD ("4") Exceeds the standards much of the time							
Average Increase Limit **5%**		6–8%	5–7%	4–6%		3–5%	2–4%	
Expected Population **60%**	AT STANDARD ("3") Generally meets and sometimes exceeds standards							
Average Increase Limit **3%**		4–6%	3–5%	2–4%		2–3%	2%	
Expected Population **10%**	BELOW STANDARD ("2") Meets most, but not, all standards Is in need of some improvement				MID-POINT	(2)		
Average Increase Limit **2.5%**		0–3%	0–2.5%					
Expected Population **10%**	UNSATISFACTORY ("1") Does not meet standards		(2)					
Average Increase Limit **0%**								

(1) This column denotes the typical distribution of personnel in each of the performance categories.

(2) Group President along with VP Human Resources must approve increase recommendations for individuals outside the guidelines.

Increases are largest for employees performing substantially above what is expected for their position. Adherence to the merit budget of 3 percent is attained by distributing the "percent" in accordance with the normal distribution recommended by the above matrix.

MARTIN-STRAIGHT COMPRESSORS (B)

Elsa Franks, marketing manager for custom stationary compressors, was frustrated. Bill Smith had just left her office, after informing her that the 5.2 percent average merit increase she had recommended for her 10 direct reports could not be approved. She knew it wasn't Bill's fault. He was responsible for managing the merit process, but when it came to the 3 percent ceiling he was simply the messenger. However, she could not help but feel badly for her people, given how hard they had pushed themselves over the past 12 months. The order book reflected the fruits of their efforts (a 14 percent increase, with 50 percent of it derived from a substantial natural gas pipeline order). Production, quality, and delivery remained problems over which marketing had little control, but at least her group had succeeded in addressing the issue of declining sales. The last thing Elsa wanted to do was precipitate more turnover.

Elsa pulled out the spreadsheet that she used for merit planning purposes and the corporate matrix (see Exhibits 16.3 and 16.4). She felt comfortable justifying the performance ratings she had assigned to each of the subordinates. Given the quarterly reviews she had instituted with team members, there should be no surprises here. However, she also knew that most of the members had been pushing themselves very hard. Giving them an average merit increase of 3 percent in the face of their efforts would not go down well.

There was no avoiding it further. She had to make the merit assignment decisions, and the total could not be more than 3 percent of the salary budget for the 10 people. She also needed to think through how to handle the feedback sessions. Finally, she wanted to consider changes to the merit process for next year that she could recommend to senior management in Chatham.

Exhibit 16.4
Merit Planning Sheet

Name	Job Title	Hay Points	80% Min	100% Mid	120% Max	Ratio	Current Salary	% Last Increase	Date Current Increase	Defined % Inc	New Yrly Inc Amount	New Yrly Salary	New Comp Ratio	Perf. Rating
Atkinson, John	Project Manager	365	40 959	51 199	61 439	127%	65 000	0.00	03/01/00		0.00	65 000.00	1.27	5
Berman, Paul	Administrative Assistant	220	31 341	39 176	47 011	95%	37 178	4.50	03/01/00		0.00	37 178.00	0.95	4
Brill, Jean	Sr. Prod. Planner Stationary	324	38 187	47 734	57 281	99%	47 380	3.00	03/01/00		0.00	47 380.00	0.99	1
Ferris, Jane	Prod. Spec. Stationary	347	39 742	49 678	59 614	109%	54 000	9.60	03/01/00		0.00	54 000.00	1.09	2
Harris, Richard	Project Manager	605	57 185	71 482	85 778	92%	66 000	9.00	03/01/00		0.00	66 000.00	0.92	3
Marcott, Nell	Project Manager	605	57 185	71 482	85 778	109%	77 772	3.00	03/01/00		0.00	77 772.00	1.09	3
Marillo, Joseph	Project Eng. Stationary	409	43 934	54 918	65 901	115%	63 000	9.45	03/01/00		0.00	63 000.00	1.15	4
Ortez, Juan	Project Eng. Stationary	409	43 934	54 918	65 901	98%	54 000	20.00	03/01/00		0.00	54 000.00	0.98	3
Richards, Gary	Procurement/Costing Specialist	365	40 959	51 199	61 439	98%	50 168	2.50	03/01/00		0.00	50 168	0.98	2
Wong, Richard	Project Manager	605	60 950	76 188	91 425	69%	52 275	10.00	03/01/00		0.00	52 275	0.69	4

Total Salary   566 773

Total Available Dollars (Budget 3%)   17 003

Total Increases Distributed   0.00%

Performance ratings are identified in the last column.

Evergreen Technologies Ltd. (ETL)

Pauline Brockman

Andrew Templer

On a bright summer morning Alison Hayes, director—IT human resourcing for Evergreen Technologies Ltd (ETL), opened the ToDo folder of her Palm Pilot and began adding in the words, "Evaluate work-from-home program." Mike Tulett, president of ETL, had just popped into Alison's office, supposedly just "in passing," but had immediately let it be known that he had important matters on his mind.

"We need to address this Alison," Mike said, waving a piece of paper in the air, "but I can't talk now because I've got a conference call with the Ministry of Transportation in a few minutes. We have to find some solutions to the work-from-home program, so can we meet at the end of the day to talk?"

Alison was barely able to nod before Mike strode off towards his office. She wondered what had brought on Mike's outburst. She guessed it was probably tied to her policy memo on managing telecommuting staff (see Exhibit 17.1). Though this was still a relatively new undertaking, she had not anticipated the depth of the reaction from employees and managers who could not take advantage of the work-from-home program.

THE COMPANY

In the last 10 years, Markham, Ontario, has grown to become Canada's new high-tech capital. In addition to being home to Evergreen Technologies Ltd. (ETL), Markham has also become the address for many of Canada's most notable high-tech companies, such as IBM, Sprint, ATI, Dell, and Onyx as well as hundreds of lesser-known start-ups.

ETL, founded in 1992 by an executive team with several years of both automotive and information technology experience, was formed to harness expertise and knowledge about the challenges of vehicle emissions in North America.

In the last few decades, smog has become a serious health and environmental concern in most major cities around the world. Greater levels of ground-level ozone have been created by mixing a growing amount of exhaust emissions from vehicles together with other environmental pollutants. This ground-level ozone, when mixed with sunlight, becomes the brown haze most people refer to as smog. As a result of the direct link between vehicles and the quality of the environment, emission-related projects have become a combined effort of the Ministry of the Environment (MOE) and Ministry of Transportation (MOT) in Canada and of the Department of Environmental Quality (DEQ) and the Department of Motor Vehicles (DMV) in the United States. Together, these organizations have begun to take a strong position to immediately decrease all forms of pollution in an attempt to reverse the negative effects on the earth's ozone layer.

ETL has responded to this market opportunity by developing and marketing the hardware and software necessary to implement and effectively administer vehicle inspection programs. Although the process and standards for vehicle emission inspections vary greatly from region to region and from country to country, ETL's software, called *Inspection Lane*, has proved to be adaptable to the various types of emission inspection equipment available in North America.

Although ETL is the only company of its kind in Canada, several impressive competitors in the United States have been vying for the lucrative state and provincial contracts. Despite this tough competition, however, ETL has been very successful in growing its business and reputation under the leadership of Mike Tulett, the company's president. Since its founding almost nine years ago, ETL has secured emissions-testing contracts in Texas, New Mexico, Colorado, Vermont, Virginia, Missouri, Georgia, and most recently, Ontario, Canada.

This case is set halfway through Year 2 in the implementation of the Canadian contract. (See Exhibit 17.3.)

ONTARIO'S "DRIVE CLEAN" CONTRACT

In the late 1990s, Ontario responded to the need to reduce vehicle emissions with its own "Drive Clean" program. In terms of the program, as announced, all cars and light-duty trucks over three years of age in the Greater Toronto Area (GTA) would be required to begin scheduled vehicle-emission testing.

Owners of vehicles over three years of age would receive a notice approximately 90 days prior to their licence renewal stating that their car or light truck would require an emissions test. Owners would be required to take their automobile to a local, privately owned, licensed testing facility in their area (e.g., Canadian Tire) before the vehicle could obtain its annual licensing sticker. Vehicles would undergo the simple test, and within minutes the owners would receive a computer-generated report that stated whether the vehicle passed or failed the test, as well as an analysis of the pollutants coming from the tailpipe. An "emissions analyzer" in each facility would allow probes and other devices to capture output from the exhaust system and to check the gas cap for leaks. If the vehicle passed the test, the positive result would automatically be relayed to the Ministry of Transportation computer system so that the vehicle registration could be renewed by the deadline. If the vehicle failed the test, the owner would receive a report describing some of the potential causes of failure. Under the program, "failing" vehicles would need to be repaired and re-tested until a pass certificate was obtained.

ETL'S RESPONSIBILITY FOR THE TEST PROCESS

As the successful bidder for the "Drive Clean" program, ETL is expected to take on a wide range of responsibilities for the emissions testing process. Its key task is the writing of software according to specifications provided by the MOE and MOT so that data captured on the analyzer can be safely transferred to the MOT's central database repository.

In addition to capturing the emissions data, ETL is required to look after other aspects of the testing process such as training emissions inspectors and performing station audits. The station audits are particularly necessary to ensure that stations follow the appropriate procedures and do not cheat the system or consumers by offering faulty readings and unnecessary repair claims. The data collected and systems developed by the technology group at ETL will be used to help identify suspect stations so that an undercover auditor can investigate and analyze the emissions testing system. Because thousands of stations exist within each province or state, it would be impossible to perform an audit on each. The technology group will also be responsible for the billing aspect of the program to ensure that the government receives its share of the money paid for each emission test performed.

THE LABOUR MARKET FACING ETL

While the Ontario Drive Clean project was good news financially for ETL, it has created significant work for the IT human resourcing department. A number of new staff had to be hired to run the project—all at a time when technology employees were in high demand. Not only do the number of technology jobs easily outnumber the number of qualified personnel, it is not at all unusual for developers to switch companies every couple of years. Like the rest of the industry, ETL has also been challenged by its ability to attract and retain highly qualified individuals, especially since very few have experience in emissions testing. Over the past five years only 3 of the 15 members of ETL's original Research and Development team have remained with the company. In addition, the database and Web development teams have undergone a complete transformation with nearly all staff now having transferred to other departments or having left the company entirely.

The Drive Clean project is proving particularly difficult to staff because none of the individuals coming to the company had prior emission-related experience and hence have required a significant learning curve to understand the business. As well, the delay in having the Ontario program implemented added to the staffing complexity. Now that the program has been approved there is sudden pressure for immediate implementation.

THE CRITICAL NATURE OF STAFFING

One of the most significant challenges of a high-tech company is securing adequate levels of highly skilled staff. Whereas the information technology department is considered a support function in many traditional industries, at ETL the computer technicians, programmers, developers, and analysts are the driving force behind the company's success. Thus, high levels of turnover and unfilled positions are a source of considerable concern.

As director, IT human resourcing, Alison has been very frustrated by the company's difficulty in retaining its high-tech talent. In a few cases, the company's most mobile staff have been lured to the United States for salaries that range from US$15 000 to $55 000 more than those offered by ETL. Because ETL is in close proximity to several high-tech competitors, employees who are slightly unhappy or who continue to look for larger salaries are able to easily find other jobs. It is also a sad fact that some less scrupulous headhunter agencies make a lot of money out of work for the IT industry by placing and re-placing employees between one client and another.

The IT industry also spans nearly all cultural and ethnic backgrounds. Due to significant shortages of qualified candidates in Canada, several of ETL's latest hires have come from Europe and the Middle East. Alison has found that overcoming language and cultural barriers has been both a difficult and slow process.

THE TECHNOLOGY GROUP AT ETL

The technology group at ETL has been responsible for developing and implementing the emissions-testing systems for the Drive Clean program. The group is divided into two major areas: development/support and infrastructure/quality control. (See the organization chart in Exhibit 17.2.)

Parallel with these major areas and similar to other high-tech organizations, the technology group has been divided into several subgroups or areas to handle business in a more efficient manner.

The research and development team (R&D) is responsible for looking at the latest technologies, testing them, and piloting how they can be used in an upcoming project. The people in this team are often able to work from home because their job requires considerable investigation and thought, but not a lot of interaction with other team members. The work in this team typically requires employees to go off on their own with an idea and put in significant time and effort in order to return with the best solution. In this group, solitary work is often more productive.

The network and support team is responsible for the day-to-day operations of the business. This team consists of developers, database administrators, and network support personnel. Due to the nature of the work, this team is typically required to work on-site. Many of the programs have mandates to be operational '24-7' (24 hours per day, 7 days per week). Fines are usually incurred by this department for "system downtime" in excess of a predefined threshold (for example, 99.5 percent availability for the month). If the team is down for more than the threshold, ETL is fined by its customers for each hour of downtime.

The database team is responsible for the collection and storage of emission and program-related data. This information is the key to most of ETL's systems. This team is responsible for the database being available "24-7," ensuring system integrity, and doing new database development work. Although the team has a general framework of how the data should be stored, each jurisdiction usually has its own unique requirements that this department must implement and monitor.

The Web development team is responsible for organizing the volumes of data collected and making this information readily available for government organizations to access through the Internet. By providing its customers with simple access to the volumes of data, this team ensures clients are able to monitor the program to assure it's achieving the expected result. For instance, customers want data from a failed emissions test to match with data from a passed test after the repairs have been completed, so that a "reduction-in-pollution" can be calculated. This group can telecommute but must work closely with the database team.

As mentioned above, there has been considerable change in the technology group at ETL. The challenge has been to attract and retain highly qualified individuals. In five years, only 20 percent of the members of ETL's original research and development team remain with the company, and the database and Web development groups have undergone a complete transformation with nearly all staff having left for other departments or companies.

The Nature of the Work

Projects teams at ETL usually consist of multiple individuals from each of the different groups. Many times the various members of the technology group must work on more than one project at a time due to the length of projects and the coordination required between departments. Ensuring the right human resourcing and the right mix of time spent on projects can be, and has been, difficult for ETL to manage.

Development work can often involve a lot of thinking and require a great amount of concentration. Interruptions therefore are avoided whenever possible. A minor five-minute interruption would delay work by much more than five minutes as it is often difficult for the IT staff to get back to where they have left off. As a result, ETL encourages its staff to use e-mail first whenever possible. Before picking up the telephone to call a co-worker, staff members will often think "Do I really need the answer this minute or can I formulate this request in an e-mail?"

Members of the support group have a rotating support policy. Since systems must be operational "24-7" this might require evening work. ETL has developed a three-week rotation for each area of support. This means a staff member is "on support" for one week, "on backup" for one week, and has one week off. When a staff member must provide evening support that person is required to carry a pager and cell phone so that he or she may be contacted quickly and respond to any problems immediately. In order to compensate its staff for providing "24-7" service, ETL has given its support personnel a choice: either extra time off or extra monetary compensation.

Because ETL wants to avoid costly and inconvenient evening service calls, all staff are encouraged to create systems and procedures that require little support so staff can spend more time on development.

ETL'S WORK ATMOSPHERE

The corporate culture at ETL, and other similar high-tech companies in the area, resembles little the manufacturing giants of the 1970s and 80s. ETL's office space is designed to be unceremoniously simple for maximum capacity and efficiency. As such, the space is carefully divided into a number of equal-sized cubicles, each carefully linked together with miles of cables, networked printers, and desktop computers. Since office space in the GTA is extremely limited and expensive, ETL has found it necessary to carefully consider the peaks and valleys in its human resource requirements. At present, ETL occupies nearly 100 percent of its available office space with no opportunity to expand without a physical move to a new facility.

For the most part, the atmosphere at ETL is serious. Inside the office, noise is generated by the clicking of keyboards and the hum from printers. High-tech work is also characterized by its constant need for high-level communication and teamwork, as most projects are quite sizable and include large numbers of developers and support personnel. Employees prefer e-mail and voicemail to written memos and lengthy group meetings. Like many other companies, ETL has a flex-hour policy, which accommodates the untraditional flow of IT work. With the approach of deadlines or the implementation of new programs, staff are often required to work long or odd work hours, which can create frequent or sudden surges in the workload.

THE PLAN TO MEET THE NEEDS OF THE DRIVE CLEAN CONTRACT

In the 20 months leading up to the launch of the Drive Clean project, Mike and Alison had met several times to develop a strategy to deal with the human resource needs of the new contract. Even before the Drive Clean contract was formally ETL's, they had decided that they would need to hire an additional 30 IT specialists in addition to any staff who left to pursue other opportunities (see Exhibit 17.3, Project Timeline).

During this time Mike had become almost famous for his speech on the importance of the Ontario contract. "We need to manage this project carefully," Mike would start. "We can't afford to relax with the recent successes in the south. We knew the competition would be anxious to take the business in our own backyard. I don't have to remind anybody that the margin on the Drive Clean project is tighter than usual. We have the resources and ability to make this project a success—BUT we need to manage the details. We can't afford to have our costs get away on this one. Staffing will be our single largest expenditure and we can't afford to mismanage this asset."

After several meetings, Mike and Alison finally agreed that of the 30 new hires, only 13 of the specialists would be offered full-time, permanent employment. Mike argued that once the project progressed to the implementation phase, certain expertise would no longer be needed.

THE WORK-FROM-HOME PROGRAM

To help attract high-quality staff Alison had made a pitch to Mike to broaden the company's work-from-home program. Alison had argued that "those who would work from home can enjoy the flexibility of making their own hours while not having the expense or frustration of commuting to work each day. Thirty new hires is going to be a challenge in itself. The work-from-home program will certainly help us to attract the right employees in the job market. As well, the company will also benefit by not needing to physically expand the office area or invest in additional office furniture."

With less than ten months left until the official launch date, Mike and Alison had spent the last few weeks meeting with each of the department leaders to explain their strategy for the upcoming increase in personnel. The work-from-home program could be extended to many of the new hires as well as some of the existing staff. Each department head would be responsible for managing the telecommuting situation in his or her department, including making the decisions about who would telecommute and who would work from the office.

Although department managers were not mandated to have a predetermined number of employees work from home, on several occasions Mike made sure to reinforce the benefits of such a program. "Without the program," Mike would explain, "the company will be forced to undergo an expensive move to a new facility. Adding on to the existing building is not possible, and a move would be extremely expensive. The fact that almost half the new hires will be on a one-year contract makes the decision not to move an easy one. To keep costs in line, we simply must find a way to manage the temporary growth in personnel through the work-from-home program."

Despite a great deal of planning and communication, however, several of the department managers had begun to express concern to Alison about the expected lack of accountability, teamwork, and communication that would result from a more intensive work-from-home program. In the past, the program had been used only periodically by a select group of staff members or for a few other temporary situations. After a few days of rather intense debate about the new program, Alison decided to develop an internal document outlining the managerial implications of the program in order to quell fears and to reinforce the basis of the program (see Exhibit 17.1).

THE IMMEDIATE CHALLENGE

Up to this point, Alison's department had been successful in securing eight new programmers and developers. Most had come from the GTA and were able to offer a variety of experience and knowledge for the early stages of the Drive Clean program. In several cases, the potential for an extensive work-from-home program was a strong factor in the new hires' decision to join ETL. However, with 22 more positions vacant and a dwindling number of applications, Alison was feeling a bit overwhelmed. "How on earth can I possibly manage everything!" she wondered to herself. "We need to secure several more staff in the upcoming weeks, but in the meantime we really need to make some decisions on the work-from-home program. How is this going to work? Who's going to be involved and how well are the remaining staff going to adjust?"

Alison's train of thought was interrupted as Mike walked into her office. She realized with a jolt that she had been thinking back over these issues for almost an hour and Mike's conference call was over already.

"The Ministry of Transportation are keen for us to get going and we need to get our work-from-home program in place," Mike started, as he eased himself into a chair across from Alison. "You know we have some issues to address with our internal staff before we can really get our human resources planning finalized. You may have addressed some of the managers' fears with your recent memo," Mike offered, "but you're probably aware of the rumblings as much as I am. Staff aren't happy and I'm concerned about the effects on our ability to implement the Drive Clean contract."

Mike stood up to leave. "Staff are concerned that they will be overlooked for the work-from-home program and are speculating that communication and interpersonal challenges with all the new hires will result in the failure of the Ontario project. Shall we meet in my office at around 5 p.m. to decide what's to be done? I'd appreciate your proposals for making sure we have the human resources to complete the contract."

As Mike left her office, Alison realized that time was becoming increasingly tight to get the project off the ground. She knew she had to have some pretty convincing human resourcing proposals for her boss that afternoon and that she would have to address the issues surrounding the work-from-home program once and for all. She was beginning to wonder if the program would cause more harm than good to her human resources planning at ETL. Teleworking might be a great staffing solution in terms of cost savings and the bottom line, but not at the expense of destroying existing working relationships and processes.

Exhibit 17.1

Evergreen Technologies Ltd.

MEMO

To: Department Managers

From: Alison Hayes

Date: March 23, 20XX

Re: **The 'Work-from-Home' Project: A GUIDE for MANAGERS**

It is important for you, as a manager, to remember that close supervision does not always mean good supervision; good supervision may be achieved without being close in proximity.

Here are some specifics that will help you achieve your goals:

Management skills. The same management skills used to manage employees working in the office apply to those telecommuting.

Work Assignments. Set up a means of communicating deadlines and project requirements. Discuss the expected quality and other criteria that might affect the successful completion of tasks. Communicate to employees what must be done, when it must be done, and who is to do it. The communication may take the form of a phone call, a weekly meeting, or memo. Use whatever means of communication is most comfortable for you. As a manager of off-site employees, the time you spend communicating with the remote workers will dictate the calibre of work they produce. Spend time communicating clearly and concisely the expectations you have of those employees.

Review Work Status. Set up intermediate periods to determine the progress of the tasks the employees are performing. The assessment may be at a designated point during the program, upon completion of certain tasks, or on a recurring basis, such as once a week on Monday.

Timetables. Work with these employees to develop reasonable and timely goals. The employees will clearly understand their workload and will be more focused in their work if they are following a timetable.

Coach and Develop Employees' Capabilities. There is limited time to spend with your remote employees to reinforce behaviour. Make the most of that time. Always reinforce positive behaviour. Bring unsatisfactory performance to the employee's attention immediately. Develop employee capabilities to correct deficiencies. Use the communications tools available to you to provide your employees with timely feedback. The feedback may be via voice mail, electronic mail, a phone call, or a face-to-face conversation.

Also remember that when managing telecommuting, the focus should not be on how the employee accomplishes the task, but whether the task is accomplished in a timely and complete manner. The bottom line is…you should already be familiar with these skills and be using them while supervising your employees located in the office.

If you need any assistance, please feel to contact me directly.

Exhibit 17.2

Evergreen Technologies Limited: Organization Chart

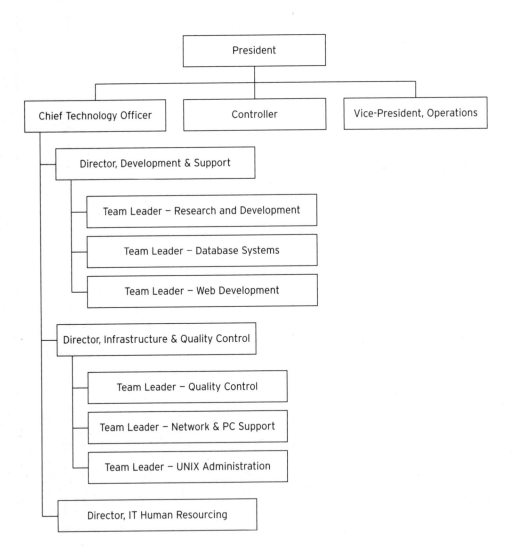

Exhibit 17.3

Project Timeline

(Appendix C) Evergreen Technologies Ltd.

Project:	Ontario - Drive Clean
Development:	Carol Kilmer
Program Mgr:	John Bergeron
Support:	Mike Mauer
Web:	Hanish Bhatia
Database:	Jarno Surmakki
	LAST UPDATED: June 20XX
HR:	Alison Hayes

STATUS UPDATE: → Recruitment is slightly behind schedule. Recruitment expected to continue until Sept or Oct.

SCHEDULE

Project timeline Gantt chart with tasks: Technical Plan Develop. (Jan 21st), HR requirement plan (Nov 3rd), Recruitment (Jan 12th – Aug 23rd), Software - Phase I (Feb 21st – June 1st), Software - Phase II (June 1st – Nov 10th), Test Facility Setup (Sept 18th – Jan 15th), Software - Phase III (Dec 10th – Feb 29th), Station Testing (March 5th – April 5th), Web Access Testing (April 5th – March 17th), Mock Launch & Testing (April 30th), Program Launch (June 15th – Proj. Complete). Columns span Year 1, Year 2, Year 3 with months Nov.–June.

## part four

Creating Positive Organizational Climates

In the previous section, we explored the development and maintenance of workforce effectiveness within turbulent and uncertain organizational contexts. This meant that simplified templates or recipes for success do not exist. These environmental realities also underpin the cases contained in Part 4, but here we focus on issues of health and safety, harassment, and managing the performance relationship when employees become viewed as marginal performers. These issues today are criticized in the development of positive, energizing organizational climates.

HEALTH AND SAFETY

One of the quickest ways to destroy intrinsic motivation is to ignore health and safety issues. Satisfaction and commitment will quickly become alienation, anger, and attrition when employees see co-workers injured or unsafe work ignored. Furthermore, problems with health and safety can have disastrous financial, legal, public relations, and community consequences.

Managers sometimes try to avoid responsibility by blaming victims, creating the illusion of initiative through hollow announcements, or turning a blind eye to health and safety matters. These tactics may make managers feel safer in the short term, but they increase employee cynicism and degrade the working climate. These practices also do little to mitigate legal responsibility and collateral damage. As well, while managers may avoid meaningful health and safety interventions, they will have difficulty repairing the damage to worker attitudes and the cultural fabric of the organization after the cynicism and alienation become firmly rooted.

It is insufficient to focus simply on ensuring that employees "feel" physically safe and secure. Because organizational members may not have experienced personal injury or seen an accident, the risk of injury may be minimized until it is too late. Even when employees feel safe, ill-trained summer students, sloppy work practices, poor housekeeping, long-term exposure to hazardous materials, and habituated unsafe practices by long-term employees set the stage for accidents, serious injury, disability claims, a soured work climate, escalating insurance premiums, death, and criminal charges.

Managers are legally and ethically required to be proactive in health and safety matters. This is a duty they share with their employees, but responsibility for the creation and preservation of a safe and secure work environment ultimately rests on management's shoulders. By law, safety committees must exist in organizations. However, the effectiveness of these committees is dependent upon the informed commitment of management to a safe workplace. Safety rules and responsibilities need to be made clear and the responsibility for enforcing rules needs to be accompanied by the authority to act to ensure compliance. Far too often, safety committees operate with little authority while the short-term need for production and profits supersedes safety concerns. Policy development in the health and safety area, employee and managerial training, access to technical/professional expertise in the health and safety area, and the application of appropriate analytic and problem-solving skills all represent important safety initiatives.

WORKPLACE HARASSMENT

In addition to traditional health and safety concerns, managers also are responsible for ensuring that the work climate is psychologically safe and secure. This gets into the domain of workplace harassment and sexual harassment. Organizations need policies and practices (including training and monitoring) that root out verbal abuse, threats, unwelcome advances and comments, ridicule, displays of offensive materials, unnecessary physical contact, assault, or other acts that embarrass or humiliate a person. Individuals are expected to desist from such inappropriate behaviours, and employers are expected to make the rules clear and to intervene when, to paraphrase the law, "a reasonable person ought to have known their behaviour would be unwelcome."

Managers also must make particular efforts to ensure that those in positions of added responsibility do not abuse their positions of power and influence vis-à-vis their subordinates. An increasingly common complaint in this area involves sexual harassment. Even when a subordinate's response is arguably consensual, there is grave risk that intimate employer-employee relationships will poison the work environment and place the subordinate, the organization, other managers, and the immediate supervisor in jeopardy.

The management of these areas is difficult and often very complex. Nevertheless, positive work environments will not exist without psychological safety.

DISCIPLINE SYSTEMS

Today, the best discipline systems are progressive. They provide warnings and opportunities for improvement before more drastic actions are taken. Oral warnings of poor performance generally precede written warnings; disciplinary suspensions precede final discharge. Managers create discipline problems for themselves by failing to be actively involved in the management of performance via goal setting, the provision of timely performance feedback, training, coaching, and counselling. Processes that begin with early intervention are far superior to disciplinary approaches that only become activated when it is impossible to continue to ignore a problem.

In order to remove the punitive connotation of disciplinary systems, some organizations have moved to embrace "discipline without punishment." In this system, problem employees are told that they are not meeting the standards and expectations of the organization and that their behaviour is unacceptable. They are invited to take time off at company expense and think about whether they really want to continue to be a member of the organization. If they so decide, they are expected to abide by company norms and expectations of acceptable work behaviour and performance. If they fail to deliver on these expectations, the working relationship is then severed.

Regardless of the specifics, human resource managers must know how to deal with issues of safety, health, and harassment, as well as inadequate performance. Managers will expect good advice from HR on their legal responsibilities. HR managers must be prepared to act as consultants and advisors in this critical area. The quality of work is often a function of the quality of work life. In turn, a positive work climate leads to that needed high quality work life.

THE CASES IN PART 4

Northern Copper Corporation presents a tragic safety situation and asks you to assess the cause(s) and develop managerial approaches that would prevent such occurrences from happening in the future.

The Friendly Boss looks at the issue of workplace harassment and its impact on performance.

Katie Lucerne explores the role of management in handling sensitive personal issues that involve performance and personal relationships between a manager and an employee in a branch of a trust company.

The final case in Part 4 (**Regulatory Review Commission**) focuses on redirecting employee behaviour when some form of progressive discipline seems to be required. The formal discipline system becomes part of performance management only when other approaches have been tried, the employee has the ability to perform, and his or her performance continues to be unacceptable.

Northern Copper Corporation

Gene Deszca

Tupper Cawsey

On January 3, two employees were poisoned and died within a week as a result of arsenic gas poisoning suffered in the electrolytic department of Northern Copper Corporation Ltd. (NCC). Fourteen other workers became ill at the same time and reported to hospital. Ten of them were admitted, three in critical condition. The deaths put the company at the centre of considerable controversy concerning corporate legal and moral responsibility for industrial safety.

Aaron Belanger, vice-president, employee relations, for NCC's parent Northern Mines, had to deal with this controversy. He knew that a coroner's inquest was to be held because of the incidents. As well, the president of Northern Mines had directed Aaron to sort out why this tragedy had occurred. He was tasked to prepare a plan to improve safety at NCC, to deal with the individuals responsible, and to recommend actions at the corporate level (see Exhibit 18.1 for a partial organizational chart of key personnel involved in the poisonings).

COMPANY BACKGROUND

NCC was situated in Québec and was a wholly owned subsidiary of Northern Mines Limited. At the time of the deaths, NCC employed 1600 production workers and was a world-scale copper refinery. The previous year's refined copper production was 127 000 tonnes. The production employees were represented by the Steelworkers International Union, Local 603.

The electrolytic department, the location of the incident, was involved in the removal of impurities from the acid used to refine copper. Arsenic gas was always given off during the purification process. The amount of arsine emitted increased as the copper in the solution was removed. The legal limit of arsine gas had been established at 0.16 mg per cubic metre of air. To protect staff operating in the area, NCC's safety supervisor, J. Thibeault, had recommended that no less than 0.5 grams per litre of copper remain in solution.

ARSENIC GAS POISONING

Since 1928, hundreds of cases of industrial arsenic poisoning had been documented in world medical literature. Well over 60 of those documented cases had resulted in death, usually from kidney failure.

Arsenous hydride is the gas produced by the smelting, refining, and galvanizing of certain metals. The gas destroys red blood cells, resulting in blockage of the victim's kidneys and liver. Arsenic poisoning symptoms include dizziness, nausea, weak legs, abdominal pains, and blood in the urine.

PROVINCIAL SAFETY REGULATIONS

At the time of the accident, Québec's provincial legislation contained the following provisions related to the safety and sanitary conditions of employees in industrial and commercial establishments.

General Provisions

- **Safety.** *Sec. 4* Industrial and commercial establishments shall be built and kept in such manner as to secure the safety of all employed in them.
- **Sanitary Conditions.** They shall also be kept in the cleanest possible manner, be sufficiently lighted and have a sufficient quantity of air for the number of persons employed; be provided with effective means for expelling the dust produced during the work, and also the gases and vapours which escape and the refuse resulting therefrom; in a word, fulfill all sanitary conditions necessary for the health of the persons employed, as required by the regulations made in virtue of the *Public Health Act*.

THE INVESTIGATION

Immediately following the arsine gas deaths of Jacques Lavel, 19, and Richard DaSilva, 32, police and provincial safety investigations were initiated. These investigations revealed that arsine gas poisoning of other NCC employees had taken place prior to the fatal poisonings and that certain company managers had knowledge of the potential dangers of arsine gas emitted during the purification process. During the investigation, key personnel were interviewed to establish the facts in the case.

Steve Smith

Steve Smith worked in the same electrolytic department as the two workers who died. He claimed that in the previous year he had been poisoned on two separate occasions in that department—on May 9 and December 16. Smith stated that he had entered the hospital on May 10, where he had stayed six days, and then returned to hospital again on May 21 because he didn't feel well. He was released from the hospital on June 10.

After returning to work, he was again admitted to hospital some seven months later, on December 17. Smith said that on both occasions he felt pain in his stomach, but attributed it at the time to strain from heavy work. He also testified that he had noticed blood in his urine.

On the day following the initial poisoning, Smith returned to the company with the intention of seeing the company doctor because he had just spent a sleepless night and had vomited repeatedly. He was informed that the company doctor was not available. A friend then drove him to the hospital because, as Smith explained, "I couldn't walk very well." Smith went on to say that he was informed a few days later by Dr. Bob Jacob, who had tested him at the hospital, that he was suffering from arsine poisoning. Dr. Jacob documented this information in a letter that was passed on to the union executive.

On June 19, Smith reported that he spoke to Gene Ellis, the company personnel supervisor, about the poisoning. Ellis told him that he "never heard of this before." Subsequently, Ellis made out an accident report for the Workers' Compensation Board. Shortly after returning to work on July 29, Smith was sent back to work in the area in which he had been previously poisoned. He informed the supervisor on duty that he wasn't supposed to work in that area (advice from his physician), but continued anyway, "because everyone said there was no danger."

When interviewed by the *Montréal Globe,* Smith said that he felt the company's investigation following the first incident had been inadequate. "They never even spoke to me," he said. "Had they asked me, I would have told them the exact spot where I got sick, but they didn't even speak to me."

The *Montréal Globe* also reported that Smith had told the doctors that the problem was due to faulty ventilation in the electrolytic department. Dr. Georges Chevalia, physician-in-chief at the hospital, also confirmed that the company had been notified at least twice in June of the definite and dangerous presence of arsine gas in the working environment and told that the situation should be investigated.

Fred Koziel

Fred Koziel was also poisoned on May 9. He was admitted to Royal Victoria Hospital on May 10, and was released May 23. Koziel said, "I was feeling pain in my stomach like someone took a knife and was cutting it out…there was a strong smell in the area where Steve and I were working, and something got caught in our eyes and made us cry." Koziel admitted that he was afraid to inform his superiors of their symptoms "because the company doesn't top up our compensation pay if someone is sick." He stated that he was unaware Smith had been admitted to the same hospital until 10 days after he himself had been admitted.

At the time of his release, Koziel was also informed by doctors that he was suffering from arsine gas poisoning. When he returned to work on June 17, he talked to the personnel supervisor Gene Ellis. Koziel reported that Ellis told him, "The tank house has 350 people and nobody gets sick, only you." He also testified that, in telling a supervisor of his poisoning, "it was the first time anyone had heard about it." Koziel said he saw Dr. J. E. Hunter, the company doctor, when he returned to work on June 17 but that "he said nothing when I told him about my condition." Two days later, he said, a supervisor made out a report of the incident.

John Walsh

John Walsh, the superintendent of the processing department, was contacted, and reported that company vice-president Bruce Adamson had rejected a "good, cheap ventilation system" proposed a full 15 months prior to the arsine gas fatalities. He went on to say that Adamson had shown very little interest in the plan even though it was likely that such a system could have been installed in five months.

Walsh stated that he began investigating his proposed ventilation system immediately after Henri Morin, the environment supervisor, detected high levels of arsine gas above the electrolytic department's purification cells. His tests had been conducted between January and July, two years earlier. The "Air Curtain" ventilation system proposed by Walsh in October of that year had been estimated to cost $100 000.

The company eventually chose a ventilation system that involved the placement of metal hoods over each purification cell (estimated cost: $450 000). The plans, however, took 20 months to complete, and final approval for the system was not received until December, just weeks before the poisoning fatalities. Walsh said that he was not satisfied with the interim measures taken, although the installation of two portable fans on each side of each cell seemed effective.

When asked whether he had stressed to his superiors the need for immediate precautionary measures, Walsh stated that he felt he had "insisted sufficiently" to put his point across. He later admitted that he had quit his job with NCC (following the deaths) because he felt he was not sufficiently involved in technical decisions at the plant.

Walsh testified that Bruce Adamson, vice-president, had the ultimate say about his recommendations and that it had appeared to him that management preferred to handle the arsine gas problem through outside advisors. "I felt we (the processing department) should have been more free in making people aware of the dangers," Walsh said. "This was one of the areas where I thought more should have been done to avoid long-term negative effects."

Later, Walsh stated that he had also recommended to Adamson that all employees working near dangerous metals be given regular medical examinations. Adamson's reaction to this had been: "We've got to tread very carefully in these matters."

The former superintendent told investigators that Adamson had called him in to his office to tell him of the arsine poisonings of Koziel and Smith the previous May. Walsh was then told that the two men had worked everywhere in the plant and that he should undertake tests throughout the plant to pinpoint the source of the arsine gas.

When Walsh was asked why he had not consulted with the stricken workers themselves to find out where they had been working, he replied, "I personally didn't ask and apparently no one else did." He then said that the tests had taken three months to complete and that the results had shown the purification cells to be the sole source of arsine gas.

Walsh also testified that he had made other recommendations that had been rejected or ignored. These included a paper safety tag, to be worn by refinery employees, which had been chemically treated so that it would turn yellow on exposure to dangerous levels of arsine gas. Another recommendation was that the copper concentration in the electrolyte solution be maintained above a minimum level of 0.5 grams per litre in the purification cells, as lower concentrations emitted more arsine gas.

Bob Rowe

Bob Rowe, superintendent of the tankhouse where the poisonings had taken place, stated that he had received a direction from someone (possibly one of the chemists) to reduce the copper concentration in the electrolyte solution to .006 grams per litre—in short, to extract a large amount of copper. He admitted he was aware that lowering the copper concentration would mean an increase in the emission of arsine gas. He said he was unaware of Walsh's recommendation to maintain the content of copper in the solution above 0.5 grams per litre.

Rowe reported that he had first learned of the arsine gas danger while attending monthly meetings with chemists, well after the first poisonings had occurred. He told the investigation that these meetings were attended by Adamson, production manager Ray Murray, and company engineers.

Gene Ellis

Gene Ellis, personnel supervisor, told the investigators that, in late May, he had received a phone call from Dr. Bob Jacob of the Royal Victoria Hospital, who told him that Koziel and Smith were in hospital suffering from arsine gas poisoning. Ellis commented that, "the doctor said the reason he called was to make us aware of the problem, so no one else would be exposed."

Ellis reported that he had informed Bruce Adamson of the matter within half an hour of the call and then dropped the subject because "I felt it was out of my hands and my superior was handling it."

He was informed on December 19 that Smith had again been admitted to hospital suffering identical symptoms as before. He then informed Adamson of the situation.

Later it was learned that Ellis had been aware that a second employee had also been admitted to hospital on the same day. However, he had not been aware at that time that it was another case of arsine gas poisoning. When Ellis learned about the second case of poisoning, he immediately informed Adamson.

Henri Moran

Henri Morin, the environment supervisor, reported that poison gas had been detected two years ago near the purification tanks. Reports on air samples taken in the purification area, dated April 6 and August 9, were submitted to the investigation.

Morin revealed that concentrations of arsine gas as high as 1.7 mg per cubic metre had been detected two years earlier—more than 10 times the legal limit.

The environment supervisor stated that the highest concentrations had been found about a metre above the purification tanks. He added that because of the relative density of arsine gas, concentrations would have been double at 10 cm above the tanks.

Further questioning revealed that Morin found the building's ventilation system inadequate to disperse lower concentrations of arsine gas. Following his first report, he had advised his supervisors that management should undertake further studies of ventilation systems, owing to the presence of higher arsine levels.

He also said he had recommended that the purification cells be checked once every three hours to make sure that copper concentration in the electrolyte solution was high enough to prevent the emission of excess amounts of arsine gas. He said, "My job is to analyze environmental problems and make suggestions. I'm not responsible for putting them into operation."

During the investigation, Joseph Petrano, pump operator in charge of the purification cells on the day the two fatalities occurred, stated that there had been no copper in five of the cells during his shift but that he had not found this situation "abnormal."

While the company studied various ventilation systems used by American refineries, Morin had fans placed in the purification area for the purpose of dispersing the gas. He admitted that the results of his August 9 sample testing were obtained after the fans were in operation. He said that plans had been developed the previous year for a ventilation system similar to one studied in a Baltimore refinery and that "the company wanted to go ahead with the plans."

When asked whether he had heard of the incidents of arsine gas poisoning in May and in December, Morin replied, "I heard about the problems in May but not the one in December." He added, "In May we started a campaign of gas tests in all the departments to determine if there was another source of gas."

Morin was then asked if he realized that concentrations of arsine as high as 1.7 mg per cubic metre represented a danger to the health of employees around the purification tanks. The environment supervisor remarked, "It's high for sure. But no workers were in the area while purification cells were operating." He added that "a lot of the tests were well below the limit."

Morin indicated that he was uncertain whether or not employees at the plant were aware of the arsine gas danger, adding that aside from a "No Smoking" sign, there were no other posted warnings in the purification tank area.

Dr. J. E. Hunter

Dr. Hunter, the company doctor, reported that he was unaware of the May and December arsine poisonings of Smith and Koziel, or any arsine gas problems in the plant, until January 4. Upon learning of the earlier incidents, he checked his files and discovered that the initial medical reports listed other reasons for the workers' absence, though subsequent documents did reference arsine poisoning. Dr. Hunter explained that he was only at the plant two and a half days a week, and, while absent, was replaced by a first-aid attendant. The doctor emphasized that he relied on his attendant to inform him about important issues that needed his attention. Thus, Dr. Hunter testified, he wasn't aware of everything that happened at the plant.

He stated that, had he been aware of the earlier poisonings, he "would have probably ordered blood and urine tests for all the employees working in the electrolytic department." Pre-employment urine tests and lung X-rays were said to be administered to all employees. However, some employees had stated that they had never been given a urine test in the pre-employment examination.

Jacques Thibeault

Safety supervisor Jacques Thibeault told the investigation that no accident reports were made about the May poisonings, and the matter had not been raised since he thought it was in management's hands. Thibeault stated that Gene Ellis, the personnel supervisor, had told him in December that he and Jean Fortier, supervisor of industrial relations, were handling the situation. Thibeault was also told that Adamson had been notified and that "they were looking into it." Thibeault went on to say that prior to the May incidents he had never heard of arsine gas and didn't know anyone was in danger. He explained, "We never had a problem like this before."

With regard to the December poisoning, Thibeault stated that Tim Williams, assistant supervisor of industrial relations, had told him not to give the accident report to the union and "to refer all questions to Fortier," Williams' supervisor. When asked if he found this odd, Thibeault replied, "It did strike me as a bit odd but I had no authority."

Ray Murray

When questioned about industrial safety instruction, Ray Murray, production manager, stated that the workers around the purification cells had never been given emergency instructions. "It wasn't right but that's the way it was," he commented. He repeated Morin's observation that no warning signs—except for a "No Smoking" sign—were posted in the area. Testimony from NCC workers revealed that employees had been given courses on industrial safety but none had mentioned toxic gases.

Bruce Adamson

When questioned about the May poisonings, Bruce Adamson, vice-president and general manager, stated that there had been no earlier incidents of arsine gas poisoning and that he presumed the poisonings occurred over a long period of time. He explained that he had no medical knowledge of the gas and had not attempted to see if the poisonings might have occurred within a short span of time. He stated that the company had been taking action to rectify the problem prior to the fatalities and that the company blamed itself for not connecting the two apparently isolated arsine gas incidents that had occurred earlier.

Alex Fournier

When questioned about the company's efforts to obtain a new ventilation system, NCC president Alex Fournier said NCC had begun looking for a ventilation system two years ago. After contacts with many companies, Fournier said he had chosen a suitable system. The system and necessary modifications were approved in December.

When asked specifically about the May poisonings, Fournier said that he wasn't aware where the men had been working but, if he had known about the dangerous gas, he would have shut down the area. He stated that he hadn't heard about the December poisonings at the time. When questioned about worker safety instruction, Fournier admitted that the pump operators should have been aware of the danger and been trained appropriately but, he explained, "The president can't be with every worker." Fournier said he was unaware of regulations stipulating that toxic-gas-producing systems must be covered with huts and that the head of an establishment must inform plant workers of the risks involved in their work.

Fournier went on to report that he always knew the problem of arsine gas would arise some day, but "it simply hadn't yet." He said he was aware of reports by Henri Morin, the environment supervisor, warning of arsine gas danger, but explained that his own knowledge about arsine gas was somewhat limited and "no one in our company knew very much about it either." He acknowledged that Morin knew about arsine gas dangers, but stated that his own knowledge about its medical characteristics were somewhat limited. When asked how far behind the company was in implementing its plans for a new ventilation system, he answered, "Roughly 20 years." Twenty years ago he had co-authored a report advocating safety measures and explaining the danger of arsine gas.

When questioned about decision-making authority and responsibility within the organization, Fournier stated that NCC's policies were those of its parent company, Northern Mines, and that targets were established by the parent. Fournier said his ultimate responsibility was to the NCC Board of Directors. He also had a responsibility to develop the Québec refinery to accomplish the goals set out by head office. Questioned about the responsibilities of Bruce Adamson, he stated, "Bruce Adamson, the vice-president and general manager, is more in charge of the day-to-day operations. He also has ultimate responsibility in safety matters."

Jean Fortier

Jean Fortier, the supervisor of industrial relations, testified that he had had some knowledge of the arsine gas problem but believed that technical decisions had been made that would rectify the problem. He based this belief upon the fact that Adamson had been made aware of the earlier events and that proposed technical changes had been approved. He admitted that he had at first decided not to inform the bargaining unit of the matter because he wanted to confirm the nature of the problem, and he did not want it to become a bargaining issue. However, once events were confirmed, it was his recollection that he had authorized the release of the information to the bargaining unit through the in-house medical services, and he did not know why the bargaining unit had not been informed of the matter.

Alain Dufresne

Alain Dufresne was the local president of the NCC bargaining unit (Steelworkers International Union, Local 603). He testified that he had some awareness that there may have been gas problems in certain parts of the plant but that he had been unaware of the seriousness or magnitude of the problem. Further, he had been led to believe by management that the problem was in the process of being rectified and that interim steps had been taken (fans and minimum copper concentration levels) to ensure that no one was at risk. He could not recall who specifically had told him this, but he thought it was likely Morin or Walsh. He noted that many people were involved in safety-related matters at NCC, and he confirmed that formal procedures and policies existed. However, he noted that procedures were often not followed and that informal processes were often used to resolve matters. When asked why the union had not pushed for more activity in this area, he stated that it had, but that the organization had responded that NCC's track record (no fatalities and lower-than-normal compensation accident rates) demonstrated that the current approach was serving the needs of employees.

AARON BELANGER'S TASK

Aaron Belanger knew the seriousness of the situation. He knew his plan must correct the problem and deal fairly with the individuals involved. As well, it was obvious that such accidents must never be allowed to happen at NCC again.

Exhibit 18.1
Northern Copper Corporation: Partial Management Staff Organization

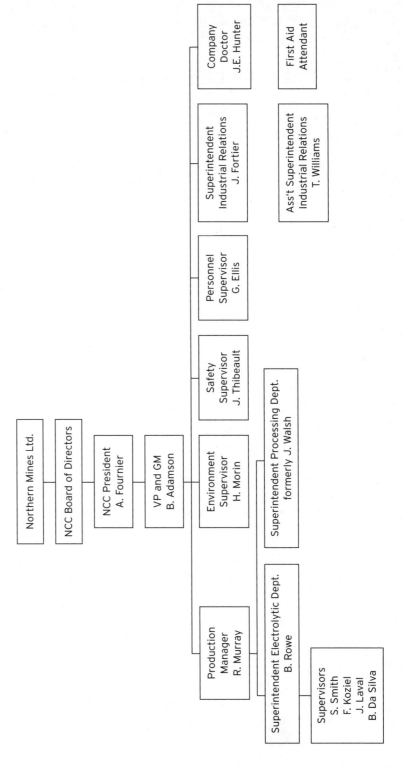

The Friendly Boss (A)*

Bernadette Schell

Tupper Cawsey

Kathleen Cawsey

Jan Wu, Ontario regional manager of human resources for Ignis Canada, Ltd., dialled the number for the Kingston branch of Ignis.

Tracey Eagles, the Kingston branch's executive assistant, answered, and Wu told her that she would be coming to the Kingston office the following Monday. She tried to make a point of stopping by every branch in Ontario once a month or so, to give employees and managers a chance to speak to her directly if they needed to.

"Sure, Jan," Eagles answered. "I'll let people know."

"Good," Wu said. "Can you be sure that Victoria is in that day?"

"No problem." Eagles' cheerful voice paused. "But did you hear she's retiring?"

"Really? When did this happen?"

"Oh, I dunno, I think she's been thinking about it for a while. Ever since all this stuff's been happening. But in June she'll reach the 20-year mark, so maybe she just wants to take her pension and get out. Twenty years is a long time with a company, these days."

*Part B of this case is provided in the Instructor's Manual.

"Hmm," Wu said. "Well, thanks Tracey. I'll see you Monday."

Wu hung up the phone and sat back thoughtfully. She hoped Victoria Markham had indeed chosen to retire because she had reached the 20-years-of-service pension bonus, and not because of the situation with her boss, David Rostini. Wu had thought the whole issue had pretty much been resolved—but what if it hadn't? And if it was a factor in Markham's retirement, as Tracey Eagles seemed to think, should Wu do anything about it?

THE SITUATION

Over a year before, in January 1997, Victoria Markham had approached Wu on one of the HR manager's regular visits to the Kingston branch. Markham was the human resources administrator in Kingston, a position she had held for nearly seven years.

Markham told Wu that she was concerned about the recent behaviour of her boss, David Rostini, manager of the Kingston branch of Ignis. Rostini had become "overly friendly" lately, Markham said, often complimenting her about her clothes or job performance, stopping by to see if she'd had her coffee break yet, calling her on a business matter but then continuing to chat with her about personal matters once the business was done.

"Lately he's even started calling me at home," Markham said. "And I feel like he's always watching me."

At the time, Wu had been unsure of how serious Markham's complaint was. Ignis Canada was a relatively large corporation, with offices in most major cities, and had comprehensive policies in place to deal with harassment issues. These included the requirement to take every complaint seriously, however minor; to protect the confidentiality of both complainant and accused; and to maintain a zero tolerance approach to the following behaviours:

- unwanted sexual advances or requests for sexual favours
- unwelcome verbal or physical conduct of a sexual nature
- insinuations, suggestions, or threats that the employee's response to such behaviour might influence employment decisions, such as hiring, promotion, raises, and so on.
- the creation of an intimidating, hostile, or offensive working environment through such acts as sexual, lewd, or profane remarks; body touching; staring; or obscene or pornographic photos.

In accordance with this policy, Wu and Markham met confidentially several times to determine the course of action Markham wished to take. They discussed various options, ranging from approaching Rostini about his actions, to filing a formal complaint of sexual harassment.

Markham decided to deal with the issue herself rather than involving the head office in Toronto. She spoke with Rostini about her concerns, and he apologized for his behaviour.

Over the next few months, Wu made sure to visit the Kingston office regularly, and to check in with Markham about the situation. "It's not a problem," was Markham's usual response.

However, Wu also kept her ears open—as much as she could without breaking any confidences—when around the other Kingston employees. Tracey Eagles was a close friend of Victoria Markham, and she told Wu that she didn't think the situation had changed much.

"The whole office can see it," she said. "He's completely infatuated with her. Acts like a love-sick teenager, mooning around after her. It's kind of embarrassing, really, seeing as they're both married. She's stopped taking coffee breaks, because he manages to time his to coincide, and I usually pick up her line on the phone, pretending she's on the other line, so she doesn't have to talk to him directly."

Eagles thought for a minute when Wu asked her if Rostini's behaviour had ever seemed aggressive or threatening. "He's a nice man," she said. "He always acts like a gentleman, always wears a suit and tie. He once called me into his office because I swore when I accidentally stapled my thumb, and he said such language was not tolerated in this office. I think he's just really infatuated."

Another time, Wu noticed Markham's desk had been moved. Markham herself just shrugged when Wu asked about it, but Eagles said she had moved because the new location could not be seen from Rostini's open office door.

In September 1997, another employee approached Wu on an unrelated issue. Andrew Molnar was process coordinator at the Kingston branch, and he wanted to know if there might be an opening in a similar position at another branch. He felt underappreciated in the Kingston office and was frustrated that his efforts to contribute came to nothing. Molnar believed that Markham had too much influence in staff meetings, and that Rostini deferred to her judgment to the exclusion of anyone else's.

"He even listens to her on financial or accounting issues, areas completely beyond her jurisdiction," Molnar said. "I mean—no offense—but what business does an HR person have in a finance meeting?"

"I like David, personally," he continued. "He goes to my church; we belong to the same gun club. But this infatuation is getting out of hand—he's letting her control him completely. Nobody else around here matters. And I'm not the only one to notice it. Ask anybody—morale in this office is really low."

In December 1997, Markham reported to Wu that Rostini had given her a potted plant, but that she had returned it. "I feel silly reporting something like this," she told Wu. "I mean, he has a perfect right to give me a plant. But it just feels…squirmy."

In light of these incidents, Wu wondered if Rostini had an "ongoing infatuation" with Markham, and in January 1998, she recommended to her superiors that he be moved to a different branch, despite Victoria Markham's statements that things were "fine" and her disinclination to take further action.

As of April 1998, however, no openings had become available. Moreover, Rostini had received a poor performance appraisal during the last employee evaluation. A confidential employee survey revealed that the employees had little confidence in him as a manager. Rostini had been informed of these results, and his superior at head office had sent him a letter stating that, despite his 25-year service with the company, a change was required in his performance or he could face dismissal.

Jan Wu swivelled back and forth in her chair as she considered the Kingston situation. On the one hand, Victoria Markham's retirement was probably a good thing, since the situation would essentially disappear once Markham left. On the other hand, if Markham's retirement had been prompted by the situation in the office, Wu wondered what responsibility, if any, she herself held, and what the company might owe its employee. Before Monday, she decided, she would have to choose whether to simply allow things to take their course and let Markham retire, or whether to take some sort of action.

Katie Lucerne

Bill Cooper

The Island is a pleasant agrarian community linked to the City by a ferry service. It is closely knit, with most residents aware of, and interested in, the daily activities of their fellow islanders. Island-wide social events are always well attended; it has its own weekly newspaper; and its residents clearly identify with the Island. Its chief exports are milk and people. While many of its youth remain to farm the gently rolling land, most leave to work on the mainland, but often return to vacation at home in the summer.

Katie Lucerne grew up on the Island and attended school there until she was 13. Thereafter, she and her schoolmates commuted to the City on the ferry to attend high school. She was a good student, graduating in the top quarter of her class, and she was well liked by her classmates. After a year of clerical training at the local community college, she found a job as a junior clerk in the Trust Company. When she began her job she moved to the City, but after two months moved back to the Island to live with her parents.

BACKGROUND

The Trust Company was a branch of a national financial institution that dealt in personal loans and mortgages. It had branches in most large and many medium-sized cities in the country. In an attempt to differentiate itself from its competitors, it stressed its friendly attitude toward customers and the "small-town" approach in its advertising copy. The internal counterpart of this was a personnel policy that stressed staff friendliness towards customers and high visibility of its employees (particularly managers) via community service. When Katie joined the City branch there were 15 employees. A partial organization chart is shown in Exhibit 20.1.

Katie's first job at the branch involved teller activities and keeping customer accounts up to date. She learned this job quickly, and after six months became the head clerk. As head clerk she was responsible for keeping records according to the procedures manual and doing minor supervision of the two junior clerks. The performance appraisal done after her first year of employment showed that she was rated as above average in all categories. She was energetic and frequently the centre of conversation during coffee breaks. A note by the branch manager, Martin House, showed that he found her to be a good employee with the potential to take on more responsibility. Within three months of her anniversary evaluation, she became head cashier. In this position she was responsible for keeping track of the cash flow.

Shortly before Katie became head cashier, a new assistant manager, Leo Madden, joined the branch. Leo had also grown up on the Island but was five years older than Katie. As an Islander, he had known her vaguely before he left to join the Trust Company on the West Coast. His appointment as assistant manager was a promotion to a position in which he would be responsible for running the clerical aspects of the office. He was pleased with the appointment, both because of the promotion and because it returned him to his home area. Leo quickly established himself as a promising manager who had an eye for managing systems and procedures, detecting work errors, and also for noticing available females.

Leo and Katie were immediately attracted to each other. Both were single, not seeing anyone seriously, and soon were sharing lunches together in the park. Initially out of convenience, but later for other reasons, they shared car rides to and from work via the ferry. Everyone in the office, including Martin House, knew of the romance between Leo and Katie. The relationship posed no particular problem, at least not initially, because it did not interfere with work and both were good, reliable employees. The other single females teased Katie about the relationship, but clearly regarded Katie as lucky.

By the time of Katie's second anniversary evaluation, her performance had settled into being that of a steady, above-average employee. If she was no longer the eager, bright trainee she had been two years earlier, neither was she a problem employee. She would occasionally have cash imbalances, but these were infrequent, small, and as likely to be long as short on cash. For his part, Leo's work record was steady and reliable. If the usual career pattern ran its course, he would likely remain as assistant manager for another year and then be promoted to branch manager of a small branch somewhere in the region.

Once the affair between Katie and Leo became established, most of the employees accepted it. The dominant view was that both were young, attractive, and suited to each other, and it would be a happy office event if they were married. Among the older married staff, a somewhat different view was held. At least two of them saw Leo as an experienced man taking advantage of Katie's relative innocence. While these employees would be pleased if Katie and Leo were married, they remained skeptical about this happening, and fully expected Leo's eventual transfer and promotion to be neither preceded nor followed by his marriage to Katie.

EARLY JUNE

Katie's stable pattern changed dramatically during the first week of June. The week began with a cash shortage much larger than usual ($40). She had no explanation for the shortage and was visibly shaken by the slip-up. By Wednesday, she was acting very coldly towards both the customers and her fellow workers, including Leo. On Wednesday she asked Leo for an extra hour at noon, which was granted. She came back at 2 p.m. and seemed somewhat more relaxed, greeting her co-workers pleasantly on her return. Again on Thursday, she requested an extra hour, but this time returned pale and tense. Her work that afternoon was seriously deficient. She had been preparing a report on the patterns in cash flows for Martin House, which she gave him at the closing of business on Thursday. He reviewed the report at home Thursday evening and found a large number of errors. He spoke to Katie about the mistakes on Friday morning. She was embarrassed by the mistakes and took the report with her, promising to return it corrected and redone on Monday afternoon. She worked on the report through her lunch hour on Friday, leaving work at 4 p.m., again with Leo's permission. Twice during the afternoon, Katie suddenly went to the women's lounge, wiping her eyes with her handkerchief.

MONDAY MORNING

On his drive into the City on Monday morning, Martin House thought about what to do. He was alarmed at the sudden decline in the quality of Katie's work, but was largely mystified as to its cause. His only idea was that it was a serious personal problem that might be connected with her relationship with Leo Madden. One thing that bothered Martin about this possibility was that, for the past three months, he had heard rumours from a number of people, including several customers, that Leo and Katie's relationship had become more serious. The most startling statement had come in a conversation between Martin and the ferryboat captain, a regular customer at the branch. He had told Martin that on a number of occasions he and others had seen Katie and Leo engaged in what he described as "activities which are not usually carried on in public view" while in Leo's car on the ferry home. The captain also told him that, while the Island community was generally tolerant towards its youth, the escalation in these amorous activities had been the subject of much discussion, the bulk of which was unfavourable towards both Katie and Leo. To his knowledge, however, no one had spoken directly to either of them about their displays.

This information initially upset Martin, but on thinking about it, he decided that it was not sufficiently the company's business for him to say anything to either of them. The office rumours that they were engaged helped to alleviate some of Martin's worries, but he also noticed that Katie wore no engagement ring, and no announcement had been made. His one direct piece of information was an overheard conversation between Leo and one of the clerks in which Leo jokingly denied any knowledge of the engagement. This, coupled with the fact that Martin had seen Leo walking hand-in-hand with another woman only two weeks ago, led him to suspect that Leo's marital expectations might be considerably different from Katie's.

By the time Martin arrived downtown, he had decided he must take some action. Katie's work was now unacceptable. Martin's relationship with Katie was, much like his relationship with all his employees (including Leo), a mixture of supervisor-subordinate and casual friend. He had daily contact with her, knew her personal background, and felt fairly comfortable with her. While Martin's primary responsibility was generating new business for the branch, he also had final authority for hiring, promoting, disciplining, and firing employees. If anyone were going to take action, it was going to be Martin.

Martin took out his keys to open the office door but found it unlocked. Inside was one of the older clerks, Barbara Weiver, sitting having a cup of coffee. Martin thought maybe she could help with the Katie Lucerne business. He poured himself a coffee and sat down. After exchanging pleasantries about their respective weekends, Martin awkwardly cleared his throat and said, "Barbara, I've noticed that Katie's not been herself lately. Do you know anything about it? I'm a little worried about her." Barbara took a long time to reply. Finally, without looking up from her mug of coffee, she said, "I don't know if I should tell you this, Mr. House, but I think you should know. I've been worried myself, and on Saturday I ran into Katie downtown. We had coffee at the Scarecrow, and as we were leaving she burst into tears and told me she was sure she was pregnant. But apparently the pregnancy tests have been inconclusive for some reason, and..." At that moment Katie and Leo quietly came through the door. Martin and Barbara's conversation quickly reverted to a discussion of their weekends. Martin then excused himself, went to his office, and shut the door.

He sat for quite a while checking over Friday's business but wasn't paying much attention to what he was reading. Katie's problem was not exactly what he had expected, but he was not altogether surprised either. His thoughts were interrupted by a telephone call. It was from the branch manager of another local trust company confirming their noon luncheon appointment.

Putting down the telephone, Martin looked at his appointment calendar and mentally blocked out the 2–3 p.m. section for a meeting with Katie. He didn't know what he would say nor how he would say it, but he knew he had to talk to Katie now. He also suspected he would end up talking to Leo as well, perhaps to them both together. Martin House rose from his chair, walked to the window, and thought about what he would rather be doing on the warm June morning. He would much rather be shooting a set of rapids in his kayak rather than preparing to deal with this messy problem. He reluctantly turned from the window, sat down at his desk, and began to sketch out how he wanted to conduct the interview(s).

Exhibit 20.1

Partial Organization Chart: The Trust Company

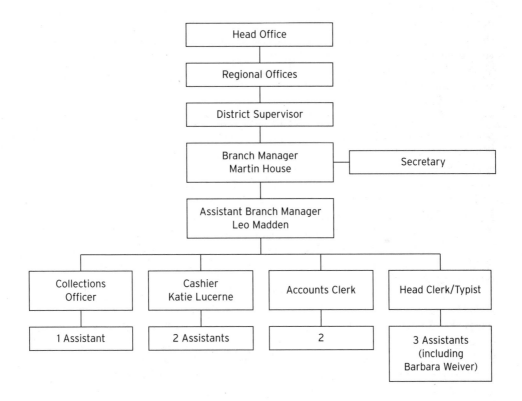

Regulatory Review Commission

Tupper Cawsey

Monique Ricard and Brian Coffey are both employees of the Regulatory Review Commission (RRC), a department of the government. Work in a government office is different from many job situations in that an employee's job security is virtually ensured unless he or she can be proven to be incompetent (see Exhibit 21.1 for the RRC's guidelines and requirements for dismissal). However, as Brian's supervisor, Monique was concerned about his performance. She wondered what action she should take to correct the situation.

BACKGROUND

Although the RRC was reorganized fairly often, Monique and Brian worked within a stable group of employees known as the operations centre. The centre's employees had worked together for several months and had developed into an effective, results-oriented team. From the manager down, an effort was made to ensure that all employees were kept informed of policies and procedures and the reasons behind changes or special requests. The pattern established was one of trust on the part of both supervisors and subordinates (see Exhibit 21.2 for an organizational chart for the operations centre, a division of operations information and change control).

The operations centre was responsible for receiving, accumulating, and disseminating status reports on all major policy and operational projects within the RRC. Consequently, much of the information handled was considered to be highly confidential and high priority. Because the centre also operated as a clearing house for urgent requests for information and as a central point for dissemination of emergency reports, it had to be staffed on a continuous basis during office hours (8:15 a.m. to 4:30 p.m.). Under normal conditions, both Monique and Brian were physically located in the centre, which was off-limits to all unauthorized personnel. If Brian had to leave the centre, Monique had to remain until he returned, and vice versa (see Exhibit 21.3 for a layout of the operations centre).

BRIAN COFFEY

Brian was hired over a year ago as a casual employee; he was hired for an indeterminate period and could be discharged at any time. However, the RRC has a policy stating that, when there is no more work for a casual employee in a given job, all possible efforts should be made to place him or her where there is a requirement for an employee of comparable qualifications. Brian started as a statistical clerk, graduated to correspondence clerk, and finally won a competition for a post requiring statistical and analytical expedience at the CR4 (clerical and regulatory classification, level 4) level. Employees at the CR4 level were expected to work with a minimum of direct supervision but under general guidelines and, occasionally, in a supervisory capacity. (For purposes of comparison, a mail delivery person is a CR1, whereas the supervisor of the mailroom is a CR5.)

Brian's six-month probationary period in this permanent appointment was to expire in August. However, because the personnel requirements in his section were reduced in May, he was put on a transfer list and assigned to the operations centre in June.

At the time, Brian was 21 years old and had taken some university courses in psychology, which he had not completed. He hoped to join the Royal Canadian Mounted Police (RCMP) and had already been through several interviews with their recruiters, although the prospects for his acceptance into the RCMP were slim.

Before Brian began work, Monique studied his personnel file and noticed that no appraisal had ever been done on him, and that a letter of reprimand had been written by his first supervisor concerning his attendance and motivation. His last supervisor, Bob Wilson, indicated that he had experienced the same problems, although he had never put anything in writing. Since Monique and Bob's sections operated on the same floor, she had already had occasion to observe Brian's work habits.

MONIQUE RICARD

Monique was 24 years old and had a BComm. After spending a summer on a large construction site in Labrador and a winter in Europe, she had done various odd jobs before joining the RRC as a clerk in December, over a year ago.

After four months, she was made head of change control and, eventually, supervisor of the newly formed operations centre. At this time, she was also in the process of training her replacement in change control.

BRIAN COFFEY AT WORK

When Brian joined the operations centre, his first job description stated that he was expected to plan and develop charts and statistical formats analyzing and incorporating information received in status reports. After an orientation session, he was given a list of assignments for which he would be responsible.

His first assignment was to develop and draw originals for wall charts that would be used to graph project status. Although the quality of the final product was excellent, it was completed much more slowly than Monique or her supervisor (who had experience in Brian's job) considered necessary. Only after repeated proddings did Brian finally get the charts printed and mounted on the walls. Within two weeks, a pattern had emerged: He would get his assignments done either after or just before stated deadlines, never as soon as he could. After Brian had been on staff for three weeks, Monique had a formal interview with him. They discussed the time it took him to respond to requests, his frequent extended lunch and coffee breaks, and late arrivals. (Brian was so concerned about his time off that he had installed a clock on his desk that was set to ring at noon and 4:30 p.m.). Although he was agreeable during this session, his behaviour did not change.

In early July, Brian was away from the office on Monday and part of Tuesday without advising Monique of his absence or the reasons for it. When he returned, Monique again spoke with him about appropriate behaviour for the staff in that department and his unacceptable attitude. When she wrote up her notes of the interview, detailing Brian's commitment to improve his behaviour, and submitted the memo to him for signature, he refused to sign it. He wrote his own memo to personnel indicating his disagreement with Monique's opinions and statements about his performance.

MONIQUE RICARD'S DECISION

Brian's probationary period would expire within three weeks, after which he would be considered a permanent employee. Considering the difficulty of discharging permanent employees, as well as the time constraints under which she was operating, Monique was now in the process of identifying her alternatives and choosing a course of action.

Since Brian had been working with her for less than two months, she wasn't sure that she had sufficient proof to justify a recommendation to discharge him. If she did initiate the process, however, she knew it would occupy much time—which she could hardly spare. She would also have to face the prospect that during that period, Brian would be virtually useless to her. Moreover, she could not add a new staff member to carry out Brian's duties. She could put Brian's name on a transfer list and hope that his qualifications were required elsewhere. However, because of the way reputations travelled in the building, she felt reasonably sure that no other section would accept him.

A third alternative would be to request that his probationary period be extended, so that she would have more time to either document his behaviour or improve it, if possible. Monique wasn't sure which alternative would be most advantageous to Brian and to the organization.

Exhibit 21.1

Extracts from RRC Requirements for Dismissal (English only)

Section 33

Administrative Actions

Subject 1

Demotion or Release for Incompetence

(1) Definition

Incompetence is defined as being unable to perform duties satisfactorily according to the job requirements and PS Selection Standards and the RRC, performance problems due to physical or mental health or misconduct.

(2) Policy

1. Where an employee is incompetent in the performance of his duties and where management has made every reasonable effort to assist that employee to improve his performance, management has the authority to remove that employee from his job.

2. Where management decides that the employee can competently perform duties of a lower level position and such a position is available, action is then taken to demote that employee to the lower level position under Section 31 (1)(a) of the Public Service Employment Act. This action is subject to appeal. See Section 30 of this Manual.

3. Where management decides that the employee could not competently perform duties of a lower level position, action is taken to release that employee under Section 31(1)(b) of the Public Service Employment Act. This action is subject to appeal. See Section 30 of this Manual.

4. Administrative action of this type is technically an appointment.

(3) Procedures

1. Before deciding to proceed with the administrative action referred to above, management is obliged to ensure that there is documented evidence of incompetence as well as documented evidence of efforts to assist the employee. Documented evidence would include:

a) performance appraisal;
b) statement of objectives to correct problem signed by employee;
c) examples of incompetence.

Without this information, it is unlikely that efforts to release or demote will prove successful. However, with such documentation, these procedures can be effectively utilized.

2. District managers *must* consult the RPA. Head office directors and chiefs *must* consult the HQ-PA. Personnel must review documentation and corroborate validity of case.

3. RPSa and HQ-PA should observe Part D, Appendix 15, of the PS Staffing Manual.

(4) Pay Action

Demotion for Incompetence. Where an employee is demoted involuntarily to a lower level position, he must be paid at the minimum rate of pay for that position. However, where circumstances are such that management wishes to pay at an incremental level above the minimum, representation may be made to Treasury Board. Such requests should be made *after* demotion action has been successfully concluded in that the appeal period has expired without appeal or the appeal has been dismissed.

Exhibit 21.2

RRC Staff Organization: Operations Information and Change Control

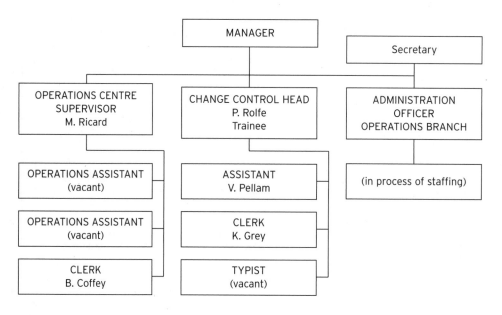

Exhibit 21.3

RRC Layout of the Operations Centre

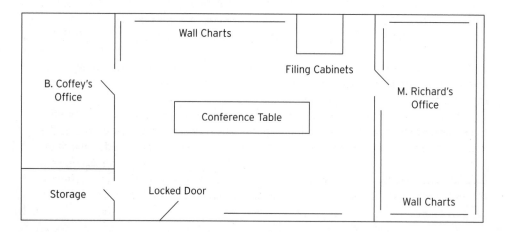

## part five

New HRM Horizons

The economic slump of the early 1980s and 1990s and the rising influence of NAFTA, the European Union, and the World Trade Organization have focused attention on the need for competitiveness in both the local and international marketplaces. Organizations (including government ministries, hospitals, schools, and not-for-profit organizations) are functioning within highly competitive environments that demand systems thinking, strategic foresight and ingenuity, and services that are cost-efficient, effective, and responsive to market changes and customer needs. All of this must fit with an internal organizational environment that honours the principles of fairness, equity, and due process. Organizations are expected to create and deliver superior value to their customers in a timely and profitable manner by developing and acting on their understanding of their customers and the environment. HRM professionals must create and add value to their organizations by delivering superior value to their clients—from the CEO to the front-line employee.

The future career success of senior HRM professionals will depend on their ability to demonstrate their value by providing superior HR services. They must overcome the belief that most human resource management functions are non-value-added activities. When staff services are effective, the value of their contribution to the end customer is indirect and supportive. To become valued, trusted, contributing HRM professionals, senior HR managers must work collaboratively with their partners/customers and focus

on ensuring that the underlying value of what they do is real and apparent to their primary customers—the employees and managers of the enterprise.

Senior HRM managers will either be seen to engage in close working relationships with
senior executives, line managers, and front-line employees that add value, or they will find
themselves "squeezed out" along with others whose activities are considered unnecessary or
better provided by external suppliers/consultants. Relevance will be determined largely by
whether or not senior HRM managers are seen as partners who contribute to the strategic
focus of the organization and facilitate the pursuit of complex—and potentially conflicting—
objectives. Those objectives include efficiency, effectiveness, equity, and the strategic alignment of HRM initiatives with the business objectives of the organization. Those who effectively address these matters will contribute to both their own and their organization's success.
Those who fall short on these deliverables will find themselves trapped in lower-level technical and/or administrative roles, or they will be replaced, outsourced, or ignored.

THE CHALLENGES OF CHANGE

Heightened levels of competitiveness, environmental turbulence, and ambiguity are creating unprecedented opportunities for HR practitioners to be of increased relevance and
value to their organizations. The pressures include globalization, the blurring of industry
boundaries, technological change, "rightsizing," outsourcing, the emergence of new organizational forms (networks, alliances, flattened structures, self-managed work teams),
mergers and acquisitions, workforce diversity, demographic changes in the workforce,
changes in workplace legislation, and the growing importance of developing "smart,"
adaptive organizations.

One manager said, "Organizations would be much easier to run if it were not for the people who inhabit them—particularly when they have to change and adapt rapidly." However,
organizations are very much human institutions. While capital, technology, systems, and
processes are key ingredients in determining performance, people have a profound impact on
what transpires and the ultimate success or failure of the enterprise. If congruence is not
developed between Human Resources and other aspects of the organization, organizational
effectiveness will suffer. When it comes to "people issues," HRM plays a critical role in
determining whether or not desired organizational outcomes are achieved. As accelerating
rates of change increase uncertainty and complexity, the challenges inherent in managing
human resources in ways that increase efficiency and effectiveness also intensify.

Efficiency, effectiveness, and equity are absolute requirements for the long-term success of North American organizations. Lacking efficiency and effectiveness, firms fail to
innovate and compete successfully. Lacking equity, they risk employee discontent,
turnover, and legal problems. These requirements underlie many of the programs introduced within HRM, such as quality of worklife, self-managed teams, quality management,
continuous improvement, outplacement, and equal opportunity. Self-managed teams and
quality-of-worklife programs, for instance, aim to reduce the power and status differences
within organizations while increasing opportunity and productivity. Their intent is to make
employees an integral part of the organization. Proponents argue that they improve both
equity and efficiency over the long term by minimizing hierarchy and encouraging respect,
learning, commitment, and innovation.

Changing demographics will drive the human resource function in the near future. HR executives must learn to live with an aging, more educated, diverse (race, ethnicity, gender) workforce is faced by HRM executives who are attempting to cope with accelerating rates of retirement at all levels within their organizations. The rate of retirements has been made worse by the use of early retirement exit packages, little hiring, and limited internal training and development for the past 15 years. Competition will be stiff for talented individuals with the requisite skills, because so many organizations that were practising variants of "lean management" for the past decade and a half will find themselves actively attempting to recruit and develop individuals over the next several years. This task will be easier if they have been successful at fostering a "lean and keen," rather than a "lean and mean" work culture. Unfortunately, that has not been the case for many public- and private-sector enterprises.

Finally it is no longer sufficient for organizations to mouth platitudes about equity in their practices. Provincial and federal human rights provisions guarantee the right to equal treatment (including equal pay for work of equal value). Recent legislation demands that organizations actively monitor equity and abolish sexual and other forms of discrimination in the workplace. Gender, race, colour, nationality, national or ethnic origin, sexual orientation, religion, marital or family status, and disability are some of the common areas of discriminatory concern. Given the growing need of organizations to access talent at a time of diminishing supply, it is in the best interests of all concerned to remove roadblocks to the active and equitable participation of all qualified candidates. Human resource managers can obviously play an important role in advancing organizational policies and practices in these important areas.

What does all of this have to say about the new horizons that HR managers will be expected to navigate? What skills and abilities do they need?

- First, they need to develop their ability to think in terms of systems, processes, and open systems as a whole.

- Second, they need to be able to think strategically and to be able to build strategic coherence between the strategy of the firm and the human resource systems and processes that are needed to support it.

- Third, they need to be able to engage in both micro and macro levels of analysis and to be able to translate that into strategically and operationally valuable HR initiatives.

- Fourth, to identify and address their clients' needs, they must be able to build partnerships/relationships with their clients and with others who can assist them in this regard.

- Fifth, they need to think and learn in cross-functional terms and not allow themselves a retreat into a human resource world that is narrowly and technically defined.

- Sixth, they need to be committed to creating value and adept at managing the polarities and tensions that value creation, value reinvention, and organizational change will give rise to.

- Seventh, they need to have well-developed skills in the traditional areas of HR, including skills in the development and application of metrics that can be used for assessment, learning, and action planning in the HR area.

THE CASES IN PART 5

The cases in this section examine some of the current issues faced by human resource managers. **Pacific Mines Limited: Brian Boydell's Letter** describes a company that has introduced innovative work arrangements. It has eliminated levels of management and re-defined the responsibilities of employees and managers. The question for participants is, what is the purpose and value of continuing with the arrangements, given the problems that have already arisen?

Self-Managed Work Teams at South Australia Ambulance Services is also a case about the implementation of innovative work arrangements, but here the context is a large, geographically diverse, complex, public-sector service organization. Readers are left to consider what the changes should be and how they should be structured, implemented, assessed, and refined. In what way can work teams bring value to ambulance services?

The final case in this section, **The Case of the Amalgamated Laboratory**, involves the merger of three smaller laboratories. Questions related to merger, integration, and change lie at the forefront of this case. Since the purported benefits of changes of this sort often vanish in the aftermath of merger announcement, readers are challenged to assess the situation and develop action plans that increase the likelihood of success.

Pacific Mines Limited:
Brian Boydell's Letter

Tupper Cawsey

As he left the office for the day, Brian Boydell felt pleased with himself. Everything seemed to be going well at last. The eight plant operators were back from Holland and Texas and were now writing training manuals. He felt proud of the way the operators were developing as a team. "I've done my best to be open and above board with them," he thought. "It's been hard work but I think we finally have the relationship we need to make the team concept work."

PLANT BACKGROUND

As Brian recalled the past year, he remembered how apprehensive and excited he'd been when he had accepted his new post in the fall. Pat Irving, project manager, had asked him to join a group of people who were devising a training program for the operators of Pacific Mines Ltd.'s new plant in Carseland. He knew then that he would be the management person working with the developing operations. Pacific Mines, specializing in ammonia-urea fertilizer production, was opening the new $540-million plant 40 km east of Calgary in September of next year. It was to be highly automated, with a total operating group of eight workers on each of the five shifts, and 20 maintenance people on a day shift. Its capacity would be 430 000 tonnes of ammonia or 475 000 tonnes of urea per year. Initially, the consulting engineers would be responsible for the start-up of the operation, but the operating teams would take over the running of the plant after it had been checked out.

The new plant would use a well-known process to produce ammonia and urea. Natural gas fuelstock and nitrogen would be converted into ammonia in a high-temperature, high-pressure continuous flow process. Ammonia would then be combined with carbon dioxide to produce urea.

The competitive advantage of the new plant would result from the scale of the operation and the efficiency of production. The latter would depend primarily on fine-tuning a complex set of interdependent processes and upon the elimination of "downtime"—the period of time when the plant computer was not functioning. Estimates of the cost of downtime were based on the cost of lost production. Contribution per tonne of ammonia was estimated at $500 per tonne. Refining the process would allow for an increase in production tonnage. There was generally no product differentiation and, consequently, the price for ammonia and urea was set as a commodity.

The eight operators would be expected to play an important role in diagnosing problems in the plant and eliminating downtime. In theory, the computer was supposed to run the plant. However, if something did go wrong, it would be up to the operators to take action—from manually adjusting valves and production flows to shutting down the plant if the automatic controls failed. Plans had been made to have the operators periodically take over control of the plant from the computer in order to sharpen their skills. In a similar plant in Holland, virtually all problems were handled by the computer, and operators did not get the chance to control the plant under normal conditions.

THE TEAM CONCEPT

The new plant was to be run on the basis of "team concept." There were to be no supervisors. Elected, unpaid team representatives would be responsible for voicing concerns, jobs would rotate on a periodic basis, salaries would be based on knowledge and training, not on job position, and there would be training provided in team building.

Pat Irving had really sold Brian on the concepts, saying that the traditional styles of management were passé today. Pat was fond of reiterating four questions he'd picked up from some management course at an Eastern business school:

1. What are we trying to do?
2. What is my part in it?
3. What is keeping me from doing better?
4. What am I doing about it?

Brian agreed that these questions seemed to keep everyone on track, and he agreed with Pat that leaders in an organization should be "first among equals." The new "servant leadership" approach to management, as Pat described it, meant that while those with ability should lead, leadership should become service to others. Under such a system, traditional hierarchies would be eliminated.

The new plant was to be organized without supervisors, and Brian sincerely felt that the team was making progress towards self-management. The team concept could only be beneficial to the employees, he mused. Pat had expressed the opinion that the employees had a claim on the business, along with the shareholders, the customers, and the community. If any group was being shortchanged, it would act to increase its share of return. The team concept was an attempt to give the employees a fair share of the pie.

So far, Brian had been pleased with how well the team building was going. He knew that the training team or "core" team (see Exhibit 22.1) hadn't met with the operators as often as he would have liked, but everyone was very busy working on the technical side of the new plant. Except for the last few weeks, he'd had frequent contact with the operators. It would be good when Bruce Floyd and the rest of the core team were together in one location. Bruce had been a central figure in the project for several years, and he was frequently away on technical matters. It would be the end of August before he moved to Calgary.

The first team-building session held in Banff last May had produced the Employee Relations Document (see Exhibit 22.2 for excerpts). It had been developed by the members of both the operating team and the core team and expanded on Pat's ideas. "How many drafts did we work through?" Brian asked himself. "Was it four or five? We really put a lot of effort into that document. Thank heavens, head office in Vancouver approved it." And the organization development people had put on a good program. Normally, he didn't trust those guys. They were too "touchy-feely" for him. The operators had liked the opportunity to work on the issues. During the week they had focused on Pat Irving's four questions as well as engaging in team-building exercises. Brian had been worried when only a few of the core team could attend but that did not seem to matter now. The after-hours socializing that week seemed to strengthen the group and make everything more fun (see Exhibit 22.3 for the training schedule for operators).

One thing did bother Brian slightly. It was now four months since they had hired the first eight operators and gone through the team-building session, and it would be difficult to start again. "The cost alone is scary," thought Brian. "I wish we had some guarantee that things would work out. The training is my responsibility, so the $4.5-million program had better pay off. Not using the team concept would have saved us a lot of money and meant that we could have started training later" (see Exhibit 22.4 for a breakdown of the training costs developed in July of the previous year, prior to the adoption of the team concept).

Brian also thought that the operators' trips to Holland and Texas had been a little unnerving. Four operators had travelled overseas for three weeks, and four had visited the U.S. for four weeks to observe plants similar to the new Carseland operation. "I wonder how much they got out of the three weeks there?" Brian reflected. "Three weeks is a long time away from home, and we had hoped they wouldn't party so much. It's surprising that Jim Cuttle and Mike Irving, who also went, didn't ensure that they worked harder. The group doing the instructing didn't seem to help much either." Several of the operators had mentioned that the trip to the U.S. could have been shortened since there was nothing to do at night in Borger, where the Texas plant was located. However, the Texas group indicated they had learned a lot about ammonia production on the trip.

Brian congratulated himself and the core team on getting the operators involved—they seemed to be caught up in working out the technical details of the new plant. Brian had been pleased when Bill Gillies had asked Craig Taraday, the instrumentation expert, to bring in the computer person from head office to talk to the operators. And the operators had liked being a part of the recent recruiting process to hire 18 more operators. They had provided a major source of information since 36 of the 42 applicants were personally known to them. In fact, many operators with steam certification in Alberta knew each other because there were so few in the province. Four of the eight operators hired had come from the same company and knew each other well (see Exhibit 22.5 for a brief description of the operators).

Brian also believed that the operators' role in decision making was expanding. Doug Ames, one of the eight, had suggested moving everyone from the team room, where they had been working, to the empty offices upstairs. (The group was sharing the building with the Calgary operators until the Carseland buildings were ready in December.) The team room led to a lot of group cooperation, but it was crowded and those operators who were trying to write their manuals were easily disturbed by the others. Brian wondered if too much group interaction was dangerous. He knew that the operators had developed the habit of going drinking together on occasion and was concerned that the group might become more socially than work oriented.

BRIAN BOYDELL'S PLANS

Brian was aware that he would have to get to work on the new salary schedules. The "pay for knowledge" concept was a good idea but it created difficulty in establishing rates, as there were no comparable jobs. Usually compensation was tied to a particular job. Estimates were made of the job's difficulty, its skill and education requirements, and the working conditions involved. A salary was determined accordingly. Under the "pay for knowledge" plan, an operator would be paid for the amount of training and knowledge he or she had, regardless of the job performed. Competencies became key. Thus a low-skill job would provide a high salary for a trained individual. This plan increased flexibility, as people could be switched quite easily from one job to another. At the same time, it allowed the operators to earn more money through their own efforts as they developed more competencies.

"It looks as if we will have to pay more money if we want to hire good people in September," Brian mused, "especially if we hope to get 18 more. Who knows what the pay will be when we hire the final 14 in December? Wages really seem to be getting out of hand. I'll be glad when the October 1 raise comes through. It will make my job of hiring easier. Setting the pay schedule for these operators took from last December until April, before we got approval from head office. I wonder if the reorganization announced last week will speed up the process? Ron Holmes, the new VP, has a reputation of being a hard-nosed but fair and extremely competent manager. He must be, to be where he is at 44. I hope he knows what we're trying to do, but I'll bet he doesn't, considering his background at General Coal Co. with its strong union. I guess I'll find out when I meet with him next week on the suggestion that we review salaries three times rather than twice a year."

As Brian left the building, he noticed a car coming towards him. It was one of the operators. Brian was surprised to see him, as most of the operators had been on a writing course at the Southern Alberta Institute of Technology (SAIT). The writing course was designed to help the operators develop the skills needed to write the training and operating manuals and was held at the other end of town. Pat and Brian believed that by having the operators write their own manuals, the final product would be intelligible to other operators and would encourage everyone to be more committed to the project.

When the car pulled up, the operator handed Brian two envelopes saying, "I've been delegated to hand these to you." One envelope was addressed to him and the other to Pat Irving. As he read the letter (see Exhibit 22.6 for a copy of the letter), Brian's feeling of dismay turned to anger: "How could they do this to me? They aren't following the team concept at all! What are they trying to pull, anyway?"

Exhibit 22.1

The Carseland Plant:
Training and Operating Staff

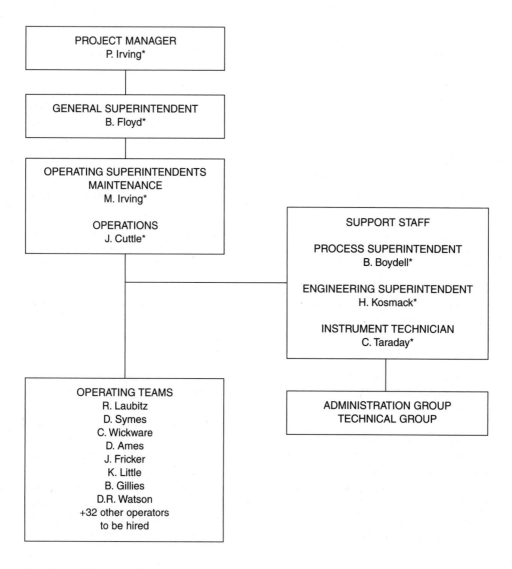

PROJECT MANAGER
P. Irving*

GENERAL SUPERINTENDENT
B. Floyd*

OPERATING SUPERINTENDENTS
MAINTENANCE
M. Irving*

OPERATIONS
J. Cuttle*

SUPPORT STAFF

PROCESS SUPERINTENDENT
B. Boydell*

ENGINEERING SUPERINTENDENT
H. Kosmack*

INSTRUMENT TECHNICIAN
C. Taraday*

OPERATING TEAMS
R. Laubitz
D. Symes
C. Wickware
D. Ames
J. Fricker
K. Little
B. Gillies
D.R. Watson
+32 other operators
to be hired

ADMINISTRATION GROUP
TECHNICAL GROUP

*Members of the core team.

Exhibit 22.2

Extracts from Employee Relations Document

General

Objective

The basic objective of the employee relations system is to ensure safe, highly efficient, and uninterrupted operations with an integrated approach to the management of human resources. The system must respond to the needs, interests, and aspirations of people.

Management Philosophy

The following statement of management philosophy represents the type of environment and relationships for which we are striving:

> Company competitors differ from each other in the degree of creativity and initiative shown by their employees. Each person has an obligation to use all his or her capacities and those of his or her colleagues in contributing to the growth and betterment of the company's operations at Carseland.

> Management has an obligation to provide an environment in which each person has freedom to develop and to use all his or her capacities.

Management Style

All levels of management will be expected to operate on a team basis and to support an integrated approach within and among teams, while encouraging personal initiative and responsibility.

A high value will be placed on obtaining sound creative decisions through understanding and agreement by team members. Decision making will take place by those who are close to the source of the problem and have the appropriate know-how. Ideas, opinions, and attitudes of people will be sought out in the continuing process of improving operating and administrative techniques. When conflict arises, every effort will be made to deal with it in an open manner, and to identify and resolve its underlying causes. Emphasis will be placed on developing talent and potential and encouraging, by example, a high degree of effort and participation. Openness, courtesy, and respect will be expected in all interpersonal relationships.

Human Resources Policies and Programs

Organization

The organization will be designed in such a way as to establish a relationship among jobs which promotes flexible, integrated work teams. This goal will be achieved in the Carseland organization by means of the following:

1. The number of authority levels will be kept at a minimum.

2. All employees will be encouraged to develop their job-related skills.

3. Versatility of operating and maintenance people is considered essential and will be encouraged by such innovations as block training, job rotation, and cross-trades training.

Exhibit 22.3

Training Schedule for Operators

Time Frame	Task	Duration
April 1	Hire first eight operators	
April	Introduction to the company	1 week
	Training techniques	1 week
	Team building (Banff Springs Hotel)	1 week
	Ammonia familiarization	1 week
May	Urea familiarization	1 week
	Specialty training–ammonia or urea	
	(Four operators for each specialty)	3 weeks
June	Visits to Geleen, Holland, and Borger, Texas	3–4 weeks
July	Return home	
	Writing of training and operating manuals begins	
August-September	Writing of training and operating manuals	6–8 weeks
September-October	Begin training other operators	8 weeks

Exhibit 22.4

Pat Irving's Memo of January 28
The Carseland Plant: Training Costs

January 28

Memorandum

To: Vice-President, Pacific Region, Vancouver

From: Manager, Operations

Subject: Appropriation of Pre-Production Expenses

This is a request for funds to carry on with pre-production training.

The amount requested is $4.5 million as outlined in my memo of July 24, attached. We are negotiating with the Alberta Department of Manpower and Labour to share this cost. We, therefore, request that $4.5 million be appropriated and $3.5 million be authorized at this time.

A budget is being prepared and monthly control statements will be issued.

P.W. Irving: mb

Enc.

cc   B. Floyd
      B. Boydell
      J. Homes
      P. W. Irving

Exhibit 22.4 (continued)

Pat Irving's Memo of July 24
The Carseland Plant: Training Costs

July 24

Memorandum

Subject: Training Costs

It is important that those people who will be operating the new plants receive adequate training. Any operating errors will be extremely costly. The cost of this training should be carried as a separate cost centre to allow proper control.

The operators now involved—Irving, Floyd, Kilborn, Boydell, Hind, and Mintsberg—are not taken into account here. The cost of pre-production training at the plant is also not included in this estimate.

The estimated breakdown is:

For 24 months:

1 supervisor @ $9600/month	$231 000	
Expenses and travel $3000/month	$ 72 000	
		$ 303 000

For 21 months:

6 shift supervisors @ $84 000/ year	$882 000	
3 maintenance supervisors @ $105 000/year	$552 000	
1 assistant supervisor @ $75 000/year	$131 000	
		$1 565 000
Expenses @ 40%	$626 000	
Total staff air fares		$2 494 000
	$100 000	
		$2 594 000

Purchase of 2 Carmody trainers (simulators) has been included in the capital estimates.

Exhibit 22.4 (continued)

Programming of trainers	$ 60 000	
Labour of Murray Williams (trainer)		
4 months @ $20 000/month	$80 000	
Training films, tapes, etc.	$10 000	
Total training equipment		$ 150 000
4 junior engineers		
6 months @ $75 000/year		$ 150 000
Operator Training:		
10 operators		
1 year @ $60 000/year	$600 000	
20 operators		
6 months @ $60 000/year	$600 000	
Steam engineer training	$110 000	
Total operator training		$1 310 000
Total		$4 204 000
Unaccounted and contingency		$ 300 000
		$4 504 000

P.W. Irving:ft

cc: F.A. Moore, Vancouver
     B. Floyd, Head Office

Exhibit 22.5

Operators' Profiles

Doug Ames

Married, two children
Third Class Certificate
District manager of distillery sales for two years
Operator and shift supervisor of Calgary ammonia plant for seven years
Plant operator for 11 years
Hobbies: hockey, golf, curling, fastball
Member of Fraternal Order of Eagles

Keith Little

Married, two children
Second Class Certificate; St. John's First Aid Certificate
Plant operator for five years
Previous supervisory experience
Hobbies: ball, golf, curling, swimming

Joe Fricker

Married, one child
Second Class Certificate; SAIT Power Engineering Diploma; one year university
Operator of two different thermal power electrical generating stations for four years
Hobbies: curling, badminton, mechanics

Dave Symes

Married, two children
Second Class Certificate; one year university
Operator of ammonia plant for four years, including gas and steam plants (Calgary)
Worked as salesman for Western Canada Steel (summer job)
Machine operator on railroad tie gang and signal helper for three summers
Hobbies: tropical fish, astronomy, oil painting, cave exploring
Member of Moose Lodge

Exhibit 22.5 (continued)

Rob Laubitz

Married, two children

Third Class Certificate; Part A, Second Class, NAIT Gas Technology Diploma;
St. John's First Aid Certificate

Operator in steam, and process of sulphur recovery and gas processing plant at
Okotoks for three years

Engineering technologist with oil company for three years

Hobbies: woodworking

Chris Wickware

Married, two children

Operator for eight years

Millwright at Edmonton Steel Mill for five years

Hobbies: hunting, fishing

Member of Royal Canadian Legion, Fraternal Order of Eagles

Union steward of several years

Don R. Watson

Married, three children

Third Class Certificate; two years university engineering

Operator of fertilizer plants in Calgary for five years

Hobbies: skiing, snowshoeing, motorcycling, member of YMCA

Bill Gillies

Married, two children

Second Class Certificate

Operator and relief shift supervisor in Calgary ammonia plant for 10 years

Operator in Fort Saskatchewan ammonia plant for three years

Hobbies: hunting, football, carpentry, mechanics

Member of Western Coop Social Club, and Canton Meadows Community
Association

Exhibit 22.6

Brian Boydell's Letter

July 21

Dear Mr. Irving:

During the latter part of June and early July, in response to our earlier request, Brian Boydell indicated the possibility of a July pay raise. However, this morning, Brian indicated that a raise in July would be impossible.

We, of the operator training team, respectfully submit this letter of discontent regarding the negative feedback to our request.

The reasons for the raise are as follows:

(1)   All of us took wage cuts to come to the company.

(2)   The cost of living has escalated substantially.

(3)   We are receiving lower wages than competition staff for similar jobs.

(4)   We have a desire to maintain a *strong* and *loyal* team.

We also note that a 37.3-hour workweek has been adopted by numerous companies. We believe that Pacific Mines should not be among the exceptions.

We feel confident that you will give this letter your every consideration.

Sincerely,

The Operating Team
Doug Ames
Chris Wickware
Don R. Watson
Joe Fricker
Dave Symes
Keith Little
Rob Laubitz
Bill Gillies

cc Mr. Brian Boydell

Self-Managed Work Teams at South Australia Ambulance Service

Tupper Cawsey

Ray Main pondered the box of questionnaires received from the ambulance officers (AOs). Normally a 45 percent response rate would be considered a good response to a survey. But in 35 of the 60-plus teams, less than half of the AOs in the team responded. Without the input of more than half of their team members, he didn't feel he could provide representative feedback to the station teams.

Next Wednesday, October 22, 1997, the workforce empowerment implementation team was meeting to hear his report on the survey. He knew they would want recommendations regarding the next steps in moving South Australian Ambulance Service (SAAS) to an empowerment culture.

SOUTH AUSTRALIAN AMBULANCE SERVICE

SAAS provides emergency paramedic and advanced life-support services as well as routine ambulance transfers throughout the state of South Australia on a self-funding basis. The service is provided by 600 full- and part-time staff and some 1100 volunteers in areas difficult to service. Emergency calls go to one of four communications centres, which pass the message to one of 19 metro teams in Adelaide, to one of the 20 country teams, or to one of the 60 to 70 volunteer teams.

Until the late 1980s, SAAS was an integral part of the St. John Ambulance Service (under the St. John Priory) and was staffed by both full-time AOs and volunteers. Full-time employees worked Monday to Friday from 9 a.m. to 5 p.m. Volunteers handled all evening and weekend work.

One manager described the old culture in strong terms:

> SAAS was a traditional, hierarchical organization with nine managerial levels for approximately 650 employees and 1500 volunteers. We were very inward-looking in our approach. It was lots of "jobs for the boys" and as long as you were obedient and followed orders you were OK.

A senior executive described SAAS as a "militaristic" organization with "an extreme number of levels: regional superintendent, assistant regional superintendent, regional director, assistant regional director, station officer, assistant station officer." Most decisions were made by the three managers at the top of the organization, who then had difficulty getting things implemented because of the powerful middle managers and station officers.

In 1989, a strike by the full-time employees led to the professionalization of the service and the beginning of its separation from the St. John Ambulance Service. After the strike, the use of volunteers was minimized and full-time employees operated the service 24 hours per day, seven days per week.[1] This change required an influx of several hundred new AOs and an increase in their professionalism and training. All full-time AOs were now required to complete a three-year program leading to a diploma through the TAFE college system.

In 1992 a new CEO, Ian Pickering, was appointed to reorganize the service and to complete the separation of SAAS from the St. John Priory. His mandate was to improve the clinical expertise in SAAS and to make it the best ambulance service in Australia. Shifting the organization from the old military model to an empowerment one was a key part of his strategy to achieve excellence.

The South Australian government passed legislation on March 16, 1993, changing the nature of SAAS. On March 17, 1993, Pickering restructured SAAS. Nine levels of management were reduced to four. All middle and lower-level managers were invited to apply for the new positions that were created, but there were no job guarantees. Retirement packages were offered and many managers took them. The day lives in organizational memory as "the St. Patrick's Day Massacre."

At the same time, all employees were organized into teams: 19 metro AO teams, 20 country AO teams, 20 support staff teams, and 60-plus volunteer teams. (See Exhibit 23.1 for a partial organization chart.) The team leader positions often went to younger, better-qualified, and newer employees, since many older employees needed to retrain to qualify for team leader positions.[2]

---

[1] Full-time employees provided ambulance services, except in difficult-to-serve rural areas. South Australia has vast areas of outback with few people. Providing service to these areas is costly.

[2] One senior manager speculated that the really good AOs did not apply for the team leader position initially because they wanted to become paramedics first.

In 1993 a strategic plan was developed. As one manager put it, "It was the first time we asked ourselves, 'What is our mission? Why are we here?' Never before had we defined patient service (as opposed to patient care)."

This strategic plan was reworked in 1995 (see Exhibit 23.2 for a summary of the vision, mission, key objectives, and major strategies). The plan included a commitment to "an empowered and accountable workforce." Seven cross-functional project teams were established to help implement the strategic plan: the workforce empowerment implementation team, the workforce development team, the information technology team, the commercial team, the structure team, the volunteer team, and the business development team. Chris Lemmer, regional director (Metro), headed the workforce empowerment implementation team with Ray Main seconded full-time as project coordinator.

The 1995–1996 Annual Report stated that "a restricted patient transport licence was granted to another patient transport service" for non-emergency ambulance transfers, introducing a potential competitive threat to SAAS from a for-profit organization. The St. John Priory continued to withdraw its links with SAAS. And a new amalgamation with the SA Metropolitan Fire Service was proposed but had not been acted on.

By 1997, SAAS had changed significantly. Paramedic courses had been run for the first time, and 35 AOs had received this higher-level qualification. An advanced life support qualification had been developed as an intermediate step between basic AO training and paramedic training, and many AOs had completed this qualification. Clinical performance had improved dramatically. Survival statistics for ventricular fibrillation arrest, for example, had improved from 4.1 percent in 1994 to 26 percent in 1997. Performance measures can be found in Exhibit 23.3 and financial statements in Exhibit 23.4.

THE JOB OF THE AMBULANCE OFFICER

Two ambulance officers were assigned to each vehicle. In the Metro area, most stations had two emergency vehicles plus one or two routine transfer vehicles. Each station had kitchen facilities, a lounge area, sleeping areas for night shifts, and exercise rooms. When an AO began his/her shift, assuming the previous crew was in the station, they would ensure that the vehicle was ready for a call. A lengthy, detailed list of supplies had to be checked. Materials used had to be replaced.

A typical Metro morning shift is described in Table 23.1.

Getting to a call was considered urgent and was carried out at speeds up to 100 km/h. On arrival, AOs unloaded the emergency equipment (in the cases above, oxygen, electrocardiograph, and stretcher) and entered the house. One AO took the lead in each case, making decisions on the immediate response demanded by the patient's condition (e.g., if blood pressure was down, should a saline drip be attached?).

AOs prided themselves on their clinical skills. They had developed sophisticated medical protocols to assist in the diagnosis and were skilled in asking relevant questions about the individual's medical history. Paramedics had eight or nine drugs at their disposal to help deal with cardiac patients, where speed was essential. As one paramedic described, "We can begin the healing process on the road so when they reach the emergency room they are in better shape than when we arrived."

While AOs were trained to present themselves as confident professionals to reassure anxious patients and relatives, they were also able to listen closely to the patient and any others present to understand the circumstances of the patient's difficulty and improve their

Table 23.1 A Typical Morning Shift for a Metro AO Team	
08:00	Arrival
08:00–08:30	Checking and restocking vehicle
08:30–08:40	Relaxation
08:40	Communications moves the vehicle to a central location in the Metro area
08:40–09:00	Wait at location
09:00 (approx.)	"Shortness of breath" call
09:00–10:30	Travel at high speed to call, attend patient, take patient to hospital
10:30–11:00	Travel to SAAS workshop to have air-conditioning switch replaced
11:00–12:15	Assist a second AO team in a pickup
12:15–12:45	Return to station, quick lunch
12:45	"Fainting patient" call
12:45–14:00	Travel at high speed to call, attend patient, take patient to hospital
14:00.....	Continue

diagnosis. Often, prior to any treatment, the AOs would carefully explain what they were going to do and its consequences. For example, if an AO was attaching a saline drip, she would state why she was doing this: "With your blood pressure a little low, you need some fluids, and we are just going to give you some." She would describe what to expect and the consequences of her actions: "I need to inject this needle. It will hurt, but only for a moment. The fluids will help your blood pressure and you won't feel so dizzy."

Friday evenings and holiday weekends were often the most stressful times to be an AO. Major car accidents occurred, and some family disputes became violent. Often AOs then dealt with people with severe injuries. In car crashes, extraction of the injured could be a problem. In family disputes, violence could continue during their intervention. SAAS had counsellors available to help AOs deal with the trauma they faced.

AOs had complained for years that they dealt with emergency situations, made life-saving decisions, and could commandeer thousands of dollars of equipment (including helicopters) in an emergency, but couldn't order a shirt for themselves if one was ripped. Someone "in authority" had to authorize it.

By 1997, SAAS had evolved a customer-service orientation. Its definition of success went beyond the survival rate of its patients to include thoughtful treatment of relatives, effective relationships with hospital medical staff, and considerate patient care. In terms of emergency services, the aim was to have "a patient ready for ongoing treatment delivered in the best possible condition with accurate information about the patient's health." Exhibit 23.5 shows the cause-and-effect chart leading to having a patient ready for ongoing treatment.

Key performance indicators were developed with success measures for each of the indicators, as shown in Table 23.2.

THE EVOLUTION OF TEAM MANAGEMENT

A key component of the strategy articulated for SAAS was an empowered workforce. CEO Ian Pickering changed the structure of the organization as one of his first and most dra-

Table 23.2 Key Performance Indicators and Success Measures		
Key Performance Indicator	Measurement	Method of Measurement
Patient ready for ongoing treatment	Patient condition on delivery Accuracy of information to hospital	Monthly sample of cases by peer audit and hospital feedback Monthly sample of cases by peer audit and hospital feedback
Timeliness	Time from emergency call to arrival at hospital Delay in meeting Ambulance Transport Service commitments	Response time + scene time + transport time for each trip Contracted time minus actual time for each trip
Communication with patients	Communication with patients	Sample of cases by patient and hospital feedback on interpersonal skills, etc.
Cost	Cost relative to best practice	Monthly figures from each department
Revenue	Revenue	Monthly revenue
Preparedness for disasters	Preparedness for disasters	Rolling three-monthly survey to rate staff knowledge of roles and availability of equipment and supplies
Community awareness	Community confidence rating	Annual community survey
Staff satisfaction	Employee satisfaction rating	Annual survey of staff and volunteers

matic moves. Because of the suddenness of the transition to team management, the organization was not fully prepared. As one manager put it, "The catchword was empowerment. We didn't know what it meant, but we told everyone."

Pickering articulated the reasons for team management in an address to a community group. (See Exhibit 23.6 for a summary of the speech.) One enthusiastic supporter stated, "Team is the only way I will survive. One peer of mine is looking so old. He does things I just won't. For example, he drove hundreds of miles just to discipline a person, to tell them off. My aim is to be an invisible manager, to influence, and to be a facilitator and let the teams do their own thing. It seems to be working, as I spend most of my time educating, encouraging, and modelling."

In the Metro area, teams comprised 10 to 13 members, organized by stations. Some larger stations had two teams of 10 to 13 members each. The rationale for this was that it took that many people to operate two ambulance teams 24 hours per day, seven days per week, including time off for vacation, illness, training, and other absences. Metro teams often were constantly on the road responding to emergency calls. As well, because of the shift schedule, it was very difficult for Metro teams to meet. As one AO put it, "We suffer from a tyranny of roster that prevents us from really forming and acting as a team." (See Exhibit 23.7 for a sample roster rotation.)

Country teams, on the other hand, found it much easier to meet. Often there were only five AOs in a station, and they had considerable unoccupied time together. Calls were not as frequent. When they did come, they could involve major traffic accidents and could be very traumatic for the AOs involved. But in a "routine" day, there was time to engage in team planning. Teams could develop detailed procedures and plans for the next year. If they needed to learn about a topic (such as budgeting), there was time. As one manager described it, "If someone wants to study and learn, then they should come to the country, as there is lots of time if you use it. I got books and a laptop and began to improve myself."

Several teams "raced ahead" in acting as empowered teams and then became frustrated when they couldn't operate as they felt appropriate. For example, one team immediately decided to assign to team members all the responsibilities previously held by the station officer. The team met and made decisions and individual team members carried them out. Unfortunately, SAAS organizational systems were not prepared for this, and team members were refused service or stores because they did not have the correct authorizing signature.

Another team decided to do away with the team leader (TL). As one would expect, leaders emerged anyway. Interpersonal issues arose that the team couldn't resolve. Factions developed and the team couldn't handle the resulting conflicts. As well, health and safety regulations required an individual with formal responsibility for these areas—assigning the responsibility to the "team" was unacceptable.

Other teams decided to choose their team leaders by voting. It became a popularity contest. One team dismissed their team leader because "they didn't like him." In this case, the union played a significant role in reconciliation. The union asked the team members how they would feel if management dismissed one of them because they didn't like that person. In this case, the TL did resign—he felt he could not be effective without the support of the team. But the union intervention was critical in increasing the employees' understanding of the responsibilities that went with empowerment.

Bernie Morellini, the staff development officer, held workshops on the concepts of empowerment and quality management. In these two-day workshops, teams developed vision and mission statements and began identifying key objectives for their team. (See Exhibit 23.8 for a sample team vision-mission-values statement.) While these seminars were greeted with enthusiasm, AOs often left them uncertain about how to use these ideas in their operations. Who had what authority remained unclear.

Nevertheless, SAAS developed increasing confidence in itself with the introduction of paramedics. It had taken considerable skill on Pickering's part to convince the medical advisory committee to accept the need for and usefulness of paramedics. This move enabled the team leaders to focus on clinical expertise rather than the formal hierarchy.

A major marketing campaign was created to announce the change in SAAS. The launch was held at the Adelaide Festival Theatre with major television coverage. Uniforms were to be redone, ambulance vehicles were to be repainted, all to symbolize the change to more professional, empowered services. Unfortunately, changes at the political level prevented the complete implementation of the plans. This failure encouraged the cynics who "had seen change attempts before and nothing really would happen." These skeptics were more than willing to derail any move to team management.

Teams improved their clinical practices with the introduction of a case card audit.[3] The case review process protected AOs from individual liability as it was assumed that the AOs did the best that was possible under the circumstances.

---

[3] A case card audit is a review of the write-up (the card) of each case dealt with by the service. That is, after each call, a case card describing the situation and what was done is produced. The audit is a team review in order to learn and improve.

PROGRESS TOWARDS SELF-MANAGEMENT ACROSS SAAS TEAMS

The progress towards self-management varied considerably across teams. Summaries of interviews with four teams are given below.

Team A[4]

Team A declared that "the team is us."

> In the first year, our team had some personnel problems. The team leader was a nice guy but he didn't seem to be working for the team. He expected us to come up with concepts, and when we did he would say "that's a silly idea." Or when we brainstormed, he would say, "That's not going to work!" There were some personal issues, as well. He kept an "I'm all right, Jack" attitude when it wasn't. For example, he would do all the administrative work without help. He would be in here until all hours of the night working. And even then, the paperwork didn't get done on time. He would ask our opinion and then change things. He and one of the other team members started annoying each other and this put this team member under a lot of pressure. Finally, this team member couldn't handle being questioned, and he would start yelling at other team members and demanding details of any calls. We weren't sure what was going on until after the TL had left. We were too close to the situation.

> Once the TL had left, there was a bit of a vacuum. We decided to take a step "back" and we had three team meetings. We were spending too much time on "in-house" activities and not enough on developing the team. We spent a lot of time on maintenance activities—who is going to clean up the station; sheets aren't being signed like they are supposed to.

> The person who was in a dispute with the TL has been much better since the TL left.

> Finally, we got rid of the station-running stuff and moved onto learning and improving. But there were no measures for each thing we were doing so we drew up our practices manual and focused on three areas: human factors, customer service, and cost. We have to revamp this now as only a few of us were here when the original planning was done.

> The process started when we had a day session with Bernie. This got us going but we needed another day to really put together some plans. We realized that if we want something we have to cost it and put a proposal together. If we want a training day per month, we have to show how it helps and how to get it done. If a member wants time off, we decide. Soon we will have the training plan for next year finalized. We will have it finished by the end of the year.

> We wrote our station work practice manual so it contained a statement of team focus, a vision, mission statement, guiding principles, and values and key objectives in the three critical areas. (See Exhibit 23.8.)

Team B

> The idea and concept is good but getting there could have been better. Two years ago they started the team concept. We thought it was "about time" as we had hinted long ago we shouldn't have a boss. We were all sort of lost when teams started. We were told to document what we did,

---

[4] Team information is representative of real teams. The names have been removed to retain anonymity.

make up the rules. So, we said "OK" and began meeting once each week. Perhaps we needed more education to make the transition easier.

There was some attempt to educate us. Each centre sent one person to a course. But by the time he got back, the message was confused. Most AOs had been here a long time and were confused by what was taught.

We are starting with our own mission and vision and standard operating practices. We are starting to make our own rules. It used to be a computer would arrive and we would wonder "why and when." Now we talk about what we need and put it in a budget. Before, the attitude was "we don't care where money goes as long as I get paid." Now we are accountable for budgets. So if we put a hole in the wall, we have to pay for fixing it. We are allowed to talk to DMs as humans and get respect.

We meet monthly or every 6 weeks or so. We put the holiday list up and get input. This year we got joint input on the budget. Next year individuals will do sub budgets.

Next year we will really have a clear picture of the team concept and fully understand it and be comfortable operating as a self-directed team. Sometimes we lacked confidence and expected to get a "no." Instead, we were asked "what took you so long to ask?"

We worry about vehicle maintenance as a team. Station usage is also our responsibility now, and we get others to use it. We have set our vision and mission and now we are just working on how to specify objectives and how to achieve them.

I'm sure that we can become pace setters.

Team C

We always ran as a team. The old station officer (SO) discussed things with us and we had input. When the SO went away, one of the team got to see the administrative work he did. Now we all see some of it and get a bigger picture. Now there is more input.

At our team meetings, we solve problems. For example, we had a communications problem in the region and decided the best solution was a satellite phone (which wasn't budgeted for). So at the team meeting we figured out how to get support and raised $3000 of the $4200 cost.

We work on documenting our procedures. This gives us a benchmark against which we can improve our practice. We create graphs and track our performance. Work practices have been developed for 32 of our procedures. Other teams have asked for copies, but we have refused. If they just took ours, they wouldn't own them. We think that each team has to develop their own procedures to really make them their own. You can see on the wall our system for duty roster. We organize it by week with a list of responsibilities that have to be done for each job, and the person checks them off when they are done.

We are concerned as we have just had two new members added to our team, and we need to figure out how to include them in the team. We aren't certain how comfortable the new members are with the team concept. We sure hope that we get along as well as previously. We need to make certain that we don't assume too much. We have planned a team-building day where we will get to know one another, and then we can discuss how we want to operate. Only after all this will we look at the 32 work practices to see if changes should be made.

We think we can handle most things. We did have to get help with a team dispute that got out of hand—but we did try our procedures first. We do most things. We develop and implement our own training program. Our budget is zero-based and we spend a lot of time figuring out what we need and how that should be budgeted for. For example, we figure out how much to budget for tires based on the condition of the tires—head office could never figure that out.

Team D

We are not sure what we are supposed to do with this team management stuff. We think we do a good job as AOs—our clinical performance is excellent, we think. And that's what our job is.

We are on the road most of the time responding to calls. That keeps us busy. I don't know what they expect us to do—come in on our days off to build a team with people I never see from one week to the next? Most of the guys don't want to do that. And how will the ambulance transport service AOs fit in? They don't even do the same job that we do.

We are out there dealing with people who need our help. I find that by the time I am finished my shift—particularly if it is a Friday night, I just want to leave this place and escape. Some of the things we have to deal with are pretty gruesome and I want to get out of here. The last thing I need is to spend time talking about something that isn't important.

If it will affect our clinical practice then we should be trained properly. If it isn't part of our clinical practice, why are we doing it?

They tell us to manage our own budget but there's nothing in there that helps pay for overtime so we can meet. If we wanted to get together as a full team, we would have to ask for money for it and it's not worth it.

THE ROLE OF THE TEAM LEADER

As was mentioned earlier, many team leaders were uncertain of their role. Some team leaders became adept at talking team and empowerment language but not doing it. AOs were used to making decisions on the spot (in emergency situations) and continued doing so as team leaders. Old autocratic habits died hard, particularly when a station officer switched roles and became a team leader. In one team, the station officer had been particularly dominant. That person carried on that behaviour. The team continued to look at him and ask, "Is this OK?" even though there was encouragement for the team to take responsibility.

One station officer who became team leader completely reversed his style. He wouldn't do anything without team input. This slowed all decisions and frustrated the AOs. He believed that everyone had to be "nice" to each other and agreeable. It took a while before he realized that teams and team leadership didn't mean being nice; rather it meant using teams and team skills to improve the service.

Another team leader saw his role as being a facilitator and providing guidance when a team needed it. If the team had a problem, the team leader helped them to solve it rather than solving it for them. He described his role as follows: "Often, I present the team with new and different alternatives to broaden their thinking. Or I ask some questions to get them to consider aspects of an issue that I think they haven't covered. Much of my role is ensuring I learn and then passing that on to the team. So I have been taking courses and have taught them about Pareto charts, fishbone analysis, and PDCA (plan, do, check, act). This gives them the tools to improve their own performance.

A more typical response was confusion over the team leader role. One team leader commented, "I had little experience and education about working in a team. And there doesn't seem to be any support for me when I need help. I know the vision and what we are trying to do, but I don't feel I have the tools to get there. I think some team leaders have no idea whether they are doing well or not—they have nothing to refer to."

One team leader questioned how he was to operate: "I can't get my team together because of the shifts we are on. How can I get team decisions? My guys want to do good AO work and they aren't certain how this empowerment stuff fits in. Finally, I just rented a hall and had everyone come to a session where we talked about team issues. I just sent them (management) the bill and said, 'Pay it.'"

One team leader went to a team referred to as "Jurassic Park" because the AOs had been there so long. Many of the misfits had gravitated to this team and most managers predicted this individual would not be able to make things work at that location. However, he listened and got stuff done. He convinced the team to be patient for changes and always explained why he was doing things.

This team leader was frustrated enough to summarize his feelings in a memo to AOs in March 1996:

> The honeymoon is over!! Team members feel that the team concept is failing—dismally. Team members believe that the new clinical team leaders are station officers with a new title. The team does not believe they are empowered to make any team-based decisions.....Empowerment implies ownership. Ownership implies responsibility. Responsibility implies that there is no one else to blame. If the team accepts empowerment, they also accept the responsibility.

> How does my team become empowered?

> Team meetings will be held with the district manager and clinical team leader. The purpose of these meetings is to establish what station activities the teams are willing to take responsibility for. Once these areas are identified, the team and team members are locked into a commitment to ensure that those tasks are undertaken....It should be noted that teams will not be forced to accept responsibility if they so desire....As stated previously, having items such as time sheets and leave approvals signed by the clinical team leader is somewhat questionable. Under the team empowerment concept these and many other tasks would become the responsibility of the team. This would allow the clinical team leader to perform the function that they were employed to do—that is facilitate the training requirements as identified by the teams and to provide clinical support.

The Workforce Empowerment Implementation Team

This cross-functional team headed by Chris Lemmer, Metro regional director, was created as a result of the strategic planning sessions in 1995. Members had been chosen because of their expertise and their interest in the project. Nine people were on the team, representing key areas of the organization (two team leaders from operations, two district managers, and a representative each from the training college, the communications team, the workshop, and administration). Initially, the team had met biweekly. Now with the survey being tabulated, it had been about two months since the last meeting. At the quarterly strategic planning reviews held by Ian Pickering, each task force team had to report on its progress.

The workforce empowerment implementation team stated its mission as: "We are committed to the development of systems, processes, and resources to enable work teams to become self-managed."

The workforce empowerment team believed that the first stage in moving to an empowered culture was the structure change that had occurred. The second stage would entail teaching the workforce about "empowerment." In order to develop a "baseline" for the change, the workforce survey was developed. Exhibit 23.9 shows a sample feedback sheet that could be made available to the teams depending on the decisions made at the upcoming meeting.

The implementation team believed that an education program for team leaders and the teams was necessary. The workforce survey would provide information to assist in the design of an education package and would enable a "re-measurement" after training in order to judge the progress towards self-managed teams.

Ray Main, as mentioned earlier, had been seconded to the team as project coordinator for two years. He had been an operational AO for nine and a half years in the Metro area and was TL of the City station for two years prior to his secondment. Ray had also been involved in the implementation of quality principles in SAAS operations as a member of the quality steering committee. His responsibilities included coordinating, planning, and implementing the systems to educate and develop work teams along the road to empowerment, in concert with the implementation team. A preliminary allocation of $165 000 for the 1997 year had been set up to support the implementation team's activities.

Ray Main's Dilemma

As a previous team leader, Ray had been frustrated by the apparent lack of systems and support for the move to an empowered culture. Now he was in a position to create that support. But where to begin? Should he work with the teams that wanted to evolve as a team and help them develop plans? What should be done about the teams who had ineffective team leaders? Should that be the district manager's or the regional manager's responsibility? How could the Metro teams be helped when they couldn't even meet?

As he sat there, he pulled the pile of surveys over and wondered how they could best be used.

Exhibit 23.1
Partial Organization Chart

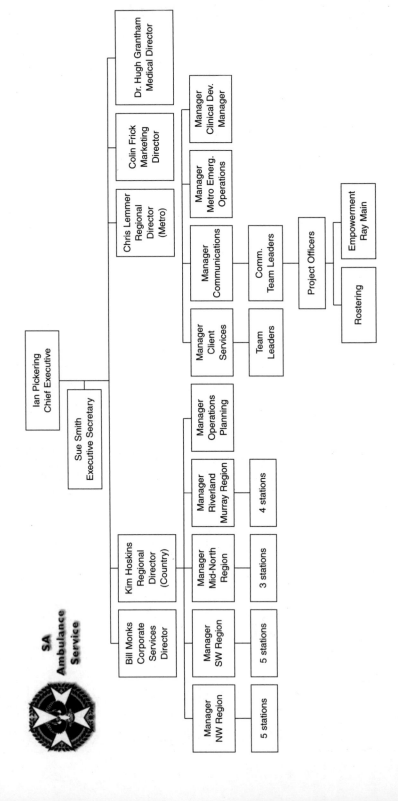

Exhibit 23.2

SA Ambulance Service–Strategic Plan 1996 to 2000

VISION

Our aim is to provide the best Ambulance Service in the Asia Pacific region and maintain this position into the 21st century

MISSION

The SA Ambulance Service is committed to the provision of total quality clinical care and transportation of patients.

GUIDING PRINCIPLES AND VALUES

We will be focussed and responsive to the needs of our patients and customers in both clinical and commercial terms.

In all things we do will maintain our leadership and expert status on all pre-hospital patient care matters and be recognised as the best by both our peers and the community

We will be innovative in our approach to business and strive to add value to the services we provide to our patients and clients.

IMPLEMENTATION

The implementation of our plan depends on all of us.
Implementation is being carried forward by seven project teams:

Workforce   Information Tech
Structure   Commercial
Volunteers   Structured Comm.
Diversification

The teams are implementing our Strategic Plan using Continuous Quality Improvement principles, bringing together the results of our detailed organisational assessment.

Key Objectives	Major Strategies
We will have an empowered and accountable workforce (that is committed to achieving the vision)	Creating an understanding and commitment to the team concept which will include processes for staff awareness, and staff development. Identifying and implementing the most appropriate structure to support and enable teams and to define relevant roles and responsibilities.
We will ensure our selection, placement, competencies and personal development of staff matches the challenges facing the organisation.	Identifying the competencies and/or educational requirements of all positions within the structure identified in the empowerment review. In cooperation with teams, overcome obstacles that restrict the development of team performance. Reviewing selection and promotion procedures. Implementing a staff development plan that incorporates succession planning, performance review, management towards objectives and encourage and supports lateral and upward relief and external exchange programs.
We will support our volunteer ambulance services in all aspects of the business.	Creating an awareness of the state-wide Ambulance Service which incorporates career and volunteer staff. Creating an awareness of the value of volunteers to the organisation. Linking the Country Volunteer structure to the empowerment goal as part of our workforce objective. Ensuring that all strategic objectives apply to country volunteer Systems. Marketing the value of the SA Ambulance Service volunteers to the community in order to promote recruitment of country volunteers. Adequately resourcing the promotion of country volunteer recruitment industries.
We will investigate issues associated with the withdrawal of St. John Priory and amalgamation with the Metropolitan Fire Service.	Researching and developing an understanding of relevant legislation including the Ambulance and South Australian Metropolitan Fire Service Acts. Define and recommend to the Minister for Emergency Services and Ambulance Board our future status.
We will implement structural changes associated with amalgamation with the Metropolitan Fire Service being cognisant of cultural issues.	Recommend to the Minister for Emergency Services and Ambulance Board necessary structural changes. Developing an understanding of each other's culture. Preserving our identity and promoting our culture. Including amalgamation in Enterprise Bargaining negotiations.
We will have IT systems to support our new structure and processes.	Ensuring compatibility in IT Systems. Developing understanding, actively lobbying and promoting the service needs and timetables for Whole of Government initiatives. Resourcing and supporting the IT plan. Ensuring the IT plan is updated to meet any new objectives. Formulating service level agreements for IT services. Developing staff development programs for IT systems.
We will have a cost effective service.	Developing business units to perform within a commercial environment. Training leaders in business issues. The devolution of budget and accountability to teams, ensuring realistic targets are set and reviewed regularly.
We will effectively manage our assets—replace, maintain, upgrade.	Developing an asset management policy (cognisant of the SA Government Strategic Asset Management Plan) Recommending to Government, asset strategies that support the best interests of the Service. Optimising the location of our assets. Establishing internal service level agreements.
We will have a well informed public and staff	Reviewing and improving our internal communication systems. Obtaining commitment from the Executive and the Ambulance Board to continue to fund commercially justifiable marketing industries. Developing product specific marketing. Putting in place real time Information Systems.
We will retain and expand existing revenue generation.	Obtaining government funding commitment for 5 years. Identifying specific areas in SAAS for the responsible allocations of cost savings in a timely manner. Advising the Minister for Emergency Services and Ambulance Board of the most commercially viable fee rates. Putting in place Information Systems to manage revenue and reserves.
We will establish a Trust for securing funding of development initiatives.	By setting up a Trust structure. Developing guidelines for funding of development initiatives.
We will diversify our business.	Financing a Research and Development Study of market opportunities. Developing an action plan based on outcomes of study. Implementing a business development plan.

Exhibit 23.3

Performance Meaures for SAAS (extracts from SAAS Annual Report)

1. Ambulance Response to Patients by Priority

Elective	33%
Clinic	4%
Urgent/Life-Threatening	31%
	(90% life-threatening/critical, 10% urgent)
Immediate Attention Required/Non-Life-Threatening	32%

2. Number of Staff Employed

Ambulance Operations	72.5%
Administration and Clerical	12.3%
Communications	6%
Operational Administration	4.2%
Directors	1%
Logistics	4%

Career Staff (Executive)

6 Males (4 contract, 2 permanent)

Ambulance Cover Members

1995	147 735
1996	161 590

---

3. Number of Ambulance Patients Transported

1991/92	102 000
1992/93	100 000
1993/94	102 000
1994/95	104 000
1995/96	106 000

Exhibit 23.3 (continued)

4. Priority One Response Times

Criteria	Performance
Metropolitan: • 50% responded to within 7 minutes • 95% responded to within 14 minutes	Metropolitan: • 50% of cases are responded to within 7.62 minutes • 95% of cases are responded to within 13.88 minutes
Country: • 50% responded to within 8 minutes • 95% responded to within 18 minutes	Country: • 50% of cases are responded to within 5.45 minutes • 95% of cases are responded to within 22 minutes* *Country performance figures are influenced by a few very long distance transports*

5. Patients Transported by Region

Metropolitan	78%
Country Paid	15%
Country Volunteer	7%

6. Emergency Casetypes

Other Medical Condition	32%
Trauma/Non-Vehicle Accident	15%
Cardiac	16%
Urgent Transfers	12%
Neurological	9%
Respiratory	9%
Vehicle	7%

7. Revenue 1995–1996

Ambulance Transport	57%
Government Contributions	24.5%
Subscriptions	14%
Other Revenues	4.5%

8. Expense 1995–1996

Operating	76%
Administration and Finance	17.7%
Depreciation	6.3%

Exhibit 23.4

Financial Statements

Operating Statement

For the Year Ended 20 June 1996

	1996 $ 000	1995 $ 000
REVENUE		
Ambulance transport	24 385	24 731
Subscriptions	6 052	5 699
Government contributions	10 502	9 371
Other revenue	1 918	1 962
	42 857	41 763
EXPENSES		
Operating	32 482	32 007
Administration & finance	7 606	6 170
Depreciation	2 687	2 968
	42 775	41 145
	82	618
Operating surplus before abnormal items		
Abnormal items	–	(620)
Operating surplus after abnormal items	82	(2)
Accumulated surplus at the beginning of the financial year	2 616	2 523
Aggregate of amounts transferred from reserves	567	971
Total available for appropriation	3 265	3 492
Aggregate of amounts transferred to reserves	908	876
Accumulated surplus at the end of the financial year	2 357	2 616

Exhibit 23.4 (continued)

Statement of Financial Position

As at June 1996

	1996 $ 000	1995 $ 000
CURRENT ASSETS		
Cash	8 658	8 232
Receivables	2 990	2 977
Investments	412	419
Inventories	169	166
Other	718	944
Total current assets	12 947	12 738
NON-CURRENT ASSETS		
Investments	29	–
Property, plant, and equipment	8 432	8 334
Total non-current assets	8 461	8 334
Total assets	21 408	21 072
CURRENT LIABILITIES		
Creditors	1 236	1 800
Provisions	4 042	4 050
Unexpired subscriptions	2 028	1 805
Total current liabilities	7 306	7 655
NON-CURRENT LIABILITIES		
Creditors	60	–
Provisions	4 042	4 050
Unexpired subscriptions	2 028	1 805
Total non-current liabilities	2 028	1 805
Total liabilities	7 306	7 655
Net assets	11 782	11 700
EQUITY		
Capital	6 298	6 298
Reserves	3 127	2 786
Accumulated surplus	2 357	2 616
Total equity	11 782	11 700

Exhibit 23.5
Patient Ready for Ongoing Treatment

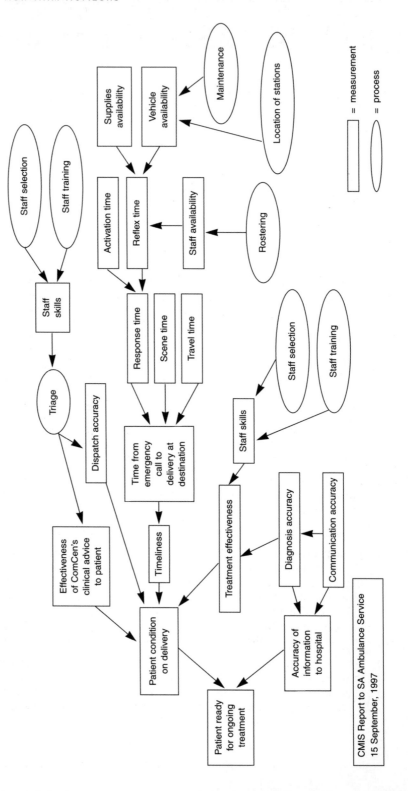

CMIS Report to SA Ambulance Service
15 September, 1997

▭ = measurement

⬭ = process

Exhibit 23.6

Address by CEO Ian Pickering, SAAS

Imagine…you are looking to buy a business.

This business is a parcel pickup and delivery service. You may be required to pick up parcels from different locations at the same time. However, neither parcel can be left longer than 10 minutes or it may be ruined. Not only that, you will be seriously criticized in court if you fail in this mission.

You will get no warning of the need to pick up these parcels. Sometimes people will call you to pick up parcels that are dropped in the street. Even if it is dark and raining you have to go. You will not know the size or condition of the parcel until you arrive. You will have to wrap the object before you pick it up. It may be dirty—it may be leaking—it may swear at you or even attack you.

You will have to make sure someone of above-average intelligence sits with the parcel and keeps checking in case it deteriorates in transit. There is no "use by" date to let you know how delicate the situation is.

It is acknowledged that it will cost you a lot of money to do this but people think you should do it for nothing. Does this sound familiar? Would you buy this business?

It's all a matter of perception. Perceptions can be deceiving.

I contend you cannot run a business such as this on a para-military-style structure. If you are honest with yourself, you will agree that the majority of decisions that impact on the desired outcomes of an ambulance service are made by the crew of an ambulance. Therefore, it follows that the endeavours of an ambulance organization should be directed at supporting a well-educated and empowered workforce at the sharp and so those decisions are timely and appropriate. Not a series of approval processes that both delay and dilute critical decisions.

Ambulance services of today operate in an increasingly competitive environment in which the medical and community expectations demand the continual identification, definition, and improvement of the most appropriate levels of care and service. Today's ambulance officers are better educated, different in culture, work history, and work ethic from their predecessors.

So, what did we see when we took a long, hard look at ourselves?

PROBLEMS.

The SA Ambulance Service has introduced radical changes to its management principles, moving away from a para-military culture to a culture that is based on quality of service, best practice, empowered work teams, an organization that is able to continually look at itself and the way it goes about its business, so that it learns from its experiences.

What did we do?

The outwardly obvious strategies included the adoption of a "Commercial Charter," the introduction of new style uniforms (dispensing with rank markings) and redesigned vehicle livery, together with a public awareness campaign based on a "Going Green" theme.

However the major culture changes had to come from within. The priority is to develop an organization that recognizes and values the importance of constantly striving for a cost-effective best practice ambulance service, while at the same time tangibly acknowledging the fact that the majority of decisions affecting the core business of the service (i.e., saving lives) are made by two officers crewing an ambulance.

Fundamental to our plan is the belief that all of our people should have the opportunity to influence decision making and be able to confidently accept the accountability that comes with empowerment.

Empowerment is a "buzz word"—misused in many instances—it is not handing over the budget for chocolate biscuits. It means being treated like intelligent adults who are capable of making reasonable decisions given the parameters in which to operate.

SA Ambulance Service has a vision—and we believe we know how to get there.

Exhibit 23.7

Rotating Roster for Metro Region

This roster assumes four groups, each with four days on and four days off.

Nine members are needed to operate the team. One person would be on annual holidays, one person would be on other duties, and one or two persons are spare, ill, or have other responsibilities.

Persons 1 & 2	Day	Day	Night	Night	Off	Off	Off	Off
Persons 3 & 4	Off	Off	Day	Day	Night	Night	Off	Off
Persons 5 & 6	Off	Off	Off	Off	Day	Day	Night	Night
Persons 7 & 8	Night	Night	Off	Off	Off	Off	Day	Day

Examining this chart shows the amount of interaction between members and the difficulty in getting together as a team of 11 to 13.

Exhibit 23.8

Ambulance Team—Strategic Plan 1997-2004

Vision

The aim of the Nalkry Ambulance Team is to be the best team within the SA Ambulance Service and to maintain this position into the 21st century.

Mission

The Nalkry Ambulance Team is committed to the provision of clinical care and customer and community service.

Guiding Principles and Values

1. We will be focused and responsive to the needs of our patients and community.
2. In all things we do we will maintain our knowledge, skills, and attitude to ensure a professional relationship with our peers and our community.
3. We will strive to lead, compete for, and deliver a service that is innovative and value-adding to our patients and our community.

Implementation

The implementation of our plan depends on all of us. We are implementing our Strategic Plan using the principles of continuous quality improvement principles.

Clinical Care

We will ensure that our knowledge, skill base, and attitudes are being continuously developed to provide total quality clinical care to our patients.

ALS

- We will be fully ALS qualified by the completion of 1998.
- If appropriate or required, the cost of training will be incorporated into the next financial year.
- Knowledge and skill maintenance will be incorporated into the station-based study plan and skill practice plan.

Exhibit 23.8 (continued)

Paramedic

- We will have at least one team member Paramedic qualified by the end of the year 2000.
- As part of the station study plan we will incorporate knowledge which will guide us towards Paramedic status.
- The cost of Paramedic training will be budgeted into the appropriate fiscal year.

Tools

- We will maintain and upgrade our existing station library.
- We will subscribe to associated periodicals.
- We will subscribe to the Internet.
- We will build a medical-associated CD library.
- We will develop an "Adopt-a-Doc" program.
- We will ensure the maintenance and availability of training equipment. This may be coordinated through the CTL.
- We will utilize the resources of the Ambulance Service Education Unit.
- We will involve the district manager and CTL appropriately.
- We will have an annual review of the acceptability and relevance of current tools.

Continued Education Program

- We will develop a program for each module to meet the needs of the CEP in consultation with the CTL.
- This program must meet the individual needs of each team member.
- At the end of each module we will review the effectiveness of the program.

Study Plan

- We will develop a yearly plan, based on our teams' aims and objectives for the coming year.
- The plan will consist of monthly and weekly topics. These topics will be value-adding to our knowledge.
- The plan will incorporate a series of short and long written questions. The appropriateness of these questions will be determined by the team.
- The effectiveness of the plan will be reviewed bimonthly at team planning days.
- This plan may be reinforced by the CTL through station visitations.
- We will develop a review program which incorporates:

Exhibit 23.8 (continued)

1. Identifying Key Performance Indicators
2. Conducting monthly case reviews
3. Conducting continuous case card audits
4. Recognition of measurable results
5. Six-month review of station-based and associated clinical training
6. Ensuring the CTL is programmed into our station-based program to provide regular useful feedback

Skills Practice

- We will develop a monthly review program which incorporates skills not included in the current CEP. This will be done in consultation with the CTL.

- We will develop a program which fosters integration and skills review with our volunteer sub-branches.

- We will develop a program which encourages skill-sharing with allied health professionals, e.g., doctors, nurses, District Nurses, CAFHS nurses.

- We will initiate a clinical placement program with the Health Services.

- We will maintain a skills log book recording protocols as they are performed in the field and in practice.

Exhibit 23.9

Sample Feedback Sheet for SAAS Teams

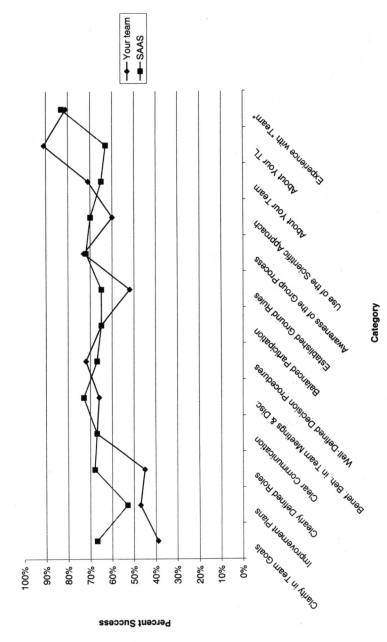

The Case of the Amalgamated Laboratory

Céleste Brotheridge

Joyce Johnston

Claude walked quickly into his office and locked the door behind him. He closed the blinds, lunged into his chair, put his head in his hands, and started shaking uncontrollably. He had just met with his supervisor who had ordered him to "get the situation in the lab under control by the end of the year 'or else.'" Claude was expected to improve productivity twofold, stop the hemorrhaging of employee resignations, and bring a "calm, friendly disposition" to his work unit within six months—all without any increase in budget allocation. "I feel betrayed," Claude thought to himself as he cried in despair. He has been the manager of the Amalgamated Laboratory for only four months. Prior to this assignment, Claude had been the successful manager of a similar operation in another city. He has 20 years of experience working in a laboratory, moving his way up the career ladder from being a laboratory technologist, a supervisor, and, finally a lab manager for the past five years. During the employment interviews, Claude's supervisor had described his prospective work situation as "an exciting and challenging opportunity to work with a team of motivated professionals in building a world-class laboratory in a progressive health district." "It's challenging all right," Claude muttered to himself, "But it's also a war zone with heavy casualties, and I'm going to be the next casualty if I don't figure out what to do."

BACKGROUND

One year prior to Claude's arrival at the Amalgamated Laboratory, the medical laboratories of three acute-care hospitals, one rehabilitation centre, and numerous private facilities were amalgamated into a single laboratory. This centralization effort was one of several initiatives undertaken by an urban health district as a means of reducing health-care costs and in direct response to decreased provincial and federal funding to the district. The implementation of the amalgamated laboratory was phased in over a three-year period. The centralized laboratory was designed as a multi-site laboratory and was situated primarily at two of the acute-care facilities due to the shortage of space at any one site and the lack of funding to develop a separate site. The centralized laboratory was expected to provide an efficient, high-volume centre for the entire health district, meeting both its day-to-day and specialized laboratory requirements.

This restructuring was planned by the health district's senior management team in a series of planning meetings. They frequently dispatched representatives to "talk to the staff" as a means of providing the laboratory staff with a certain level of involvement. During these staff meetings, the management representative would describe management's plan and then solicit comments and ideas from the staff. Although the staff members were pleased with the opportunity to voice their concerns and opinions, when the final restructuring plan was announced, it became evident that their input had been discarded.

THE PLAN

It was determined that the multi-site laboratory would consist of a high-volume core lab and small stat labs at two acute-care facilities. These latter facilities required stat labs in order to respond to urgent requests for lab work. Also, 13 collection centres with minimal testing capability would be provided to the community (as a replacement for privately operated laboratories). The laboratory at the rehabilitation centre, which had previously provided a "full-service menu" to the centre, would be providing only collection services, and this would result in the layoff of one full-time medical laboratory technologist. Of the three acute-care facilities, one was slated for closure one and one-half years following the completion of the project. Because this facility provided trauma care that required laboratory service, a stat lab was to be maintained until the trauma service was relocated to another centre.

The Amalgamated Laboratory required the development of three new specialities: (1) the laboratory information system (LIS); (2) the order entry area; and (3) the call centre, which would handle inquiries. Within each section of a laboratory were supervisory personnel who acted independently under the general guidance of the institution's laboratory manager. Prior to the amalgamation, there were four laboratory managers, each of whom was made an assistant manager in the new centralized laboratory, with one to be selected as the overall laboratory manager. In addition to supervisors, each lab section had also had two other levels of medical laboratory technologists. In the Amalgamated Laboratory, 19 separate sections were to be combined to form seven sections. However, during the restructuring, these seven sections were further combined to form four units. Thus, the 19 supervisory positions were replaced by four unit manager positions. Unit managers were responsible for all of the existing supervisory duties and also for the unit budget. Only two of the four unit managers who were hired were past supervisors. The other two unit managers were a biochemist whose job had been discontinued and a level-one laboratory technologist (the lowest level of the medical laboratory technologist job classification). Another biochemist whose job was discontinued became the LIS manager.

The supervisors who were not hired into the new unit manager positions became "working level senior technologists"—a step down in the hierarchy. These staff members were "grandfathered"—retained at their current salary level. In addition to performing routine bench work, these senior technologists were given responsibilities associated with the laboratory information system for their areas. They were also required to perform relief supervisory functions in the event of the unit manager's absence. Former level-two technologists became level-one technologists (grandfathered at their current wage rate) and were no longer required to perform any supervisory activities, but were expected to work all the shifts that were previously level one duties.

All laboratory staff belonged to different locals of the same union, and union permission was required in order to shuffle staff to various facilities throughout the district. Negotiations with the union were currently under way that would see the laboratory staff become members of a single local. Staff employed at the acute-care centre scheduled to close would not lose their jobs, but would be retained by seniority. However, the junior staff members at the remaining facilities were threatened with the possibility of being "bumped" from their jobs. Management had assured the staff that the overall number of staff would not be reduced to any great extent past the normal level of attrition for the laboratory, including normal and early staff retirement. The total number of technical, office, and support staff within the hospital laboratories prior to the amalgamation was 237 and would be reduced to 195. The majority of the job loss would be at the privately owned labs, which would be reduced to collection centres only (i.e., no testing performed). The development of the new areas would result in fewer medical laboratory technologist positions and more "non-medical" staff in the overall projected numbers for staffing the new centralized laboratory.

The Implementation

Each unit met to standardize procedures and formulate plans for their implementation. Training for the implementation of the LIS and for the movement of staff between sections was initiated. The amalgamation was to proceed in steps over a three-year period, with sections moved as soon as the renovation of their area was complete. However, in some cases, some sections were moved "just to test the waters" even before their area was fully renovated. Some sections were shuffled before the LIS was in place and operational, but the bulk of the movement of staff occurred when the LIS became functional. Within two years, the new sections were implemented and the core lab came into existence. As planned, the laboratories at the other two acute-care centres became stat labs. One entire "unit" was located at the acute-care facility that would not be closed, and the remaining three units were centred at the facility with the "high-volume" core lab. The staff worked hard and within a few months were ready to take on the increased workload from the community.

ONE YEAR POST-AMALGAMATION

When Claude arrived at the laboratory, the amalgamation had already been in place for a year. He found that, although the restructuring appeared to be successful "on the surface," many troubles were brewing within the laboratories. Staff morale was exceedingly low. The technical staff (the laboratory technologists) within the units were accusing the other units of having too many staff members, having staff who did nothing or didn't do what they were hired to do, not working shift work, or, more generally, having better working conditions. Intra- and interunit conflict within the laboratory erupted on a continual basis.

This conflict was fuelled by the existence of distinct cultures in the laboratories prior to the restructuring. The laboratory at Institution 1 had been the only CAP-accredited facility. (CAP) is a prestigious designation, which certifies that a laboratory adheres to extremely high standards of quality. In order to qualify for and maintain this certification, the staff had been required to put in many extra hours of work to write and adhere to stringent procedures of quality assurance. In contrast, the laboratory at Institution 3 had maintained a very relaxed and casual atmosphere. This congenial atmosphere had facilitated the development of a very close working relationship with the other specialties within the institution and served to ease a potentially very stressful work situation. The culture at Institution 2 fell somewhere between those of Institutions 1 and 3.

In one particular unit, the antagonism between members who were previously employed by different laboratories had undermined the well-being of the unit. The unit existed as three cultures within one. Each sub-culture retained its own methodology and techniques and each refused to cooperate with the other or adopt the "standardized procedures." The sub-cultures used different specimen logging (numbering) practices and refused to cover for each other at break time. Also, one sub-culture would discard another's reagents and stains because "they were not labelled correctly." As a result of this year of ongoing discord, the frustrated and berated unit manager had resigned.

Claude has also had to contend with the issue of vacation and sick leave benefits usage. Employees were making full use of their sick leave benefits to the extent that, on any given day, every unit had one or more staff members away on sick leave. Also, the laboratory staff were some of the most senior staff within the health district and had accumulated four to six weeks of vacation leave. Many had carried over their vacation time from the previous year as a means of boosting staffing levels during the amalgamation process. Now that the restructuring was completed, many employees were applying for vacation leave.

A higher-than-normal level of attrition occurred throughout the laboratory as staff chose to move into other jobs within the district or into positions in different organizations. Unfortunately, those individuals who have departed from the laboratory were among its most talented and qualified. Although staffing shortages were being experienced throughout the Amalgamated Laboratory, staffing levels in one particular unit plunged to a critically low level.

In response to this urgent problem and as a means of ensuring that minimal staffing levels were maintained, Claude reallocated staff from other sections and hired casual staff as needed. These measures, however, required that existing staff (who were already burdened by an excessive workload) train and closely supervise the new, inexperienced, and generally underqualified staff members. In addressing the issue of the heavy workload, Claude decided to streamline the frequency and availability of testing services. Whereas in the past some tests were performed on several samples, they were now limited to being performed on only one sample. Also, testing now became available "at regular hours only" rather than at all times as needed by other specialities within the health-care system.

Unfortunately, this measure seems to have backfired. Staff seem to have a reduced level of pride in their work and in the service provided to clients. Also, the removal of some laboratory services from several institutions has made it difficult for the medical and nursing staff from these institutions to obtain information on testing and specimen collection from laboratory staff. This situation stands in stark contrast to previous service levels where laboratory staff provided services in person and with pride, so that overall quality of patient care was improved. Laboratory staff no longer view themselves as members of a team working towards improving the health of a patient. Rather, they feel like they are part of a bureaucracy, just trying to get as much work done as possible.

Since his arrival four months ago, Claude has been attempting to familiarize himself with his new work situation and has been responding to situations and incidents on a continual basis. He has met with staff members as a group and individually (where possible) to discuss options for improving the performance and the morale of the laboratory. These meetings seemed futile, however. They consisted of a great deal of talk, blaming, and demands for higher staffing levels. The staff appear to be drowning in a sea of confusion—unable to look beyond their more immediate needs. But another important issue looms on the horizon. In the next two months, an acute-care facility will close and its laboratory staff will need to be absorbed within the Amalgamated Laboratory. Claude was determined to resolve the problems of the Amalgamated Laboratory. "After all," he thought to himself as he adjusted his tie in the mirror, "I'm a winner and winners never quit."